Also of interest from the Urban Institute Press:

Prisoners Once Removed: The Impact of Incarceration and Reentry on Children, Families and Communities, edited by Jeremy Travis and Michelle Waul

Juvenile
Drug Courts
AND TEEN SUBSTANCE ABUSE

THE URBAN INSTITUTE PRESS
Washington, D.C.

THE URBAN INSTITUTE PRESS
2100 M Street, N.W.
Washington, D.C. 20037

Library of Congress Cataloging in Publication Data

Juvenile drug courts and teen substance abuse / edited by Jeffrey A. Butts and
   John Roman.
         p. cm.
   Includes bibliographical references and index.
   ISBN 0-87766-725-X (alk. paper)
   1. Juvenile courts--United States.   2. Drug courts--United States.   3. Juvenile
delinquents--Drug use--United States.   I. Butts, Jeffrey A.   II. Roman, John, 1969-
III. Title.

   KF9794.J875 2004
   345.73'081--dc22   2004019669

Printed in the United States of America
10 09 08 07 06 05 04   1 2 3 4 5

THE URBAN INSTITUTE is a nonprofit, nonpartisan policy research and educational organization established in Washington, D.C., in 1968. Its staff investigates the social, economic, and governance problems confronting the nation and evaluates the public and private means to alleviate them. The Institute disseminates its research findings through publications, its web site, the media, seminars, and forums.

Through work that ranges from broad conceptual studies to administrative and technical assistance, Institute researchers contribute to the stock of knowledge available to guide decisionmaking in the public interest.

Conclusions or opinions expressed in Institute publications are those of the authors and do not necessarily reflect the views of officers or trustees of the Institute, advisory groups, or any organizations that provide financial support to the Institute.

Contents

Preface ix

Acknowledgments xv

1 Drug Courts in the Juvenile Justice System 1
Jeffrey A. Butts and John Roman

2 American Drug Policy and the Evolution of
Drug Treatment Courts 27
John Roman, Jeffrey A. Butts, and Alison S. Rebeck

3 What Juvenile Drug Courts Do and
How They Do It 55
Shelli Balter Rossman, Jeffrey A. Butts, John Roman,
Christine DeStefano, and Ruth White

4 Drug Court Effects and the Quality of
Existing Evidence 107
John Roman and Christine DeStefano

5 Defining the Mission of Juvenile Drug Courts 137
Jeffrey A. Butts, Janine M. Zweig, and Cynthia Mamalian

6 Identifying Adolescent Substance Abuse 185
Daniel P. Mears

7 Shaping the Next Generation of Juvenile
Drug Court Evaluations 221
Jeffrey A. Butts, John Roman, Shelli Balter Rossman, and
Adele V. Harrell

8 Building Better Evidence for Policy and Practice 267
John Roman and Jeffrey A. Butts

Appendix 279

About the Editors 355

About the Contributors 357

Index 361

Preface

Juvenile justice officials across the United States are embracing a new method of dealing with adolescent substance abuse. Importing a popular innovation from adult courts, state and local governments have started hundreds of specialized drug courts to provide judicial supervision and coordinate substance abuse treatment for drug-involved juveniles. The number of youth affected by these new juvenile drug courts is small compared with the more than one million cases handled each year by traditional juvenile courts, but the programs are spreading rapidly and their presence is changing the way practitioners and policymakers think about the challenge of adolescent drug use.

Drug courts give offenders an opportunity to change their behavior and stop their use of illegal drugs before they receive serious legal penalties. Those who stop using drugs and complete a rigorous program of treatment may have their charges dismissed or their sentences reduced. To ensure that program participants complete drug treatment as ordered, drug courts assume responsibilities that go beyond the traditional role of a criminal court. They coordinate client case management and probation supervision for every case. They hold regular review meetings and frequent court hearings to monitor each offender's situation. They use graduated sanctions and tangible rewards to motivate offender compliance, and they check for violations by conducting numerous random or unannounced drug tests.

Beginning with a small number of experimental programs, the drug court concept quickly grew into a full-scale movement in the United States. Less than a decade after the first program started in 1989, there were more than 1,000 drug court programs in operation across the country. The first drug courts were designed for adult defendants, but in the mid-1990s state and local jurisdictions began to develop juvenile drug courts as well. By 2003, approximately 300 juvenile drug courts had opened and another 100 were being planned.

As often happens in the justice system, juvenile drug courts became popular long before evaluation researchers were able to demonstrate that they were effective. In fact, researchers have only begun to test whether juvenile drug courts "work," in the sense that they stop or reduce substance abuse more effectively than the current approaches used for similar youth. Such evidence is hard to assemble, and it takes lengthy research studies with long-term follow-up periods to generate real proof of program effectiveness. Until very recently, juvenile drug courts had not been around long enough for evaluators to complete studies with long-term outcomes. The number of juvenile drug court programs was small until the late 1990s.

Fortunately, adult drug courts appeared five years before juvenile drug courts and the evaluation literature on adult programs has had more time to develop. These studies suggest the drug court concept itself may have merit. At the very least, drug courts seem to affect offender behavior enough to pay for themselves through reduced crime and drug abuse. It is not clear, however, whether the growing evidence about adult drug courts can be applied to juvenile drug courts. Many important policy questions about juvenile drug courts have not been answered. Should juvenile programs differ substantially from adult drug courts? Should they use different treatment models? Should courtroom routines be designed and managed differently? How can juvenile drug courts effectively motivate young offenders to reduce their substance abuse behavior? How should their procedures and strategies be adapted to incorporate the important role of family and school in the lives of adolescents?

The most important unresolved issue may be whether the juvenile justice system really needs juvenile drug courts. Adult drug courts were a significant innovation for the criminal justice system. They introduced a problem-solving approach to a system accustomed to fact finding and punishment. Rather than simply weighing the evidence in a single case and imposing a sentence, drug courts use the leverage of judicial authority to motivate offenders to change their drug-using behavior. But this approach is not exactly revolutionary in the juvenile justice system. In fact, it is standard operating procedure in traditional juvenile courts. Justice experts even refer to drug courts as "juvenile courts for adults."

Further, adult drug courts usually handle seriously addicted offenders who have been abusing drugs and suffering the consequences for years. Offenders in adult drug courts have often lost housing, jobs, family, and friends because of substance abuse. Very few juveniles will have experienced anything so severe by the time they are referred to a juvenile drug court program. The typical youth referred to a juvenile drug court is 15 or 16 years old and has been drinking alcohol and smoking marijuana for a few years at most. Teenagers are not likely to respond well to a program designed to intervene in an adult-style downward spiral of addiction and dependence. Drug-involved youth usually need improved relationships, exciting recreational opportunities, job preparedness, and perhaps family counseling to support them in making positive choices. In short, drug-involved youth are much like youth in general.

Why then does the juvenile justice system need a "new" court model to handle drug-involved youthful offenders? Perhaps because juvenile courts have strayed too far from their historic problem-solving mission to mimic the "just deserts" orientation of criminal courts. The drug court process may be an important change in style and procedure for today's juvenile courts, albeit one that returns them to their traditional mission. Maybe the introduction of juvenile drug courts allows local juvenile justice systems to acquire treatment resources they otherwise would not be able to access. Juvenile drug courts may be valued not because they offer a new or innovative court process for juvenile offenders but because they enable local officials to leverage new resources for responding to teen drug use.

Whatever factors explain the appeal of juvenile drug court for policymakers and practitioners, specialized courts for juvenile drug users are clearly a popular and growing program model in the United States. We do not know whether they are actually more effective than traditional juvenile courts in accomplishing their mission of reduced substance abuse among adolescent offenders, but until evaluation researchers produce better studies of program impact, juvenile justice officials will probably continue to fund and implement juvenile drug courts without sufficient evidence. The contributors to this book hope that their work will encourage practitioners and policymakers to think carefully about the role that drug courts can or should play in the juvenile justice system. They also hope the chapters in this volume will encourage evaluation researchers to produce better studies that will begin to fill the current evidence gap about the impact and effectiveness of juvenile drug courts.

Contents of the Book

Most of the material presented in this book was produced for the National Evaluation of Juvenile Drug Courts (NEJDC) project at the Urban Institute in Washington, D.C. The project was funded by the U.S. Department of Justice's National Institute of Justice and conducted by researchers affiliated with the Urban Institute's Program on Youth Justice. The NEJDC project was designed to facilitate future evaluation research on juvenile drug courts and to encourage policymakers and practitioners to examine the impact and effectiveness of the juvenile drug court process. Together, the chapters in the book highlight the most important factors in the effectiveness of drug courts for juveniles and encourage future evaluation researchers to formulate and test explicit hypotheses involving those factors. The contributing authors hope that their work will encourage policymakers, researchers, and practitioners to ask tough questions about juvenile drug courts and their effectiveness.

In chapter 1, "Drug Courts in the Juvenile Justice System," Jeffrey A. Butts and John Roman introduce the key concepts behind drug courts and describe the emergence of juvenile drug courts, one of the most recent and fastest growing manifestations of the American drug court movement. They scrutinize the uncertain mission of juvenile drug courts and challenge policymakers and practitioners with an implicit query, "If juvenile drug courts are the answer, what is the question?"

In chapter 2, "American Drug Policy and the Evolution of Drug Treatment Courts," John Roman, Jeffrey A. Butts, and Alison S. Rebeck describe the proliferation of drug courts during the 1990s. They argue that the drug court concept was evolutionary, not revolutionary. Drug courts were a natural extension of moving substance abuse treatment beyond the exclusive domain of social services and into the criminal justice arena.

In chapter 3, "What Juvenile Drug Courts Do and How They Do It," Shelli Balter Rossman, Jeffrey A. Butts, John Roman, Christine

DeStefano, and Ruth White review the practices and policies of juvenile drug courts. They describe the typical ingredients of juvenile drug courts and analyze differences within the general model based upon the daily operations observed in six programs studied by the Urban Institute.

In chapter 4, "Drug Court Effects and the Quality of Existing Evidence," John Roman and Christine DeStefano examine the results of drug court evaluations and the limitations of available research for linking drug court components with participant outcomes. They review the strengths and weaknesses of existing studies, identify areas that deserve further exploration, and propose strategies for improving future drug court evaluations.

In chapter 5, "Defining the Mission of Juvenile Drug Courts," Jeffrey A. Butts, Janine M. Zweig, and Cynthia Mamalian analyze several important policy issues related to the uses and possible misuses of juvenile drug courts. They review available evidence about the nature of adolescence and current patterns of illegal drug use among young people, and they question the appropriateness of juvenile drug court programs when they are used for teens that do not show signs of serious drug and alcohol problems.

In chapter 6, "Identifying Adolescent Substance Abuse," Daniel P. Mears reviews the diagnostic instruments used by practitioners to decide when juveniles have drug and alcohol problems that require treatment. He analyzes the current state of research on the accuracy and utility of screening and assessment tools and describes which ones are used most often in the juvenile justice system.

In chapter 7, "Shaping the Next Generation of Juvenile Drug Court Evaluations," Jeffrey A. Butts, John Roman, Shelli Balter Rossman, and Adele V. Harrell present a new conceptual framework for evaluating juvenile drug courts. The framework is designed for researchers who want to develop and test explicit, theoretically derived hypotheses about not only if drug courts influence youth behavior, but also why and how they do it.

In chapter 8, "Building Better Evidence for Policy and Practice," John Roman and Jeffrey A. Butts consider the significance of juvenile drug court research for future policy and practice, and propose several steps needed to advance the quality and applicability of research evidence.

Acknowledgments

This book was developed from a series of reports produced for the Urban Institute's National Evaluation of Juvenile Drug Courts (NEJDC) project, which was supported by a grant from the National Institute of Justice, a component of the U.S. Department of Justice Office of Justice Programs. The principal investigators were Jeffrey A. Butts and Shelli Balter Rossman. The NEJDC project investigated juvenile drug court programs in six states: Florida, Montana, New Jersey, New Mexico, Ohio, and South Carolina. The purpose of the investigation was not to assess or evaluate the programs, but to observe and learn from the judges, staff, and practitioners in each site and to develop a new conceptual framework for evaluating juvenile drug courts. Researchers from the Urban Institute examined court operations and drug treatment services and mapped the network of agencies and individuals involved in programs for substance-abusing offenders. The insights and observations developed from these activities guided the formulation of the project's conceptual framework.

The editors and contributors are grateful for the patience and efforts of the many practitioners and local officials who hosted the Urban Institute's site visits and helped the researchers understand the key ingredients of juvenile drug courts. In particular, the study could not have been conducted without the support of the project's principal contacts in each of the six jurisdictions:

- Judge Jose Rodriguez and Annmarie Karayianes from the juvenile drug court in Orlando, Florida;
- Judge John W. Larson and Brenda Desmond from the youth drug court in Missoula, Montana;
- Judge Salvatore Bovino and Linda Coppola from the Jersey City, New Jersey, juvenile drug court;
- Judge Larry Ramirez and (formerly) Ann Wallace from the Third Judicial District Juvenile Drug Court in Las Cruces, New Mexico;
- Judge Michael Murphy and Domina Matthews of the Montgomery County Juvenile Drug Court in Dayton, Ohio; and
- Judge F. P. Segars-Andrews and Julius Scott from the juvenile drug court program in Charleston, South Carolina.

Other individuals in the six communities were vital to the project's efforts to understand the background and operations of the juvenile drug court programs. The Urban Institute research team is grateful for the time and efforts of the following individuals:

Orlando, Florida

Ken Allison, Center for Drug-Free Living
Bob Pickerill, Coalition for a Drug-Free Community
Judge Belvin Perry, Ninth Judicial Circuit Court of Florida
Terry Turner, drug court administrator
Tammy Austin, Orange County Youth and Family Services
Joanne Nelson, case management supervisor
Brendan Arlington, case manager

Missoula, Montana

Margaret L. Borg, Chief Missoula County Public Defender
Leslie Halligan, Deputy County Attorney
Charity Claramunt, Juvenile Supervision Officer
Bonnie Fergerson, school representative
Geoffrey Birnbaum, Missoula Youth Homes
Emily McCrea, Attention Home
Laurie Hunt, parent educator

Dudley Dana, psychologist
Carol Lee Engler, social worker
Brenda Johnson, Missoula Youth Court
Murray Pierce, Juvenile Supervision Officer
Ellie Greenwood, Community Programs Coordinator
Anne St. Hilaire, St. Patrick Addiction Treatment
Glen Welch, Chief Juvenile Probation Officer

Jersey City, New Jersey

Joseph C. Mollica, Superior Court
James A. Sharrock, Hudson County Sherriff's Office
Steven Sladen, Assistant Prosecutor
Cathy Wasserman, Office of the Public Defender
Sgt. Joseph Coyle, Jersey City Police
Lou DeStefano, Jersey City Police
Michael J. Paolello, St. Mary's Hospital
Robin Semel, St. Mary's Hospital
Martha Santiago, Jersey City Schools

Las Cruces and Anthony, New Mexico

Rosie Medina, administrative assistant
Mark Filosa, Special Master
Thomas Cornish, former children's court judge
David Proper, Program Public Defender
Anamarie DeLovato, Assistant District Attorney
Terese Lahann, Assistant District Attorney
Mark Whitehead, former clinical director
Ron Nestle, former substance abuse counselor
Stacy Reynolds, former substance abuse counselor
Efrain Lara, former surveillance officer
Barbara Reyes, surveillance officer
Juan Salcido, surveillance officer
Cynthia Ramirez, surveillance officer
Dan Rosales, court liaison
Tom Schnebley, Las Cruces Police Department

Melissa Molina, Las Cruces Police Department
Lance Shepan, Dona Ana County Sheriff deputy
Jerod Zuniga, Dona Ana County Sheriff deputy
Marv Allen, Las Cruces Public Schools liaison
Carolyn Scott, Chief Juvenile Probation and Parole Officer
Esther Aguirre-Stewart, probation officer
James Turner, probation officer

Dayton, Ohio

Voletta Gaston, The Better Way Program
Keith Vukasinovich, Partnerships for Youth
Scott Harting, drug court
Richard Rapp, Wright State University
Robert Offutt, drug court
Melissa Sanders, drug court
Angela Zanolli, drug court
Kay M. Rosario, Office of the Public Defender
Steven Ring, Assistant Prosecuting Attorney
Luigi Dodieu, drug court
Karen Slorp, drug court
Tamara Mannix, juvenile court

Charleston, South Carolina

Scott Henggler, Medical University of South Carolina
Phillippe Cunningham, Medical University of South Carolina
Jeffrey Randall, Medical University of South Carolina
Lynn West, Medical University of South Carolina
Robert Pickering, Charleston County Schools

NEJDC Advisory Committee

Other people assisted in conceptualizing and designing the materials in this book. One important source of guidance was the advisory committee for the National Evaluation of Juvenile Drug Courts project. Members of the advisory committee reviewed the research team's overall approach to the work and provided critical comments about the products of the effort.

Dr. David Altschuler, Johns Hopkins University
Dr. Steven Belenko, Treatment Research Institute
Hon. Sharon Chatman, Superior Court of California
Dr. John Goldkamp, Temple University
Dr. Doris MacKenzie, University of Maryland
Dr. David Rottman, National Center for State Courts
Dr. Howard Snyder, National Center for Juvenile Justice

Urban Institute

Several current and former employees of the Urban Institute played critical roles in the development of this book, including Jeremy Travis, President of John Jay College and former senior fellow at the Urban Institute and director of the National Institute of Justice (NIJ). Although the NEJDC project began after Jeremy left NIJ, his vision and leadership helped nurture the ideas that resulted in the project.

Dr. Adele Harrell, the founding director of the Justice Policy Center at the Urban Institute, helped conceptualize the methods and research approach used for the NEJDC project. Adele was an able and always entertaining advisor and mentor throughout the development of this book and many other products from the Justice Policy Center.

The editors and authors are also grateful to Dr. Terence Dunworth, director of the Justice Policy Center since 2002. Terry provided helpful guidance and essential support during the latter stages of this work and remains a constant presence, peering over the shoulders of every JPC researcher—if only metaphorically.

Rob Cryer, Dionne Davis, and Erika Jackson played key administrative roles in this project along with their responsibilities for keeping the JPC show on the air. William Turner, formerly of the Urban Institute, assisted in preparing materials for several chapters in this book.

U.S. Department of Justice

The NEJDC project that led to this book benefited from significant contributions by people in the U.S. Department of Justice, most importantly the project's program manager at the National Institute of Justice, Janice Munsterman. The NEJDC project was a demanding effort that involved extensive program visitation and observation, without the standard cycle of data collection, analysis, and reporting. Janice helped the project focus on the goal of producing a useful conceptual framework for future juvenile drug court evaluations and making the work as responsive as possible to the needs of policymakers and practitioners. Her steady hand and easy giggle are the real energy behind many of the nation's most important research projects on crime and justice.

The former Drug Courts Program Office (DCPO) within the U.S. Department of Justice provided critical support for the project, and several members of its staff were pivotal in helping guide the development of this work, including Marilyn Roberts, former director of DCPO, Jennifer Columbel, and Stephen Antkowiak.

Finally, the editors and authors are grateful for the leadership and support of Sarah Hart, director of the National Institute of Justice, and Deborah J. Daniels, Assistant Attorney General for the Office of Justice Programs within the U.S. Department of Justice.

1

Drug Courts in the Juvenile Justice System

Jeffrey A. Butts and John Roman

I n just over 10 years, drug courts have exploded across the United States as a popular new way to deal with substance abuse and crime. The drug court concept is widely praised, from the White House to state-houses and city halls all over the country. Now the drug court movement is spreading to the juvenile justice system. Are drug courts for juveniles needed? Are they effective? Do they reduce the problems associated with juvenile crime and adolescent drug abuse more effectively than the tra-ditional juvenile justice process? Unfortunately, there are no clear answers to these questions because evaluation research on juvenile drug courts has not been able to keep up with the speeding train of federal funding and program diffusion.

In the next decade, policymakers, practitioners, and researchers will have to work together to improve the evidence on juvenile drug courts. The harm that can result from teenage drug abuse motivates all Americans to search for effective drug abuse programs for youth, but judging effec-tiveness requires more than good intentions and public testimonials. It takes well-designed evaluation research to establish empirical links between program efforts and changes in youth behavior, and it requires programs that know how to focus their efforts where they are likely to do the most good for youth, families, and communities. Judged by these standards, juvenile drug courts today would have to be described as experimental.

The Drug Court Movement

Growing numbers of drug arrests during the 1980s and 1990s led law enforcement agencies and courts to support new approaches for dealing with substance abusing offenders. Many jurisdictions turned to drug courts, a program model that emerged from Florida in the late 1980s. The idea behind drug courts is relatively simple. They offer defendants an opportunity to have their charges dismissed or their sentences modified in return for completing a course of drug treatment under court supervision. Some drug courts order treatment in lieu of more severe sentences; others make participation in treatment part of sentencing. Essentially, drug courts use the threat of legal sanctions to order good behavior from drug-involved offenders.

Drug courts employ various techniques to ensure that offenders complete their treatment as directed. They use case management to coordinate all services for each client. They require drug tests to monitor offender behavior and detect new drug use, and they hold periodic review hearings in open court. During these hearings, a judge reviews the progress of each case and discusses recent developments with the program staff, the defendant, and sometimes the defendant's family. Offenders are usually involved in the drug court process until they have established a sustained period of program compliance and a lengthy record of clean drug tests— often 12 to 18 months.

The drug court concept is very popular. Less than a decade after the first program opened in 1989, drug courts were operating in hundreds of communities across the United States. By November 2003, there were more than 1,000 drug courts in operation and 400 more in planning stages (Office of Justice Programs 2003). Drug courts were first used for adult offenders, but drug courts for juveniles began to appear in the mid-1990s. As of November 2003, 294 juvenile drug courts were operating in 46 states and the District of Columbia; another 112 were being planned (figure 1.1).

There are many reasons for the rapid expansion of drug courts in the United States. First, drug arrests nearly tripled during the 1980s and 1990s. According to law enforcement data collected annually by the Federal Bureau of Investigation, the total number of drug arrests in the United States grew from 580,900 to 1,579,600 between 1980 and 2000.[1] With more drug offenders coming to court, officials were ready for new ways of dealing with them, and the drug court concept seemed to fit the bill. Funding

Figure 1.1. *The Number of Juvenile Drug Courts in the United States Grew Quickly*

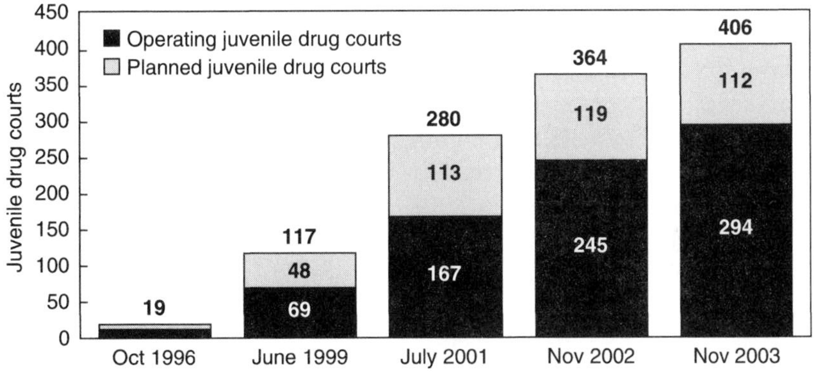

Sources: Office of Justice Programs (1996, 1999, 2001, 2002, 2003).

was also a powerful impetus. The federal government invested heavily in promoting and implementing drug courts. Federal funding for drug courts was first authorized in Title V of the Violent Crime Control and Law Enforcement Act of 1994 (PL 103-322). The U.S. Department of Justice then established a Drug Courts Program Office to administer the funds and provide leadership for program development.[2] By 1997, federal appropriations for drug courts had grown to $30 million annually. The 2003 budget increased that support to $68 million, bringing the total federal investment in drug courts to more than $330 million since 1994. When federal and state expenditures are combined, more than a billion dollars have likely been invested in drug courts.

Drug courts continue to be popular. In 2004, the White House National Drug Control Strategy Update described the creation of drug courts as "one of the most promising trends in the criminal justice system" (The White House 2004, 6). Federal funds are helping support a clearinghouse for drug court information and technical assistance at The American University in Washington, D.C. (http://www.american.edu/justice). The National Association of Drug Court Professionals (http://www.nadcp.org) and the National Drug Court Institute (http://www.ndci.org) continue to promote drug courts nationwide and promulgate standardized policies and procedures for drug court programs. Interest in drug courts at the federal, state, and local levels remains high.

Different Courts, Different Missions

Drug courts represent a significant change in the philosophy and orientation of the criminal justice system. In a traditional criminal court, defendants (through their attorneys) and the state (through prosecutors) engage in an adversarial contest with clearly defined rules. Each side defends its position and interests. There are winners and losers. A neutral judge determines the outcomes based on the facts presented at trial, unless the defendant specifically waives his or her right to trial by pleading guilty, often in accord with an agreement between the prosecution and defense. When the process ends, whether by the completion of a trial or a plea agreement, the parties' responsibilities are complete and the case is over.

In drug courts, on the other hand, there are no winners and losers. Attorneys and treatment providers work with the judge as a team to develop and monitor client treatment plans. They focus on the offender and his or her ability to become and remain drug-free.

The collaborative, problem-solving approach used in drug courts is revolutionary for the criminal court system, but it is very similar to the traditional juvenile court process developed more than a century ago (table 1.1). America's system of juvenile law was founded on the premise that—owing to their immaturity—young people accused of crimes should be handled differently from adults, with less concern for their guilt and more effort to correct their illegal behavior and address the problems that led to it (Bernard 1992; Fox 1970; Watkins 1998). In theory, the sanctions imposed in juvenile court were designed to do more than punish wrongdoing. They were to address the causes of a youth's misbehavior and restore the youth to full and responsible citizenship. Juvenile court judges were expected to base their decisions on the unique circumstances and needs of offenders rather than simply the severity of their offenses.

To give juvenile courts the flexibility to fulfill this mission, lawmakers allowed the original juvenile courts to meet significantly lower standards of evidence and due process. Before the 1960s, juvenile court judges were not required to follow detailed procedures or adhere to complex legal rules (Manfredi 1998). With fewer legal formalities, juvenile courts were free to intervene quickly and comprehensively with each youth. Even with a juvenile merely suspected of criminal involvement, a judge was empowered to take jurisdiction over the matter, place the youth on probation, or even order a period of incarceration. Of course, juvenile courts today are far more regulated than courts of the 1960s. In recent decades, state and

Table 1.1. *To Conduct Sound Evaluations, Researchers Need to Understand How Juvenile Drug Courts Differ from Adult Drug Courts and Traditional Juvenile Courts, and How They May Complement or Conflict with Juvenile Justice Goals*

	Traditional criminal court	Adult drug court	Juvenile drug court	Traditional juvenile court
Governing goal	Retribution	Public safety	?	Youth development
Operational objective	Appropriate punishment for offense	Crime prevention through penalties and rehabilitation services	?	Promoting a law-abiding lifestyle through educational and rehabilitation services
Crime control strategy	General and specific deterrence/incapacitation	Specific deterrence and rehabilitation	?	Rehabilitation
Formality	Formal determination of guilt	Often informal, after admission of guilt and plea	?	Individualized mix of formal and informal procedures
Interactional style	Adversarial	Formal, collaborative	?	Informal, collaborative
Behavioral focus	Specific offense	Offense-related factors and specific problem behavior	?	General pattern of risky behavior

(continued)

5

Table 1.1. *Continued*

	Traditional criminal court	Adult drug court	Juvenile drug court	Traditional juvenile court
Sentencing	Defined by offense and criminal history as specified by guidelines and statutes	May be mitigated in exchange for compliance with treatment and other conditions	?	Based on perceptions of future risk—often indeterminate
Monitoring of compliance	Probation or correctional agency	Judge or case manager	?	Judge, probation, social services
Consequences for noncompliance	Jail/prison or administrative sanctions	Graduated sanctions, increased monitoring, changes in treatment plan	?	Administrative sanctions, changes in treatment plan

Source: Urban Institute National Evaluation of Juvenile Drugs Courts, based on an idea suggested by Dr. Adele Harrell.

federal lawmakers have blended the original philosophy of the juvenile court with the rules and procedures of the criminal court. Many states have reduced the confidentiality of juvenile court proceedings and juvenile court records, increased the legal formalities used in juvenile court, and shifted the focus of the juvenile justice process away from individualized intervention and rehabilitation (Butts and Mitchell 2000). Much like criminal courts, juvenile courts today focus on public safety and offender accountability.

In many ways, however, the juvenile court process remains different from that of the criminal court. The official purpose of the juvenile court process is still to decide whether a youth should be *adjudicated* (or judged) delinquent, not whether he or she is *guilty* of a criminal act. Juvenile court decisions are based partly on evidence, but also partly on an assessment of each youth's situation. When a youth is adjudicated delinquent, the juvenile court does not simply impose a sentence commensurate with the severity of the offense. The court determines the best overall response to the whole situation. That response—or *disposition*—could include punishment, but it also may involve individual and family services, educational and vocational rehabilitation, and other forms of treatment.

Why Juvenile Drug Courts?

If the "new" drug court process was similar to the traditional juvenile court, why did so many jurisdictions develop juvenile drug courts? The sudden supply of federal funding is probably responsible for some of the demand for juvenile drug court programs. Judges may have also learned to value juvenile drug courts as a way to coordinate existing services more effectively and hold agency partners accountable. It is also possible that juvenile justice officials simply wanted to emulate adult drug courts, which were becoming increasingly popular with policymakers and the public. Whatever reasons explain the growth of juvenile drug courts, it appears they will continue to affect the juvenile justice system for years to come.

Juvenile drug courts (or JDCs) share many characteristics with adult drug courts. Both provide intensive supervision of drug-involved offenders and use an array of treatment and social services to assist (or coerce) offenders to stop using illegal drugs. In juvenile as well as adult drug courts, shared hearings are a central part of the process. All aspects of the drug court process convey to participants that the only way to avoid more severe sanctions and deeper involvement with the program is to follow the rules and make a sincere effort to change.

There are also important differences between juvenile and adult drug courts. JDC programs place a greater emphasis on the role of the family in all facets of court operations, from assessment and treatment, to courtroom procedures, to the structure of rewards and sanctions. Juvenile drug courts usually include more significant outreach to each offender's home and community. They are more likely to mobilize the efforts of other significant people in youths' lives to create teams of program partners that can teach, supervise, coach, and discipline youthful offenders. Ideally, JDC programs also incorporate development-based treatment strategies that take into account the age and cognitive capacity of each client, and they consider each offender's school performance and peer relationships as well as work and family obligations. Juvenile drug courts reflect the key features of the juvenile justice process. They are founded on the notion that adolescents are different from adults and that the root causes of adolescent substance use often are found in developmental and family-related risk factors.

The juvenile drug court process is similar to that of traditional juvenile courts, but with three important differences: (1) judicial oversight of case progress is greater; (2) there are many more court appearances; and (3) the purposes and goals of substance abuse treatment are closely integrated with the entire court process. In a traditional juvenile court, a series of court hearings is used to establish an offender's responsibility (or guilt). The court then orders an appropriate mix of sanctions and services, perhaps including probation supervision, restitution payments, community service, or even incarceration. There may be one or two review hearings to evaluate a youth's status, but much of the court's work is finished once the final disposition in the case has been ordered.

The JDC process, on the other hand, is a repeating cycle of court hearings (figure 1.2). Cases usually begin with an arrest, followed by some form of screening and assessment to determine each youth's eligibility for drug court. The court meets with each offender regularly, often weekly in open hearings. Before each hearing, the judge may meet with the drug court team (probation officer, case manager, prosecutor, defense attorney, treatment provider, school representative, and so on) to review the sanctions and services ordered for each youth, assess their effectiveness, and make any needed modifications in treatment and supervision arrange-

Figure 1.2. *The Drug Court Process Involves Repeated Cycles of Case Staffings, Team Meetings, Hearings, Sanctioning, and Testing*

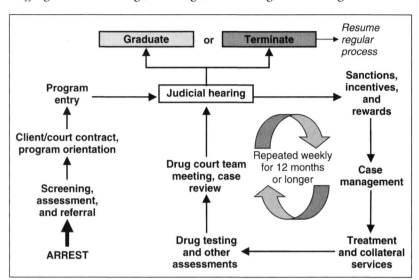

Source: Urban Institute National Evaluation of Juvenile Drug Courts.

ments. The weekly cycle continues until the judge and other program staff believe that a young offender has succeeded in changing his or her drug-related behavior or has met other predetermined treatment goals. The court may then hold a graduation ceremony to celebrate the youth's accomplishment. Youth who fail to change their behavior are usually released from the program, only to face disposition in juvenile court on their original charges.

Beyond their general similarities, JDC programs have developed a variety of different features. Some involve very traditional courtrooms where the judge wears a black robe and speaks formally to participants. Others are much more informal; some judges even use humor and drama during court hearings. Many JDCs rely on traditional drug treatment modalities, such as individual and group counseling, but others employ alternative interventions, including wilderness experiences, acupuncture, and animal therapy. Few, however, extensively refer juveniles to either residential treatment or AA/NA, as adult drug courts do. In some programs, offenders and their families are allowed to leave the courtroom as soon as the judge finishes discussing their particular case. Other programs require every client to stay throughout the court session and observe the court's response to other cases. Researchers have yet to determine whether these program variations affect JDCs' abilities to achieve their principal objective—changing the drug-related behavior of youthful offenders.

Asking Critical Questions

As the number of juvenile drug courts continues to grow, policymakers must have credible answers to two central questions: (1) Do juvenile drug courts reduce substance abuse among the youth who enroll in them; and (2) Can communities trust juvenile drug courts to help them deal with their teenage drug abuse problems? The answer to the first question is "probably." The answer to the second question is "not necessarily," given how juvenile drug courts are designed and used across the country.

On the question of individual effects, researchers are beginning to find evidence that drug courts, when implemented properly, can help stem substance abuse among program participants. Few studies have produced anything more than limited support for this conclusion, but the results to date are promising (see Roman and DeStefano, in this volume). Drug courts are not a miracle cure, but enough studies have found evidence of beneficial effects for policymakers to continue to experiment with improving the drug court model.

Proving the existence of community-level benefits is more problematic. How well JDC programs deal with adolescent substance abuse depends on how they are deployed (see Butts, Zweig, and Mamalian, in this volume). In particular, who are the juveniles sent to JDCs and how severe are their drug problems? What can communities expect to gain in the aggregate by controlling drug use among those youth sent to juvenile drug court? Many JDCs do not target their efforts to substantially benefit the community. They accept youth with limited criminal histories and no indications of severe drug problems. A single arrest for marijuana possession could be enough to qualify a youth for drug court in many jurisdictions. Were it not for the availability of the drug court program, such youth would not be so deeply involved in the juvenile justice system.

Of course, for some of these youth, an experience with drug court may help them avoid future drug abuse and legal trouble. For others, however, drug court could turn out just as damaging to them as drug use. They could be harmed by the stigma and deviant self-identity that result from formal court processing and a lengthy regimen of court-ordered treatment. Formalized legal intervention with adolescents is not risk-free. Young people who are arrested and brought to court may be more likely to become adult criminals than similar youth who are allowed to discover for themselves how to be law-abiding and drug-free (Bernburg and Krohn 2003). If a JDC program were to accept many clients without serious drug problems or criminal involvement, the program would not significantly affect drug-related crime in the community and it could actually harm some youth.

What Is a "Drug-Involved" Offender?

Whether JDCs turn out to be a good solution for youth and their communities, there is no doubt the issue of substance abuse is highly relevant in the juvenile justice system. At the very least, prolonged substance use increases the odds that a young person will be arrested and referred to the juvenile justice system. Even for teenagers charged with non-drug crimes, substance abuse may contribute to the scale and trajectory of their involvement with other illegal behaviors. The social, educational, and vocational problems associated with chronic drug abuse can also make it harder for young offenders to participate in the rehabilitative programs designed to help them stay out of trouble.

The number of young people arrested and charged with drug-related offenses increased in recent decades. Between 1990 and 1997, the arrest rate for juvenile drug violations in the United States more than doubled (figure 1.3). After the mid-1990s, juvenile drug arrests did not decline as much as did arrests for violent crime. The number of juveniles charged with violent crimes dropped so much in recent years that by 2002, the violent juvenile arrest rate was similar to rates from the 1970s. The arrest rate for juvenile drug offenses, while falling, remained higher than in previous years.

Increasing numbers of juvenile drug arrests mean that juvenile courts must deal with more drug cases. Indeed, the number of drug offense cases referred to U.S. juvenile courts grew sharply in recent years (Stahl, Finnegan, and Kang 2002). In 1985, juvenile courts handled approximately 74,000 drug offense cases, accounting for 6 percent of all delinquency cases that year. By 2000, the number of drug cases had nearly

Figure 1.3. *Unlike Violent Crime Arrests, Juvenile Drug Arrests Have Not Returned to Pre-1990 Levels*

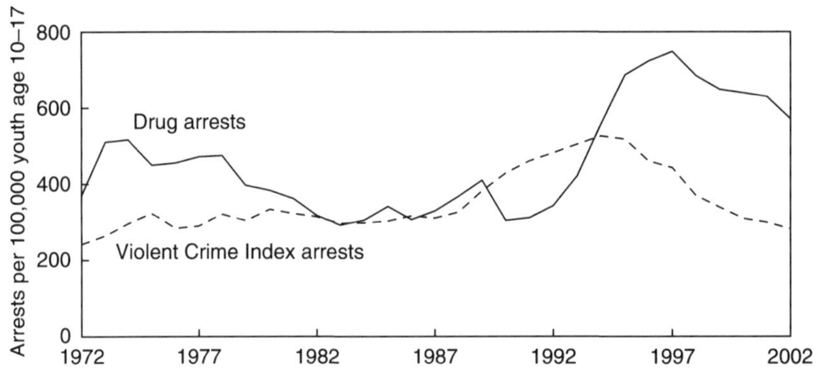

Source: Urban Institute analysis of data from the Federal Bureau of Investigation, Uniform Crime Reporting Program.

tripled to 198,500, accounting for 12 percent of all delinquency cases handled by juvenile courts across the country.

To say that illegal drugs are highly relevant in the juvenile justice system, however, is not to say that drugs and crime are synonymous. Most adolescent drug users, in fact, are never arrested or prosecuted. The number of youth who have used illegal drugs is far larger than the number of drug users in the juvenile justice system. Findings from the National Survey on Drug Use and Health (SAMHSA 2003) suggested that nearly half (47 percent) of all 16- and 17-year-olds have tried an illegal drug at least once.[3] The drug most often used by adolescents is cannabis or marijuana (39 percent of 16- and 17-year-olds). Other drugs are used by far fewer youth, including Ecstasy or MDMA (8 percent), cocaine (6 percent), LSD (6 percent), and methamphetamine (3 percent). This impression of adolescent drug use is confirmed by other national surveys. In 2003, nearly one in four high school seniors reported at least some illegal drug use within the past month—again, mostly marijuana (figure 1.4).

Illegal drug use is probably more pervasive among young people involved with the juvenile justice system, but exact levels of substance abuse by juvenile offenders are difficult to estimate because there are no consistent or broadly available data on the question. Some information is available from drug tests taken by newly arrested youth. Findings from a statistical data series once managed by the National Institute of Justice,

Figure 1.4. *Because Marijuana Is the Most Commonly Used Illegal Drug,
Trends in Youth Drug Use Are Dominated by Marijuana Trends*

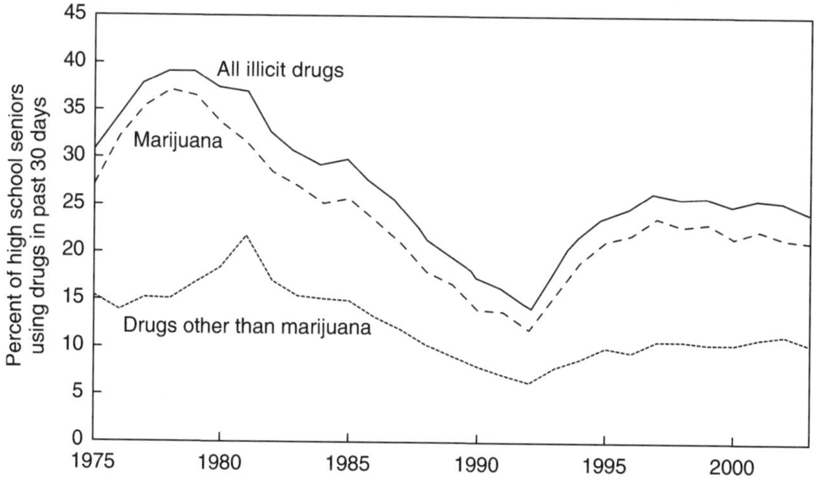

Source: Johnston, O'Malley, and Bachman (2003).

the Arrestee Drug Abuse Monitoring (ADAM) program, suggested that half of all juveniles arrested and taken into custody by law enforcement officials had recently used illegal drugs, mostly marijuana (table 1.2).[4] Of course, youth taken into physical custody may not be representative of all juvenile offenders. Some arrested youth are released by law enforcement and directed to appear for a juvenile intake process later. In addition, a positive drug test merely indicates recent use, not substance abuse or dependence. Researchers who have used diagnostic measures to estimate substance abuse among more representative samples of youthful offenders have found prevalence levels far lower than 50 percent.

In one study of juvenile intake cases in Texas, clinically sophisticated interviews detected "substance use disorders" in 25 percent of a randomly selected sample of 991 juvenile offenders, and most were alcohol and marijuana users as opposed to users of other substances (Wasserman et al. forthcoming). Abuse and dependence disorders involving drugs other than alcohol or marijuana were seen in 3 and 3.6 percent of the sample, respectively. Another recent study measured past-year substance abuse disorders among youth involved with the juvenile justice system but not necessarily adjudicated or detained (Aarons et al. 2001). Even considering

Table 1.2. *In Many Large Cities, Half the Male Juveniles Arrested and Taken into Custody Test Positive for at Least One Illegal Drug, Primarily Marijuana*

Jurisdiction	Any illegal drug	Marijuana
Birmingham, AL	45%	43%
Cleveland, OH	62%	60%
Denver, CO	62%	59%
Los Angeles, CA	54%	52%
Phoenix, AZ	69%	62%
San Antonio, TX	56%	53%
San Diego, CA	57%	53%
Tucson, AZ	56%	53%

Source: National Institute of Justice (2000).

that past-year disorders should be far higher than current prevalence rates, the study found fewer drug problems than would be suggested by drug tests of recent arrestees. Using clinical interviews, the study found past-year "alcohol use disorders" in 28 percent of the sample and cannabis use disorders in 15 percent. Disorders involving other drugs were less prevalent. Disorders involving cocaine, for example, were detected in just 0.5 percent of the sample.

The Marijuana Problem

Any serious investigation of substance abuse in the United States must confront an uncomfortable but obvious reality—American drug laws are not governed by the dangers associated with specific drugs. Drug laws are not about pharmacology. They are an imperfect mixture of fear, anger, and moral judgment. If drug laws were a carefully calibrated response to the individual or societal costs of drug use, the strongest legal penalties would be reserved for alcohol, heroin, and certain prescription drugs, such as Oxycontin. These drugs are easily abused, highly addictive, and in large doses cause sudden death. Yet, their social and legal status ranges from extreme condemnation (heroin) to commercial and cultural celebration (alcohol).

Then, there are non-dangerous drugs that can result in severe legal penalties. The prime example, of course, is marijuana (or cannabis). Despite years of government-sponsored advertising suggesting that marijuana is harmful and dangerous, scientific reviews have found that the most dangerous thing about smoking marijuana is the smoke itself (e.g., Earleywine 2002; Iversen 2000). After a thorough review of the scientific literature, the National Academy of Science's Institute of Medicine recently came to a similar conclusion. The alleged harmful effects of cannabis (including those related to cognitive functioning) turn out to be trivial, temporary (lasting only as long as inebriation), or produced only by immense doses that are impossible to achieve outside a laboratory setting (Joy, Watson, and Benson 1999). The most significant and lasting risks for a typical marijuana smoker are associated with the tar in unfiltered smoke and its effects on the lungs.

If marijuana laws cannot be justified by the effects of the drug itself, why are thousands of young people arrested every year for marijuana possession and use? Many policymakers and juvenile justice practitioners argue that cannabis is a "gateway" drug that leads to the use of more dangerous drugs. This belief, however, has been refuted by research (Labouvie and White 2002; Morral, McCaffrey, and Paddock 2002; Wagner and Anthony 2001). The notorious gateway effect is a misreading of the natural consequences of the friendship networks that form among illegal drug users. Marijuana smokers are more likely to be around when other illegal drugs are offered, but this does not mean marijuana users are chemically or psychologically compelled to try them. Once opportunity is statistically controlled, they are no more likely to escalate their drug use.

So, why are marijuana laws still enforced and why are marijuana users still arrested and even incarcerated? There are several possible explanations. Policymakers who support the continuing enforcement of cannabis prohibition may be acting with imperfect information. They may believe that marijuana is truly harmful despite all evidence to the contrary. They may be equally unaware of research showing that enforcing marijuana laws costs society more than marijuana use itself does (Miron 2004). On the other hand, they may be less concerned with science than they are with electoral politics. Few public officials want to be labeled as "soft" on drugs. The politics of drug prohibition may also accurately reflect public attitudes. For whatever reason, many people simply don't approve of marijuana use. Finally, elected officials may be heeding the warnings of the drug treatment industry, which helps foster negative attitudes about marijuana use because it is in their interest to do so. Obviously, a sizeable portion of drug treatment revenues would suddenly disappear if adolescent marijuana users were no longer subject to arrest and coercive treatment.

Whatever reasons explain the continuing prosecution of marijuana use, how are juvenile justice officials to know when a youth's marijuana use has truly become a "problem" for the youth and not merely a behavior scorned by others? Certainly, abusive and chronic marijuana use can be a problem, but marijuana use itself is not sufficient proof of a drug problem. Juvenile justice officials must weigh their response to marijuana users carefully and proportionally to their overall efforts to stem adolescent substance abuse. Over-intervening with casual marijuana users would clog juvenile drug court programs and prevent them from dealing effectively with youth who have serious drug problems. They key question is, which users are the serious users?

Which Youth Have "Serious" Drug Problems?

Policies and programs to address teen drug abuse are often justified with terrifying stories of overdoses and young lives ruined by addiction. Drug treatment providers in particular advertise their services with disturbing tales about altered brain chemistry and the deleterious effects of abusing cocaine, methamphetamine, and Ecstasy. Many Americans would be surprised to learn that most drug-using youth in the juvenile justice system are actually nondependent alcohol drinkers and marijuana smokers. Youth who abuse more serious drugs can be found in the juvenile justice system, but they are far from typical. Truly addicted juveniles, in fact, are rare. Most juvenile offenders—as with teenagers in general—use alcohol and marijuana only and very few could be described as addicted or dependent. During the development of this book, Urban Institute researchers routinely asked juvenile drug court officials about the drug use behavior of their clients. The consensus view was that 80 to 90 percent of the youth referred to juvenile drug courts were nondependent users of alcohol and marijuana (see Butts, Zweig, and Mamalian, in this volume). The lowest estimate these practitioners ever mentioned was 75 percent.

Of course, all "drug-involved" juvenile offenders are "at risk" of more serious problems, just as everyone who drinks alcohol is at risk of alcoholism. The critical policy question is, are the risks faced by youth who have been *arrested* for drug use significantly greater than those faced by

teen drug users in general? Can we assume that a juvenile arrested for marijuana use is, by definition, at greater risk of long-term harm from substance abuse than thousands of other teen marijuana smokers who manage
to avoid arrest? Is arrest a useful proxy for the clinical severity of substance
abuse? Certainly, other factors could increase the probability of detection
and arrest for teen drug users—such as race, gender, neighborhood, social
and economic class, parental education and labor status, the amount of
leisure time spent in public areas versus private homes or motor vehicles,
educational enrollment and achievement, verbal ability, and so on. Are
these factors considered when weighing the significance of drug arrests?

As more teenagers are compelled to participate in the juvenile drug
court process, policymakers, practitioners, and parents should clarify
what the goals and purposes of JDCs should be and how they should
target their efforts. Clearly, the nation cannot afford a system of drug
courts designed to intervene with all youth at the first sign of illegal
drug use. The average JDC handles 40 to 50 cases a year. According to
the U.S. Census Bureau, there are approximately 17 million American
residents between the ages of 14 and 17.[5] Based on national rates of
teen drug use, 15 percent of youth that age (or 2.5 million) would be
expected to have used an illegal drug at least once in the past 30 days
(SAMHSA 2003). Given that most teen drug users are marijuana users,
and given that marijuana is detectable in bodily fluids for up to several
weeks, this would mean perhaps as many as 2 million Americans age
14 to 17 would test positive for illegal drugs at any given time. If just
one in five of these drug-using teens was arrested and sent to juvenile
drug court each year, the United States would need 8,000 to 10,000 new
juvenile drug courts to handle the caseload. The number of needed
programs would grow exponentially if juvenile drug courts were
expected to handle all teenagers that drink alcohol illegally.

Even if the United States could afford to provide a drug court for every
juvenile that needed one, there is no clear consensus about who those juveniles are. Some juvenile drug courts accept clients with drug behaviors
similar to a broad cross-section of American youth. Many programs use
only vague terms to denote the degree of substance abuse necessary for a
juvenile to be referred to drug court. They rely on nonclinical judgments
about drug "problems" or drug "involvement." The National Drug Court
Institute and National Council of Juvenile and Family Court Judges
recently suggested that JDC clients could include any young offender
"identified as having problems with alcohol and/or other drugs" (NDCI/
NCJFCJ 2003, 7). This suggests that the use of alcohol alone could

qualify a young person for juvenile drug court and that the severity of behavior necessary for a JDC referral is open to interpretation by each jurisdiction. In fact, the report noted explicitly that NDCI/NCJFCJ decided not to distinguish "use" from "abuse" in order to recognize that youth appearing before juvenile drug courts are likely to have different "levels of use" (p. 2).

Even diagnostic guidelines provide little assurance that JDCs focus their resources on youth with serious drug problems. Most screening and assessment instruments used in the juvenile justice system rely on the American Psychiatric Association's *Diagnostic and Statistical Manual of Mental Disorders* (DSM) to identify varying levels of drug use according to severity or harm (see Mears, in this volume). Few policymakers appreciate how much the DSM changed in recent decades. As recently as 1980, the DSM largely relied on objective criteria to distinguish drug use from drug abuse and drug dependence. Today, the procedures for identifying drug abuse and dependence are not limited to medical, pharmacological, or even clearly defined behavioral indicators. They are normative judgments, subject to practitioner interpretation, cultural bias, changing social mores, and shifting policy views.

In 1980, the third edition of the DSM differentiated substance abuse from "non-pathological substance use." An abuse diagnosis required the presence of "impairment in social or occupational functioning" that lasted for at least one month. To declare a person's use of marijuana as "abuse," the DSM required a clinician to report social or occupational impairment lasting for at least one month *and* "pathological use—intoxication throughout the day; use of cannabis nearly every day for at least a month; episodes of Cannabis Delusional Disorder." By definition, very few adolescents qualified.

By 1994, the concept of non-pathological use had been removed from the DSM, and the criteria for abuse had been weakened so much that abuse could be indicated by any single item on a list of four behavioral indicators, as long as that indicator was present at some point during the previous 12 months. The four indicators were

- recurrent substance-related legal problems (e.g., arrests for substance-related disorderly conduct);
- recurrent substance use in situations in which it is physically hazardous (e.g., driving an automobile or operating a machine when impaired by substance use);

- continued substance use despite having persistent or recurrent social or interpersonal problems caused or exacerbated by the effects of the substance (e.g., arguments with spouse about consequences of intoxication, physical fights); and
- recurrent substance use resulting in a failure to fulfill major role obligations at work, school, or home (e.g., repeated absences or poor work performance related to substance use; substance-related absences, suspensions, or expulsions from school; neglect of children or household).

Overall, these revisions "lowered the bar" and made the DSM criteria for drug abuse increasingly social. Legal problems alone could now qualify an individual for a substance abuse disorder, even in the absence of tolerance and withdrawal, and without any indications of school problems, occupational troubles, or family strife. The new criteria have profound consequences for youth, depending on their community context. Young drug users from communities where drug laws are strictly enforced would naturally be more likely to encounter "recurrent legal problems." Thus, the chances of being labeled a drug "abuser" rather than a drug "user" would be partly determined by the strength and consistency of law enforcement in one's city or neighborhood.

If any young person who receives a DSM diagnosis of drug "abuse" is considered appropriate for juvenile drug court, millions of American teenagers could qualify for drug court. If the "net" of drug court intervention is cast that wide, many youth could end up in a JDC program for nonproblematic drug use, and the cost-effectiveness of drug courts would be lost. Moreover, when too many teen drug users are considered potential drug court clients, the juvenile justice system will by necessity have to select juvenile drug court referrals from a very large pool of eligible youth. How can policymakers be certain that the criteria used to make these selections are free of diagnostic inaccuracy, racial and class bias, and the self-interest of drug treatment providers who depend on a constant stream of amenable clients for their livelihood?

The Need for Research Evidence

The explosion of drug courts across the United States is proof enough that the programs are popular and are supported by a wide range of practitioners and policymakers. But are they an effective addition to the juvenile justice system? Researchers must begin to address many unanswered questions about juvenile drug courts and their compatibility with the juvenile justice system. Is court-ordered drug treatment for adolescents always better than treatment offered without the backing of judicial authority? Which youth respond well to the drug court process and which do not? How serious should a youth's drug behavior be to justify the added expense and treatment intensity of juvenile drug court? Should the use of alcohol and marijuana alone be enough to send a youthful offender through a 12-month program of supervision and treatment? If so, how severe should the use of alcohol and marijuana be to qualify a youth for drug court?

What happens to young offenders after they leave juvenile drug court? Do JDC programs provide tangible benefits unavailable in traditional juvenile courts? Do they change youth behavior enough to offset their operating costs and the negative effects they may have on young offenders? Surprisingly, there are no good answers to these questions. Juvenile drug courts have developed so rapidly that evaluators have not had time to generate empirical support for their effectiveness. Policymakers do not know whether juvenile court drug courts are effective and whether they are different enough from criminal courts and juvenile courts to warrant their own program models and funding streams. Although the drug court concept is firmly established throughout the country and professional organizations and membership groups have been actively promoting drug courts for nearly 10 years, evaluation findings remain scarce. Jurisdictions working to start new drug courts usually rely on anecdotal "best practice" ideas. New juvenile drug courts in particular tend to pattern their policies and procedures after other reputedly successful programs, regardless of whether those reputations are backed by sound evidence.

Evaluating drug court effectiveness presents many challenges. Their relatively small caseloads, the lengthy duration of each offender's involvement, and the need for long-term behavioral follow-up mean that completing a drug court evaluation can take four to five years. Even studies that include adequate follow-up do not always address critical questions. Few drug court researchers have even attempted to conduct theory-based evaluations, partly because there is no clear consensus about the theoretical rationale for drug court effectiveness. Unless data collection and measurement efforts are guided by an articulated theory of how drug courts change offender behavior, it is nearly impossible for evaluators to establish evidence of program impact (i.e., the empirical connection between program participation and subsequent behavior). Instead, researchers are likely to settle for "black box" studies that compare outcomes among drug participants and nonparticipants without disentangling the value of individual program elements (figure 1.5).

The absence of compelling evidence should not be surprising at this stage in the development of drug courts. Before federal funding was available, most drug courts were local reform projects pursued by individual judges or other court officials. Well into the 1990s, most drug courts were busy getting their programs organized and trying to secure operational funding. Program staff did not have time to participate in complex research projects. Even today, many juvenile drug courts are not suitable for evaluation because they handle small caseloads of carefully selected clients, leaving evaluators to cope with inadequate sample sizes, limited statistical power, and inappropriate or nonexistent comparison groups. Small programs have to run for many years to accumulate enough cases for reliable evaluation findings. Juvenile drug courts also vary in the types of offenders they handle, the duration and intensity of their treatment programs, their use of sanctions and incentives, and their policies regarding client termination. These factors make it difficult to generalize the results of one study to juvenile drug courts in general.

No evaluation of juvenile drug courts has yet been able to test an explicit hypothesis of how program operations affect offender behavior. Proponents offer numerous reasons why they think drug courts work—the effects of drug treatment, the personal involvement of judges, and the structured monitoring of treatment compliance, to name a few—but there is no clear consensus about which program features are most important for which client outcomes. How should evaluators measure the key ingredients of the drug court process? How should they draw a conceptual

Figure 1.5. *Typical "Black Box" Drug Court Evaluation Framework*

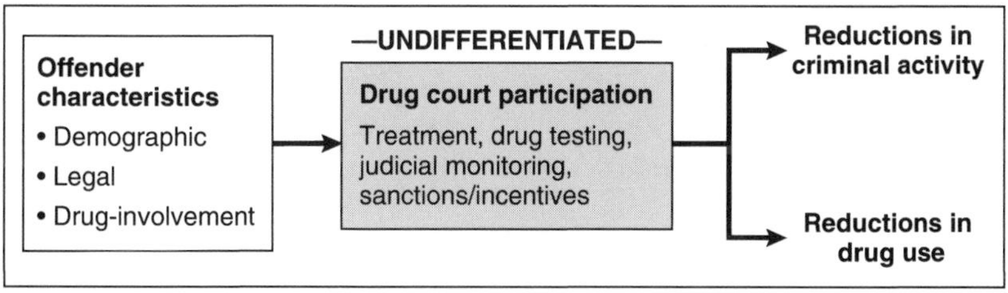

Source: Urban Institute National Evaluation of Juvenile Drug Courts.

boundary around a drug court program and specify the causal chain of events that leads to program impact? Is the treatment provided to offenders the essence of drug court, or do courtroom activities and case managers have independent effects? Is case management part of treatment? Does client behavior change in response to the actions of judges, prosecutors, defense attorneys, or probation officers? If teachers coordinate educational plans with treatment goals for students involved in juvenile drug courts, does this mean schools should be considered part of drug courts?

Juvenile drug courts were established in part because of the widespread belief that reducing substance abuse among youthful offenders will reduce recidivism. Positive findings from drug treatment research have led policymakers and practitioners to endorse an expanded role for drug treatment in the justice system. The drug court process is thought to keep clients engaged and attached to the treatment process, and client retention is paramount for positive treatment outcomes (Hubbard et al. 1989; Siddall and Conway 1988). These hypotheses are likely behind the popularity of the drug court concept, but they need to be tested by well-designed, theoretically oriented evaluations, and some of that research needs to focus on the application of drug courts in the juvenile justice system.

Conclusion

Drug courts are one manifestation of a broad, national movement to develop new specialized courts, including community courts, mental health courts, and domestic violence courts (Berman and Feinblatt 2001). These "problem-solving" courts have introduced new ways of thinking to the criminal justice system. Courts are no longer limited to establishing facts and imposing sentences. They use their legal authority to identify and solve problems at the individual, family, and community levels. Ironically, the traditional juvenile court pioneered this "new" approach with young offenders more than a century ago. Juvenile drug courts, however, are not the same as juvenile courts. Juvenile drug courts involve greater judicial oversight of service delivery and case progress. Offenders make far more court appearances, and treatment goals are the primary concern of the court process. In fact, juvenile drug courts may reflect the original ideals of juvenile justice more closely than do contemporary juvenile courts.

To understand these issues and to clarify what makes juvenile drug courts effective, researchers must begin to investigate juvenile drug courts more carefully. Future evaluations should be designed using theoretically informed conceptual frameworks. The findings of nontheoretical studies are encouraging, but little information is available about the key components of the juvenile drug court process. Researchers are only beginning to investigate drug court operations and effectiveness, and many important questions about juvenile drug courts have not been answered—or sometimes even asked. The remaining chapters in this book examine the development and operations of juvenile drug courts and suggest ways that evaluation research could help clarify their mission and document their influence.

NOTES

1. *Crime in the United States,* annual series. Washington, D.C.: U.S. Department of Justice, Federal Bureau of Investigation. Online: http://www.fbi.gov/ucr/ucr.htm.

2. In November 2002, the former Drug Courts Program Office was abolished and its functions were moved to the Bureau of Justice Assistance within the Office of Justice Programs.

3. The National Survey on Drug Use and Health was previously known as the National Household Survey on Drug Abuse.

4. Federal funding for the Arrestee Drug Abuse Monitoring program was eliminated in 2004.

5. Found at http://www.census.gov/population/www/index.html, as of March 2004.

REFERENCES

Aarons, Gregory A., Sandra A. Brown, Richard L. Hough, Ann F. Garland, and Patricia A. Wood. 2001. "Prevalence of Adolescent Substance Use Disorders across Five Sectors of Care." *Journal of the American Academy of Child and Adolescent Psychiatry* 40(4): 419–26.

American Psychiatric Association. 1994. *Diagnostic and Statistical Manual of Mental Disorders,* 4th ed. Washington, DC: American Psychiatric Association.

APA. *See* American Psychiatric Association.

Berman, Greg, and John Feinblatt. 2001. "Problem-Solving Courts: A Brief Primer." *Law & Policy* 23(2): 125–40.

Bernard, Thomas J. 1992. *The Cycle of Juvenile Justice.* New York: Oxford University Press.

Bernburg, Jön Gunnar, and Marvin D. Krohn. 2003. "Labeling, Life Chances, and Adult Crime: The Direct and Indirect Effects of Official Intervention in Adolescence on Crime in Early Adulthood." *Criminology* 41(4): 1287–1318.

Butts, Jeffrey A., and Ojmarrh Mitchell. 2000. "Brick by Brick: Dismantling the Border between Juvenile and Adult Justice." In *Boundary Changes in Criminal Justice Organizations,* vol. 2 of *Criminal Justice 2000,* edited by Charles M. Friel (167–213). Washington, DC: U.S. Department of Justice, National Institute of Justice.

Earleywine, Mitchell. 2002. *Understanding Marijuana: A New Look at the Scientific Evidence.* New York: Oxford University Press.

Fox, Sanford J. 1970. "Juvenile Justice Reform: An Historical Perspective." *Stanford Law Review* 22:1187–1239.

Hubbard, Robert L., Mary Ellen Marsden, J. Valley Rachal, Henrick J. Harwood, Elizabeth Cavanaugh, and Harold M. Ginzburg. 1989. *Drug Abuse Treatment: A National Study of Effectiveness.* Chapel Hill: The University of North Carolina Press.

Iversen, Leslie. 2000. *The Science of Marijuana.* New York: Oxford University Press.

Johnston, Lloyd D., Patrick M. O'Malley, and Jerald G. Bachman. 2003. *Secondary School Students.* Vol. 1 of *Monitoring the Future: National Survey Results on Drug Use, 1975–2002.* Bethesda, MD: National Institute on Drug Abuse.

Joy, Janet E., Stanley J. Watson Jr., and John A. Benson Jr. 1999. "First, Do No Harm: Consequences of Marijuana Use and Abuse." In *Marijuana and Medicine: Assessing the Science Base,* edited by Janet E. Joy, Stanley J. Watson Jr., and John A. Benson Jr. (83–136). Washington, DC: National Academies Press.

Labouvie, Erich, and Helene R. White. 2002. "Drug Sequences, Age of Onset, and Use Trajectories as Predictors of Drug Abuse/Dependence in Young Adulthood." In *Stages and Pathways of Drug Involvement: Examining the Gateway Hypothesis,* edited by Denise B. Kandel (19–41). Cambridge, U.K.: Cambridge University Press.

Manfredi, Christopher P. 1998. *The Supreme Court and Juvenile Justice.* Lawrence: University Press of Kansas.

Miron, Jeffrey A. 2004. *Drug War Crimes.* Oakland, CA: The Independent Institute.

Morral, Andrew R., Daniel F. McCaffrey, and Susan M. Paddock. 2002. "Reassessing the Marijuana Gateway Effect." *Addiction* 97:1493–1504.

National Drug Court Institute and National Council of Juvenile and Family Court Judges. 2003. *Juvenile Drug Courts: Strategies in Practice.* NCJ187866. Washington, DC: U.S. Department of Justice, Bureau of Justice Assistance.

National Institute of Justice. 2000. *1999 Annual Report on Drug Use among Adult and Juvenile Arrestees: Juvenile Program Findings.* Washington, DC: U.S. Department of Justice, Office of Justice Programs, National Institute of Justice. http://www.ncjrs.org/pdffiles1/nij/181426.pdf.

NDCI/NCJFCJ. *See* National Drug Court Institute and National Council of Juvenile and Family Court Judges.

Office of Justice Programs. 1996. *Juvenile Drug Courts: Preliminary Assessment of Activities Underway and Implementation Issues Being Addressed.* OJP Drug Court Clearinghouse and Technical Assistance Project. Washington, DC: American University. http://www.american.edu/spa/justice/publications/juvsum.html.

———. 1999. *Juvenile Drug Court Activity Update: Summary Information.* OJP Drug Court Clearinghouse and Technical Assistance Project. Washington, DC: American University. http://www.american.edu/spa/justice/publications/Juvoverviewinsert.htm.

———. 2001. *Juvenile Drug Court Activity Update: Summary Information.* OJP Drug Court Clearinghouse and Technical Assistance Project. Washington, DC: American University. http://www.american.edu/justice/publications/juvenilecourtactivity.pdf.

————. 2002. *Summary of Drug Court Activity by State and County, Juvenile and Family Drug Courts.* OJP Drug Court Clearinghouse and Technical Assistance Project. Washington, DC: American University. http://www.american.edu/justice/publications/Juvsumchartgamze.pdf.

————. 2003. *Summary of Drug Court Activity by State and County, November 7, 2003.* OJP Drug Court Clearinghouse and Technical Assistance Project. Washington, DC: American University. http://www.american.edu/justice/publications/drgchart2k.pdf.

SAMHSA. *See* Substance Abuse and Mental Health Services Administration.

Siddall, James W., and Gail L. Conway. 1988. "Interactional Variables Associated with Retention and Success in Residential Drug Treatment." *The International Journal of the Addictions* 23(12): 1241–54.

Stahl, Anne, Terrence Finnegan, and W. Kang. 2002. "Easy Access to Juvenile Court Statistics: 1985–2000." Pittsburgh, PA: National Center for Juvenile Justice. http://ojjdp.ncjrs.org/ojstatbb/ezajcs/.

Substance Abuse and Mental Health Services Administration. 2003. *Summary of National Findings.* Vol. 1 of *Results from the 2002 National Survey on Drug Use and Health.* NHSDA Series H-22, DHHS Publication No. SMA 03-3836. Rockville, MD: Substance Abuse and Mental Health Services Administration.

Wagner, Fernando, and James C. Anthony. 2001. "Into the World of Illegal Drug Use: Exposure Opportunity and Other Mechanisms Linking the Use of Alcohol, Tobacco, Marijuana, and Cocaine." *American Journal of Epidemiology* 155(10): 918–25.

Wasserman, Gail A., Larkin S. McReynolds, Susan J. Ko, Laura M. Katz, and Jennifer R. Carpenter. Forthcoming. "Gender Differences in Psychiatric Disorders at Juvenile Probation Intake." *American Journal of Public Health.*

Watkins, John C. Jr. 1998. *The Juvenile Justice Century.* Durham, NC: Carolina Academic Press.

The White House. 2004. *National Drug Control Strategy, Update, March 2004.* Washington, DC: The White House. http://www.state.gov/documents/organization/30228.pdf.

2

American Drug Policy and the Evolution of Drug Treatment Courts

John Roman, Jeffrey A. Butts, and Alison S. Rebeck

The first drug court in the United States was established in Dade County, Florida, in 1989. The program was based on a simple yet powerful idea. The court offered to dismiss pending drug charges for offenders that completed a program of substance abuse treatment. The program integrated social service delivery with substance abuse treatment, blended court processing with a schedule of graduated sanctions and incentives, and used a case management approach to place nonviolent drug-involved defendants in judicially supervised treatment and supervision programs.

Court systems in the late 1980s were overwhelmed with drug cases and drug-involved offenders facing charges of all types. Crowded court dockets and growing jail and prison populations forced criminal justice systems to explore alternatives to conventional case processing. Extending the idea of specialized court dockets for drug offenders that began in the 1970s, drug courts were designed to reduce caseloads and break the cycle of drug use and crime. Although the expressed purpose of drug courts was often reducing drug use, their true mission included controlling burgeoning court caseloads. The guiding premise was relatively simple: if drug-involved offenders could be made to stop using drugs, then pressure on the court system could be dramatically reduced. By the mid-1990s, hundreds of U.S. cities and counties had started drug court programs. Many communities were beginning to set up drug courts for juvenile offenders as well.

Drug courts were believed to be a cost-effective way to deal with large numbers of drug-using offenders. Traditionally, the criminal justice system handled drug users much like other offenders. Unless they were arrested again or violated probation, drug users were seen as typical offenders, albeit with risky behavior. Even those who continued to use drugs while under court supervision suffered few consequences unless their behavior resulted in a new arrest. Drug courts offered a new way to hold drug offenders accountable, to supervise their behavior during court-ordered treatment, and perhaps to reduce crime and substance abuse in the community. The drug court concept was the most prominent example of what later became a large movement of specialized, or "problem-solving" courts, including community courts, mental health courts, and domestic violence courts (Berman and Feinblatt 2001). These courts introduced a new philosophy to the criminal justice system. Courts were no longer limited to establishing facts and imposing sentences in a strictly adversarial process. They could use their legal authority to identify and solve problems in the community.

The rapid spread of drug courts in the United States might suggest that their growth was governed by a well-defined plan, but this was not the case. Drug courts emerged through an adaptive process; no central authority ordered their implementation. As jurisdictions struggled to deal with drug-involved offenders, the idea to link nonviolent offenders to court-supervised treatment instead of incarceration had an obvious, practical appeal. Once the basic concept was established and drug courts were widely publicized, federal agencies began to offer funding and training to develop even more drug courts.

The growth of *juvenile* drug courts (or JDCs) occurred for slightly different reasons from those motivating the development of adult drug courts. Drug courts for adults provided a new way to deal with drug-involved offenders, but the traditional mission of the juvenile court was already similar to this "new" approach. Juvenile court judges had always been able to supervise cases closely and review each offender's progress in treatment. The juvenile court had always diverted many offenders from formal sanctioning in return for their participation in treatment programs. Most important, the central purpose of the juvenile court process had always been to change each offender's behavior using a combination of sanctions and services. Punishment for past crimes was not the juvenile court's primary mission. Of course, juvenile courts varied in their ability (or inclination) to conform to the classic model of juvenile justice (Fox

1970; Watkins 1998). Some jurisdictions never fully embraced it, and many states took legislative actions during the 1980s and 1990s to undo key elements of their juvenile court systems (Butts and Mitchell 2000). But even after these reforms and policy changes, the juvenile court process resembled drug courts far more than criminal courts.

Why then did so many jurisdictions develop juvenile drug courts? Funding was an important impetus. Once adult drug courts were established, federal funds to start new drug courts increased, and some of these funds were designated for juvenile programs, leading to greater demand for juvenile program models. Some juvenile court judges may have viewed the new drug court concept as a way to leverage new resources for treatment. Others may have wanted to use the drug court process to exert greater influence over community agencies. It is also possible that juvenile justice officials simply wanted to be part of the drug court movement. As anecdotal evidence of drug court success began to accumulate, policymakers may have been persuaded that the combination of services and supervision made possible in drug court might also improve juvenile outcomes.

Understanding the Drug Court Mission

The proliferation of drug courts during the 1990s was not prompted by a revolutionary change in American social values, nor did it reflect a sudden shift in drug policy. It resulted from a century-long evolutionary process that gradually moved policies and programs to reduce substance abuse beyond the exclusive domain of social services and into the criminal justice arena. Drug abuse was criminalized during the 20th century because people believed punishment was the only useful way to control drug problems. When new treatment approaches emerged and people began to see their effects, policymakers and practitioners saw new potential for drug treatment within the criminal justice system. As the justice system embraced its new mission, it had to devise new organizational strategies.

James Q. Wilson pointed out that "organization matters" when developing effective bureaucracies (1989, 14). In *Bureaucracy*, Wilson argued that three concepts drive a public agency's effectiveness: how the organization performs its critical tasks, how widely the sense of mission is shared within the organization, and how much autonomy exists to respond to challenges to the organization's mission. A successful public agency fluidly integrates mission and tasks, and grants sufficient (but not excessive) authority to practitioners to implement programming. An agency's history is often the best guide to understanding the relationship between its mission and methods. Historical context may reveal why an agency does certain things; evaluation research may shed light on whether those things work as intended.

Drug courts were designed to manage caseload pressures in the criminal justice system by addressing the underlying substance abuse problems of criminal offenders. Drug-related stresses on criminal caseloads derive from several sources: increases in substance abuse among the general population, increases in the number of people arrested as a result of substance use behavior, increases in the type and range of problems brought into the justice system by arrested drug users, and increases in the number of offenders incarcerated for substance-related offenses. Drug courts could be configured to address varying combinations of these pressures. The mission of any one drug court will directly relate to how local officials perceive sources of strain on the justice system.

A drug court designed to manage one source of pressure may not effectively control pressure from another. For example, if a drug court were implemented to alleviate overcrowding in correctional facilities, it would likely incorporate a set of elements in its design (such as long participation periods, few incarceration-based sanctions, minimal responses to relapse, and high graduation rates) that support that particular mission. In doing so, the court might reduce the use of jail beds. However, it may not be able to meet other goals, such as intensively treating addicts and helping them achieve and maintain sobriety. Understanding the mission of drug courts is critical to developing hypotheses about their intended effects and how they attract the support of local practitioners and policymakers.

Drug Users in the Justice System

Three plausible hypotheses may explain why juvenile drug courts took hold in the 1990s and became a popular program model for juvenile justice systems. First, rising numbers of arrests could have led to increases in juvenile court caseloads, and the system responded to these pressures by looking to innovations like JDCs. Second, increases in drug use prevalence among adolescents may have led to societal pressures on the court system to implement more alternative programs for drug-involved youth. Third, juvenile drug courts may have provided an opportunity for juvenile justice officials to widen the net of intervention and deal with larger numbers of offenders. That is, increases in the availability of treatment for drug-involved juveniles may have enabled the system to respond to more juveniles overall.

Historical accounts of the drug court phenomenon typically attribute the growth and development of drug courts programs to increases in the number of drug offenders entering the justice system, and not only those charged with drug offenses. Not all drug-involved offenders are arrested for drug offenses. Many are charged with other crimes, including property offenses and violence. The population of drug users in the justice system is far larger than the number of individuals arrested for drug offenses. In fact, drug-testing data from the recently discontinued Arrestee Drug Abuse Monitoring (ADAM) program suggested that in many of the largest U.S. cities, half of all arrestees tested positive for at least one illegal drug at the time of arrest (National Institute of Justice 2000). Drug offenses usually account for less than one in four arrests nationwide.

Drug use prevalence statistics for arrestees are unavailable in most communities, but trends in drug offense arrests are a reasonable indicator of changes in the volume of drug-using offenders. Based on trends in these cases, there is support for the notion that drug courts were invented to deal with growing caseloads of drug-using offenders. Indeed, courts experienced a sharp increase in drug offense cases in recent decades, much of it associated with the surge in cocaine use during the mid-1980s. Between 1975 and 1990, the number of drug arrests made by U.S. law enforcement agencies jumped from approximately 600,000 to just over 1 million a year (table 2.1). Drug arrests involving juveniles, on the other hand, actually fell between 1975 and 1990 but climbed sharply after 1990. After remaining stable at around 75,000 cases a year between 1985 and 1992, the volume of drug offense cases disposed by juvenile courts rose sharply beginning in 1993, reaching nearly 200,000 cases annually by 1997 (Stahl, Finnegan, and Kang 2003). As discussed below, the growing numbers of drug offense cases in juvenile courts did not simply reflect an increase in juvenile drug use. They were partly the result of changing law enforcement practices, much like in adult courts.

The number of drug offense arrests nationwide climbed dramatically for young adults during the 1980s and peaked in 1989, just as the adult drug court movement began to take hold across the country (figure 2.1).

Table 2.1. *Drug Arrests in the United States*

Year	All ages	Under 18
1975	601,400	145,400
1980	580,900	109,700
1985	811,400	92,800
1990	1,089,500	81,200
1995	1,476,100	189,800
2000	1,579,600	203,900
2002	1,538,800	186,600

Source: Urban Institute analysis of data from the Federal Bureau of Investigation, Uniform Crime Reporting Program.

Note: Weighted, national estimates.

The number of juvenile arrests for drug offenses remained relatively unchanged throughout the 1980s but grew steadily after 1991—and the first juvenile drug courts started in 1995. Between 1990 and 1995, the number of juveniles arrested for drug offenses more than doubled. By 1995, the number of juvenile arrestees was higher than in the late 1970s. The per capita rate of drug arrests among young adults swelled during the 1980s, just before the emergence of adult drug courts, while a similar increase in arrest rates among juveniles occurred in the early 1990s, just before juvenile drug courts were launched in 1995.

Of course, the impetus to start drug courts did not come entirely from caseload increases, or rather, not from the size of the caseload. In the years before drug courts were implemented, the nation's courts were also seeing a different type of drug offender. Law enforcement efforts to deal with the rise in cocaine use during the 1980s shifted the profile of drug offenders referred to courts. Cases involving cocaine or heroin grew from just over 10 percent to more than 50 percent of all drug arrests between 1982 and 1988 (figure 2.2). Proportionally, marijuana offenders fell from 70 percent to 30 percent of all drug arrests. It would not be surprising if the shifting caseload was partly responsible for the growing interest in new methods for dealing with drug offenders during the late 1980s and early 1990s. However, by the time JDCs began to appear, marijuana was once again the most common type of drug charge.

Drug use patterns have changed markedly over the past two decades and do not precisely match changes in arrests. When drug *arrest* informa-

Figure 2.1. *Juvenile Drug Arrest Trends Are Dominated by Trends among Young Adults*

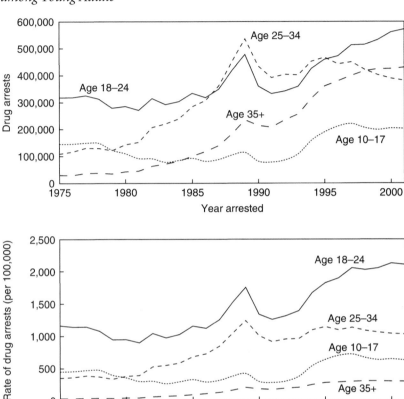

Source: Urban Institute analysis of data from the Federal Bureau of Investigation, Uniform Crime Reporting Program, national estimates.

tion is juxtaposed with drug *use* information, it becomes clear that drug offense caseloads were not climbing in the nation's courts because of a general increase in drug use among the population. In fact, the prevalence of illegal drug use in the United States (or, the overall percentage of people using drugs) was generally falling throughout the 1980s. Drug use by most age groups was either falling or relatively steady well into the 1990s (figure 2.3). Among juveniles, however, the prevalence of drug use jumped, from just over 10 percent admitting drug use in 1992 to nearly 20 percent in

Figure 2.2. *The Surge in Cocaine Arrests during the Late 1980s Changed the Composition of All Drug Arrests*

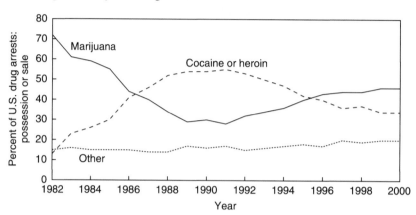

Source: U.S. Department of Justice, Federal Bureau of Investigation, Uniform Crime Reporting Program, as compiled in the Sourcebook of Criminal Justice Statistics Online.

1997. This increase could explain the growing number of drug offense cases handled by U.S. juvenile courts (figure 2.4).

There are various explanations for the changes in policy and practice leading to the invention of drug courts during the 1980s and 1990s. The crack epidemic of the 1980s certainly contributed to the growing number of drug-involved offenders referred to the court system. Changes in sentencing (i.e., longer sentences for drug crimes) and an increased police focus on disrupting the supply of drugs most likely had an impact as well. The public's perception that crime and violence are drug-related may have also affected policy. Whatever the exact combination of forces that brought about the birth of juvenile drug courts, their appearance was both an innovation in court administration and a manifestation of long-term trends in U.S. drug policy.

A Brief History of U.S. Drug Policy

Until the first American drug policies were created in the early 1900s, recreational drug use was socially acceptable in the United States (Musto 1999). The use of chemicals and plants to alter consciousness and mood was nearly a thousand years old (Earleywine 2002). By the 1800s, many

Figure 2.3.   *Unlike Other Age Groups, Reported Drug Use among Juveniles Increased during the 1990s*

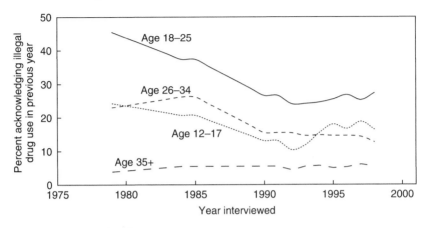

Source: SAMHSA (2000).

Figure 2.4.   *Drug Offense Cases in U.S. Juvenile Courts Grew during the 1990s*

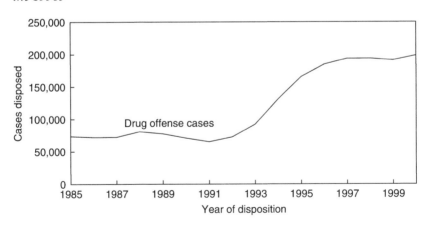

Source: Stahl, Finnegan, and Kang (2003).

Europeans and Asians were using opium; Americans tended to prefer alcohol. Even in the United States, however, there was a thriving trade in legal narcotics, including heroin and cocaine. Attitudes toward drugs and alcohol began to change during the Industrial Revolution as the need for increased efficiency in industry proved incompatible with chronic alcohol use. Increasing awareness of the economic and social damages caused by alcohol abuse was partly responsible for the first public recognition of alcohol's addictive properties, which led in turn to the development of the first disease models of addiction (Hoffman 2000).

The use and abuse of psychoactive substances other than alcohol became prevalent in America during the Civil War. The development and use of narcotics began to grow earlier in the early 19th century, and the use of marijuana and opiates had been recognized for hundreds of years, but the widespread use of morphine to treat wounded soldiers during the Civil War was associated with the first broad reports of drug addiction in the United States (Nolan 2001). In 1884, cocaine was discovered to be an effective anesthetic and it soon replaced morphine in many medical procedures. With growing medical acceptance and no regulation, entrepreneurs saw the commercial potential of cocaine and various suppliers began to offer the drug as a diuretic, a treatment for respiratory problems, and even a suppressant for opiate addiction (MacCoun and Reuter 2001; Musto 1999). The recreational use of opiates and cocaine increased during the late 1800s and early 1900s. A wide array of commercial products (e.g., Coca-Cola) contained opiates or cocaine, and intravenous drug paraphernalia was sold by mainstream retailers (Musto 1999). Soon, however, the problems of drug abuse and dependence became apparent. Family members, neighbors, and local officials began to observe that cocaine users, for example, sometimes exhibited aggressive behavior. In the worst cases, continued use of narcotics seemed to produce chronic physical and mental deterioration.

Many in the medical community initially saw drug addiction as a disease, characterized by physical cravings and a physiological change in the nervous system. The disease model encouraged physicians to view drug use itself as a loss of control by the addict. The search for effective treatments focused on developing new drugs that could counter the addictive properties of narcotics. These remedies proved generally unsuccessful, however, and in some cases simply added new addictive substances to the market.

Eventually, researchers began to believe that substance abuse was not a physiological condition at all, but a psychological and moral problem. The new model of addiction led to changes in treatment protocols and had a profound effect on social policies toward drug users and addicts (Nolan 2001). The new model linked substance abuse with social deviance in a new way, leading to a shift in social policies (MacCoun and Reuter 2001). The physiological model had suggested substance abuse and addiction caused deviance. The addict's behavior was beyond his or her control. The new paradigm reversed the causal link between drug use and deviance. Moral turpitude and psychological pathology were thought to cause drug use, and only the most deviant individuals were likely to become substance abusers and addicts. Experts suggested that drug use indicated an antisocial mental disorder, based on the tautological premise that a psychologically healthy individual would not use or abuse drugs. Once substance abuse and deviance were considered under the control of the individual, fundamental changes in drug policy soon followed, including the criminalization of drug use.

From Tolerance to Punishment

Between 1910 and 1930, the federal government created an assortment of new laws and policies to govern the production, sale, and use of various drugs. The first American drug policies were largely regulatory, designed to ensure product safety and fair trade. Until Theodore Roosevelt was sworn in as president in 1901, there were no federal laws restricting drug use in any form. Only a handful of state and local laws were in place, and those were often racially or ethnically motivated, such as laws targeting the opium houses used by Chinese immigrants (MacCoun and Reuter 2001; Hoffman 2000). In response to a growing awareness that drug use and other forms of social deviance were often linked, President Roosevelt appointed an anti-narcotics advisor and launched an educational campaign to warn the public about the dangers of drug use. The United States Congress next passed a series of bills creating the first federal drug policies, including a law to regulate the use of drugs, the 1906 Food and Drug Act. The law required drug manufacturers to use labels that properly identified the contents of their products. It did not, however, target specific illicit substances.

Congress enacted the first national anti-drug legislation, the Harrison Narcotics Tax Act, in 1914. The Harrison Act required distributors and consumers of narcotics to register with the federal government and pay a special tax. In addition, it placed legal limits on the amounts of drugs permitted to be sold by type, limited distribution of narcotics to prescriptions issued by professionally trained physicians, and limited narcotics prescriptions to medicinal purposes (MacCoun and Reuter 2001). The Harrison Act effectively shifted decisionmaking about the commercial availability of drugs from the medical to the legal arena. Still, while the law limited the quantity of drugs that could be prescribed, it did not ban any specific drug use.

The restrictions imposed by the Harrison Act immediately raised concerns that drug users might use illicit means to acquire drugs or money for drugs. In response, a few states established drug distribution clinics that provided small doses of narcotics to addicts in order to manage their behavior until the medical community could develop an effective treatment for addiction. Such treatment proved elusive, however, and the federal government outlawed drug distribution clinics in 1925 (Nolan 2001).

The Harrison Act also marked a fundamental change in societal attitudes that eventually led to laws prohibiting drug use outright. In 1915, California, Utah, and Texas were the first states to prohibit marijuana possession. In 1923, five additional states passed similar laws, and by 1931, 29 states prohibited the use of marijuana for nonmedicinal purposes. Federal legislation prohibiting marijuana emerged in 1937 with the passage of the Marihuana Tax Act (Bonnie and Whitebread 1999).

Instead of restricting drug consumption, however, federal drug policy after 1914 focused on alcohol consumption. In 1919, Congress passed the Volstead Act, subsequently adopted as the Eighteenth Amendment, outlawing the manufacturing, sale, import, and export of alcohol. The law's effects were mixed. While alcohol-related fatalities and alcohol consumption among the working class declined slightly during 14 years of prohibition, consumption by the wealthy increased, and enforcement was modest overall (MacCoun and Reuter 2001; Hoffman 2000). The most extreme sign of alcohol abuse (deaths from liver cirrhosis) dropped only 10 to 20 percent during Prohibition (Miron 2004). Yet, alcohol prohibition continues to affect drug policy today. First, the repeal of prohibition codified alcohol as legally different from other drugs. The political failure of prohibition helped foster contemporary drug policies that focus almost exclusively on narcotics (Hoffman 2000). Second, prohibition statutes acknowledged the widespread problems of alcohol dependence, leading to the first treatment protocols resembling current therapies, including the development of Alcoholics Anonymous in the 1930s.

During alcohol prohibition, the federal government attempted to incorporate treatment for drug offenders into the criminal process. The

Director of the Federal Bureau of Prisons urged Congress to establish "narcotic farms" for drug offenders that would serve as narcotic treatment facilities for convicted offenders, probationers, and voluntary patients (Lipton 1995). The first narcotics farm, opened in Lexington, Kentucky, in 1935, was intended to provide education and rehabilitation in addition to substance abuse treatment. The Lexington farm and a second farm in Fort Worth, Texas, represent the first significant collaborations between the legal system and the medical/treatment community. This experiment, however, was unsuccessful. Residents were treated more like prisoners than patients, and the narcotic farms were quickly closed (Nolan 2001).

By the mid-20th century, drug policy had become more punitive, placing drug users squarely in the arena of the criminal justice system. One of the most important developments in drug policy during the 20th century was the 1930 appointment of Harry J. Anslinger as Commissioner of Narcotics within the newly created Federal Bureau of Narcotics (Musto and Korsmeyer 2002). Anslinger remained commissioner until 1962, serving in five administrations. Over the course of his long tenure, he was instrumental in establishing and shaping retributive drug policies, based on the idea that drug addiction is a form of voluntary deviance. During his four decades of leadership, no federal measures offering treatment to drug offenders were implemented, and drug offenders received no special consideration in sentencing or while incarcerated (box 2.1).

While alcohol prohibition inspired therapeutic approaches, narcotics policy focused on punishment. The Marihuana Tax Act (1937) was the first federal policy to prohibit the possession of a drug (earlier statutes regulated distribution only). Subsequent laws regulated the manufacturing and distribution of drugs and gave the federal government greater control of the industry. The Boggs Act of 1951 and the Narcotics Control Act of 1956 were the first bills in a long series of federal legislation that established severe penalties for the possession and use of narcotics (Keel 1993; Nolan 2001). With few exceptions, state and federal drug policies focused on punishment throughout the 1950s and 1960s.

The Next Era in Drug Policy

As recently as the 19th century, the United States had no national drug policy. Mind-altering chemicals were legal to produce and consume. Growing awareness of drug abuse problems in the early 1900s reduced

---

Box 2.1. Drug Policies Enacted during the Tenure of Harry
Anslinger, Commissioner of Narcotics, 1930–62

1937 *Marihuana Tax Act:* Requires all handlers of cannabis to register and pay a
special occupational tax of $1 per ounce. Nonmedicinal, untaxed posses-
sion or sale of cannabis is outlawed. Violations are punishable by a fine, a
prison sentence, or both. Some industrial uses are exempt from the tax.

1938 *Food, Drug, and Cosmetic Act:* Gives the federal Food and Drug Administration control over drug safety and redefines drugs as substances that
affect the body even in the absence of disease. Establishes class of drugs
available by prescription. (Pharmaceutical company determines status.)

1942 *Opium Poppy Control Act:* Attempts to regulate synthetic equivalents of
opium and cocaine.

1946 *Narcotics Act:* Increases penalties for distribution. Does not address penalties for users.

1951 *Boggs Act, Amendment to the Harrison Act:* Institutes mandatory mini-
mums for drug-related convictions. First offenses carry penalty of 2 to
5 years; second offenses receive 5 to 10 years; third offenses receive 10 to
20 years. No distinction made among types of drugs.

1951 *Durham-Humphrey Amendment:* Establishes more specific guidelines for
prescription drugs: habit forming, safety, and evaluation of new drugs.

1956 *Narcotics Control Act:* Imposes more severe penalties for narcotics violations. Gives juries the death penalty option for drugs sold to minors. Permits
federal narcotics agents to carry firearms.

---

the societal acceptance of recreational drug use and prevalence rates
declined, but treatment for drug-related problems was not yet available.
Because medical treatments for addiction were unknown, most experts
concluded that drug abuse was simply a behavioral or moral condition.
For most of the 20th century, drug policies were strongly influenced by
this view. Drug abuse was believed to arise from a lack of self-control and
the voluntary adoption of deviant values.

In the closing decades of the 20th century, a second transformation
in American drug policy emerged. For certain categories of drugs and
particular types of drug offenders, the criminal justice system began
augmenting its approach to drug policy with treatment-oriented, court-

supervised rehabilitation, often under the rubric of "therapeutic jurisprudence" (Hora, Schma, and Rosenthal 1999). This second transformation was partly inspired by widespread frustration with the volume of drug-related cases in the courts, but it also reflected changing perceptions about the efficacy of substance abuse treatment. Policymakers began to believe that treatment programs could produce (or at least support) positive behavioral change in drug users. Although some public officials remained skeptical about drug treatment, it became clear that for many drug-involved offenders the punitive approach to drug use was no more effective than treatment, and much more expensive. The marriage of justice and treatment began to appeal even to skeptics.

Although the criminal justice system was always interested in modifying behavior, these changes in drug policy, and the resulting adaptation of therapeutic approaches by the courts, altered how the justice system attempted to change behavior. Drug courts eventually emerged as an innovative way to intervene with drug-involved offenders, not just to punish past wrongs but also to prevent future harms. The procedures used by drug courts grew out of this new and unique mission.

Drug Treatment and the Legal System

The severity of the penalties enacted in the 1951 Boggs Act and its inclusion of mandatory minimum sentences prompted the American Bar Association (ABA) to initiate the first investigation into the effects of federal drug policy. An ABA committee charged with investigating drug policy proposed that the ABA and the American Medical Association (AMA) jointly urge Congress to reexamine the Harrison Act (King et al. 1961). The joint AMA/ABA committee analyzed international drug policies and concluded that most western nations experienced lower addiction rates while employing less retributive policies than the United States. Their study also reported that, in other nations, the medical community generally set drug policy including oversight of drug distribution. The committee concluded that punishment was not an effective deterrent to drug use, that imposing criminal penalties could lead to greater levels of criminal offending, and that drug dependence was best addressed by physicians.

The AMA/ABA recommendations were the first in a series of research initiatives that gradually led to efforts to apply treatment principles to drug offenders. In 1962, President Kennedy held a conference to evaluate drug research, laws, and policy. The conference led to the establishment of a commission charged with generating recommendations for legislation to reduce drug abuse. The conference proposed protocols for rehabilitating drug abusers, described the need for greater coordination between agencies to address drug addiction, and presented a list of suggestions for future research.

While the Kennedy administration was investigating new approaches to drug policy, the Supreme Court issued a ruling that would eventually permit the integration of drug treatment into criminal case processing.[1] *Robinson v. California* challenged a California statute that defined narcotic addiction as a crime punishable by imprisonment. In overturning the California statute, the Court ruled that drug addiction was an illness and that imprisonment of addicts for their addiction alone was cruel and unusual punishment in violation of the Fourteenth Amendment (Nolan 2001). Four years later, Congress passed the Narcotic Addict and Rehabilitation Act of 1966, giving courts the freedom to use treatment facilities as alternatives to incarceration (Keel 1993; Nolan 2001).

The Nixon administration continued the transition away from purely punitive sentencing and toward substance abuse treatment. Drug policy under President Nixon contained a mix of punitive and rehabilitative approaches. The administration supported the Comprehensive Drug Abuse and Control Act of 1970, which replaced and updated all previous laws governing narcotics and serious drugs. The new laws strictly limited legal narcotics dosages and generally expanded prison sentences for most drugs (box 2.2). However, perhaps as a result of *Robinson v. California,* federal budgets during the Nixon administration also included increased funding for prevention, education, and treatment.

In 1973, two agencies were created that separated treatment oversight from criminal justice enforcement: the Alcohol, Drug Abuse, and Mental Health Administration (ADAMHA) and the Drug Enforcement Administration (DEA). The ADAMHA brought together the National Institute for Mental Health (NIMH), the National Institute for Drug Addiction (NIDA), and the National Institute on Alcohol Abuse and Alcoholism (NIAAA) into one organization. The newly formed DEA was a modified Bureau of Narcotics and Dangerous Drugs.

At about the same time, Robert Martinson, under the direction of the New York State Governor's Special Committee on Criminal Offenders, conducted a literature review of treatment evaluation studies from 1945 to 1967. The study was meant to develop a model for successful rehabili-

---

Box 2.2. Drug Policies Enacted Following the Tenure of
Commissioner Harry Anslinger

1970 *Comprehensive Drug Abuse and Control Act:* Replaces and updates all previous laws concerning narcotics and other dangerous drugs with a stronger emphasis on law enforcement. Calls for harsher prison sentences but lessens penalties for possession of marijuana.

1972 *Drug Abuse Office and Treatment Act:* Establishes federally funded programs for prevention and treatment.

1973 *Heroin Trafficking Act:* Increases penalties for distribution but does not address penalties for users.

1974 *Methadone Control Act:* Regulates methadone licensing.

1978 *Amendments to 1972 legislation:* Further increases federal funding for prevention and treatment programs.

1978 *Alcohol and Drug Abuse Education amendments:* Establish education programs for drug addicts within the Department of Education.

1980 *Drug Abuse Prevention, Treatment, and Rehabilitation amendments:* Further extend prevention, education, and treatment programs.

1984 *Drug Offenders Act:* Sets up special programs and organized treatment for offenders.

---

tation that New York could implement in its prisons. Martinson found mixed results in his literature review, and concluded, in part, "nothing works" in treating substance abusers. Despite the ambiguous study results, state and local policymakers widely accepted the idea that nothing works in treatment, leading to a resurgence of punitive policies for drug users and limiting the development of treatment-oriented policies.

Federal policies, however, continued to support expansion of treatment services for addicts within the criminal justice system. The expansion of available treatment services throughout the 1970s created incentives for a few innovative designs in treatment programming to emerge. These innovations included alternatives to incarceration that could reroute drug offenders from the court system into treatment facilities, and community supervision programs that would discourage continued drug use through persistent oversight. Most programs attempted to link the legal system with the medical community through a combination of drug treatment and criminal sanctions.

Alternatives and Innovations

During the 1970s and 1980s, a few small but important treatment-oriented interventions emerged within the criminal justice system. Three factors seemed to lead to these innovations. First, the criminal justice system experienced rapid growth in the number of drug offenders entering the system. Second, perceptions about the ineffectiveness of incarceration as a general and specific deterrent intensified during the 1970s and 1980s, when the use of imprisonment for drug offenders was exploding. Third, a growing body of social science research using sophisticated analytical approaches identified treatment protocols that were empirically linked with better outcomes for substance abusers. This combination of opportunities and challenges spurred much of the innovation during this period.

Early program models usually focused on either enhancing treatment or increasing criminal justice supervision. Comprehensive programs that wholly integrated treatment and justice models were rare. Over time, the most innovative programs, regardless of their original orientation, tended to become more collaborative. The descriptions that follow highlight two of the most widely implemented programs (TASC and ISP) and two other approaches ("N Parts" and EDCM) that were precursors to the drug court model. The development of drug courts in the late 1980s was the result of an organic evolution of these treatment-justice partnerships rather than a wholly new approach to drug policy.

Treatment Alternatives to Street Crime

Treatment Accountability for Safe Communities (TASC), originally called Treatment Alternatives to Street Crime, was developed with funding from the 1972 Drug Abuse Office and Treatment Act. Since then, TASC's goals have been to develop alternative programs to divert drug offenders from the court system into treatment and provide a link between the judicial system and treatment services. Participants completing the program often have their initial offense dismissed (Nolan 2001). Anglin, Longshore, and Turner (1999) described the four goals of the

TASC program as (1) a collaboration between the criminal justice and treatment systems to help drug-involved offenders; (2) the use of legal sanctions as an incentive to enter and remain in drug treatment; (3) referral of offenders to appropriate treatment providers; and (4) intensive monitoring of offenders' progress in the program.

An outcome evaluation of five TASC programs investigated the effectiveness of TASC in reducing recidivism and drug use among participants (Anglin et al. 1999). Four programs worked exclusively with adult offenders and the other focused on juveniles. The study found fewer self-reported drug-related crimes in two of the five sites, and no difference in the other three. Official arrest records showed no differences between TASC participants and the comparison group at three sites: Canton, Chicago, and Orlando. In Birmingham and Portland, there were signs that TASC participants were more likely to be arrested or commit a technical violation in the six month follow-up period than the comparison group.

Analysis of drug use behavior showed no difference in two of the five sites. Of the three sites reporting improved outcomes, the results from Chicago (the juvenile site) and Birmingham indicated a reduction in drug use for TASC participants. On most measures reported by Anglin, the participants in the juvenile site appeared to fare better than their counterparts in the adult TASC programs.

A separate evaluation of the Colorado TASC program found no significant differences in recidivism rates in the first and second years following program participation (Owens et al. 1997). The authors concluded the program was not effective in reducing recidivism.

Intensive Supervision Probation

Intensive Supervision Probation (ISP) placed drug offenders under intensive community supervision as an alternative to incarceration. ISP goals were to minimize prison crowding, conserve resources, protect the safety of the public, and provide more rigorous punishment than regular probation (Tonry 1990). In theory, ISP programs also accepted offenders onto probation who otherwise would not have been released from prison, to reduce prison crowding. In practice, this latter goal was rarely met and most ISP participants would have received traditional probation. Overall, the ISP concept tended to divert jail- and probation-bound offenders (rather than prison-bound offenders).

Tonry (1990) found that some judges used ISP as an alternative to regular probation, not incarceration. These judges perceived regular supervision as ineffective, and used ISP to apply stricter supervision for offenders that should have been the norm under regular supervision. Had ISP been used in this manner (e.g., as an alternative to general probation rather than to prison) the program would likely have had a minimal effect on prison crowding and potentially increased costs. In cases where ISP was not used as an alternative to probation, some judges sent borderline cases to jail and then recommended they apply to ISP (Tonry 1990).

In monitoring participants, ISP imposed curfews, mandated employment, conducted random drug tests, and provided counseling. Evaluation of ISP suggested that the level and intensity of treatment was minimal and failed to affect participant drug involvement (Petersilia, Turner, and Deschenes 1992; Turner, Petersilia, and Deschenes 1992). ISP participants had higher rates of technical violations than comparable groups of parolees under regular supervision, even though the latter group was subjected to fewer drug tests and minimal supervision. Because ISP participants were more closely supervised than general parolees, rules violations led to increased incarceration rates, rather than alleviation of prison overcrowding. The lack of an integrated treatment program may have been partly responsible for the unintended increases in corrections populations. Researchers hypothesized that had treatment been provided, technical violations resulting from negative drug tests might have been reduced, thus reducing the rates of re-incarceration (Tonry 1990; Petersilia et al. 1992; Turner et al. 1992).

"N Parts"

In 1987, in response to the increasing number of drug offenders entering the system, New York City created specialized drug courts, called "N" or Narcotics Parts. These specialized drug case dockets were designed to expedite drug cases through the court process, thereby reducing disposition time and easing caseloads. The program had more limited goals than a typical drug court, and did not incorporate an explicit drug treatment component. The New York City "N Parts" were successful at reducing the case processing time to disposition, and reduced costs to a level about one-third the regular cost for processing a case (Belenko and Dumanovsky 1993). Although reducing recidivism was not a stated goal of the program, there was no significant difference in recidivism rates between offenders processed in "N Parts" and in other court parts (Belenko and Dumanovsky 1993). Evaluations to date have not isolated any programmatic effects, and it is unclear if differences in outcomes were a function of preexisting differences between offenders sent to "N Parts" and those sent through regular court processing.

Expedited Drug Case Management

The Expedited Drug Case Management (EDCM) program was developed in the late 1980s in response to the significant increases in incarceration rates for drug offenders and limited prison and jail space. Funded by the Bureau of Justice Assistance (BJA) and piloted in three counties—Middlesex County, New Jersey; Montgomery County, Pennsylvania; and Multnomah County, Oregon—the program differed from the "N Parts" approach by incorporating both treatment and rehabilitation into the case disposition process. BJA listed nine key program components:

- case differentiation criteria;
- case-processing track and procedures;
- early defendant screening for substance abuse;
- pretrial release and alternative sanctioning;
- coordination between the court and treatment providers;
- mobilization of community resources;
- mechanisms for interagency coordination;
- program management and monitoring; and
- judicial system leadership.

The EDCM pilot programs were found successful at expediting cases through the court, reducing bench warrants, reducing the number of days spent in pretrial detention, and providing treatment services for individuals (Cooper 1994). The program was then implemented in many jurisdictions and is sometimes referred to as the "second" drug court model (Belenko and Dumanovsky 1993). However, the two drug court models, the drug treatment court and the EDCM, differ in their primary objective and their emphasis on treatment. The EDCM program is designed to improve the efficiency of the courts by expediting cases through the system, and places little emphasis on treating social and psychological problems associated with drug abuse (Guerin et al. 1998; Hora et al. 1999).

The Bureau of Justice Assistance developed the EDCM model intending to use the specialized dockets to comprehensively intervene with drug-involved offenders, and the program ultimately intended to include a focus on treatment (Cooper 1994). The pilot EDCM program in Middlesex County included several components similar to the drug court model: the judge had a central role in most aspects of the program, and the programming included community and organizing treatment services for offenders. However, limited resources led to the end of the EDCM experiment before the program was comprehensively evaluated.

Drug Court Expansion

Most reviews of drug court history attribute the initial development and rapid growth of drug courts to the substantial increases in the numbers of drug-involved offenders entering the criminal justice system in the late 1980s and early 1990s. Clinton Terry, in *The Early Drug Courts*, suggested that drug courts were a response to increased caseloads resulting from policies undertaken by the Reagan administration. During this period, the criminal justice system changed briefly from a movement toward more treatment and prevention programs to one focused on more intensive law enforcement efforts. Terry argued that new enforcement-oriented policies led to dramatic increases in arrest rates for drug abuse, a concurrent increase in drug-related caseloads, and a significant reduction in the efficiency of case processing (Terry 1999).

Studies of how the first drug court developed in Miami suggested that caseload pressures led to its creation. Nolan's (2001) study of drug courts documented the creation of a commission, headed by Associate Chief Judge Herbert Klein of the Eleventh Judicial Circuit of Florida, to study how to respond to an influx of drug-involved offenders without sacrificing public safety. The commission recommended creating a specialized court in Dade County as the direct result of "growing numbers of felony drug cases in Miami" (39). Schwartz and Schwartz (1998) offered a similar analysis, noting that "the frequency of drug offenses by drug users, the over-crowding of jail space, and a diminishing sense of community well-being" along with "the escalation of criminal activity associated with substance abuse" were primary factors in the development of the first drug courts. In their analysis of drug courts, Hora, Schma, and Rosenthal (1999) suggested that by addressing a combination of these problems, including "more efficient case load management, reduced system costs and jail crowding and decreased rates of recidivism," the drug court concept received an "enthusiastic reception" (456).

Federal funding for adult drug courts was authorized five years later through Title V of the Violent Crime Control and Law Enforcement Act of 1994 (PL 103-322), which allowed the attorney general to make grants to states, state courts, local courts, units of local government, and Indian tribal governments to establish drug courts. Eligible drug court programs were expected to incorporate continuous judicial supervision of nonviolent substance abusing offenders with intensive treatment and other integrated services and sanctions. As part of the process, the attorney general established the (now defunct) Drug Courts Program Office (DCPO) within the Office of Justice Programs (OJP) to administer the drug court grant program and provide grants for financial and technical assistance, training, leadership, and related programmatic guidance. Funding became available the following year.

DCPO awarded grants through a competitive discretionary process. In 1995, the first year of funding, DCPO awarded 52 grants for planning, 5 for implementation, and 7 for enhancement. Another 9 implementation and 7 enhancement grants were awarded with FY 1996 funds. Nationally, 12 jurisdictions were using these FY 1995 and FY 1996 funds for juvenile drug court planning or implementation. By FY 1997, Drug Court Grant Program appropriation was up to $30 million. As of October 2000, there were 1,222 drug courts in the United States (in operation or planned), including 326 juvenile and family drug courts (OJP 2002). Drug courts were operating or being planned in 49 states plus the District of Columbia, Puerto Rico, Guam, and two federal jurisdictions, including more than 30 Native American tribal courts.

Juvenile drug courts appear to have evolved directly from the adult drug court model, rather than as an adaptation of typical juvenile case processing. Although adult drug courts are generally accepted to have grown out of a grassroots movement prompted by anecdotal evidence of program success, the emergence of the juvenile drug court appears less organic. Perceptions of positive outcomes in adult drug courts led many localities to try to transfer their success to a juvenile model in much the same way jurisdictions adopted adult drug court models based on evidence from other jurisdictions. The need for specialized case processing for juveniles followed many of the same precursors that occurred in the adult system: rising caseloads and perceptions of the growing efficacy of treatment. In addition, case dockets appearing before juvenile courts were increasingly complex as substance abuse issues became harder to separate from other family issues (OJP 1998). Juvenile drug courts also offered juvenile courts a way to return to the fundamental principle of juvenile case processing—individualized rehabilitation—in a system that had become increasingly adversarial and punitive. Finally, the availability of funding from many different sources—private, local, state, and eventually federal—probably spurred much of the development.

For juveniles, two separate and distinct court models were developed, juvenile drug courts and family drug courts. Juvenile drug courts focus on juvenile delinquency (criminal matters) and status offenses (truancy) that involve nonviolent substance-using juveniles. Family drug courts deal with cases involving parental rights. Parents are the litigants, and they may come before the court through either the criminal or civil process. The issues heard before this court arise from a parent's substance abuse, and can include custody and visitation disputes, abuse, neglect and dependency matters, petitions to terminate parental rights, guardianship proceedings, and other loss, restriction, or limitation of parental rights. The first juvenile/family drug court started on October 1, 1993, in Monroe County, Florida (Key West).

Juvenile and family drug courts began appearing across the country in early 1995, when federal funding became available for the first time. A juvenile drug court opened in Kent and Newcastle counties in Delaware in January 1995 (OJP 1998). Other courts started soon thereafter in Jefferson County, Alabama (Birmingham), in January 1995; Clark County, Nevada (Las Vegas), in March 1995; Lake County, Indiana (Gary), in June of that year; Washoe County, Nevada (Reno), in July; and Tulare County, California (Visalia), and Salt Lake City, Utah, in October 1995 (OJP 1998, 2000). As of October 2000, there were 154 juvenile and family drug courts in existence and another 172 in the planning stage (OJP 2002).

Drug courts specifically targeting juvenile offenders first received federal funding through Title I, Subchapter XII-J of the Omnibus Crime Control and Safe Streets Act, as amended under 42 U.S.C. 3796, in 1995. This law modified the original by specifically including nonviolent substance-abusing juvenile offenders in the grant process and establishing a process for awarding and disbursing federal funds for juvenile drug courts that was identical to the adult process (OJP 2002). The enactment of the Adoption and Safe Families Act of 1997, which mandated the termination of parental rights for children who had been in foster care for 18 of the preceding

22 months, also spurred juvenile drug court development. The combination of the relatively short time period of supervision and the need for consistent judicial supervision, coordination of services, and accountability of the services provided to juveniles and families in crisis is believed to have led court systems throughout the country to adopt juvenile and family drug courts rather than create entirely new program models (OJP 1998).

Conclusion

As juvenile drug courts enter their second decade of operations, it is instructive to reflect on their history as one expression of American policies to deal with the connected problems of drug abuse and crime. The creation of juvenile drug courts reflects the nation's changing beliefs about drug use and criminality. As beliefs change, new laws and policies emerge that reflect those beliefs. New laws and policies lead to new program innovations. Eventually, new bureaucracies are formed to translate those innovations into standard practice. Juvenile drug courts are fast becoming a central part of the new bureaucratic model for responding to youth drug use.

While no single problem can be cited as the dominant factor leading to the development of drug courts, increases in the number of drug-involved offenders clearly correlate with their development. This broad association between higher arrest and incarceration levels and drug court development is generally unchallenged in the drug court literature. Pressure from rising caseloads led courts to innovate, and this innovation was driven by a belief that drug treatment could reduce the number of future drug offenders.

However, if rising caseloads were the key factor that defined the mission of drug courts, it would follow that communities facing varying sources of pressure and different offender populations would have developed a range of program models. If a jurisdiction faced rising numbers of drug-related crimes, then its drug court would likely be designed to deliver intensive treatment services to addicts with the goal of addressing their dependence and ultimately reducing drug-related crime. If a jurisdiction faced rising numbers of offenders charged with drug trafficking, then that jurisdiction might design a court to create more efficient case processing. If a jurisdiction found that probationers and parolees constituted an abnormally large percentage of drug-involved offenders, then that drug court might be integrated into the reentry process. Finally, if a community was faced with rising rates of drug use among adolescents, a drug court might focus on prevention.

Drug courts, however, did not evolve a diversity of program models. The missions of most drug courts appear uniform: to reduce drug use through treatment for a population of nonviolent drug users that are identified at the point they enter the criminal justice system. While there is some variation across drug courts, most have adapted a uniform model, albeit one adapted to particular community contexts. The consistency of drug court practices suggests that there is more to the story of drug court development than a simple response to increased rates of arrest and incarceration. Procedural requirements linked with federal funding and training provided by national organizations may have led to the establishment of relatively rigid operational norms. The homogeneity of drug court operations across communities with different drug use and offending patterns is striking.

The lack of a formal theory to articulate the relationship between drug court programming and outcomes contributes to the difficulty in understanding drug court goals. If drug courts are a direct response to rising offender populations, it stands to reason that drug courts would target their resources on drug offenders in proportion to their risk of reoffending. Instead, most drug courts spend their treatment resources in proportion to each offender's substance abuse severity. While substance abuse severity and risk of reoffending are linked, the correlation is not understood well enough to justify this strategy if the main intent of drug courts is to reduce recidivism. Most drug courts pursue a mission that falls somewhere between reducing recidivism and providing effective treatment, and the determination of this balance may be a function of each court's history.

NOTE

1. *Robinson v. California: Appeal from the Appellate Department.* 370 U.S. 660 (1962).

REFERENCES

Anglin, M. Douglas, Douglas Longshore, and Susan Turner. 1999. "Treatment Alternatives to Street Crime: An Evaluation of Five Programs." *Criminal Justice and Behavior* 26(2): 168–95.

Belenko, Steven, and Tamara Dumanovsky. 1993. *Program Brief: Special Drug Courts.* Washington, DC: U.S. Department of Justice, Office of Justice Programs, Bureau of Justice Assistance.

Berman, Greg, and John Feinblatt. 2001. "Problem-Solving Courts: A Brief Primer." *Law & Policy* 23(2): 125–40.

Bonnie, Richard J., and Charles H. Whitebread. 1999. *The Marijuana Conviction: A History of Marijuana Prohibition in the United States.* New York: Drug Policy Alliance.

Butts, Jeffrey A., and Ojmarrh Mitchell. 2000. "Brick by Brick: Dismantling the Border between Juvenile and Adult Justice." In *Boundary Changes in Criminal Justice Organizations,* Vol. 2 of *Criminal Justice 2000,* edited by Charles M. Friel (167–213). Washington, DC: U.S. Department of Justice, National Institute of Justice.

Cooper, Caroline S. 1994. *Expedited Drug Case Management.* Washington, DC: OJP Drug Court Clearinghouse and Technical Assistance Project, School of Public Affairs, American University.

Earleywine, Mitchell. 2002. *Understanding Marijuana: A New Look at the Scientific Evidence.* New York: Oxford University Press.

Fox, Sanford J. 1970. "Juvenile Justice Reform: An Historical Perspective." *Stanford Law Review* 22:1187–1239.

Guerin, Paul, Robert Hyde, Laurel Carrier, Kristine Denman, Rebecca Frerichs, Jeff Halsted, Sarah Kurhajetz, Audrey Merriweather, Jeff Mix, and Jessica Neely. 1998. *Final Report: Process Evaluation of the Administrative Office of the Courts Drug Court Programs: First Judicial District Court, Third Judicial District Court, and Bernalillo County Metropolitan Court.* Albuquerque: University of New Mexico, Institute for Social Research.

Hoffman, Morris B. 2000. "The Drug Court Scandal." *North Carolina Law Review* 78:1437–1534.

Hora, Peggy F., William G. Schma, and John T. A. Rosenthal. 1999. "Therapeutic Jurisprudence and the Drug Treatment Court Movement: Revolutionizing the Criminal Justice System's Response to Drug Abuse and Crime in America." *Notre Dame Law Review* 74(2): 439–537.

Keel, Robert. 1993. *Drug Law Timeline: Significant Events in the History of Our Drug Laws.* St. Louis: University of Missouri at Saint Louis.

King, Rufus, Edward J. Dimock, Abe Fortas, C. Joseph Stetler, Robert H. Felix, and Isaac Starr. 1961. *Drug Addiction, Crime or Disease? Interim and Final Reports of the Joint Committee of the American Bar Association and the American Medical Association on Narcotic Drugs.* Bloomington: Indiana University Press.

Lipton, Douglas S. 1995. "The Effectiveness of Treatment for Drug Abusers under Criminal Justice Supervision." Paper presented at the annual Conference on Criminal Justice Research and Evaluation, Washington, D.C., July 21–24.

MacCoun, Robert, and Peter Reuter. 2001. *Drug War Heresies: Learning from Other Vices, Times, and Places.* New York: Cambridge University Press.

Miron, Jeffrey A. 2004. *Drug War Crimes.* Oakland, CA: The Independent Institute.

Musto, David F. 1999. *The American Disease: Origins of Narcotic Control.* New York: Oxford University Press.

Musto, David F., and Pamela Korsmeyer. 2002. *The Quest for Drug Control: Politics and Federal Policy in a Period of Increasing Substance Abuse, 1963–1981.* New Haven: Yale University Press.

National Institute of Justice. 2000. *1999 Annual Report on Drug Use among Adult and Juvenile Arrestees. Juvenile Program Findings.* Washington, DC: U.S. Department of Justice, Office of Justice Programs, National Institute of Justice. http://www.ncjrs.org/pdffiles1/nij/181426.pdf.

Nolan, James L. Jr. 2001. *Reinventing Justice: The American Drug Court Movement.* Princeton, NJ: Princeton University Press.

Office of Justice Programs. 1998. *Juvenile and Family Drug Courts: An Overview.* Washington, DC: OJP Drug Court Clearinghouse and Technical Assistance Project, School of Public Affairs, American University.

———. 2000. *Juvenile Drug Courts: Preliminary Assessment of Activities Underway and Implementation Issues Being Addressed.* Washington, DC: OJP Drug Court Clearinghouse and Technical Assistance Project, School of Public Affairs, American University.

———. 2002. *Summary of Drug Court Activity by State and County.* Washington, DC: OJP Drug Court Clearinghouse and Technical Assistance Project, School of Public Affairs, American University. http://www.american.edu/justice/publications/Juvsumchartgamze.pdf.

OJP. *See* Office of Justice Programs.

Owens, Stephen J., Kelli J. Klebe, Sheila A. Arens, Robert L. Durham, Joel Hughes, Candace Moore, Maureen O'Keefe, Janis Philips, Julie A Sarno, and Joe Stommel. 1997. "The Effectiveness of Colorado's TASC Programs." *Journal of Offender Rehabilitation* 26(1–2): 151–76.

Petersilia, Joan, Susan Turner, and Elizabeth Piper Deschenes. 1992. "The Costs and Effects of Intensive Supervision for Drug Offenders." *Federal Probation* 35(4): 12–17.

SAMHSA. *See* Substance Abuse and Mental Health Services Administration.

Schwartz, John R., and Linda P. Schwartz. 1998. "The Drug Court: A New Strategy for Drug Use Prevention." *Obstetrics and Gynecology Clinics of North America* 25(1): 225–68.

Stahl, Anne, Terrence Finnegan, and W. Kang. 2003. "Easy Access to Juvenile Court Statistics: 1985–2000." Pittsburgh, PA: National Center for Juvenile Justice. http://ojjdp.ncjrs.org/ojstatbb/ezajcs/.

Substance Abuse and Mental Health Services Administration. 2000. "National Household Survey on Drug Abuse: Main Findings 1998." NHSDA Series H-11, DHHS Publication No. SMA 00-3381. Rockville, MD: Substance Abuse and Mental Health Services Administration.

Terry, W. Clinton III. 1999. "Broward County's Dedicated Drug Treatment Court: From Post-adjudication to Diversion." In *The Early Drug Courts: Case Studies in Judicial Innovation,* edited by W. Clinton Terry III (77–107). Thousand Oaks, CA: Sage Publications.

Tonry, Michael. 1990. "Stated and Latent Functions of ISP." *Crime and Delinquency* 36(1): 174–91.

Turner, Susan, Joan Petersilia, and Elizabeth Piper Deschenes. 1992. "Evaluating Intensive Supervision Probation/Parole (ISP) for Drug Offenders." *Crime and Delinquency* 38(4): 539–56.

Watkins, John C. Jr. 1998. *The Juvenile Justice Century.* Durham, NC: Carolina Academic Press.

Wilson, James Q. 1989. *Bureaucracy—What Government Agencies Do and Why They Do It.* New York: Basic Books.

3

What Juvenile Drug Courts Do and How They Do It

Shelli Balter Rossman, Jeffrey A. Butts, John Roman,
Christine DeStefano, and Ruth White

The U.S. Department of Justice selected six juvenile drug courts (JDCs) in Florida, Montana, New Jersey, New Mexico, Ohio, and South Carolina to participate in the National Evaluation of Juvenile Drug Courts (NEJDC), conducted by the Urban Institute in Washington, D.C. The NEJDC project aimed to develop a new conceptual framework for evaluating juvenile drug courts. Researchers investigated the procedures of these programs to fashion a more effective approach to evaluating the outcomes and effects of juvenile drug courts.

Drug courts deliver court-supervised substance abuse treatment for nonviolent, drug-involved offenders that meet certain eligibility guidelines. Drug courts seek to reduce recidivism by using the authority of the court process to coerce offenders into stopping their use of illegal drugs, and providing offenders with treatment and services to support a drug-free lifestyle. Juvenile drug courts, like drug courts for adults, depend on communitywide partnerships that blend the efforts of public safety organizations with those of treatment and rehabilitation agencies. These partnerships

- hold offenders accountable for their drug use and other illegal behavior;
- address whatever social and behavioral problems may be contributing to offenders' substance use;

- support offenders and their families in developing positive community relationships and sustaining crime- and drug-free lives; and
- ensure effective coordination of the justice system with related service providers.

Young offenders enter drug court programs by various paths. Many are offered drug court as a pre-adjudication (i.e., pretrial) diversion alternative. Others go to drug court after adjudication (i.e., conviction) in juvenile court, but with their final disposition (or sentence) postponed pending completion of drug court. Still others are referred to drug court as a post-disposition diversion program, perhaps as part of a probation revocation hearing. Participation in juvenile drug court is nearly always voluntary. Young offenders choose to go through drug court rather than the usual legal process. When offenders select drug court, they may have their charges dropped (in pre-adjudication programs) or their sentences vacated (in post-adjudication drug courts), or they may receive a less severe disposition once they graduate from the program. Graduating from drug court is generally contingent on completing a recommended amount of treatment. In addition, youth are often required to pass randomly ordered drug tests, comply with program rules, and meet other criteria including school attendance, finding employment, and the like.

The juvenile drug court process is a cycle of treatment and supervision, often lasting one year or longer. Judges oversee the progress of each case through frequent, often weekly, hearings. Each youth's compliance with court orders is closely monitored by court staff in collaboration with a case manager or treatment coordinator who ensures treatment plans are implemented. Judges in juvenile drug court play an interactive role, bringing together the key players in the justice and treatment systems, including probation, substance abuse treatment, schools, physical and mental health, and other agencies that have contact with youth and families. Judges also try to develop a close alliance with the parents and family of each offender. Empowering families is critical for sustaining the positive effects of drug court once a youth has graduated from the program.

Juvenile drug court programs vary in some important ways. Policies and practices evolve over time. Procedures favored in one jurisdiction may not be acceptable in another. Programs vary in the assortment of individuals and agencies involved in the drug court partnership. They may use different procedures for screening, assessing, and referring youth for treatment. Their case planning and case management approaches may differ, just as their courtroom operations, treatment and collateral service provision, compliance monitoring, and rewards or sanctions may vary. Some major areas of difference among juvenile drug courts include the following:

- *Legal eligibility.* Some drug courts are limited to misdemeanor cases or first-time offenders. Others accept felony cases and offenders with long criminal histories.
- *Legal incentives.* Program participants may be offered case dismissal, shorter periods of probation, or probation instead of incarceration.
- *Drug use severity.* Drug courts may require a medical diagnosis of abuse or dependency based on a professional clinical substance abuse assessment, or they may admit offenders that report drug use, test positive for drugs, are arrested for drug charges, or request treatment.
- *Judicial monitoring.* The timing and frequency of court reviews vary according to court policies. The courtroom docketing of cases and other aspects of the judicial review process may differ.
- *Sanctioning and termination.* Participants may be terminated from drug court for a variety of reasons, such as admission to residential treatment, a new arrest, leaving treatment (or failing to report for treatment), positive drug tests (the number varies), or failure to appear at court hearings. Some courts permit youth to reenter after an unsuccessful termination.
- *Treatment.* Treatment approaches (e.g., therapeutic models, individual versus group settings, frequency and duration of treatment) vary from one program to another. Some difficult populations (e.g., youth with co-occurring disorders or sexual offenders) may be excluded from treatment.
- *Collateral services.* Juvenile drug court programs provide various services, or links to services, beyond those required for substance abuse treatment (e.g., educational, occupational, health, or recreational).
- *Drug testing.* Frequency of testing may depend on treatment modality and phase. The specific drugs included in testing programs often vary.
- *Family involvement.* The role of the parents in their children's lives creates an element of complexity that does not exist in adult drug court models. Juvenile drug courts differ in how they manage parental involvement in treatment and court proceedings. When the behavior

of parents or other family members may undermine treatment goals, courts differ in how they create accountability for parents and juveniles without creating new problems for the family.

- *Family-friendly strategies.* Juvenile drug court programs have diverse family-friendly practices (e.g., hearings are scheduled during times family members can be present, transportation and child care are provided, treatment agencies offer evening or weekend hours and are conveniently located, services are compatible with parental discipline and are culturally competent).

This chapter describes the practices and procedures used in juvenile drug courts by examining six programs in (Charleston) South Carolina, (Dayton) Ohio, (Jersey City) New Jersey, (Las Cruces) New Mexico, (Missoula) Montana, and (Orlando) Florida. The information presented here was gathered by the Urban Institute during visits to each court during 2001 and 2002 and from document reviews, courtroom observations, and interviews with key stakeholders (judges, program coordinators, case managers, and so on). The Urban Institute investigated the composition of the drug court team in each community, the procedures used for screening and assessing youth, the conduct of judicial hearings and how cases are coordinated, the use of rewards and sanctions, drug testing procedures, and the provision of treatment and collateral services (box 3.1).

Drug Court Teams

Juvenile drug courts marry intensive judicial supervision with community-based interventions to reduce substance abuse. The exact configuration of such efforts may vary. The National Drug Court Institute and the National Council of Juvenile and Family Court Judges (NDCI/NCJFCJ 2003) suggest that drug court teams should include judges, court administrators, prosecutors, defense attorneys, management information staff, and evaluators and researchers, as well as representatives from local law enforcement and probation, treatment providers, social service agencies, the schools, and other key community-based entities.

The six programs examined for this study differ somewhat in the constellation of their team members, the roles of key actors, how decisions are made, and the stability of team members over time. Some programs have experienced substantial turnover in treatment agencies, case

Box 3.1. Programs Participating in the National Evaluation of Juvenile Drug Courts

Charleston Juvenile Drug Court

The Charleston Juvenile Drug Court, under the direction of Judge Charlie Segars-Andrews, is located in Charleston County, South Carolina, a metropolitan area with more than 300,000 residents. The juvenile drug court began in September 1997 and can serve 60 youth at a time.

Dayton Juvenile Drug Court

The Montgomery County Juvenile Drug Court is presided over by Judge Michael Murphy, and has been operating in Dayton, Ohio, since January 1998. The program serves populations in and around Dayton, a large metropolitan area of more than 500,000 surrounded by rural and farming districts.

Jersey City Juvenile Drug Court

The Jersey City Juvenile Drug Court, led by Judge Salvatore Bovino, is located directly across the Hudson River from Manhattan Island in New York City. The program began in February 1998 and is part of the Family Division of the Superior Court of New Jersey. It was the first juvenile drug court in the state.

Las Cruces Juvenile Drug Court

The Las Cruces Juvenile Drug Court is led by Judge Larry Ramirez and operates in two locations in Dona Ana County, New Mexico. Court sessions are held in the city of Las Cruces, which has a population of 80,000 people, as well as in the rural community of Anthony. The programs have been operating since 1996.

Missoula Youth Drug Court

The Missoula County Youth Drug Court opened in October 1996 under the leadership of Judge John W. Larson. The court is located in the county seat of Missoula, Montana, a largely rural area, where most of the 96,000 residents are concentrated in or around the Missoula city limits. The court serves 25 youth at a time.

Orlando Juvenile Drug Court

The Orange County Juvenile Drug Court, directed by Judge Jose Rodriguez, serves Orlando, Florida, and surrounding communities. The county has a population of approximately 920,000. The juvenile drug court started in August 1997 and works with 50 youth at a time.

Source: Urban Institute National Evaluation of Juvenile Drug Courts.

managers, and treatment or service personnel. Judicial leadership, on the other hand, appears relatively stable. Most judges have overseen their juvenile drug court since its inception. In two study sites—Missoula and Charleston—the current judge helped found the drug court program. All six JDCs, however, benefit from dedicated judicial leadership. The judges strongly support the concepts underlying juvenile drug court, including the principles of therapeutic and restorative justice. In all six programs, the judges supervise courtroom hearings and attend most pre-hearing meetings of the drug court team where cases are reviewed and strategic responses to individual clients formulated. Most judges closely monitor the practices of the public and private treatment providers affiliated with their programs.

In addition to strong judges, most JDCs rely on program coordinators that are responsible for day-to-day program operations. Typically, the program coordinator also supervises the management information system, either automated or manual. The JDC coordinator usually performs initial eligibility screenings and referrals of clients, arranges for psychosocial assessments and evaluations, prepares participant contracts, schedules drug court orientations and participant/family attendance for routine hearings, and maintains the record keeping system. School liaisons and police officers may help with services for program participants, but generally do not play key decisionmaking roles. A prosecutor often makes referrals to the program, but may have no further involvement with the juvenile drug court. The public defender in Jersey City usually becomes involved with juvenile drug court clients only when they fail to complete the program successfully. Similarly, juvenile probation officers are not generally a part of the program, but could become involved under special circumstances.

Unlike most of the other juvenile drug courts in this study, the Missoula Youth Drug Court does not include a full-time program coordinator. Instead, the judge in Missoula is the program leader, assisted by a judicial aide, a standing master (or magistrate), and a community program coordinator. A specialized juvenile probation officer (JPO) and the director of juvenile probation also play central roles. Every agency involved with the juvenile drug court is in close, regular contact with these key staff members. Another key member, the community program coordinator (CPC), liaises between the court, schools, and the community, and coordinates required treatment programs. In the Missoula program, the judge interacts regularly with nearly everyone in the juvenile drug court network.

While his most frequent contacts—nearly daily—are with the CPC and JPO, he also speaks frequently with the public defender and the local prosecutor. The CPC and JPO play central roles in the drug court network, talking with each other and other agency representatives at least weekly. Other individuals interact less frequently but all members of the network are readily accessible, in part because Missoula is a relatively small community and most people in the local network work near one another.

Prosecutors and public defenders (or other defense counsel) participate in most of the JDC programs visited by the Urban Institute. The extent of their involvement, however, varies. Often, attorneys from these offices are involved in determining client eligibility and making referrals to drug court, but they are less likely to attend team meetings or play a day-to-day role once youth are enrolled in the program. In Dayton, Ohio, for example, the judge leads the juvenile drug court and makes most treatment decisions. Because the court is a post-adjudication program, prosecutors do not routinely participate in drug court proceedings. Prosecutors generally appear in court only when a program youth is rearrested and faces the possibility of new charges. Public defenders play a similar role. Most drug court hearings involve only the judge, the court clerk, the case management agency (Treatment Alternatives for Safer Communities, or TASC), the youth, and his or her parents or guardians.

Similarly, in Orlando the state attorney's and public defenders' offices play limited roles in the day-to-day details of the juvenile drug court program. Key program staff include the presiding judge, the drug court coordinator, the director of the treatment facility used by the drug court (Center for Drug-Free Living), case managers, the case management supervisor, family and substance abuse counselors, and mental health agency staff.

In contrast, prosecutors and public defenders are quite active in the Las Cruces juvenile drug court. All the key players in Las Cruces work in nearby offices and see each other often, even outside the contact required to handle court cases. The judge, program director, and the program director's assistant play central roles and regularly contact most people in the network. Surveillance officers from local law enforcement agencies also play important roles and have almost daily contact with the program director and her assistant. Community police officers, sheriff deputies, assistant district attorneys (ADAs), and the public defender communicate weekly with the program director and her assistant, as do the local treatment agencies. In addition to reviewing all legal documents and motions related to the juvenile drug court process, the public defender in Las Cruces co-chairs the Juvenile Drug Court Advisory Committee and advises the team on culturally sensitive issues. Several ADAs work on juvenile drug court cases and are responsible for reviewing program documents and making decisions regarding referrals. A representative from the district attorney's office attends all drug court meetings and case reviews.

Several drug court programs visited by the Urban Institute include law enforcement representatives as central members of the drug court team. Juvenile probation officers also play key roles in some programs; for example, both the Missoula and Jersey City programs have full-time juvenile probation officers assigned to juvenile drug court. In Jersey City, a juvenile probation officer performs curfew checks, conducts urinalysis testing, and assists with cases where youth have educational and employment issues. A Missoula probation officer performs similar functions and supervises all record collections (including assessments). In Las Cruces, police officers and deputy sheriffs supervise the community service projects of drug court clients, actively promote pro-social activities, and serve as mentors.

A handful of officers from the Jersey City Police volunteer to attend drug court sessions and perform home, work, and school checks. Each officer monitors juveniles living in his or her district twice weekly, conducting curfew checks and developing mentoring relationships with the youth. If a juvenile drug court client is caught in a minor delinquent act during a curfew check, the officer typically handles the matter informally with a "curbside or station house adjustment." Youth caught participating in serious crimes, such as drug possession, are arrested. The officers believe that the relationships they develop with youth help foster communication and trust.

Despite wide recognition that school attendance and educational achievement are critical to the success of youth in juvenile drug courts, school personnel are not always key players in JDC programs. In Jersey City, however, a school liaison links the four major schools in the area with the staff of the juvenile drug court. The liaison, a full-time employee of the District Court, interacts with substance abuse counselors at each school and meets routinely with all students involved with the juvenile court system, including those participating in juvenile drug court. Charleston also incorporates school representatives into its drug court process.

School representatives actively monitor drug court participants, attend case meetings as needed, and provide educational progress reports on juvenile clients at status hearings. School representatives communicate frequently with the drug court coordinator and report weekly on students' academic progress, behavior, and attendance. Charleston school officials support the juvenile drug court program because they believe its oversight of youthful offenders reduces school expulsions and improves school order.

Screening, Assessment, and Referral

Only one of the six juvenile drug courts (Jersey City) is purely a diversion program (i.e., pre-adjudication), and only one (Dayton) works strictly with post-adjudication cases. The remaining four programs, like many JDCs, accept a mixture of pre- and post-adjudication cases, with the bulk of their caseloads focused on post-adjudication.

Several activities usually occur before youth are accepted into a juvenile drug court program, although the order and substantive scope of these events varies from one program to another. Candidate cases must be screened to ascertain whether charges and other circumstances meet the court's admissions criteria. Youth must undergo some form of drug and alcohol assessment to determine their suitability for program participation as well as their individualized treatment and collateral service needs. Key stakeholders must establish consensual agreement to enroll eligible and suitable juvenile offenders—often denoted by contracts signed by the youth and family.

Referral

Referrals to the six JDCs visited for this study originate from many sources. Most Jersey City participants are referred by the assistant prosecutor after arrest. Police officers, parents/guardians, schools, public defenders, and the judge could also refer juveniles to the New Jersey program, but do so infrequently. In Orlando, the state attorney's office (or prosecutor) usually refers pre-adjudication cases, while a probation officer or a judge likely refers post-adjudication cases as a condition of probation. Occasionally, other sources, including family members and the public defender's office, refer youth. In Charleston, Las Cruces, and Missoula, referrals come from various sources inside or outside the justice system, but are most likely to stem from a probation agreement.

Eligibility

Policies to determine client eligibility are usually based on legal criteria and developed collaboratively by judges, prosecutors, defense attorneys, and even treatment providers. Partly because of federal funding requirements, eligibility policies often exclude offenders charged with violent or other serious crimes. Some offenders are excluded because of their extensive criminal histories or the severity of pending charges. Eligibility standards vary, however, reflecting local estimates of public tolerance for community-based treatment of drug offenders. Program guidelines can include other factors as well, such as individual characteristics perceived to favor or impede treatment success, resource constraints that would undermine a program's ability to provide satisfactory service to a wider range of clients, and judicial or team preferences regarding program priorities.

Most of the programs studied by the Urban Institute have formal eligibility criteria that are applied uniformly across all candidates (table 3.1). Only one jurisdiction (Jersey City) makes eligibility determinations on a flexible, case-by-case basis. The district attorney's office in Jersey City works closely with the program coordinator to determine the best candidates for juvenile drug court. In many cases, the DA refers cases based solely on the coordinator's recommendation.

Some drug courts have altered their eligibility criteria over time. The Orlando, Florida, program began with mostly diversion cases (pre-adjudication) involving first-time offenders. As the drug court evolved, eligibility expanded to post-adjudication juveniles, and these cases soon accounted for nearly 80 percent of program participants. Similarly, low rates of referral and enrollment led the Jersey City program to expand its eligibility criteria and begin accepting second- and third-time offenders with detainable offenses.

Many juvenile drug courts concentrate their efforts on juveniles whose offenses are directly related to alcohol and drug use, but other programs accept youth with a range of substance abuse problems, regardless of whether their offenses involved drug use. To be referred to the Las Cruces juvenile drug court, for example, youth offenders must have committed a drug-related offense. Eligibility requirements in Dayton stipulate that youth must have been charged with a drug-related offense *or* have been

Table 3.1. *Eligibility Requirements and Exclusions for Juvenile Drug Court Programs*

Program	Caseload type	Eligibility requirements	Eligibility exclusions
Charleston	Pre- or post-adjudication	Age 13 to 17 Alcohol- or drug-related crime Drug dependence[a]	Violent offenses Sexual offenses
Dayton	Post-adjudication	Age 13 to 17.5 Drug dependence[a]	Violent offenses History of 4+ offenses TASC termination within prior 6 months
Jersey City	Pre-adjudication	Age 13 to 18 Extensive history of possession charges Detainable offenses	Violent offenses Drug dealing Probation violators
Las Cruces	Pre- or post-adjudication	Age 14 to 18 Drug dependence[a] Drug-related offenses with minimum 9-month sentence	Violent offenses Drug dealing
Missoula	Mostly post-adjudication	Age 14.5 to 17.5 Extensive juvenile justice history Drug use or abuse	Violent offenses First-time offenders
Orlando	Pre-adjudication, first-time offenders Post-adjudication cases accepted if case profile includes drug use	Age 14 to 18 Drug dependence[a]	Violent offenses Felony offenses (cases with more than 3 prior felonies *may* be excluded) Misdemeanor assault and battery Drug dealing Sexually abused youth

Source: Urban Institute National Evaluation of Juvenile Drug Courts.

a. Not synonymous with conventional notions of "addiction." The definition of "dependence" has become more subjective in recent years owing to changes in diagnostic criteria (see Butts, Zweig, and Mamalian, in this volume).

found to have a drug problem by a formal assessment. Charleston's drug court program focuses on youth referred for alcohol- or drug-related charges and tests potential clients to determine whether they meet the American Society of Addiction Medicine (ASAM) criteria for level I or level II treatment. The Orlando program, on the other hand, accepts referrals for youth with substance abuse problems, but does not require that their most recent offense is drug-related. The Orlando judge believes his program is an attractive alternative for juvenile offenders that otherwise would be unable to afford substance abuse treatment. The Orlando program even accepts youth with co-occurring disorders (substance abuse and mental health) as long as they comply with medication regimens. Many juvenile drug court judges consider their programs "problem solving" courts with a mission to target underserved juvenile populations.

Drug courts that receive funds from the U.S. Department of Justice have been required to exclude offenders with pending charges or prior convictions for violent offenses, but staff members of several programs visited for this study note that they consider this requirement unnecessary, at least in certain cases. Some programs have developed methods of filing charges to avoid eliminating youth from juvenile drug court eligibility. In one site, a case management agency had been performing all the preliminary screenings for the juvenile drug court and had rigidly denied eligibility based on charge severity, as instructed by the prosecutor. The judge believed that the process ignored important mitigating circumstances, and he worked with local prosecutors to create a more flexible charging process. Because of the judge's intervention, the program began to accept youth who otherwise would have been declared ineligible.

A number of other eligibility restrictions apply in each study site. Jersey City, Las Cruces, and Orlando exclude youth charged with selling illegal drugs. Charleston excludes youth with sexual offenses. The Dayton program turns away any juvenile with four or more prior offenses, those with limited intellectual capacity, and anyone who has been terminated from the TASC program in the previous six months.

Several drug courts pay particular attention to the age of potential program participants. The Las Cruces program rarely accepts youth who are likely to reach age 18 during their participation in drug court. The Missoula drug court initially accepted juveniles between ages 13 and 18, but later restricted eligibility to youth between 14.5 and 17.5. Program staff in Missoula report that younger youth struggle to understand and comply with Moral Reconation Therapy®, while older youth have independence issues that run counter to program requirements (e.g., curfew rules and regulations against smoking tobacco while in the program). The Orlando juvenile drug court typically accepts youth between ages 14 and 18, but the program does not enforce a strict lower age limit and accepts younger candidates based on their maturity level, education level, and social and family resources.

Screening and Assessment

Screening and assessment practices differ from one jurisdiction to the next (table 3.2). The six juvenile drug courts involved in this study use varying assessment protocols. Some use standardized instruments, while others rely on tools developed in-house or crafted by local treatment providers. The courts in Las Cruces and Dayton combine several standardized instruments. Jersey City, Missoula, and Orlando prefer to use in-house instruments constructed from standardized protocols. In addition to an in-house screening tool and chemical dependency assessments performed by treatment providers, the Missoula drug court uses a strengths-based inventory that youth complete during the early phases of program participation (box 3.2).

In Jersey City, once the district attorney's office has determined legal eligibility for juvenile drug court, the program coordinator conducts an initial screening of each youth. The coordinator interviews the offender and a parent or guardian; examines the youth's family, drug, and arrest history; and scrutinizes the individual's attitude and willingness to participate in the program. If the coordinator believes the youth is an appropriate candidate, the case is referred to a treatment provider for a more thorough bio-psychosocial assessment and an individualized treatment plan. The assessment includes information about the youth's academic record, substance abuse history, employment status, legal status, and family and peer information. It also covers general health information, such as the juvenile's nutritional background and history of medical or mental problems. The Jersey City process gives parents the opportunity to assess their children's behavior before and after program participation. Using a brief behavior assessment questionnaire, parents rate their child's behavior on several dimensions, including obedience to family rules, compliance with curfews, school attendance, frequency of substance use, association with known substance users, lying, irritability, loss of temper, sadness or depression, and criminal activity.

Table 3.2. *Screening and Assessment Practices of Juvenile Drug Courts*

Program	Responsible for screening	Responsible for assessment	Instruments used
Charleston	Program staff	Treatment providers	American Society of Addiction Medicine
Dayton	Juvenile court intake: all adjudicated youth receive SASSI and urinalysis screen for nine drugs	Juvenile Automated Substance Abuse Evaluation (JASAE) conducted if screening detects positive urine Diagnostic assessments by treatment providers TASC home visits	SASSI JASAE Youth Level of Service/ Case Management Inventory
Jersey City	Program coordinator	Treatment providers	Instruments developed by staff/providers
Las Cruces	Children's court judge or Juvenile Pre-Prosecution Diversion Program in District Attorney's office	Licensed substance abuse counselors	SASSI Teen ASI Children's Functional Assessment Rating Scale Life Purpose Questionnaire Short Sensation Seeking Scale
Missoula	Juvenile probation officer	Treatment providers	Instruments developed by staff/providers Strengths-based inventory completed by youth
Orlando	Juvenile Assessment Center Review by State Attorney's office	1–3 days comprehensive in-patient assessment at juvenile addictions receiving facility	Instruments developed by staff/providers based on TCU Prevention Management and Evaluation System

Source: Urban Institute National Evaluation of Juvenile Drug Courts.

Notes: Screening is a brief investigation using instruments and established criteria to determine eligibility and suitability of potential program participants. Assessment is a comprehensive bio-psychosocial appraisal of youth and family by trained professionals using multidisciplinary approaches.

Box 3.2. Missoula Youth Drug Court Self-Administered
Strengths-Based Assessment and Inventory of Personal Resources

1. Describe what is best about you.
2. What's the best thing you've done in your life so far?
3. When are you at your best? What does it look and feel like?
4. Describe the best thing about your family.
5. What does your family do well together?
6. Describe the people who have had the biggest impact on you, who do you look up to?
7. Who is the most positive person in your life right now? What do you get from him or her?
8. Describe a time when you successfully solved a problem.
9. Describe the most important thing you've learned about life so far.
10. What does being happy mean to you? When was the last time you felt truly happy?
11. Where would you like to be: a) one year from now? b) five years from now? c) ten years from now?
12. What skills or qualities do you have that the community may not know you have?
13. You have identified the following skills and talents. How can you use these skills in the future to benefit the community or people around you?
14. What is most important for people, including the YDC team, to know about you?
15. In signing the contract for drug court it is assumed that at a minimum you want to have your charges expunged if you are successful in this program. To do that you will need to do a lot of hard work and complete a variety of required and individually selected programs. What do you feel you need from your family and friends to do that?
16. What can the drug court team or the judge do to help you be successful in this program?
17. Imagine that when you get up tomorrow morning everything that was wrong with your life is now magically gone. In fact, everything is okay now. What does it look like? Can you get there?

Source: Urban Institute National Evaluation of Juvenile Drug Courts.

In many JDCs, a treatment provider performs screenings and assessments after youth have been referred by the program. In some programs, the local juvenile justice system screens all youth arrested in the jurisdiction, regardless of whether they are expected to have further contact with a treatment provider. In Orlando, for example, all arrested youth are immediately sent to a 24-hour multiservice juvenile assessment center (JAC) for preliminary evaluation. There, juveniles are considered for detention placement, screened for substance abuse, and assessed for social service, mental health, and family needs. First-time offenders are usually released with instructions to appear for court, often within 30 days of arrest. Juveniles with substance abuse problems are referred to the state attorney's office (SAO), which determines case processing within a few days. If the SAO determines a juvenile is eligible for drug court, information from the JAC assessment (as well as all pertinent social, health, and criminal records) is sent to the juvenile drug court judge and the public defender's office. At this point, the juvenile attends a detention hearing and is either accepted for drug court or sent back to the regular juvenile court process. For eligible youth, the addictions receiving facility conducts a one- to three-day evaluation, including a mental health assessment and in-home visits. At this point, a treatment plan is developed and either outpatient or residential treatment services may be ordered.

In Dayton, all adjudicated youth must provide a urine sample at the TASC laboratory and complete a Substance Abuse Subtle Screening Inventory (SASSI) administered by a substance abuse specialist. If an individual meets drug court eligibility requirements—and is charged with a drug-related offense, has a positive urinalysis, or has a SASSI assessment indicating drug use—he or she is screened using the Juvenile Automated Substance Abuse Evaluation (JASAE) instrument. If the JASAE identifies a drug or alcohol problem, the youth is considered a possible drug court referral and is sent to a specially designated nurse assessor, who functions as a member of the drug court's assessment team and performs detailed diagnostic assessments. If the assessor determines the youth requires at least level 1 care, that information is forwarded to the TASC coordinator, who assigns a TASC case manager. Within three days of assignment, the case manager performs a home visit and exchanges additional information with the youth and family. The case manager administers the Youth Level of Service/Case Management Inventory (YLoSI) to determine the youth's needs and risk factors, and then completes a disposition investigation report that includes the youth's social history. All this information is then available at the youth's first drug court hearing.

Admission

Sometimes the entire drug court team makes final decisions about program admissions, and sometimes the judge makes them. In Jersey City, when substance abuse counselors conclude that they cannot work with a particular juvenile or the youth does not look like an appropriate candidate for the drug court program, the case is not likely to be accepted, but the judge has the final say. If a juvenile is not accepted, the case is returned to the Family Division of the District Court for adjudication.

Youth found appropriate for drug court are advised of the voluntary nature of their participation, the court requirements, and any other expectations that could factor into their ability to graduate successfully from the program. This orientation generally includes a contract that must be signed by the youth and possibly his or her parent(s). Sometimes the judge provides the orientation for youth and their families. The drug court judge in Orlando, for example, believes that it is particularly important for him to "sell the program" to families in a way that ensures their voluntary participation. He is sensitive to the fact that members of minority communities may distrust the legal system. For that reason, he feels that it is critical to talk with parents about the services the drug court provides that could help them and their child, and not just to focus on the legal problem that brought the family into contact with the court. As part of the admissions process, some programs give youth a handbook with information about the drug court staff, rules and requirements, treatment phases, drug testing procedures, and courtroom routines.

In the Las Cruces program, orientation begins at a youth's first drug court review. The judge introduces the youth and family to all team members and explains the program requirements, including sanctions and incentives. This introduction is followed by an orientation week organized by the treatment provider, during which the youth is given a copy of the program contract, his or her monthly schedule, and the participant handbook (box 3.3).

In Missoula, once a juvenile is determined eligible, the public defender discusses the legal consequences of participating in the youth drug court with the juvenile and his or her guardian(s). Each juvenile and family is given the opportunity to decline the program and return to the regular juvenile court (called "youth court" in Montana). If all parties agree to participate, a contract is signed and the juvenile and family attend an orientation provided by the community programs coordinator. Families are advised that because of limited treatment funds, participants with adequate resources or insurance are expected to pay some or all of the treatment costs. During the orientation, families eligible for Medicaid or CHIP

Box 3.3. Las Cruces Juvenile Drug Court Rules

1. Do not use or possess drugs or alcohol or tobacco products. Sobriety is the primary focus of this program. Maintaining a drug-free lifestyle is very important in your recovery process. If you are prescribed any medications by your doctor, you must notify your counselor immediately.
2. Attend all ordered treatment sessions. This includes individual, family, and group counseling, educational sessions, required AA meetings, community service projects, and your committed community volunteer work. If you are unable to attend a scheduled session, you must contact your treatment counselor and they must authorize your absence.
3. Be on time. If you are late, you may not be allowed to attend your counseling session and will be considered noncompliant. You must contact your assigned counselor if there is a possibility you may be late.
4. Do not make threats toward other participants or staff or behave in a violent manner. Violent or inappropriate behavior will not be tolerated and will be reported to the court. This may result in termination from the Juvenile Drug Court Program.
5. Dress appropriately for court, community service, and treatment sessions. As a participant, you will be expected to wear clothing that is appropriate for what you are participating in. Clothing bearing drug-, alcohol-, or gang-related themes are not tolerated.
6. While in court, remain quiet and seated at all times unless you are asked a question by the treatment team or by the judge. You are to seat yourself in the jury box.
7. Parents (guardians) must attend scheduled court reviews and the required parenting groups. When unable to attend, the court needs to be advised of legitimate reason for absence in advance or as soon as possible.

Source: Las Cruces, New Mexico, Juvenile Drug Court, *Participant/Parent Handbook: Reaching for the Stars* (Las Cruces: Juvenile Drug Court, 2001).

---

are required to apply for coverage. At the time of the Urban Institute visits, no juveniles in Missoula had been refused participation because of inability to pay.

In Jersey City, the juvenile drug court coordinator conducts client orientations to discuss the roles and responsibilities of youth and their guardians, court procedures, and the key requirements of the program. At the end of the orientation, each participant is given a copy of the program schedule, which includes the dates of treatment sessions, court appearances, and other appointments. After completing orientation, juveniles begin a two-week trial period. During this trial period, youth begin treatment and attend drug court sessions before officially becoming a participant by signing the contract. If a youth decides not to participate, the case is returned to District Court.

By comparison, parents/guardians and youth in Orlando are required to sign a drug court contract before their participation can begin. If a youth breaks this contract, he or she is subject to sanctions or dismissal from the court program. If a juvenile is dismissed, the case is returned to the regular juvenile court process or the youth is subject to the requirements of a preexisting probation agreement, which could include time in secure detention.

Judicial Hearings

Juvenile drug court hearings vary greatly. The courtroom setting, the frequency and scheduling of court appearances, attendance of drug court team members, courtroom processes and routines, and the nature and extent of youth and family involvement, not to mention the individual styles and personalities of the judges themselves, may differ. Despite their variety, JDCs as a group are quite different from traditional juvenile courts. They are less confrontational, more interactive, more attuned to the principles of therapeutic jurisprudence, and more likely to emphasize the theatrical dynamics of the courtroom.

Most juvenile drug court hearings observed by the Urban Institute were held in relatively standard courtroom settings, but the facilities varied from the well-appointed, state-of-the-art courtroom used by the Orlando court to the school library in Las Cruces that was hastily configured before each court session. Some courtrooms were completely packed with youth and their relatives, and it was impossible to hear everything being said. Others had space for everyone and the proceedings were well amplified. Some courts were forced to reduce overcrowding by permitting participants to leave at the end of their status hearings instead of requiring everyone to remain for the entire session to benefit from exposure to other proceedings. In some programs, the limitations of the courtroom facility prompted staff to hold less frequent status hearings—that is, court was convened weekly, but some cases were heard less frequently based on the amount of court contact needed for that youth.

Many JDC programs follow a formal protocol. The judge dresses in a traditional black robe. A bailiff announces the beginning of each court session, and those in attendance are directed to behave appropriately. In other courts, the proceedings are considerably less structured. The judge, team members, and family participants are less restricted, conversing informally and moving around the courtroom so much that at times the environment becomes somewhat chaotic. In some programs, the court does not even wait until everyone is seated before convening the first session, and late arrivals may cause disruption. Youth may be periodically pulled out of the courtroom for drug testing, leading to considerable side conversations among audience members. Boxes 3.4, 3.5, and 3.6 describe typical court sessions in three juvenile drug court programs.

Regardless of their varying physical characteristics and different levels of formality, most programs try to preserve the authority and dignity of their proceedings, while recognizing youth lifestyles in clothes, language, and demeanor. Several, but not all, programs visited for this study have written standards for courtroom behavior and personal dress. In Charleston, for example, parents and youth are instructed in the proper way of speaking to the judge (e.g., respectfully and with no hands in pockets), and are told to dress appropriately (e.g., pants should be clean and without holes, shirts should be tucked in, shorts or short skirts are not permitted).

Some programs have standard routines for the material addressed during court hearings. For example, in Charleston, every hearing includes a parental report and teacher ratings of the juvenile's school performance, including his or her attendance, preparedness for class, and classroom conduct. Each JDC hearing concludes with an open discussion of the youth's progress to date and a request that the youth pay a court administration fee for the hearing. Some other courts have similar regimens, but others approach each case individually, guided by the information discussed during a pre-hearing case staffing.

Although some programs expect all youth to remain throughout each court session, others do not. In these courts, the ordering of cases assumes great importance. Some judges prefer to hear noncompliant cases first, so all participants hear the issues involved and the consequences that follow. In Las Cruces, for example, where youth are allowed to leave at the end of their own case reviews, new cases are heard at the end of the session to give

(text continues on page 80)

Box 3.4. A Day in Missoula County Youth Drug Court

The county courthouse in Missoula, Montana, occupies a square in the middle of town. A traditional, official-looking building built during the early 20th century, the courthouse is several stories high and includes a central atrium that is open from the lower to upper floors. The courthouse has one main entrance with a set of concrete stairs that open onto a formal courtyard. One can enter the courthouse through several side entrances as well, and except for a small sign with a list of items not allowed in the building, there is no apparent security. The bottom level of the building contains the courtrooms, including the one used for the weekly meetings of the Missoula Youth Drug Court (YDC), while the other levels include administrative offices and a small eatery.

On most days, the Missoula courthouse is quiet, but on Wednesday afternoons, when the YDC sessions take place, the lower hallways are abuzz with conversation and adolescent energy. Just before 3:30 P.M., the doors of the courtroom are unlocked and everyone files in to claim their seats. Several church-style, wooden pews begin to fill up with youth and their family members. Participants enter the room from the rear, behind the pews. The raised parapet where the judge will be seated is at the front of the room and dominates the physical space. A podium is positioned at the front of the room where each youth will soon stand to face the judge and address the court. There are several long tables just behind the podium and in front of the spectator pews. A juvenile probation officer and the prosecutor share one table, while a public defender sits at the other with an empty chair reserved for each juvenile as he or she takes a turn before the judge. Other case managers and treatment providers sometimes sit at a table to the judge's right.

On the judge's left is a row of five or six wooden chairs with their backs against the wall and in plain view of the spectators. A few minutes after everyone is settled into the pews, a door opens behind these chairs and uniformed correctional officers escort several youth into the courtroom. The youth are dressed in orange jumpsuits, handcuffs, and leg shackles. They have just arrived from the county's locked detention center. Most were ordered into detention during a previous drug court hearing, often for violating program rules or testing "dirty" on a urinalysis. The shackled youth generally seem bored or embarrassed, but occasionally one of the older boys looks at a friend seated in the pews and the two exchange grimaces and grins to signal their disdain for the proceedings.

At precisely 3:30 P.M., Judge John W. Larson enters the room from a side door. He is dressed formally, in black robes. Judge Larson moves to his chair on the raised bench area. The courtroom is noisy before the judge arrives, but as he enters the noise quickly subsides. The bailiff asks everyone to rise and announces that the court is in session. Judge Larson quickly scans the room, asks everyone to be seated, and the court proceedings begin.

Most spectator conversations end immediately, although several young people near the back of the room continue to whisper. During the proceedings, it is some-

(continued)

Box 3.4. *Continued*

times hard to hear people who speak to the judge while facing away from the spectator pews. Only the juvenile, the attorneys, and the judge are given microphones.

Judge Larson begins the court session by calling a young woman and her mother to the podium. The girl is dressed in jeans and an oversized sweatshirt, with her hair in a ponytail. Her mother is also dressed casually. This particular youth is trying to get into drug court in lieu of inpatient treatment, where she is currently placed. The judge decides that YDC is not appropriate at this time and that she should continue with her treatment. The girl begins to cry and Judge Larson offers her sympathy and advice before calling the next case.

The next juvenile is dressed in wrinkled khakis and a large jersey with a team logo. He and his mother are called to the podium and the judge greets the youth by name in a friendly and familiar manner. He asks the young man to give the court an update on his status. The young man says he has been on house arrest, but that he has been attending all his appointments and classes. He asks the judge's permission to go to a job interview. Judge Larson briefly reviews why the youth was on house arrest (a dirty drug test) and then grants permission for the job interview. The judge tells the youth that if he obtains the job, he will be released from house arrest to go to work.

Judge Larson continues to call each participant to the podium. In each case, he verbally reviews the youth's status and recent progress. The other drug court team members provide information to the court as well. The judge discusses the youth's overall progression through the drug court program, often stopping to explain to the other spectators why each decision is being made. In some cases, community service hours are added. In others, a dirty drug test or a missed appointment results in house arrest, or even detention. Some cases showing progress are rewarded with reduced time in court and gift certificates; those who have done particularly well might receive a round of applause, prompted by the judge.

The judge seems to have a good rapport with the youth, and they in turn treat him with respect. He offers sympathy, advice, and admonishments when necessary, but he generally tries to focus on the positive and encourages each youth to succeed. He also addresses the parent or guardian to ask about behavior at home and parenting concerns.

Overall, the courtroom atmosphere is serious, but not oppressive. As it becomes obvious that the court session will soon close, people become distracted, and the noise level increases. Judge Larson finishes speaking with the last participant and then finishes the proceedings by telling the juveniles that he'll see them again soon.

Source: Urban Institute National Evaluation of Juvenile Drug Courts.

Box 3.5. A Day in Montgomery County Juvenile Drug Court

It is a warm Thursday morning in August. The Montgomery County Juvenile Drug Court is about to meet in the courtroom of Judge Michael B. Murphy, the administrative judge of the juvenile division of the Common Pleas Court of Montgomery County in Dayton, Ohio.

The juvenile division is located at 303 West Second Street in downtown Dayton, across the street from the main criminal court building for Montgomery County, and a few blocks from Interstate 75, which runs north and south through central Dayton. Both court facilities are easily accessible by public transportation. A parking lot is available less than a block away for any visitors who drive to court.

The juvenile court building appears to have been constructed during the 1950s or 1960s, with an attractive concrete exterior, long interior hallways, tile floors, and ample light. After going through a small security area just inside the courthouse entrance, visitors are greeted by a framed portrait of Judge Murphy that hangs on a wood paneled wall. The door to Judge Murphy's courtroom is no more than 20 to 30 feet down an adjacent hallway.

On a typical Thursday morning between 9:00 and 9:30 A.M. during the summer, about a dozen young people and their parents are gathered in the hallway awaiting the start of juvenile drug court. Promptly at 9:30 A.M., a uniformed bailiff opens the door and instructs each youth and parent to find a seat in one of the 20 to 30 chairs available in the back of the courtroom.

The room is perhaps 60 by 30 feet. The visitor area is just inside the entrance door at one end of the long room, while the judge's bench is at the opposite end. Witness tables and a speaker's podium are just in front of the visitors' area, facing the judge's bench. An elevated jury box with two rows of chairs is along one long wall. The other long wall has large windows extending nearly to the ceiling, approximately 25 feet high. Mini-blinds control the glare, but the room is otherwise bright and sunlit. Outside, a phalanx of shoulder-high shrubbery runs along the length of the courtroom wall, blocking passers-by from looking in and preventing anyone in the courtroom from being distracted by activity on the street or sidewalk.

The entire room is clean and well decorated. Visitor seating consists of modern, polished wood chairs with clean, upholstered cushions. The judge sits on an elaborate, elevated bench with all the trappings of a formal courtroom. The words, "Judge Michael B. Murphy," are emblazoned on a plaque on the front of the bench, clearly visible to all participants.

The courtroom includes an electronic sound system. Contemporary, flexible arm microphones are placed at regular intervals along the witness tables and at the speaker's podium. A court reporter sits just in front and below the judge's bench, creating a record of the proceedings. Although microphones are used to amplify the participants, visitors would have no trouble hearing the proceedings if the sound system was not used. The floor is carpeted and the room remains hushed

(continued)

Box 3.5. *Continued*

during court. There are few conversations among the participants. Those who do talk take great care to whisper.

Several youth dressed in yellow t-shirts enter the courtroom. They are escorted by uniformed correctional officers and some are released from handcuffs as they enter the room. They have been brought to court from the secure juvenile detention facility. Most were placed in detention by Judge Murphy during a previous hearing for violating the rules of juvenile drug court. The detention youth sit in the front row of the jury box, seen by the entire courtroom but separated from the other JDC youth and their parents. Other spectators (the TASC case managers and visiting researchers) are seated in the back row of the jury box.

Within a few minutes, the court clerk steps from behind her small work area next to the judge's bench and calls out, "All rise," and announces the convening of the court and the entrance of Judge Murphy. Everyone in the courtroom rises in silence and waits for the clerk to indicate that they may sit again.

The clerk calls the first case by reading the case number and noting that this particular hearing is a "progress report."

A young man named Jason [*not his real name*] stands and walks to the podium, looking disinterested and disheveled. Jason is around 16 years old. His mother follows and sits at the witness table next to the podium. Judge Murphy looks up from the case file he has been inspecting. He smiles at Jason and says, "How you doing today?" Jason mumbles, "All right." He does not return the judge's smile. A similar exchange between Judge Murphy and the youth's mother is only slightly more reciprocated.

The judge begins the case by asking Jason's TASC case manager to read her report to the court. Case managers typically know the most about each youth's circumstances and recent behavior. They see each youth at least weekly. They visit them at school and will often drop by their homes unannounced, either to check on the youth's compliance with curfews and other court rules or to collect urine samples for drug testing. Case managers also regularly communicate with other treatment professionals that may be involved in each case, such as the counselors at Partnerships for Youth, where many JDC clients receive drug treatment.

Jason's case manager reports a number of problems to the court. Jason has been out past curfew several times. His most recent drug test was positive for cocaine, and his teachers and counselors report various bad behaviors and troubling developments. The case manager finishes her report by noting that Jason's recent behavior would seem to indicate that a period of secure detention is warranted.

Judge Murphy asks a few routine questions before turning to the central issue in the case. He looks directly at Jason, who is standing at the podium looking bored. "We did a UA recently. Right?" There is no reaction. "What did it say?" the judge tries again. Jason mumbles an answer, "cocaine." "Pardon me," the judge asks, "what did you say?" "Cocaine," the youth says, raising his voice just a little, "positive." "That's

(continued)

Box 3.5. *Continued*

right," Judge Murphy responds, making a note to himself on the papers in front of him.

Turning to Jason's mother, the judge asks whether she has anything to tell the court. She appears reluctant, looking first at her son. Then she turns to the judge and says, "Been having trouble with him." She goes on to describe Jason's recent behavior around the home, including broken curfews, poor school attendance, and a generally disrespectful and sometimes abusive attitude toward her.

Judge Murphy pauses, watching the young man standing at the podium. There is no eye contact between them. Jason stares at the floor in front of him for much of the judge's exchange with his mother. Judge Murphy says nothing. There are several awkward moments of silence before the young man dares to look up.

When Jason finally looks up at the bench, Judge Murphy says plainly, "We have several problems here, don't we?" This elicits an almost indiscernible shrug of the shoulders and a barely audible, "I dunno."

The judge continues. "You are not sticking to the plan, young man. You are not going to school as you agreed to do. You are not obeying your mother's rules at home. You are treating her with disrespect, and you came to drug court last time under the influence."

The last point finally gets Jason's attention. "What?" he says, looking up for an instant, but with only the slightest affect. "You came to drug court last time under the influence, didn't you?" the judge repeats. Jason offers an explanation. "I was just tired. I didn't sleep." Judge Murphy seems interested in this statement and asks the juvenile, "Why not?" The answer comes in the form of another shrug and a slight mumble. The judge repeats, "Why didn't you sleep the night before drug court?" At this point, Jason looks up and tries to go on the offensive. "Because I knew that court wasn't going to go too well."

Jason returns his gaze to the floor in front of the podium and misses the small, understanding smile from Judge Murphy. "I believe you did know that," he says. "And guess what? Court isn't going too well today either, is it?" There is no response, but Judge Murphy continues. Addressing Jason by name, the judge informs him that he is going to be "remanded to detention today." Clearly this comes as no surprise, but Judge Murphy repeats the reasons he is ordering detention. He finishes by telling Jason that he will be held in detention "until we get this matter resolved." During the judge's statement, a uniformed deputy has wordlessly stepped behind Jason, handcuffs opened and readied.

Judge Murphy indicates that the discussion is over for the day. "Go with the deputy," he says to Jason, who continues to stare at the floor. Everyone in the courtroom sits silently as Jason knowingly extends his hands behind his back until he hears the handcuffs click onto his wrists. The deputy puts a hand around the youth's bicep. Jason turns and walks out the rear door with the deputy in tow.

(continued)

Box 3.5. *Continued*

The court remains quiet. There are no conversations, but visitors in the jury box can see several parents in the back of the courtroom glance quickly at their own teenagers, hoping to see shock or perhaps even fear that just might keep them on a better path and out of trouble.

Not every case like Jason's will end in handcuffs and detention. In a different case on the same day, Judge Murphy places another recalcitrant youth on home detention with electronic monitoring of his whereabouts at all times. One reason for the different outcome in that case is the judge's belief that the youth's parents are actively concerned about their son and that they will do all they can to enforce the court's orders and keep their son in check. The juvenile drug court program is designed to work with and support competent parents whenever possible.

Source: Urban Institute National Evaluation of Juvenile Drug Courts.

newcomers the opportunity to view the entire series of cases heard that day. At the end of the session, the judge introduces the youth and family to the surveillance officers and explains their role in monitoring youth compliance with program requirements. This information is easier for youth and their families to grasp because they have just heard several examples of how program rules are monitored and enforced.

The Orlando judge frequently permits successful youth to leave court after their cases have been heard. Newer cases are scheduled at the end of each session to give those youth broader exposure to court-room proceedings, and to ensure that they witness the judge responding to successful cases. In addition, hearings are scheduled on Friday afternoons so detention orders can be enforced immediately without interrupting a youth's schooling. The judge notes approvingly that this approach also disrupts any weekend plans that a noncompliant youth may have made prior to court.

The Importance of Process

Practitioners and researchers suggest that a critical factor in the success of the drug court model is the dynamic between the offender and the judge in the courtroom. In studying adult drug courts, for example, Hirst and Harrell (2000) found the most important characteristics of court for the

Box 3.6. A Day in Jersey City Juvenile Drug Court

The Jersey City Juvenile Drug Court holds its sessions in the main courthouse located in downtown Jersey City, minutes from the commuter train system. The large, 1950s-style concrete building looks more like an office building than a courthouse, but just inside the door, uniformed deputies screen visitors through a metal detector. The tiled hallways are busy and noisy.

The juvenile drug court (JDC) is held in a small, traditional courtroom on one of the upper floors. Each JDC session is immediately preceded by a client staffing, where Judge Salvatore Bovino and the drug court coordinator review the status of each youth they expect to see that day. Court is scheduled to begin at 4:30 P.M., but sometimes begins as late as 5 P.M. The judge sits behind a traditional judicial bench on a raised area at the front of the courtroom. Directly in front of the judge is a long table where the coordinator sits and where participants must stand when addressing the court. To the left of the bench is a small desk with a computer where a juvenile probation officer (JPO) records information during the proceedings.

The JDC proceedings are relatively informal. There are no announcements as the court convenes. The audience is not even in the room when Judge Bovino enters. When it is time for court to begin, the judge simply walks in and takes his seat. While he is dressed in a traditional black robe, it is left open in the front. The judge begins to chat with the drug court program coordinator. They seem to be finishing up a conversation from the client staffing that has just occurred.

The sheriff's deputies open the main doors for participants and their parents to file in, and as the audience gathers, the noise level in the room increases. In the rear of the courtroom are three rows of wooden benches where the juveniles and their family members sit facing the judge. The audience seating area can be rather dim as there is no lighting in this area. In addition to the youth and their parents, the audience includes several officers from the Jersey City Police Department. The officers have arrived a few minutes before the youth enter the courtroom. As they come in, several youth exchange friendly greetings with the officers.

On this day, there are 13 juveniles in court; only four are accompanied by a parent or guardian. Nearly half the juveniles in court are dressed almost identically, in black, oversized down parkas, black hooded sweatshirts, and black or blue jeans. Several also have woolen ball caps with the bills turned backward.

Speaking loudly to overcome the buzz of conversation in the room, the JDC coordinator beckons the first juvenile to stand with her at the long table in front of the Judge. She calls him twice before he hears his name. As the judge looks down to review the paperwork for the first case, most of the audience grows quiet. Several conversations continue among the police officers. Before he addresses the juvenile standing in front of him, Judge Bovino turns to the program coordinator and asks if another youth is in the room. When told that the youth is not in attendance, the judge

(continued)

Box 3.6. *Continued*

spends several minutes working with the program coordinator and the JPO to issue a bench warrant for that youth's arrest.

The first juvenile stands with his hands clasped behind his back, facing the judge. There is no formal dress code requirement for JDC, but the judge reminds the juveniles that he wants them to dress respectfully. The judge asks that today's participants tuck in their shirts, take off their hats, and make sure their underwear is not showing.

Judge Bovino asks the juvenile for his report card, and the youth indicates that it should be coming in the mail soon. The JDC coordinator briefly converses with the juvenile and the judge, but it is difficult to hear what they are saying. The judge tells the youth he is doing well and says he will see him in two weeks.

The next juvenile called to the table apparently missed a curfew during the past week. The judge admonishes him, but no sanctions are applied, and the youth is asked to take his seat.

As the third juvenile approaches the table, other court staff enter the courtroom from the judge's chambers and begin talking to the court reporter. This disruption makes it hard to hear what happens next. A recent curfew check of this youth revealed that he was not at home when he was required to be there. When questioned about this, the youth said that he had to work. However, the JPO confirmed with the youth's employer that he was not working on the date in question. During the staffing, it was decided that Judge Bovino would address this issue in court to determine if the youth would tell the truth. When questioned in open court, the youth lies once again about being at work. The judge admonishes him for breaking curfew and for lying, and the coordinator tells the judge that they can no longer accept the youth's word. The judge orders additional community service hours. As the youth turns around to return to his seat, he rolls his eyes at the audience.

The next couple of youth are doing much better in the program. They are encouraged to look for jobs, hand in their report cards, and continue to follow the rules. One asks for a later curfew time, bringing a note from his mother requesting the same. Although the judge ribs him a little, after checking with the JDC coordinator, the judge grants him a 9 P.M. curfew, one hour later than his current curfew.

The sixth juvenile, who was recently released from inpatient treatment and has tested positive for marijuana three times in the previous two weeks, is called to the front and is accompanied by his mother. He admits to using and says he is having trouble because he recently went off house arrest and has been exposed to people who are using. The coordinator says that the youth looks high now; the mother immediately reports "He's been with me all day." Nonetheless, the coordinator orders an immediate drug test, the results of which will be available the next business day. The judge discusses the possibility of sending the youth back to long-term

(continued)

Box 3.6. *Continued*

inpatient care, but the youth indicates he would rather be placed under house arrest again than have to stay at a residential program. The coordinator advocates for house arrest to give him a chance to stay at home and stop using. The judge agrees, but says that in the mean time they will look for a bed for him in inpatient, where he will go if he does not improve.

The seventh juvenile called was discussed at length in the staffing. He has been violating treatment program rules by repeatedly wearing gang colors and one black glove (another indication of gang involvement). The judge addresses the issue with him, finding him in violation and sanctioning him to Youth House for the next two days. The youth is put in handcuffs and led away by the sheriff's deputies.

There is one new participant, who is asked to approached the bench with his father. The judge briefly explains the JDC program, asking both the youth and parent if they want to participate. Both agree and sign the contract.

One participant receives verbal commendation for having just graduated from high school. The Jersey City Police Department has donated portable compact disc players as rewards for such accomplishments; however, the JDC team forgot to bring one this time. Other incentives during this session have included decreased court appearances and a more lenient curfew, while sanctions consisted of verbal admonishment by the judge, house arrest, community service, threats of detainment at Youth House, and an actual detention.

Source: Urban Institute National Evaluation of Juvenile Drug Courts.

---

clients were voice (the client is heard), neutrality (in determining sanctions and treatment), trust (between the client and court), standing (the client is treated with respect), and accuracy. Each client's perception of fair treatment within the court process, or the quality of procedural justice, was integral to the success of the drug court model. Factors that influenced a client's perception of justice included the certainty and swiftness of penalties, the accuracy of drug tests, evidence that the judge cares about the welfare of every client (although some clients believe too close a relationship undermines the effectiveness of the court), and personal involvement. All the JDC programs visited for this study operate in a manner generally consistent with the values of procedural justice. They all depend heavily on the relationship between the judge and each youth. Most hearings incorporate direct conversation between the judge and the youth, and some involve extensive interaction with the youth's parent(s) as well.

Many programs emphasize family involvement. For example, several programs report that judges have decided to hold hearings later in the day to accommodate working parents. Some programs strongly encourage parental attendance at status hearings, while others mandate it. In some programs, parents are not simply expected to attend hearings, they are key participants. The Charleston judge routinely asks parents to speak in open court about their child's behavior at home. The judge coaches parents on setting and enforcing appropriate boundaries for youth at home and in the community, and she often consults with parents regarding what sanctions the parents want the court to invoke for a child's infractions of family rules. Parents who cannot attend a particular court session are expected to send a written note to the judge beforehand, reporting on the youth's behavior. The program facilitates parental participation by providing transportation for parents who would otherwise be unable to attend court or participate in treatment with their children. Several programs have adopted family-friendly policies sensitive to cultural needs. For example, the Florida judge is multilingual and deliberately converses with parents and youth in both English and Spanish to bridge the gap for non-English speakers. Similarly, the Las Cruces program operates in Spanish at times to prevent English-speaking youth from controlling situations when parents speak only Spanish.

Judges, of course, have their own unique styles; some display considerable emotional affect (both positive and negative, as appropriate), while others are more reserved in the courtroom. All judges exercise considerable discretion regarding what they discuss in public hearings, often taking advantage of the courtroom theater to surface individual issues that permit them to make a broader point and leverage peer pressure for use in other cases. Judges often allocate more time to noncompliant cases to identify problems and ask youth to examine for themselves why something has happened and what corrective actions are needed. Youth are frequently invited to predict the consequences for certain transgressions given their current standing in the drug court program, and most youth are able to do so. This method reinforces knowledge of the program rules for all participants and allows newcomers to see the rules are neither capricious nor arbitrary.

The free-wheeling nature of some JDC judges can be problematic. Judges can extemporize in court, and sometimes they venture into a therapeutic role for which they have limited preparation. One judge observed by the Urban Institute seemed to enjoy "taking the lid off" family issues in open court, sometimes with little regard for the adverse effects on youth and families. In one hearing that left a number of stakeholders quite uneasy, the judge unexpectedly asked a youth to confirm a report that his father had recently been hostile to drug court staff attempting to make a home visit. The youth acknowledged the incident, and the judge reacted by reaffirming that home visits were a requirement of drug court participation. The youth became agitated and stated that he would rather be dismissed from the program and sent to a correctional facility than comply with home visits. The judge insisted that program withdrawal was not an option and compliance was mandatory. The youth timidly explained that his father was outraged by the perceived intrusiveness of the program, and he alluded to previous physical abuse by his father against himself and his mother. The mother then spoke up suddenly, saying that she also wanted her son to withdraw from the program and go to a correctional facility. Instead of recognizing the vulnerability of the family and the real possibility of domestic violence, the judge pushed forward, insisting that the youth go home and tell his father that home visits were mandatory and ordered by the judge. Both mother and son looked stricken, leaving observers to wonder about the repercussions that would ensue. Treatment providers later expressed concern that these issues should have been explored in a clinical setting.

Most juvenile drug court hearings are not so dramatic. Often, they are routine. Participants can become very accustomed to the routine. In one case, just as the judge was beginning to discuss the consequences for a youth's violation of program rules—but well before the sanction had actually been named—the young man quite nonchalantly dropped his head and shoulders and placed his hands behind his back, crossed at the wrists, preparing for what he knew was coming. Moments later, he was handcuffed and removed to the secure detention center. In some programs, everyone is so attuned to the courtroom routine that when the judge congratulates a youth for making progress, three-year-olds in the audience know when to start applauding at the conclusion of the judge's congratulatory statement.

Team Meetings and Case Reviews

Most juvenile drug court teams observed by the Urban Institute hold pre-hearing meetings to review the cases scheduled in court each day. The

Jersey City juvenile drug court is an exception. It does not hold traditional case reviews. Instead, the program coordinator meets with the judge before each hearing to brief him on the status of each case. More typically, however, the entire JDC team meets for case reviews before each court session. In Las Cruces, team meetings are quite large, involving all key partners, including local police. The entire team makes case decisions. The judge takes a leading role in the discussion, but he usually concurs with the recommendations of the team.

Members of Missoula's JDC team meet before each weekly court session. The judge, juvenile probation officers and juvenile probation office director, public defender (or her representative), and community program coordinator generally attend case reviews. Treatment and out-of-home placement liaisons attend as needed. The prosecutor attends some case reviews but is primarily involved in determining participant eligibility and enrollment. The prosecutor in Missoula does not have much contact with drug court clients unless they are facing program termination or likely to face secure detention for more than a few days. In all matters, the judge has ultimate decisionmaking authority, but decisions are nearly always consensual. Team members, excluding the judge, vote on weekly decisions regarding admission, expulsion, placement, sanctions, and incentives. The judge sometimes casts a tie-breaking vote.

Case reviews permit team members to discuss the status of each youth scheduled for court. The team identifies actions that should be taken during the hearing, including service modifications, drug tests, verbal recognitions and awards, or the imposition of sanctions and penalties. Sanctions are not always traditional. The Orlando judge once ordered a youth to practice his trumpet and hug his mother at least once a day. During the next review meeting, the family therapist reported that the young man had been following the judge's instructions in both regards. The judge announced this fact in open court and praised the young man in front of other participants. Judges and team members in many JDC programs rehearse how to conduct hearings for optimum effect.

Occasionally, drug court team meetings expose a lack of consensus about specific cases or highlight differences of opinion about court practices. In one case witnessed by the Urban Institute, a JDC team grappled with how to respond to two sisters. Each sister faithfully attended court, came to every treatment session, and complied with every community service requirement. Both, however, continued to drink alcohol despite repeated drug test failures and increasingly stringent sanctions. The girls had been repeatedly abused as pre-teens, and the treatment staff believed that the persistent alcohol use was related to the abuse. Some team members argued that the program was simply "spinning its wheels," and that neither sister was likely to succeed under the current arrangement. The treatment staff insisted that these cases were precisely the kinds that should remain in drug court; they suggested that the nonclinical members of the team did not fully comprehend the time and resources needed to counteract the range of negative forces in the lives of troubled youth. Ultimately, the law enforcement perspective won out. The girls were dismissed from drug court and later committed to a juvenile correctional facility.

Behavior Management

Juvenile drug courts manage client behavior with several methods. Most use a combination of incentives, rewards, and sanctions. All JDC programs attempt to match their behavioral management techniques to the unique circumstances of each client.

Incentives

Like their adult counterparts, most juvenile drug courts use incentives to encourage the participation of youthful offenders. In Jersey City, delinquency proceedings are suspended while a youth participates in drug court. Upon graduation, all charges are dismissed and the judge can terminate preexisting probation requirements. Failure to comply with the requirements of juvenile drug court, however, is likely to result in program dismissal, which sends the case back to the Family Division District Court for adjudication on the original charges. Youth in the Orlando program are enrolled after adjudication, and often as a condition of probation. Thus, dismissal of charges cannot induce youth to participate, but juveniles completing the program can have their probation supervision terminated early or their records expunged. In Missoula, youth must admit to the allegations in a delinquency petition before they are accepted into the JDC program. The disposition of the petition is suspended while the youth participates in drug court. Once the youth successfully completes the program, the petition is dismissed and the juvenile's *entire* record can be expunged. Las Cruces expunges records on a case-by-case basis, and only if the youth avoids additional legal trouble for two years after drug court graduation.

Rewards

JDC programs use rewards to acknowledge good behavior and program advancement, including verbal praise and tangible rewards. Some rewards relate directly to drug court regulations. For example, the Charleston program excuses youth from their fourth weekly court appearance in a month if they have clean drug tests during the first three weeks and otherwise comply with all program rules. Other rewards for youth include not having to pay all the court appearance fee, being allowed to skip a treatment session, or moving through the phases of drug court more quickly. As youth accumulate clean drug tests, the frequency of the tests could be reduced.

Some rewards are more tangible. Successful youth are given small rewards during court sessions, such as gift certificates and tickets to local events. In Las Cruces, the drug court rewards compliant youth with tickets to athletic events, curfew extensions, free movies or bowling passes, gift certificates provided by local businesses, and opportunities to work with the local K-9 police unit or visit a local TV news station. The Missoula and Las Cruces courts sometimes used police "ride alongs" as a reward. Youth accompany police during a patrol shift, giving them a chance to observe police activities and relate to police officers as individuals. The Las Cruces program also holds a regular gift lottery twice a month. Youth doing well in juvenile drug court are entered into the BKOM (Best Kid of the Month) lottery. At the end of that day's court session, one or two eligible youth are selected at random from the BKOM list. As the winning names are announced, the youth are called up to the judge's bench where they receive gifts more valuable than the token prizes usually available to successful clients. Past winners have received certificates for compact discs and running shoes.

Programs often celebrate client progress in open court. Like most JDCs, the Orlando program recognizes every program graduate during a court session. Each graduate is invited to speak briefly to the audience, and his or her parents then tell everyone in court about the changes they have observed since their child began the program. In Missoula, the drug court tries to individualize graduation ceremonies and often invites special guests according to each participant's wishes. In one case, a youth became particularly attached to a llama while participating in pet therapy, and the program arranged to have the llama brought into the courtroom for the graduation celebration.

To graduate from the Las Cruces program, youth must complete a four-phased treatment program, perform volunteer work with a community organization for at least two hours a week, demonstrate progress on educational and vocational goals, have four consecutive clean urinalysis tests, attend a Victim Impact panel, and attend and report on a cultural activity. After completing all requirements, graduates are asked to speak during a regular court session, addressing what they have accomplished in the program and how it has affected their lives. Each graduate receives a certificate of completion, and a community police officer presents the youth with a pair of athletic shoes donated by the police department. The shoes are the same type worn by police bike patrols, and are highly prized by the youth. In one case, when a graduate relapsed during after-care, program staff made him give back one shoe while allowing him to keep the other one to remind him of what he was working to achieve. When he regained his satisfactory program status, they returned his second shoe during his final court appearance.

Sometimes the value of program rewards is more symbolic than economic. In Orlando, the judge presents each new drug court client with a glow-in-the-dark star at his or her first court appearance. He instructs each youth to

> ask your mom for permission to put it on your dresser, your wall, or somewhere where it will be the last thing you see before you turn out the light. I want it to remind you of what you can accomplish. I also want it to be the first thing you see in the morning to remind you to never let anyone steal your shine. Some people say it's cheesy, and it is—but it's cheesy good.

Sanctions

When incentives and rewards cannot encourage client participation, juvenile drug courts rely on sanctions and penalties to clarify program expectations and reinforce program rules. Clear policies about sanctions also help ensure that other participating agencies respond to rule violations consistently and fairly. Penalties escalate in proportion to the severity of a juvenile's rule violations. The use of graduated sanctions is supported by deterrence theory, which posits that human beings are rational actors who choose their behavior based on perceptions of the costs and benefits associated with that behavior (Akers 2000; Tittle 1980). The consistent, gradual application of sanctions—that is, penalties become more severe each time an offender exhibits negative behavior—encourages individuals to change behavior to avoid the costs of unacceptable activities.

In all the juvenile drug courts visited by the Urban Institute, sanctions serve the dual purpose of holding participants accountable for their behavior while reinforcing core aspects of the programs. Youth may face sanctions for several noncompliant behaviors, including curfew violations, poor school attendance, missed individual or group treatment sessions, failure to appear for drug tests or dirty test results, and inadequate participation in required program components. Sites differ slightly in what sanctions they choose, what circumstances trigger sanctions, and how they apply sanctions. All programs, however, sanction youth using increased community service hours, and all include the threat of secure detention.

In Charleston, the juvenile drug court judge often sanctions noncompliant youth by requiring a book report or paper on a topic related to their misbehavior. The judge also believes in using court authority to facilitate family strengthening. Youth are frequently assigned household chores and parents are asked to monitor and report on the successful completion of these chores, as well as to help determine and enforce the court's response when a youth fails to perform an assignment. Other sanctions include fines, community service hours, days in detention, out-of-home placement, house arrest with or without electronic monitoring, and program expulsion. Occasionally, the judge finds it necessary to issue "pick-up orders" when youth fail to comply with program requirements. These orders are processed by investigators in the solicitor's office (i.e., prosecutors) who work with local law enforcement agencies.

In Orlando, a youth's first violation of program rules typically results in a judicial warning. With each subsequent infraction, youth receive escalating eight-hour increments of participation in Project Learn, a community service component that operates on weekends. Secure detention and electronic monitoring may be ordered for repeated or serious infractions. For youth who admit to using illegal substances without drug testing, sanctions can be reduced from what they would have been if the youth had waited until the results of a dirty drug test became known. Youth sanctioned in court for positive urinalysis tests or other major infractions automatically have their treatment extended for an additional 30 days.

In Las Cruces, program sanctions (or "consequences") typically begin with community service and increase in severity for youth that continue to violate the rules. The court often orders electronic monitoring, repeated program phases, and time in detention. The most severe response is dismissal from drug court and commitment to a residential juvenile facility. The drug court team decides sanctions on an individual basis. When a juvenile is placed on probation, parents are also named in the court petition, so the judge may impose requirements on them as well. Parents of youth in the juvenile drug court may have to perform community service. Judges may even order jail time for parents.

In Missoula, the youth drug court relies on a grid outlining the schedule of graduated sanctions for substance use, missed appointments, and unexcused absences or behavior issues at school (figure 3.1). Youth sanctioned for new drug use move quickly through warnings, community service, home arrest, and detention with each infraction, but youth misbehaving at home are likely to receive other, customized punishments. Sanctions and rewards may be blended in ways that could confuse youth. The Missoula drug court requires youth who violate program rules to perform community service. The youth meet every Saturday morning to perform three hours of community work service, including assisting

Figure 3.1. *Missoula Youth Drug Court Sanctions Grid*

	Sanctions for substance use	Sanctions for missed appointments	Sanctions for school issues	Sanctions for home issues
↓	Book report	Warning	Warning	Warning and implementation of rules
Increasing infractions	3 hours community service	Letter of apology	2 hours study hall per absence (up to 10 absences)	Uphold family rules and consequences
	6 hours community service	3 hours community service	School conference	Uphold family rules and consequences
↓	Home arrest or community service (when in group home placement)	6 hours community service	Home arrest	Home arrest
	24 hours detention	Pay for missed appointment	Home arrest	Customized sanction

Source: Urban Institute National Evaluation of Juvenile Drug Courts.

Goodwill, the Humane Society, and the Salvation Army. At the same time, all drug court participants must complete some form of community service during their time in drug court. This service, however, is not a sanction. Similarly, community service hours in Las Cruces are used as both sanction and reward. Resistant youth sometimes have to assist police officers with their holiday gift-delivery project or staff the police booth at approved block parties. Yet, these same activities are offered as rewards for youth who enjoy them.

The broad use of sanctions is partly responsible for another problem area. In all six programs visited by the Urban Institute, some drug court staff, defense attorneys, and treatment providers expressed concern about possible net widening. The enhanced supervision and sanctioning organized by drug courts is very attractive to juvenile justice decision-makers, especially for youthful offenders that would not otherwise get much attention from the court and juvenile probation staff. As word spreads in a community that the juvenile drug court employs a rigorous schedule of graduated sanctions, it becomes tempting for referring agencies to send a broader segment of the juvenile justice population to drug court. As long as the youth is involved with drugs or alcohol in some way—which is true in many juvenile delinquency cases—the referral may seem justified. This practice, however, exposes a much wider array of young offenders to the relatively intense methods and severe sanctions available in juvenile drug court.

Some local observers are particularly worried about using detention as a sanction for noncompliance. Because of graduated sanctioning, JDC youth may be sent to secure detention for program infractions that are not otherwise considered serious enough to warrant removal from the community. Incarceration, even short-term detention, can expose youth to harmful influences. Unless it is necessary for public safety, detention may create more problems than it solves. Defense attorneys report that they have advised clients against participating in drug court because the consequences of program failure could result in punishments more stringent than those associated with the youth's original offense.

Drug Testing

Frequent, court-ordered testing for alcohol and other drugs is a key component of the drug court model. Frequent testing contributes to the therapeutic process by supporting the structure clients need during the treatment process. The expectation of testing promotes abstinence and can help persuade clients to remain drug-free long enough for the positive effects of the program to take hold. Testing also allows a drug court to know how and when to administer sanctions or rewards during each client's court appearances.

Although drug tests can be targeted to look for a narrow range of illegal substances, most programs rely on general screening, including tests for cannabis, amphetamines, cocaine, and the like. The main testing methodologies, in descending order of reliability and validity, are hair tests, blood tests, and urinalysis. Hair tests have a greater retrospective time window, but are the most costly approach. Blood tests have roughly the same time window as urinalysis, but cost more. Urinalysis is the most common drug test used in the justice system, including drug courts. Although relatively accurate, urinalysis is more easily confounded by water loading, herbal detoxification, and fraud (Harrell, Cavanagh, and Roman 1998). If administered properly and frequently, however, urinalysis can be effective in determining alcohol and other drug use and aiding the overall drug court treatment process. Drug courts may also rely at times on a fourth test methodology, self-reported behavior. Asking clients to report their own drug use may be an effective component of treatment, but it is obviously insufficient as a means of monitoring actual drug use.

The six JDCs visited for this study rely largely on urinalysis, augmented by youth self-reports and Breathalyzer tests, to detect alcohol use. The courts vary in where and how often they test youth, as well as who is responsible for testing. For example, case managers perform Breathalyzer tests in the Dayton drug court, and technicians in the court's on-site testing laboratory conduct urinalysis testing. In some programs, juvenile probation officers and treatment providers conduct testing, but only the results of the probation tests are reported to the court. Treatment providers may also use their own test results to shape treatment plans.

All programs test participants at least weekly. Some programs test more frequently at the beginning of treatment, and then gradually decrease the frequency. Several programs reduce the frequency of testing as clients consistently pass their drug tests. At least one program schedules tests based on the youth's drug of choice. Since marijuana stays in the body longer, the program tests less frequently when youth are known to primarily use marijuana. In most programs, a missed drug test counts against the youth just as if he or she had tested positive.

Juvenile drug court programs differ in their philosophy of drug testing and their ability to test as often as and whenever they wish. Some program staff believe it is sufficient to test just often enough that youth would reasonably expect drug use to be detected at some point. Other staff prefer to catch drug-using youth shortly after their actual use and impose sanctions immediately. These programs try to arrange drug testing on evenings and weekends. The Las Cruces program, for example, uses surveillance officers working in teams and with rotating schedules to contact youth at random. The Missoula court participants call a telephone number daily to find out whether they have been chosen at random to come in for a drug test. Missoula performs weekday tests at the courthouse, but conducts weekend tests at a community-based facility.

As in all drug courts, quality control and assurance procedures are essential to maintaining the integrity of the drug testing process. If the results are contested in any way, each program must provide a way to verify the accuracy of the results. Sample collections are usually observed directly by a qualified expert, and the temperature and creatinine levels in urine are measured immediately to ensure against fraud. In one program, the juvenile drug court judge became concerned that the personnel administering the client drug tests were not always observing tests stringently. This concern created conflict between the court and the staff, as the staff believed that extremely careful observation was unnecessarily intrusive and embarrassing for adolescents. In programs with few staff members, the need to observe drug tests can be problematic because of the difficulty in matching youth and staff genders for tests.

Surveillance officers in Las Cruces randomly test youth at least weekly, but more often during a youth's first few weeks in the program. If a youth reoffends, fails a drug test, or fails to progress through the treatment program, he or she is tested more frequently. Testing is deliberately performed at randomly selected settings and times to minimize the likelihood that youth could prepare for the test (e.g., by flushing or carrying a false sample). Sometimes, a youth is tested twice in one day to deter youth who may otherwise believe it is safe to use drugs immediately after a random test. Surveillance officers closely observe each specimen collection and test for flushing or dilution. The on-site testing covers five drugs and costs the program $3.45 per test. If a tested youth is suspected of drug use, the surveillance officer first attempts to have the youth admit his or her usage. If a youth admits to drug use, the juvenile probation officer is notified and the youth is taken to the local detention facility for on-site testing. When a youth failing an on-site test does not admit to new use, the test sample is sent to a laboratory in Albuquerque for a $25 test that can detect alcohol, cannabis, benzodiazepines, amphetamines, opiates, barbiturates, cocaine, methadone, methaqualone, phencyclidine, and propoxyphene. Creatinine levels are also tested to detect flushing. If lab testing verifies drug use, the youth is sanctioned with detention. Surveillance officers also carry Breathalyzers to detect alcohol use, and youth can be detained solely on the findings of a Breathalyzer test in the field.

Treatment staff in one site warned that frequent drug testing could have unanticipated consequences. Youth in some drug courts quickly learn program routines, including how drug tests are conducted and for what drugs they test. In particular, youth discover that most of the affordable drug-testing protocols used by courts do not test for hallucinogens. They also learn that alcohol does not remain detectable in the body for very long, sometimes only a few hours. One treatment specialist reported that her clients had told her their time in the drug court program had turned them into "alcoholics and acid [LSD] freaks." Juvenile drug court staff members are aware of these perceptions and try to design testing procedures to discourage such reactions.

Case Management

Juvenile drug courts rely on case management to achieve several important goals. The case management role often includes assessing clients (both for program eligibility and any social and treatment service needs), linking clients to appropriate treatment programs, monitoring client progress in treatment, and reporting client status in court. Charleston is the only program in the study that does not include a formal case management function. The treatment staff, program coordinator, and school representatives in Charleston stay in regular contact with each other, and hold weekly case review meetings to assess participant progress and adjust treatment plans. Although not considered a case manager and not directly supervising the provision of client treatment, the drug court coordinator serves as the chief liaison among the judge, treatment staff, school representative, and juvenile justice agencies and is responsible for the general oversight of court activities.

By comparison, the Jersey City drug court coordinator is in charge of day-to-day case management for program participants. The coordinator determines initial eligibility and treatment referrals, arranges psycho-social assessments and evaluations, schedules drug court orientations, pre-pares juvenile drug court contracts, tracks participants through the court process, obtains school reports, prepares and presents progress reports, prepares JDC schedules for participants and their parents or guardians, and makes recommendations to the court for sanctions and incentives. Still, the program coordinator's function is more administrative than hands-on. Case management activities do not include visiting homes or schools to perform drug testing or determine youth compliance with program rules.

The Orlando juvenile drug court includes two case managers, each handling a caseload of approximately 25 clients. Case managers monitor school attendance and client participation in treatment. They monitor curfews ordered by the court and conduct at least one school visit and one home visit each month. Their typical work day begins in the late morning and concludes about 8:30 P.M., allowing them to make home contacts with their clients. The two case managers rotate their days off, so at least one is always on duty. Once a youth is assigned a juvenile drug court case manager, formal supervision by the local juvenile probation office ends, but probation officers continue to receive updates and make decisions for clients, in part because case managers lack the authority to detain youth.

In Las Cruces, the program director and assistant program director work closely with "surveillance officers" to perform day-to-day case management tasks, including coordinating and monitoring each youth's treatment regimen and probation and community service requirements. Surveillance officers work in teams for safety. The team approach also helps them avoid compromising situations, such as being alone with youth during home visits when other adults are absent. The juvenile drug court's surveillance officers maintain strong ties with local law enforcement and juvenile probation officers. Local police officers routinely call surveillance officers—their mobile phones are on 24 hours a day—if a juvenile drug court youth is picked up. The surveillance officers keep juvenile probation officers informed of case progress, particularly when youth fail drug tests or are arrested for new charges.

In the Dayton program, the TASC coordinator develops case management plans and TASC case managers provide intensive supervision for drug court youth, including monitoring them at home and at school. Case managers are required to make at least seven contacts a week with each juvenile, and to complete two or more home visits a month. Managers keep written activity logs and report all client contacts to the court and treatment providers weekly. Dayton case managers are registered with the Ohio Credentialing Board for Certified Chemical Dependency Counselors and have to fulfill stringent training requirements before working with juvenile drug court clients.

Treatment and Collateral Services

One of the most important tasks of a juvenile drug court is to design an effective approach to adolescent substance abuse treatment. Treatment protocols must be adapted to the specific needs of youthful offenders, whose level of substance use will typically fall far short of dependency or addiction. As yet, the research and treatment literature does not offer effective protocols specifically designed to serve drug-using juvenile offenders. The National Institute on Drug Abuse disseminated 13 principles of effectiveness in treating drug addiction, but was not clear about how to apply such approaches to drug-involved, but not drug-dependent, juveniles (NIDA 1999). The effect of coercing treatment for nondependent adolescents is unknown, but in many ways it violates the NIDA principles of effective treatment.

Treatment modalities for adults often include 12-step programs (NA/AA), methadone maintenance and other medicinal treatments, short- and long-term residential or inpatient models such as therapeutic communities, and cognitive-behavioral approaches (box 3.7). Many JDC programs use treatment models adapted from these adult interventions. Some approaches used in adult treatment programs may transfer well to youth populations, but others may be unsuitable. For example, the Community Reinforcement Approach (CRA) and similar approaches that target severe dependence problems appear inappropriate for adolescents. These approaches include the Matrix model, primarily an intervention for serious stimulant dependencies (cocaine and methamphetamines); day treatment with abstinence contingencies and vouchers, a long-term intervention for homeless addicts; and voucher-based reinforcement therapy in methadone maintenance treatment, an intervention for opiate dependence. Federal substance abuse agencies recommend that adolescent programs avoid adult-style relapse prevention methods that require strong responses to relapse, including the social isolation techniques often applied with groups (SAMHSA 1998).

Box 3.7. Common Treatment Modalities for Substance Abuse and Dependence

Multisystemic Therapy (MST): integrative, family-based therapeutic approach that has been used for violence and other antisocial behaviors, as well as substance abuse. MST targets family problems and provides services primarily in the home rather than a clinical environment. By identifying and correcting antisocial behavior in a broader social context, MST addresses problems in each facet of an adolescent's life, including the home, school, and community. MST can be more resource-intensive than other approaches, but it is widely used and appears to reduce drug use and rearrest.

Multidimensional Family Therapy (MDFT) for adolescents: outpatient drug abuse treatment for adolescents centered on family, peer, and community relationships. Similar to MST, MDFT focuses on developing pro-social behavior skills, such as problem solving and self-control. Skills are taught through individual and family counseling sessions. Individual sessions focus on communication as a means of self-control and personal growth. Family sessions are used to develop parenting skills appropriate to the particular needs of the substance-using adolescent.

Moral Reconation Therapy® (MRT®): cognitive-oriented treatment for substance abuse and antisocial disorders. Commonly used in correctional institutions, MRT is course-based and delivered in a classroom setting. Participants work through 16 moral and cognitive stages. Each new concept builds on previous lessons. Most research on MRT has focused on adult populations in correctional settings. Its effectiveness with adolescents in the community is less certain.

Relapse prevention: cognitive-behavioral therapeutic model. Teaches strategies for understanding and coping with drug use triggers. Drug use is seen as learned behavior. Treatment focuses on understanding the consequences of drug use and identifying and managing individuals, situations, and environments likely to cause drug cravings. Research suggests that treatment effects are stronger when combined with other treatment approaches.

Individualized Drug Counseling (IDC): generally based on a cognitive-behavioral model and similar to relapse prevention. Participants are taught to meet short-term behavioral goals. Sessions focus on the consequences of drug use and techniques for avoiding future use. May be conducted in group, individual, and family sessions. Outpatient IDC appears to be effective when combined with other treatment services, including medical, psychiatric, and employment services.

Supportive-Expressive Psychotherapy (SEP): primarily used to treat cocaine and heroin dependency and often combined with cognitive-behavioral treatment. Therapy is generally very short. Clients learn to express complex personal emotions in individual and group settings. Helps prepare individuals to participate in treatment,

(*continued*)

Box 3.7. *Continued*

and to understand the effect emotions can have on drug use and how to manage emotions to prevent use.

Motivational Enhancement Therapy (MET): variant of cognitive-behavioral treatment that focuses on developing internal motivation to stop drug use rather than the confrontational approach used in other models. Often used with alcoholics and heavy marijuana users who may not see their drug use as a problem. Based on the concept that once users learn to see the effects of their drug use, positive changes will result, including acceptance of treatment.

Behavioral therapy for adolescents: focuses on developing greater self-control among adolescents by emphasizing the benefits associated with pro-social activities and the cessation of negative behavior. Uses sanctions and rewards, case management, and drug testing. Participant responsibilities become greater as treatment progresses. Research suggests efficacy for adolescent substance abusers across a range of outcomes.

Community Reinforcement Approach (CRA) plus vouchers: a six-month treatment program for addicted individuals, often opiate users. The program includes cognitive-behavioral methods to assist addicts in becoming drug free and maintaining sobriety while learning new coping skills to prevent future drug use. Treatment helps participants with vocational and other pro-social skills to take the place of drug use. Research suggests CRA may be effective in treating opiate-addicted adults.

Source: Adapted from National Institute on Drug Abuse, *Principles of Drug Addiction Treatment: A Research-Based Guide* (Washington, DC: National Institute on Drug Abuse, 1999).

The six drug courts visited for this study vary considerably in their treatment approaches and their use of collateral services. Three courts work with more than one treatment provider (Charleston, Missoula, and Dayton), while the others (Jersey City, Las Cruces, and Orlando) rely on a single source. Regardless of how many treatment partners they report, most drug court programs have limited program and community resources, which make it difficult to offer a full continuum of treatment services. In several sites, key stakeholders expressed concerns about their ability to sustain their court's treatment component beyond the duration of their federal program grant.

Outpatient or intensive outpatient treatment is readily available as part of the juvenile drug court program in most program sites. Half the programs include at least rudimentary transitional or aftercare planning or services. Only Jersey City has reliable access to day treatment. Several programs make explicit arrangements for youth with co-occurring mental health issues requiring medication—only Las Cruces has a psychiatrist on the drug court team—and most programs report difficulties in securing sufficient resources for residential treatment, even for the small number of drug court youth that need inpatient services. In Missoula, for example, youth in need of residential treatment are sent to one of three agencies in other areas of Montana or Washington State. Jersey City has several residential treatment providers nearby, but they have long waiting lists and are unlikely to provide inpatient treatment to clients without health insurance. Youth from Dayton have to travel to a program two hours from home to obtain residential treatment.

All programs rely on some form of phased treatment to motivate participants and mark their progress toward graduating from drug court. In some programs, the shift from one phase to another not only changes the substantive focus of the intervention, but also means youth are rewarded with fewer restrictions (e.g., lowered attendance requirements). Three programs (Missoula, Dayton, and Orlando) require a minimum period of consistently clean urinalysis tests before youth may advance from one phase to another. Youth in the Missoula program must have five weeks of clean drug tests to advance from phase 3 to phase 4. Orlando youth must have 30 days of clean tests to advance. Orlando youth also have to attend all required individual and group sessions (or make up missed sessions) and complete all homework assignments received during treatment. Treatment providers in many sites informed the Urban Institute researchers that youth often took longer to complete program phases than expected. Treatment periods are often extended because of relapse or failure to comply with school requirements.

Most JDC programs provide treatment in a combination of individual and group settings. In Charleston, for example, one treatment provider uses Multi-Systemic Therapy (MST), an intensive in-home program that delivers services in the client's school and other appropriate personal settings and focuses on addressing risk factors, parenting issues, and peer associations. MST increases successful parenting, requiring both family and parent therapy sessions in addition to individual therapy sessions. A dedicated MST counselor works with each family for at least 10 hours a week, using cognitive-behavioral and contingency management techniques.

Although each program has some capacity to provide individual and home-based family counseling, most therapeutic interventions delivered through the JDCs are delivered in peer group settings. The groups vary according to each court's particular caseload, mixing genders, age groups, and youth with varying levels of substance abuse. Several practitioners noted that these group sessions need to be highly structured, with clearly specified behavioral expectations, to ensure that youth remain on task and do not disrupt or provoke one another.

The Las Cruces program uses a highly structured approach for its group sessions, involving Juvenile Moral Reconation Therapy (MRT®) as well as behavior modification, 12-step requirements, and community service or motivational activities/therapy. MRT is a structured, cognitive-behavioral program that teaches participants to make better decisions based on improved levels of moral reasoning. It is a systematic, step-by-step treatment strategy to enhance self-image, promote growth of a positive and productive identity, and facilitate the development of higher stages of moral reasoning (box 3.8).

Several programs (Jersey City, Las Cruces, and Orlando) also require youth to attend AA/NA support groups or engage in other self-help activities. There are few NA/AA groups for juveniles in Orlando, however, and because the treatment provider does not believe in sending juveniles to adult 12-step groups, it offers other options, including permitting youth to volunteer in local faith-based organizations or community centers.

The Missoula program offers the most extensive range of treatment and collateral services through its community education and wellness program. Youth are expected to complete a strengths-based inventory during phase 1 of the program. Two treatment providers—St. Patrick Hospital and Turning Point—provide outpatient treatment and aftercare services. The St. Patrick Hospital intensive outpatient program (IOP) creates individualized treatment plans with specific goals and recovery plans. The initial phase lasts about six weeks and includes group and individual counseling. The patient aftercare program lasts an average of six months, and if a juvenile does not progress in aftercare, he or she can be sent back to IOP. The education and wellness components in Missoula provide many community-based options for youth. The court's community program coordinator works to develop nontraditional treatment and wellness programs:

- *Acupuncture.* The Detoxification and Stress Reduction Clinic uses acupuncture to relieve stress-related disorders and drug

Box 3.8. Treatment in the Las Cruces, New Mexico, Juvenile Drug Court

Juvenile Moral Reconation Therapy (MRT®) was chosen as the therapeutic model for the Las Cruces juvenile drug court through a competitive process. MRT has 16 steps, 12 of which are completed during program participation. Involvement in a mandatory parenting group may begin at any time during the four phases of treatment. At all stages, any missed group sessions or appointments must be made up before a youth advances to the next stage. The program is divided into four phases:

Phase I—Introduction and Information (8 weeks): During this phase, participants attend cognitive and motivational therapy groups weekly. They must also attend six AA/NA meetings, for which verification is required. Rural areas of the county do not have as many AA meetings, so exceptions may be made for rural youth. Phase I focuses on drug and alcohol education and understanding the dynamics of denial and abstinence. MRT step 3 must be completed before a youth advances to the next phase.

Phase II—Focus on Personal Responsibility and Accountability (10 weeks): Behavior modification groups begin during this phase. Participants are also expected to continue to attend weekly AA/NA meetings. Topics addressed include issues of family origin, consequences of poor choices, harm reduction, and continued discussion of denial and abstinence. To progress from this phase, juveniles must complete MRT step 6, demonstrate progress on educational goals, and have four consecutive clean drug tests.

Phase III—Life Skills and Relapse Prevention (6 weeks): This phase emphasizes cognitive group work, as participants begin to address the behaviors that led them to juvenile drug court. Job search skills and vocational training are introduced, and AIDS/STD risks are discussed. Anger management is also introduced during this stage. For successful completion of this phase, participants are expected to continue to attend weekly AA/NA meetings, complete MRT step 9, continue to show progress on educational goals, and have a minimum of four consecutive clean drug tests.

Phase IV—Independence and Mastery (12 weeks): In the last 12 weeks, individuals develop their own aftercare plan. They are expected to attend weekly AA/NA meetings, complete MRT step 12, and demonstrate progress toward educational and vocational goals. Participants must have 30 days of continuous sobriety to pass this phase.

During the first three phases, participants are expected to engage in "motivational activities." These include but are not limited to activities that address job skill development, educational goals, self-esteem building, and parenting skills. They may take part in positive community service programs (e.g., volunteer activities) and participate in a mask-making project that uses guided imagery to encourage self-awareness and life direction.

(continued)

Box 3.8. *Continued*

The time after graduation is considered a transition phase. The drug court program may eventually include aftercare initiatives to help youth transition from intensive supervision and treatment to less structured and independent lifestyles. Participants may continue with the last four steps of MRT after graduation and activities linking youth to positive peers, education/vocation, or community are encouraged.

Source: Urban Institute National Evaluation of Juvenile Drug Courts.

---

withdrawal symptoms. All drug court participants are required to attend at least 18 acupuncture treatments (i.e., three times a week for the first six weeks of program participation), more in cases of relapse and withdrawal.

- *Writing workshop.* This program uses weekly small group meetings to achieve functional literacy and enhance analytical skills over the course of a 15-week workshop. All drug court participants are required to attend the workshop.
- *Parks and recreation adventure program.* This program uses a ropes course, outdoor trips, and special events to build trust, confidence, and responsibility, and to teach leisure and communication skills. Youth meet biweekly, generally for 10 weeks. Many, but not all, drug court participants attend the ropes course. All youth are required to attend some sort of adventure program during their drug court enrollment.
- *Parent education and support.* This six-week program builds parenting skills, promotes insight, and increases parent understanding of teenage development and the effects of drug and alcohol use. Parents are required to attend this group.
- *Conflict resolution program for parents and kids.* Juveniles and parents are required to attend this program together to learn how to handle conflict and manage anger.
- *Marijuana education group.* A youth marijuana education group meets once a week for two hours. Drug court participants are sent to the marijuana group as needed.

- *Animal-assisted therapy.* Juveniles in this program work with an individual therapist who uses interaction with llamas to build trust and responsibility.
- *Neuro-feedback.* Juveniles in this program learn how to assess their brain wave activity and change their behavior accordingly. Few drug court youth participate.

Several drug courts incorporate parental participation into their treatment methods. The Missoula program requires parents to attend a six-week parent education course that covers adolescent and young adult development, the dynamics of alcohol and substance abuse, family communication, problem solving and anger management, and methods of enhancing home discipline and youth responsibility. In addition, one Missoula treatment provider offers a parent support group and a parent education course that are open to the community.

The Orlando program also recognizes the need to assist parents. Team members have noted that the average cost of family counseling (approximately $75 an hour) is not affordable for many families referred to juvenile drug court. As a result, the court began offering in-home counseling. Initially, sessions were scheduled bimonthly. However, the need proved greater than expected, and the program soon had to offer in-home counseling for some clients up to four times a month, raising concerns about the program's capacity to sustain that pace over the long term. The drug court has also started a weekly parent group that runs concurrently with youth group sessions, and is considering launching multifamily group sessions that combine youth clients and their parents.

The treatment provider in Las Cruces estimates that approximately 60 percent of parents of youth participants are affected by substance abuse themselves, mostly alcohol. A therapist is prepared to provide individual, couples, or family counseling, but few parents have taken advantage of the service. The routine drug court treatment program combines youth and parents for some sessions. Parents are also supposed to attend six AA public information groups before enrolling in the required parenting support group. Most parents, however, attend only three or four AA meetings. The parent program in Las Cruces began as a 12-week educational support group, but soon expanded to 30 weeks. Initially, the program was established as a defined series that parents would complete in cohorts, but it became a continuous process with parents, typically mothers, rotating in and out, depending on their child's entry into the drug court and their completion of the AA information series.

Conclusion

Rapid growth in the number of juvenile drug courts and the number of juveniles served by them has led to variations within the juvenile drug court model. Operational structures and treatment approaches usually result from adaptive responses to local context. Rather than evolving in strict adherence to a well-defined drug court model, JDC programs tend to develop their policies and procedures based on available resources, perceived gaps in services, the need to manage growing caseloads, and other factors. As a result, drug court practices vary enormously from court to court.

While the anecdotal evidence about drug courts' success is positive, strict empirical research has so far produced only limited evidence of impact. The great diversity in program models is a key reason for the lack of theory-based drug court evaluations and the limited effect of evaluation results on drug court policies. Given that drug courts do not generally apply a well-developed theoretical approach to solving the drug-related problems of offenders, the great diversity in practice and the sparsity of theory-driven evaluations is not surprising. Understanding whether the drug court model can be applied effectively to other populations, such as juvenile offenders, requires addressing two issues.

First, the theoretical relationships between the drug court model and behavior changes must be clearly identified. Once such a framework is developed, evaluators may be able to test the effectiveness of drug court components, both independently and in conjunction with other components. Such evaluations will help answer questions not only about whether drug courts can effectively change behavior, but how they do so.

Second, it is important to critically examine each component with an eye toward understanding how these processes work with a juvenile population. Many operational characteristics of juvenile drug courts were developed for adult populations. Whether program models and procedures developed for adults will effectively address the needs of juveniles is unclear. Understanding how to change offender behavior in adolescents is critical in understanding whether, and how, to adapt adult drug court structures for juvenile populations.

REFERENCES

Akers, Ronald L. 2000. *Criminological Theories: Introduction, Evaluation, and Application,* 3rd ed. Los Angeles: Roxbury.

Harrell, Adele, Shannon Cavanagh, and John Roman. 1998. *Findings from the Evaluation of the D.C. Superior Court Drug Intervention Program. Final Report.* Washington, DC: The Urban Institute.

Hirst, Alexa, and Adele V. Harrell. 2000. *Perceptions of Procedural Justice by Felony Offenders in Drug Treatment.* Washington, DC: The Urban Institute.

National Drug Court Institute and National Council of Juvenile and Family Court Judges. 2003. *Juvenile Drug Courts: Strategies in Practice.* NCJ187866. Washington, DC: U.S. Department of Justice, Bureau of Justice Assistance.

National Institute on Drug Abuse. 1999. *Principles of Drug Addiction Treatment: A Research-Based Guide.* NIH 99-4180. Washington, DC: National Institutes of Health, National Institute on Drug Abuse.

NDCI/NCJFCJ. *See* National Drug Court Institute and National Council of Juvenile and Family Court Judges.

NIDA. *See* National Institute on Drug Abuse.

SAMHSA. *See* Substance Abuse and Mental Health Services Administration.

Substance Abuse and Mental Health Services Administration. 1998. *Substance Abusing Adolescents.* Issues in Brief Series. Washington, DC: Center for Substance Abuse Treatment, Office of Policy and Coordination, Substance Abuse and Mental Health Services Administration.

Tittle, Charles R. 1980. "Labeling and Crime: An Empirical Evaluation." In *The Labeling of Deviance,* 2nd ed., edited by Walter R. Gove (241–69). Beverly Hills, CA: Sage Publications.

4

Drug Court Effects and the Quality of Existing Evidence

John Roman and Christine DeStefano

D espite immense growth in the number of drug courts in the United States during the 1990s and early 2000s, and equal growth in the number of drug court evaluations, a thorough review of the drug court literature yields few solid clues about the real impact of drug courts on offender behavior. While the U.S. Department of Justice (and DOJ's former Drug Courts Program Office, or DCPO) requires drug court grantees to conduct evaluations in order to qualify for federal funding, only a handful of drug courts have been subject to high-quality, careful evaluation research. As a result, evidence of the impact of drug courts on key outcomes (such as recidivism and drug use) remains largely anecdotal.

The lack of scientific evidence is particularly acute for juvenile drug courts, which developed more recently than adult drug courts. There are still relatively few mature juvenile drug courts and they have generated even fewer outcome evaluations. Much of what is known about the effectiveness of juvenile drug courts must be extrapolated from research on adult drug courts. Juveniles are socially, developmentally, and cognitively different from adults. They may not have the same behavioral response to drug court protocols, but researchers and practitioners have not identified whether and how juvenile drug court programs should differ. Most programs simply assume that adult drug court procedures will work with juvenile populations. This assumption is based more on hope and supposition than evidence.

Research about adult drug courts has helped juvenile drug courts, particularly in the area of evaluation methodology, but the juvenile drug court literature suffers from many of the same flaws seen in the adult literature. Most drug court research focuses on overall program effects, judged by differences in aggregate rates of rearrest or recidivism. Few studies have analyzed how particular program features or activities relate to specific client outcomes.

This chapter examines the results from the drug court evaluation literature, paying particular attention to the limitations of existing research in establishing strong links between drug court components and participant outcomes. Many weaknesses in the drug court evaluation literature can be attributed to problems common to applied social research: small sample sizes, short operating histories, and inadequate resources. Despite these limitations, the strengths and weaknesses of existing evaluations can be analyzed and conclusions can be drawn from the broad, if somewhat shallow, pool of adult drug court evaluations. The following discussion reviews existing research, documents those areas of research in the drug court field that deserve further exploration, and suggests ways to strengthen drug court evaluations.

Evaluation Challenges

Only a handful of drug court evaluations were published before the mid-1990s, when adult drug courts were proliferating nationally. More evaluations were available by the beginning of the 2000s, but they did not offer policymakers clear, convincing evidence of the effectiveness of drug court programs. Most published studies focused on implementing and operating drug courts or, at best, analyzed differences in treatment enrollment and client retention. Few researchers tested the effectiveness of drug courts by comparing them with traditional courts or with nontreatment control groups (Harrell 2000). Despite the small number of successful evaluations, or maybe because of it, practitioners and policymakers continue to demand better research. To develop more rigorous studies, drug court evaluators must address three significant methodological and technical challenges:

- Stakeholders have varying requirements and expectations of evaluations;

- Most jurisdictions have limited resources for conducting evaluation studies; and
- Tracking client recidivism and other outcomes requires long time frames.

In combination, these factors often make it impossible for local jurisdictions to fund and conduct effective evaluations of drug court impact.

Stakeholder Requirements

Drug court evaluations are typically undertaken in response to specific incentives from federal, state, and local funding agencies. The U.S. Department of Justice has traditionally required jurisdictions to engage in some form of process or impact evaluation research to receive federal support for drug court programs. Before the requirements were changed in 2001 to mandate impact evaluations, most studies were process evaluations, which are rarely used to modify court operations. Process evaluations can help identify and overcome problems in implementation and development, but they are not designed to establish causal links between program interventions and client outcomes. The benefits of the new DOJ requirement for outcome evaluations have not been fully realized.

Of course, evaluations do not always produce useful evidence of program impact. Funding agencies place great pressure on drug courts to demonstrate efficacy, and it is not surprising that some evaluation protocols are biased toward positive program outcomes. For example, it is very common for drug courts to test their effectiveness by comparing the recidivism of program graduates with the recidivism of nongraduates or youth removed from drug court as a result of noncompliance. Clearly, these groups are not comparable, and under these conditions the effect of the drug court process cannot be disentangled from basic underlying differences between the groups. Evaluations of this type have helped promote drug courts as a promising program model, but they have not provided high-quality evidence of impact.

Resource Constraints

The first drug courts began as part of a reform movement that emerged in the late 1980s and early 1990s, before federal support for drug courts became available. In the earliest courts, limited resources for program operations led researchers to focus on implementation issues rather than program outcomes. The previous DOJ requirement that courts conduct process evaluations may have encouraged jurisdictions to continue to focus on descriptive analyses of drug court operations and put off questions about program outcomes and impact.

Resource constraints also limited the size of drug courts, leading to difficulties in developing meaningful comparisons for drug court evaluations. Most drug courts serve relatively small caseloads of carefully screened offenders, often fewer than 200 clients a year. Small numbers of research subjects make it difficult to detect differences between treatment and comparison group outcomes unless those differences are very large or data are collected over a very long time. In addition, because drug court clients are often carefully screened for characteristics that suggest they could succeed in a drug court setting, researchers have trouble assembling appropriate comparison groups.

Design Issues

Drug court evaluations face problems common to most applied social research efforts. Foremost among these problems, it is virtually impossible to identify and control for all factors that may be associated with client outcomes. Unless an evaluation can account for all possible causes of an individual's behavior, it is difficult to isolate the particular effects of the drug court on behavior. This problem is complicated by other critical challenges—small sample sizes, the effect of confidentiality requirements on data collection (particularly for comparison groups), difficulties identifying appropriate comparison groups (especially in small jurisdictions), and the extended duration of follow-up periods to measure the persistence of drug court effects on behavior.

One of the most difficult challenges facing drug court evaluations is the absence of obvious comparison groups. Most juvenile drug courts visited as part of the National Evaluation of Juvenile Drug Courts stated that all, or almost all, the juvenile offenders eligible for their drug courts were screened and recruited for participation. Juvenile drug court programs also report that their efforts to recruit eligible offenders are usually successful. The most common reason for recruitment failure is active refusal by offenders. Thus, nonparticipating eligible youth are very different from participating youth. Without extra referrals to create a comparison group of *eligible and willing,* but nonparticipating youth, most jurisdictions are forced to use less desirable comparison groups. Typically, evaluations have compared

- graduates with nongraduates;
- participants with nonparticipants (where both groups were eligible, but nonparticipants refused to enter the program);
- participants with nonparticipants (where nonparticipants were not eligible for drug court);
- drug court participants in one jurisdiction with nonparticipants in a nearby jurisdiction with similar socioeconomic characteristics; and
- drug court participants with an earlier group of similar youth from the same jurisdiction who went through the usual court process before the drug court was established or widely available.

In each case, these comparison groups could systematically differ from the treatment group (drug court participants) on characteristics that could meaningfully relate to the likelihood of success during an evaluation follow-up period. Any differences detected between the treatment and comparison groups, therefore, may result from these systematic differences rather than the effects of drug court. Because so much of the drug court evaluation literature is composed of studies that fail to control for these fundamental disparities, policymakers are left with suggestive, but nonconclusive, evidence of the impact of drug courts on offender outcomes.

In addition to the difficulties faced by evaluators in identifying appropriate comparison groups and designing effective studies, many evaluations find it impossible to generate findings quickly enough for policymakers and other important audiences (box 4.1). To evaluate an average-size juvenile drug court, researchers may need more than four years to collect and analyze client outcome data and report the results. Because most federal funding support for drug court programs lasts only three years, it is not surprising that few formal outcome evaluations have been completed. Further, many programs have not been in operation long enough to allow for a highly rigorous evaluation. It is common for juvenile drug courts to serve extremely small populations, sometimes only 20 to 40 juveniles a year. Recruitment periods for studies of these small programs would be even longer than in the example described above.

Even study samples of 100 drug court participants and 100 comparison subjects are likely insufficient when drug courts are associated with

Box 4.1. Time for Research?

Suppose a juvenile drug court begins operations on January 1, 2005, and expects to have an average caseload—about 100 cases a year.

The court receives an implementation grant that will cover its expenses for two years, and a continuation grant will likely provide support for a year after that (i.e., through 2007). At the end of this period, the court will require other funding, and the program director wants to plan ahead and have evaluation evidence that supports these requests for additional funding. Thus, the program director decides to include an evaluation component from the very beginning of program operations.

Unfortunately, the program director will soon confront several frustrating realities about program evaluation. First, the evaluator will likely suggest that data collection for the evaluation should not begin immediately. It is important to wait at least several months to avoid confounding the study results with early changes in the program model and other start-up issues. Thus, the evaluation will not actually begin until July 1, 2005.

To obtain a minimally effective sample for data analysis (100 juveniles in the treatment group) at the time of follow-up, it will be necessary to approach at least 200 youth during the subject recruitment period. It is likely that half the youth approached for the study sample will not be in the sample by the end of the follow-up period, because of initial refusal (nonparticipants), post-entrance refusal (subject attrition), or various other causes. Thus, it will be two full years before the last study subject is recruited at program entry, or June 30, 2007.

More time will be required for each subject to go through the drug court program. With an average in-program period of one year, plus several months of out-of-compliance time even among eventual program graduates, an evaluator would likely need to wait as long as 18 months for all subjects to complete the full course of drug court intervention. Thus, the last subject recruited for the evaluation in June 2007 may not complete the program until the end of 2008.

Finally, the whole point of the evaluation is to track postprogram recidivism. With the last subject completing the program in December 2008, the evaluation would have to collect follow-up data through December 2009 to capture 12 months of potential recidivism for all study subjects.

Even with very rapid analysis of the study data and extremely efficient production of the evaluation report, the study results would not be available until early 2010. This date is more than two years after the program's operating grants have expired, too late to be helpful in demonstrating the drug court's effectiveness in requests for new funding.

relatively small treatment effects. For instance, if the effect of a drug court is moderate, a 10 percent difference in one-year recidivism could be large enough to justify the expense of funding a drug court. However, in a small or even average-size juvenile drug court, recruiting evaluation samples large enough to detect this small difference could take several years longer than the typical three-year funding period, and if researchers underestimate subject attrition or overestimate treatment effects even slightly, it would further limit the evaluation's ability to identify group differences (box 4.2).

Subject attrition during follow-up is one of the primary challenges in evaluating any social program, and especially for drug courts. For obvious reasons, criminally involved drug offenders are not eager to have extensive contacts with law enforcement or the courts, and even if researchers explain clearly that they are not agents of the court, many research subjects will try to avoid follow-up contacts. Subjects in drug court comparison groups may be even less likely to cooperate with evaluators during an extended follow-up period. They are often involved in the same subculture as drug court participants, but without the influence of the drug court to foster their cooperation with evaluators. The small monetary incentives usually offered to study subjects are sometimes not enough to guarantee continued cooperation.

Finally, for all these reasons, drug court evaluations often rely on administrative data to measure recidivism rather than attempting to obtain repeated waves of face-to-face survey data from drug court participants and comparison group subjects. Evaluators can often collect survey data from drug court participants through the court, but may have to rely on official records for comparison group members. These records are limited to those variables most relevant to criminal justice events. Without comparable survey data for both treatment and comparison groups, evaluations are unable to detect group differences on several important variables not found in official records, such as self-reported recidivism, the type and intensity of drug use (in addition to drug arrests), family relations, and attachment to such prosocial activities as work and school.

Despite these obstacles, the research literature on the effects of drug court is growing. Although the quality of the methods and research designs varies, researchers are generating enough positive findings to provide support for the drug court model. Overall, the evidence is too thin to state definitively that drug courts work.

Box 4.2. The Importance of Power

All the statistical analysis presented in an evaluation, and all the discussion of research design, seek to maximize the confidence the reader should place in the differences that are or are not reported in the study. How clearly an evaluation can infer differences between two groups is referred to as the statistical power of the design. Three factors directly relate to statistical power: (1) the sample size, (2) the amount of variation in the study sample, and (3) the probability of detecting a difference.

Suppose an evaluator randomly assigns offenders to treatment and comparison groups and is interested in determining whether the treatment group had fewer postprogram arrests. The statistical power of the study refers to how large the difference in number of arrests among the study sample would have to be before the researcher could say with confidence that a true difference exists. Sample size and variation are directly related. Suppose that in both study A and study B the mean number of rearrests was exactly one for the treatment group and exactly two for the comparison group. However, in study A, almost all treatment group members had one arrest and all comparison group members had two arrests. Since the two groups do not overlap, it is relatively easy to detect a difference. In study B, however, equal numbers of treatment group members had zero, one, and two arrests, and equal numbers of comparison group members had one, two, and three arrests. Since there is more variation and the number of rearrests in the two groups overlap, more sample members are needed to be confident that there was a difference.

The other major factor in a study's power is the level of confidence that a difference actually exists. In study A, with a relatively small sample, one could be very confident that a difference exists because there is no variation in the sample. In study B, a much larger sample is needed to detect a difference. Since there is overlap, one would need to study a lot of members of each group to be sure that there really was a difference. This relationship between sample size and variation also influences the effect size (e.g., difference between the two groups) that can be detected. If both study A and study B had 50 sample members, researchers in study A could detect a very small difference in rearrest rates between the two groups. Researchers in study B could only detect relatively large differences between the two groups with confidence.

Researchers typically choose a 95 percent confidence level for type I errors and an 80 percent level for type II errors. This means that researchers will reject a true hypothesis only 5 percent of the time (type I error), and fail to reject a false hypothesis only 20 percent of the time (type II error).

Adult Drug Court Evaluations

Urban Institute researchers collected every drug court evaluation that was available by the end of 2003, categorized each study according to its methodological rigor, and summarized the results. The resulting review of drug court literature is not a statistical analysis or meta-analytical study. The assessment presents a descriptive review of what is known about the general efficacy of drug courts and drug court components. The review begins with the evaluation literature on adult drug courts, primarily because researchers have spent much more time investigating these programs. The adult drug court literature also contains important information that could help develop new conceptual frameworks for evaluating juvenile drug courts.

Methodology

In conducting this review of the drug court evaluation research literature, the Urban Institute obtained copies of all relevant outcome evaluations completed as of 2003. The process began with a search of databases that catalogue research published in peer-reviewed journals, including ERIC (Education Research Information Consortium), Sociofiles, and ProQuest. This search revealed only a handful of drug court evaluations.

Next, existing profiles of drug court research were analyzed. Three principal sources were identified: a 1997 drug court evaluation review report by the General Accounting Office (GAO), an annual synopsis of drug court evaluations for the National Drug Court Institute,[1] and a manuscript by Clinton Terry, "The Early Drug Court Years." A search of the Internet using Google and other search engines on a variety of keywords ("drug court" with "research," "evaluation," "assessment," "outcome," or "impact") yielded several more recent drug court evaluations. Finally, several studies were identified by contacting established drug court researchers and the American University's Drug Court Clearinghouse and Technical Assistance Project (DCCTAP), or submitting search requests to the National Criminal Justice Reference Service (NCJRS).

In addition to studies of individual drug courts, several cross-site studies were reviewed. There have been at least two attempts to conduct national evaluations of the drug court model. The National Institute of Justice funded a study by the RAND Corporation of 14 drug courts around the country. Because of limitations in data availability and other constraints, however, the evaluation was not completed. The Center for Substance Abuse Treatment (CSAT) conducted a cross-site evaluation of drug court models that targeted female and juvenile offenders. Evaluations completed as part of this project and other federally funded initiatives are included in this analysis.

Most drug court evaluations included in this review were collected directly from these sources. When complete copies of the evaluations were unavailable from these sources, study results were summarized using descriptions from secondary sources (such as Belenko 1998, 1999, 2000; and GAO 1997). These secondary sources sometimes provided only limited information. Study summaries did not always include key variables, such as program eligibility or study sample size.

While the techniques used to obtain information about drug court evaluations were reasonably comprehensive, the list of studies that resulted from these efforts may not be exhaustive. Some evaluations may have been overlooked because their results were not made available to a national audience. If drug court evaluations were released to a limited audience and not summarized or described in other publications, it is possible that they were not included in this review.

The appendix provides synopses of all evaluations collected for this review. The studies are categorized by the rigor of their study design. The few juvenile drug court evaluations conducted to date are described separately at the beginning of the appendix. Each synopsis includes the key program features, the type of research design used to evaluate the program, the evaluation's key findings, and any validity or reliability issues associated with the study's methodology.

Evaluation Typology

Evaluations were grouped according to their ability to control for competing explanations of outcomes. This grouping allows the review to identify the level of confidence associated with each evaluation's results. Confidence levels are based on how well an evaluation appears to have isolated the effects of the drug court on client outcomes and controlled for competing explanations of differences in outcomes. Isolating effects could occur in two ways: either the evaluator used a strong evaluation design, such as a randomized trial, or statistical controls allowed the evaluator to account for confounding effects. Thus, the terms "rigor" and "confidence" are synonyms for how successfully an evaluator accounted for external effects on outcomes, using either strong designs or statistical controls. These terms should not be interpreted as either subjective or pejorative judgments about a particular evaluation.

Evaluation designs fall along a continuum. On one end of the continuum are the most rigorous designs, including randomized, controlled experiments. On the other end are nonexperimental studies. In between the two extremes lie dozens of quasi-experimental designs that vary in design strength and the statistical methods used to control for confounding effects. Designating an evaluation at a particular point along the continuum does not reflect an absolute judgment about the overall usefulness or quality of the evaluation, but rather what share of reported program effects could be attributed to factors other than program participation and random chance. That is, as an evaluation moves away from experimental designs, there is an increasing chance that an unobserved factor, something other than the drug court intervention itself, may have contributed to the observed differences between the treatment and comparison groups. If an evaluation employed a weak design, but implemented statistical techniques to control for those factors not addressed in the design, the evaluation may still be placed in a strong design category.

Four classes are used in the typology of drug court evaluations, generally following the classification algorithm used in a recent review of crime prevention initiatives (Sherman et al. 1997). Evaluations are classified as experimental, quasi-experimental (strong), quasi-experimental (weak), and nonexperimental. Within each type, studies may suffer from various threats to validity. Identifying these competing explanations helps practitioners and stakeholders more accurately interpret an evaluation, especially if the threats could lead researchers to reach inappropriate conclusions about the effectiveness of an individual drug court and limit the generalization of results to a broader set of drug courts.

RANDOMIZED/EXPERIMENTAL DESIGNS

Experimental designs, also known as randomized designs, control for selection effects and reduce competing explanations for any differences between treatment and control (or comparison) groups (Boruch 1997). The most common threat to validity in evaluation arises when factors beyond the evaluator's control influence how individuals are placed into the various groups studied. It may be difficult or impossible to determine whether differences in group assignment may have led to differences in outcomes. In many drug courts, for example, once someone is found eligible to participate in drug court, he or she is asked to volunteer to enter the program. An individual's decision to volunteer may directly relate to the expected outcomes, since volunteers may be more motivated to reduce their drug use. Thus, an evaluation design that compares volunteers and nonvolunteers (refusers) could confuse differences in motivation with program effects.

Random assignment models, commonly referred to as experiments, reduce these problems by automating client selection. Experimental designs are often difficult to use in applied social research, generally because of ethical concerns about randomly withholding treatment from certain clients. Only four drug court evaluations in this review were classified as experimental.

Quasi-Experimental Designs

Quasi-experimental designs use methods other than random assignment to minimize competing explanations for observed differences in client outcomes. Unlike randomized experiments, where detected differences are assumed uncorrelated with any factor other than random chance, quasi-experimental designs assume that some set of observed and unobserved variables contributes to detected differences. Researchers use statistical corrections to control for these confounding effects. One confounding effect, selection bias, is present in most quasi-experimental designs. Formally, selection bias refers to the "possibility that [despite statistical corrections] . . . there might nevertheless be initial differences between the groups that affect the outcome and therefore become confounded with the effects of treatment" (Mohr 1995, 77).

In quasi-experimental designs, it is generally assumed that some factor or set of factors other than chance contributes to group assignment. In drug court evaluations, for example, participants' decisions to volunteer could explain some (or all) of the group differences in outcomes. Generally, quasi-experimental evaluations employ statistical methods to correct for selection bias. Of course, it may be impossible to control for all sources of selection bias. What share of the detected differences is a function of the intervention rather than other confounding factors could be difficult to determine.

Mohr (1995) identified seven types of quasi-experimental designs commonly used in applied social research. Drug court evaluations tend to use two of these approaches: comparative change and criterion population designs. Comparative change designs identify a comparison group that researchers expect to have the same characteristics as the treatment group, with the sole exception that members do not receive the intervention. In drug court evaluations, comparison groups are often composed of individuals ineligible for treatment as a result of factors unrelated to program operations and outcomes. For example, eligibility for drug court may be limited to defendants arrested in a particular geographic area, and comparison cases might be drawn from a similar, nearby neighborhood that was arbitrarily excluded from drug court.

Criterion population designs (commonly referred to as matched designs) consist of a comparison group matched to the treatment group on variables expected to affect the outcome. In this case, a comparison group is identified after the treatment group is identified. Generally, the comparison group is identified from a similar population in an adjacent area, and group members are selected based on a match with treatment group members, using a set of characteristics (generally age, race, gender, current charge, prior criminal history, and extent of substance abuse problems). Evaluators create one-to-one matches where each comparison group member shares baseline characteristics with a treatment group member. A variation on this approach creates a comparison group that matches the treatment group in aggregate across all matching criteria. Neither approach eliminates all threats to validity, as factors other than those used for matching may still correlate with both group assignment and client outcomes. Statistical corrections are needed to control for confounding effects.

It is possible to design relatively strong quasi-experiments. For example, when the pool of eligible participants is large but program spaces are limited, an effective comparison group may be selected from potential clients that did not have the opportunity to volunteer for drug court. Such a comparison group would not be expected to differ systematically from the treatment group. This approach seems especially well-suited for evaluations of drug court programs, but it is not commonly used by researchers.

Quasi-experiments are divided into strong and weak designs in this analysis. To be classified as a strong design, a study must satisfy Mohr's criteria (1995, 157) that "no known or recognizable difference between the treatment and comparison groups that might affect outcome scores and that is not controlled in the analysis" is present. In other words, the evaluation must include a carefully chosen comparison group that appears not to differ systematically from the treatment group, or adequate statistical controls must be in place to control for such differences. Fifteen quasi-experimental (strong) evaluations are identified in this review of the drug court evaluation literature.

Evaluations are classified as a weak design when the possibility of serious selection bias is apparent or the treatment and comparison groups are known to differ systematically on omitted variables related to both the outcome and group assignment. Several studies included in this category compared individuals who chose to attend drug court with others who chose not to attend. Another common evaluation design in this category involves a simple comparison of graduates and nonparticipants. This design involves serious threats to internal validity, since one would expect program graduates to have very different characteristics from the whole treatment population, and these differences would introduce a potentially large bias in favor of positive program effects. Fourteen quasi-experimental (weak) evaluations are identified in this analysis.

NONEXPERIMENTAL DESIGNS

Nonexperimental evaluations, or uncontrolled studies, examine an intervention or treatment "without any direct comparison with a similar group of patients on a more standard therapy" (Pocock 1997, 51). Nonexperimental designs have multiple, serious threats to external validity, as the results cannot be generalized to any other group because there is no way to determine whether the group being studied is representative of any larger population. Since there is no group against which to compare the treatment groups results, it cannot be determined whether any measured effects would have been observed in another group, or whether they were unique to the treatment group. In addition, nonexperimental designs may suffer from threats to internal validity, since differences detected by the evaluation cannot be attributed to the intervention. Nonexperimental research cannot be used to evaluate the effectiveness of one type of intervention over another.

In the drug court evaluation literature, the most common nonexperimental design compares program graduates to program failures. Under this design, unmeasured factors other than the intervention (such as intrinsic motivation) may explain group differences. It is inappropriate to use findings from such studies to estimate how effective a drug court will be in another jurisdiction or with a different target population. While this type of design cannot inform a comparison of drug courts with traditional court processing or other intervention, the results are not without value.

For example, an examination of the differences between graduates and failures can help programs understand how subgroups respond to treatment, and to create programming elements that address these different outcomes. Twelve nonexperimental evaluations are identified in this review of the literature.

Evaluation Results

Careful analysis of the available drug court evaluation literature identified four experimental and 15 quasi-experimental (strong) studies. A brief discussion of these evaluations is provided below, and a more complete review of the drug court evaluation literature is contained in the appendix.

Juvenile Drug Court Evaluations

To date, few evaluations of juvenile drug courts have been completed, although several are ongoing. Only seven juvenile drug court evaluations that include client outcomes could be located for this analysis. Three are categorized as quasi-experimental (weak), and two use nonexperimental designs. Only one, the Utah juvenile drug court evaluation, is classified as quasi-experimental (strong). This study matched treatment and comparison group cases on age, gender, ethnicity, and criminal history, and found a statistically significant difference between number of charges one year before the intervention and one year after discharge. Drug court participants had 1.1 fewer charges after the intervention, while the comparison group had 0.6 fewer charges after the intervention.

In addition to these studies, researchers at the University of Akron completed two randomized studies of the Summit County juvenile drug court (Dickie 2001, 2002). The evaluation found that drug court juveniles had fewer new charges than the comparison group, a higher rate of negative drug screens than the comparison group, and higher employment rates than the comparison group. However, the evaluation had very small sample sizes to begin with, and suffered from substantial attrition. Of 30 original comparison group members, data were available for only 9 at the 12-month follow-up. The authors do not control for differences between those who were present at follow-up and those who were initially included in the evaluation. Therefore, it is not possible to determine whether differences at follow-up were the result of juvenile drug court or a biased follow-up sample.

Experimental Designs

Three randomized adult drug court studies have been completed, two in the United States and one in New South Wales, Australia. The first randomized drug court study was conducted by researchers at RAND (Deschenes, Turner, and Greenwood 1995) and evaluated the Maricopa County (Phoenix, Arizona) First Time Drug Offender Program. The second study, by Gottfredson and Exum (2002), evaluated the Baltimore drug treatment court and the third studied the New South Wales, Australia, drug court (Freeman, Karski, and Doak 2000). All three studies examined differences in rearrest rates between randomly assigned drug court participants and an appropriate comparison group. Although no significant differences in outcomes were detected in the Arizona study, the Baltimore study showed significant reductions in criminal justice contacts, and the Australia study found significant reductions in drug offenses. In all three studies, offenders from the comparison group were more likely to be rearrested than were drug court participants.

The same general methodology was used in all three evaluations, but some description of their respective assignment processes is necessary in considering how to generalize from their findings. In the Arizona and Australia studies, defendants were processed through several stages to determine their eligibility for participation. Once program eligibility was determined, defendants were randomly assigned to the treatment or comparison group, and could not accept or reject their placement. The results of these studies are generalizable to a population that would meet the program's eligibility requirements, and not to a more general population of potential drug court participants.

Generalizability of results from the Baltimore study is affected by problems with assignment. Randomization was halted periodically as a result of staff turnover in one of the many court offices participating in the process. When randomization was interrupted, participants were assigned to drug court according to procedures in place before the study. The authors believe that this change in procedure might have affected generalizability, although the magnitude and direction of the bias is unclear.

In the Arizona study, almost 9 percent of study subjects randomly assigned to the treatment group never received treatment, although the authors note that "data currently being collected on treatment services received and graduation from the drug treatment court will allow for a more refined estimate of effects on recidivism" (Deschenes et al. 1995, 23). In a review of the evaluation, GAO (1997, 102) observed that, "The results, especially those involving recidivism, fail to establish strong effects of testing and treatment and part of the reason for this may be due to the fact that various programs were not always implemented as designed."

The Baltimore drug treatment court (BDTC) began operations in 1994 to serve nonviolent adult drug offenders. Participants are referred from three sources: circuit court cases, district court cases supervised by the Division of Parole and Probation, and less serious district court cases processed by the Alternative Sentencing Unit. As part of the program, defendants must take part in drug treatment provided by a registered provider in Baltimore City. In addition, all defendants enter the BDTC under "intensive" supervision and must attend hearings once every two weeks. Participants also have regular meetings with their probation agent outside of court. Routine urinalysis tests are required to validate offender compliance with rules prohibiting drug use. For the evaluation, eligible offenders were randomly assigned to one of two conditions: drug treatment court or treatment as usual. Once offenders were deemed eligible for drug court, they were given "conditional" drug court offers where participants had a 50 percent chance (for those deemed eligible through circuit court) or a 67 percent chance (for those deemed eligible through district court) of participating in drug court. One hundred thirty-nine participants were assigned to the treatment condition and 96 to the control condition. There were no significant differences between the treatment and control groups on several offense-related and social demographic variables.

The results of the Baltimore study suggest that participants in drug court had lower levels of recidivism, particularly for drug offenses. Participants in BDTC were significantly less likely than the comparison group participants to be rearrested ($p < .05$). Forty-eight percent of the treatment group was rearrested for a drug-related charge, compared with 64 percent of the comparison group. New arrests (0.9 compared with 1.3 for the comparison group) and new charges (1.6 compared with 2.4) were also significantly lower for members of the treatment group.

The drug court in New South Wales, Australia, used a randomized study design to examine drug court operations between February 1999 and June 2000. Freeman, Karski, and Doak (2000) tested the hypothesis that drug court is more effective at reducing recidivism in drug-using criminal offenders than are conventional sanctions. Offenders were referred to drug court by either a local or district court, and their drug court eligibility was determined at a preliminary trial. The treatment group (224 members) was made up of individuals who accepted entry into drug court, indicated willingness to adhere to drug court guidelines and objectives, and were approached by officials at a detoxification center. The comparison group (121 members) was selected randomly from individuals eligible for drug court but unable to participate because of space limitations at the detoxification center when they were accepted.

The study focused on two outcomes: the time to first offense, and the frequency of offending over time. The follow-up period for each subject started when the subject was referred to drug court and ended on September 30, 2000. This time period included time while incarcerated as well as time at risk (out of custody).

The mean follow-up periods were 369 days for the treatment group and 294 days for the comparison group. On average, the treatment group spent 34 percent of their follow-up time in custody while the comparison group spent 54 percent of follow-up time in custody. The average days at risk during follow-up were 243 days for the treatment group and 145 days for the comparison group.

The mean frequency of offending while at risk suggests little difference between the treatment and comparison groups. For instance, the two sample populations did not differ significantly on their frequencies of theft with drug offenses or theft offenses alone. However, there was a significant difference between the treatment and comparison groups for drug offenses ($p < .05$). The results of a survival analysis suggested no significant differences between the groups in the time to first offense (for all types of offenses). There were, however, significant differences in the time to first drug-related offense. One year after referral to the drug court, 6 percent of the treatment group had committed a drug-related offense compared with 15 percent of the comparison group.

Quasi-Experimental (Strong) Designs

Fifteen adult drug court studies were identified as strong quasi-experimental designs. Five studies either did not report the statistical significance of observed differences or reported significance levels for only a portion of their findings. Of the 10 studies reporting statistical significance, eight found statistically significant differences in favor of the drug court. Each evaluation employed rigorous quasi-experimental methods, but several caveats are warranted before interpreting the results. All studies examined differences between treatment and comparison groups. Since all studies involved voluntary assignment to drug courts, preexisting client motivation may partly explain stronger outcomes among the treatment groups. Most studies conducted only bivariate analyses to determine between-group differences in recidivism. Only a few studies (e.g., Douglas, Chester, and Hamilton County) statistically controlled for other variables known to affect outcomes (e.g., age, gender, race, and prior arrests). Because competing explanations for differences in outcomes, including baseline motivation and drug use patterns, were not controlled in the study, confidence in observed differences is attenuated.

The Denver drug court study by Granfield and Eby (1997) did not find a statistically significant difference in recidivism between the treatment and comparison groups. Slightly more than half of the subjects in each group were rearrested at least once (58 percent of the treatment cases versus 53 percent of comparison cases). According to Granfield and Eby, the results were preliminary and statistical power was limited by the small sample size (100 study participants).

The Douglas County study found a statistically significant difference, but in part it favored a comparison group. The study found that 42 percent of the treatment group was rearrested before the end of the 12-month follow-up, compared with 29 percent of clients referred to a diversion program and 61 percent of traditional adjudication clients. Before concluding that diversion outperformed drug court, the authors noted that diversion clients were lower risk offenders on average and that all three groups differed on important demographic variables. Additionally, the diversion group was from an earlier cohort of offenders and historical factors may have influenced client outcomes.

Quasi-Experimental (Weak) and Nonexperimental Studies

The results of quasi-experimental (weak) and nonexperimental evaluations can be very difficult to interpret. Study authors often compare program graduates and nongraduates when reporting results. This technique tends to enhance the apparent success of drug court. Other authors use inappropriate comparison groups (e.g., persons who refuse to participate in the drug court program). For study results to apply beyond a single court, researchers must compare equivalent samples, where one participates in drug court and one does not. As a result, an objective observer would have low confidence in the study results. A description of the studies in this category can be found in the appendix.

Measuring the Effectiveness of Drug Court Activities on Outcomes

In addition to impact evaluations that compare drug court to alternative justice system processing on drug court outcomes, a number of studies have examined the effects of specific drug court activities on outcomes. A set of studies funded by NIDA was designed specifically to examine the effect of certain drug court features on related outcomes. Other studies tested program outcomes as part of a broader evaluation. This section describes the results of both sets of evaluation activities.

Designs that isolate a particular program activity can more reliably indicate the relationship between that activity and drug court outcomes than can studies where this activity is merely a covariate in a broader model. Covariate designs include independent variables to control for competing explanations of a main program effect (generally recidivism). In these instances, it is tempting to interpret the effect of other covariates on outcomes. However, since the model *does not* necessarily include competing explanations for the direct effect of the covariate on outcomes, caution is warranted in interpreting these effects.

A number of studies designed to test the effectiveness of particular adult and juvenile drug court components have been funded recently, although results are not yet available. Two randomized trials are currently under way to test the independent effects of treatment in juvenile drug courts. Researchers at the University of Miami are conducting a randomized trial of the effects of multidimensional family therapy (MDFT) on juvenile drug court participants. Participants will be randomly assigned to either the usual juvenile drug court program or a juvenile drug court that includes MDFT. Researchers expect to complete the study in 2008.

A similar study is being conducted in Charleston, South Carolina. Researchers from the Medical University of South Carolina are studying the independent effects of multi-systemic therapy (MST) on juvenile drug court participant outcomes. Juveniles eligible to participate in juvenile drug court will be randomly assigned to one of four conditions: community service without drug court, drug court with community service, drug court with MST, and MST enhanced with the community reinforcement approach. This study is expected to be completed by the end of 2004.

Several outcome trials of adult drug courts are ongoing, one of which has reported preliminary results. A study funded by NIDA and CSAT and conducted by researchers at the Treatment Research Institute (TRI) randomly assigned drug court participants in five Delaware cities to two experimental conditions. The two groups will attend status hearings with varying frequency and intensity while all other drug court activities are held constant for all study participants. Initial findings "revealed no main effect of status hearings on counseling attendance, urinalysis results, official rearrests and re-convictions, or self-reported substance use or criminal activity during drug court or at 6 months or 12 months post-admission" (Marlowe 2003). The study did find that those with the highest risk had better outcomes when assigned to status hearings twice a week, and those with the lowest risk had better outcomes when status hearings were assigned as needed. The study will be completed in 2006. Other TRI researchers are conducting a randomized evaluation of different sanctioning protocols. The study, which TRI expects to complete in 2006, will compare outcomes for drug court participants receiving negative sanctions, positive rewards, or both.

NIDA and NIH have funded two other drug court studies. A study at the Research Triangle Institute, scheduled for completion in 2004, will test the effectiveness of varying coerced treatments in nine jurisdictions. The study may identify the impact of different methods of linking systems within the drug court model. NIDA and NIH have also funded researchers at UCLA to study vouchers as a positive reinforcement on drug court participants in California. The study will randomly assign participants to four conditions: vouchers for negative urine tests, vouchers for treatment completion, vouchers for treatment completion or negative drug tests, and standard treatment with no vouchers. This study is expected to be completed in 2004.

Two more NIDA studies are evaluating the effects of drug court on client motivation. A University of Delaware study, scheduled for completion in 2004, will analyze the effects of three different types of outpatient therapy for drug court participants (drug education, outpatient therapy, and intensive outpatient therapy). In addition, the Friends Research Institute will use a random assignment model to test the effects of Motivational Interviewing. This study will be completed in 2006.

Meta-Analysis

Two large-scale efforts to conduct meta-analyses of drug court effects have been attempted. Meta-analysis is a research technique that combines statistics from completed studies to generate consensus findings from the field. First, researchers at the University of Maryland conducted a meta-analysis of 42 drug court evaluations and found a positive effect size for 36 (Wilson, Mitchell, and MacKenzie 2002). Overall, the authors found a significant reduction in recidivism among drug court graduates, and an effect for both juvenile and adult drug courts. However, the authors noted that weak designs may have affected the results. For instance, the strongest evaluation designs (randomized trials that did not suffer from substantial attrition) showed drug courts had no effect on recidivism. Nevertheless, most studies found that drug court reduces the postprogram likelihood of a subsequent arrest and conviction, for both drug and non-drug offending.

The other meta-analysis was conducted by researchers at the Washington State Institute for Public Policy (WSIPP). WSIPP researchers examined outcomes from 29 drug court evaluations of 19 drug courts (Aos et al. 2001). Of the 26 effect sizes coded, 21 were in the direction of lower rates of reoffending and 11 had a significantly lower risk of reoffending. While these numbers suggest somewhat mixed findings, the overall effects from the full pool of studies were negative (fewer new crimes committed by drug court participants) and significant, although somewhat modest. No juvenile drug court evaluations were included and so no meta-analytic results were available for juvenile drug court participants.

Cost-Benefit Analysis

In addition to impact evaluations, another important set of data about the effectiveness of JDCs comes from cost-benefit analysis (CBA). Unfortunately, the data from CBAs are even more limited than data from other types of evaluations. CBAs are generally conducted in three steps. First, researchers conduct an impact evaluation to isolate and measure the effects of a drug court. Second, researchers simultaneously develop estimates of costs associated with drug courts. Third, those observed effects are translated into monetized estimates of program effects. The dollar values associated with program benefits are then compared to cost estimates to determine whether the program is cost-effective (Dhiri and Brand 1999; Roman and Harrell 2001; Cohen 2000; Cartwright 2000; Rajkumar and French 1997; Miller, Cohen, and Wiersema 1996).

The quality of cost-benefit analysis depends on the quality of the underlying impact evaluation. If the impact evaluation has rigorously controlled for competing explanations of program effects, then the results of the cost-benefit analysis can be interpreted with much greater confidence. However, if the cost-benefit analysis cannot isolate the effects of the drug court and attribute those effects to the drug court, then differences in outcomes are accepted with much less confidence. In these situations, assigning costs and benefits may only serve to compound specious findings. Since both the impact results and the cost and benefits estimates must be developed independently, it is even more difficult to conduct rigorous cost-benefit analysis than to conduct an outcome evaluation.

In general, most cost-benefit analyses estimate only the monetary effects of a drug court for the criminal justice system, not the costs and benefits to participants, victims, and other community members. These populations are generally excluded because of the difficulty in measuring costs and benefits that accrue to them. Among other difficulties, much of the cost of crime (and benefit of preventing crime) takes the form of changes in pain and suffering, fear, and other factors that are intrinsically difficult to measure. However, these costs and benefits are also critical in evaluating the effectiveness of drug courts. Since they are generally excluded even in sound cost-benefit analyses, the results from drug court CBAs should be interpreted with that fact in mind.

Three studies make up the cost-benefit literature related to drug courts, and all focus on adult drug courts. The most rigorous CBA was conducted by Steve Aos and colleagues at WSIPP. The WSIPP researchers created an innovative meta-analytical approach to measuring the costs and benefits of Washington's criminal justice system (WSIPP 2003). First, they used meta-analytic techniques to estimate the effects of drug court from 30 published drug court studies. These courts reduced recidivism by about 13 percent (Aos et al. 2001). Next, they evaluated the impacts of six drug courts in Washington state, and found similar reductions in recidivism. These results were then combined with independent analyses of the economic costs and benefits of drug courts on the Washington criminal justice system. Overall, WSIPP researchers found that the drug courts saved the state almost $4,000 per participant over regular court, a savings of about $1.74 for every $1 invested.

Two recent cost-benefit analyses of drug courts suggest larger program effects. An evaluation of the St. Louis drug court found that on average the adult drug court cost almost $1,500 more than regular probation when comparing drug court graduates and probation completers (Loman 2004). In the two years after completing their program, drug court graduates were significantly less likely to have a felony rearrest (an average of 1.7 for drug court graduates and 2.1 for probation completers). This led to a savings of $2.80 for every $1 invested in drug court. The study compared probation completers and drug court graduates using a matched sample. No differences between the groups were detected at baseline. Although it is possible that some unmeasured factor was related to both group assignment and outcomes, no selection effects were apparent.

The other recent cost-benefit analysis is a study of a drug court in Portland, Oregon (Carey and Finigan 2004), that studied the same court reviewed in a 1998 cost-benefit analysis (Finigan 1998). The 1998 study found that the program saved $5,629 per participant enrolled. However, it is possible that some of the difference in outcomes (benefits) was the result of baseline differences between the treatment and comparison groups. The 2004 study also found significant cost savings from drug court. Using a somewhat different methodology from the approach used in other studies, Carey and Finigan found that the drug court was both less expensive to operate and yielded benefits in the postprogram period. However, this study compared drug court participants to individuals who refused drug court. Since motivation to enter drug court may correlate with motivation to avoid future offending and drug use, some observed differences in outcomes may be the result of these selection effects. Therefore, some differences in economic outcomes (costs and benefits) may result from baseline differences among participants.

In addition to these cost-benefit analyses of drug courts, the Urban Institute conducted a cost-benefit analysis of the Washington, D.C., Superior Drug Court Intervention Program (SDCIP). The SDCIP cost-benefit analysis was built on a randomized design that assigned drug-involved arrestees to one of three conditions: a business-as-usual condition, a treatment program, and a sanctions program (Roman and Harrell 2001). The sanctions program used drug court–type sanctions but did not include a treatment element, and the treatment condition did not include a sanctions component. Attrition in the treatment group made comparisons impossible, but comparing the sanctions program to the business-as-usual program found a savings of $2 for every $1 invested in the program. However, much of the savings was from averted alcohol-related crimes (such as drunk driving) rather than drug-related crimes.

Difficulties Interpreting Variation in Existing Studies

The knowledge gained by examining a broad set of independent evaluation studies is limited by how reliably the studies implement consistent methods. Over the past decade, evaluations have measured the effects of drug court programs at various stages of development and using a variety of program models. Many evaluations focus on particular program components that may not be common to drug courts in general. Generalizing from the results of these studies can be precarious.

Drug court programs vary in how they define key processes and outcomes. For instance, the point at which a participant is considered "in" a program may be the moment he or she is assigned to the program or it may be when treatment actually begins. The difference may be a matter of weeks, or even months, which can have important effects on key outcomes. Even when outcomes are consistently defined, definitions of enrollment status may create inaccuracies in reporting. Belenko (1999) pointed out that many evaluations measure graduation and retention according to GAO guidelines. According to the GAO algorithm, retention rates are the sum of the number of graduates plus the number still active in the program, divided by the number of total participants.

The GAO method does not control for time in the program: all active participants are counted alike, whether they have been in the drug court for one month or 12. Some share of those recently entering a drug court program will end up being terminated, so the GAO method could artificially inflate the success rate. A more useful method of measuring retention would be to choose a cohort of participants that have entered the drug court over a certain period, say six months or a year, and follow them for a sufficient length of time until all have either graduated or been terminated. This would enable researchers to calculate accurate retention rates for various periods as well as the total share of admitted participants that graduate.

The operational structures and polices of drug courts vary widely. Drug courts vary in the characteristics of the offenders they accept, the duration and intensity of intervention, and what share of intended services are actually provided. Some courts accept only first-time offenders, while others focus on chronic, drug-abusing offenders. The severity of offenders' drug problems, the types of drug they use, and the duration of their abuse could have major effects on program retention, completion, and outcomes. Treatment access and quality also vary across drug courts, ultimately affecting outcome findings.

A related issue surrounds the type of intervention received by the comparison group. In the simplest evaluation case, the criminal justice system uses a standard approach for drug-involved offenders within a jurisdiction, and assigns a subset of that population special treatment in the form of a drug court intervention. In reality, many courts offer several alternative interventions with dynamic eligibility criteria and operational characteristics: that is, there is no business-as-usual approach. In addition, many jurisdictions create programs that serve an entire population (e.g., all defendants with a certain set of charges and criminal history), making the creation of an appropriate comparison group a challenge at best.

Problems with Existing Impact Evaluations

The previous section highlighted the limits of existing studies examining the effectiveness of drug courts in reducing recidivism and drug use. In addition to issues about the analytical approaches to evaluating drug courts, the evaluation literature has yet to clearly articulate how drug court components, separately and as a whole, contribute to program outcomes. That is, there has been a distinct lack of theory-driven evaluation. Few, if any, evaluations have included explicit hypotheses of how drug court operations might change criminogenic behavior.

Drug court proponents and practitioners point to elements they believe are critical to a successful drug court: access to high-quality and appropriate treatment, judicial interest in offender progress in treatment, frequent drug testing, and graduated sanctions and rewards. Each of these practices, independently and in combination, may contribute to a drug court's success or failure in changing behavior. Their roles certainly deserve more attention, yet researchers have not examined how these practices relate to offender behavior from the perspective of crime control and human behavior theory. Even if one accepts that drug courts are successfully placing offenders in treatment, retaining them longer in treatment, and reducing criminal activity, almost no research has addressed why drug courts are successful. Evaluations need to consider the effects of specific drug court policies and how drug court procedures and treatment influence outcomes.

Rather than a theory-based approach to evaluation, drug court evaluations have typically employed a simple "black box" model, in which outcomes are examined as a function of participation in drug court and offender characteristics. These evaluations have focused on measuring reductions in drug use during drug court participation (based on drug test results) and reductions in arrest during and following drug court.

To open the black box of drug court interventions, researchers must test theoretical propositions about why these practices influence offender behavior. Understanding how offender behavior changes could then lead to more informed hypotheses about the effects of specific drug court procedures on outcomes. In practical terms, identifying the relationships between individual drug court activities and outcomes and combinations of activities and outcomes can lead to improvements in programming, and ultimately achieve longer-term reductions in drug use and crime.

Conclusion

Research on drug courts has so far produced only limited evidence of drug court impact. Reasons for the lack of persuasive evidence include problems in designing and supporting drug court evaluations, lack of attention to conducting theory-based evaluations, and difficulty generalizing from evaluations given the wide variation in drug court operations. This review of the evaluation literature underscores the importance of rigorous, theory-based evaluation research for future policy and practice. Continued funding for new and existing drug courts, combined with the widespread promulgation of the drug court model, suggest that drug court programs will continue to grow. Researchers must continue to develop theory-based evaluation designs to advance the understanding of drug court impact.

NOTE

1. The reports by Dr. Steven Belenko entitled "Research on Drug Courts: A Critical Review" have appeared annually beginning in 1998 in the National Drug Court Institute Review, and are also independently published by the National Center on Addiction and Substance Abuse at Columbia University. A similar review in 2000 by Dr. Kenneth Robinson was also included in the literature review.

REFERENCES

Aos, Steve, Polly Phipps, Robert Barnoski, and Roxanne Lieb. 2001. *The Comparative Costs and Benefits of Programs to Reduce Crime,* Version 4.0. Olympia: Washington State Institute for Public Policy.

Belenko, Steven. 1998. "Research on Drug Courts: A Critical Review." *National Drug Court Institute Review* 1(1): 1–42.

———. 1999. "Research on Drug Courts: A Critical Review 1999 Update." *National Drug Court Institute Review* 2(2): 1–58.

———. 2000. *Drugs and Drug Policy in America: A Documentary History.* Westport, CT: Greenwood Press.

Boruch, Robert F. 1997. *Randomized Experiments for Planning and Evaluation: A Practical Guide.* Thousand Oaks, CA: Sage Publications.

Carey, Shannon, and Michael Finigan. 2004. "A Detailed Cost Analysis in a Mature Drug Court Setting: A Cost-Benefit Evaluation of the Multnomah County Drug Court." NCJ 203558. Portland, OR: NPC Research.

Cartwright, William S. 2000. "Cost-Benefit Analysis of Drug Treatment Services: Review of the Literature." *The Journal of Mental Health Policy and Economics* 3:11–26.

Cohen, Mark A. 2000. "Measuring the Costs and Benefits of Crime and Justice." In *Measurement and Analysis of Crime and Justice,* Vol. 4 of *Criminal Justice 2000* (263–315). Washington, DC: U.S. Department of Justice, National Institute of Justice.

Deschenes, Elizabeth Piper, Susan Turner, and Peter W. Greenwood. 1995. "Drug Court or Probation? An Experimental Evaluation of Maricopa County's Drug Court." *The Justice System Journal* 18(1): 55–73.

Dhiri, Sanjay, and Sam Brand. 1999. "Analysis of Costs and Benefits: Guidance for Evaluators." Crime Reduction Programme Guidance Note 1. London: Research and Statistics Directorate, Home Office.

Dickie, J.L. 2001. *Summit County Juvenile Drug Court Evaluation Report: July 1, 2001–June 30, 2001.* Akron, OH: The Institute for Health and Social Policy, University of Akron.

———. 2002. *Summit County Juvenile Drug Court Evaluation Report: July 1, 2001–June 30, 2001.* Akron, OH: The Institute for Health and Social Policy, University of Akron.

Finigan, Michael. 1998. *An Outcome Program Evaluation of the Multnomah County S.T.O.P. Drug Diversion Program.* West Linn, OR: Northwest Professional Consortium.

Freeman, Karen, Ruth Lawrence Karski, and Peter Doak. 2000. *New South Wales Drug Court Evaluation: Program and Participant Profiles.* Sydney, NSW: NSW Bureau of Crime Statistics and Research.

GAO. *See* U.S. General Accounting Office.

Gottfredson, Denise C., and M. Lyn Exum. 2002. "The Baltimore City Drug Treatment Court: One-Year Results from a Randomized Study." *Journal of Research in Crime and Delinquency* 39(3): 337–56.

Granfield, Robert, and Cindy Eby. 1997. *An Evaluation of the Denver Drug Court: The Impact of a Treatment-Oriented Drug Offender System.* Denver, CO: University of Denver, Department of Sociology.

Harrell, Adele. 2000. *Evaluation of the D.C. Superior Court Drug Intervention Programs.* Washington, DC: U.S. Department of Justice, National Institute of Justice.

Loman, L. Anthony. 2004. "A Cost-Benefit Analysis of the St. Louis City Adult Felony Drug Court." St. Louis, MO: Institute of Applied Research.

Marlowe, Douglas. 2003. "Matching Services to Client Needs in Drug Court." Application to the National Institute on Drug Abuse. http://crisp.cit.nih.gov/crisp/crisp_query.generate_screen enter 'drug court.'

Miller, Ted R., Mark A. Cohen, and Brian Wiersema. 1996. "Victim Costs and Consequences: A New Look." National Institute of Justice research report. Washington, DC: U.S. Department of Justice, National Institute of Justice.

Mohr, Lawrence B. 1995. *Impact Analysis for Program Evaluation,* 2nd ed. Thousand Oaks, CA: Sage Publications.

Pocock, Stuart J. 1997. *Clinical Trials: A Practical Approach.* New York: John Wiley and Sons.

Rajkumar, Andrew S., and Michael T. French. 1997. "Drug Abuse, Crime Costs, and the Economic Benefits of Treatment." *Journal of Quantitative Criminology* 13(3): 291–323.

Roman, John, and Adele V. Harrell. 2001. "Assessing the Costs and Benefits Accruing to the Public from the Washington, D.C. Superior Court Drug Intervention Program." *Journal of Law and Policy* 23(2): 237–68.

Sherman, Lawrence W., Denise Gottfredson, Doris MacKenzie, John Eck, Peter Reuter, and Shawn Bushway. 1997. *Preventing Crime: What Works, What Doesn't, What's Promising.* NCJ 165366. Washington, DC: U.S. Department of Justice, Office of Justice Programs.

Terry, W. Clinton III. 1999. "Broward County's Dedicated Drug Treatment Court: From Post-adjudication to Diversion." In *The Early Drug Courts: Case Studies in Judicial Innovation,* edited by W. Clinton Terry III (77–107). Thousand Oaks, CA: Sage Publications.

U.S. General Accounting Office. 1997. *Drug Courts: Overview of Growth, Characteristics, and Results.* Report to the Committee on the Judiciary, U.S. Senate, and the Committee on the Judiciary, House of Representatives. Washington, DC: U.S. General Accounting Office.

Utah Substance Abuse and Anti-Violence Coordinating Counsel. 2001. *Salt Lake County Drug Court Outcome Evaluation.* Salt Lake City: Utah Substance Abuse and Anti-Violence Coordinating Counsel.

Washington State Institute for Public Policy. 2003. *Washington State's Drug Courts for Adult Defendants: Outcome Evaluation and Cost-Benefit Analysis.* Document no. 03-03-1201. Olympia: Washington State Institute for Public Policy.

Wilson, David B., Ojmarrh Mitchell, and Doris Layton MacKenzie. 2002. "A Systematic Review of Drug Court Effects on Recidivism." Paper presented at the annual meeting of the American Society of Criminology, Chicago, Nov. 12–16.

WSIPP. *See* Washington State Institute for Public Policy.

5

Defining the Mission of Juvenile Drug Courts

Jeffrey A. Butts, Janine M. Zweig, and Cynthia Mamalian

Nearly half of all adolescents in the United States try illegal drugs before they reach age 18. Judging from the sheer number of youth who try drugs during their teen years, it is obvious that the majority of juvenile drug users are able to control their own behavior, avoid the consequences of prolonged drug abuse, and have adult lives free of serious substance abuse problems (Bachman et al. 2002). While some youth develop severe problems as a result of drug use, most do not. This fact is equally true for delinquent and nondelinquent youth. To be cost-effective and socially responsible, juvenile drug courts must focus their treatment resources on those delinquent youth least able to control their own behavior and most at risk of prolonged and harmful substance abuse. To accomplish this goal, juvenile justice officials should understand the nature of adolescent development, the incidence and prevalence of substance use among teenagers, and the interventions used to change drug-related behavior and reduce harmful substance abuse.

Drug Use among American Teens

There are many types of adolescent drug users in the United States, beginning with the legions of American teenagers who smoke tobacco and drink alcohol. Illegal drug use, however, is also very common. More than half of all high school seniors have tried at least one illegal drug; nearly half have tried cannabis or marijuana (figure 5.1). Millions of teens— one in four overall—have tried drugs other than marijuana, ranging from inhalants and prescription drugs to cocaine, MDMA (or Ecstasy), methamphetamine, hallucinogenics, and opiates. Some of these youth may become chronic or abusive drug users just as some youth who try alcohol will go on to become abusive drinkers and alcoholics. Even among juveniles that try illegal drugs other than marijuana, however, most will avoid serious substance abuse problems.

Which youth should be referred to juvenile drug court? Clearly, the justice system cannot afford to devote the high level of time and resources demanded by the juvenile drug court process to all adolescent substance users just because they happen to have been arrested. Strategic decisions must be made to focus limited resources where they will do the most good for youth, their families, and the entire community. Juvenile drug courts

Figure 5.1. *More than Half of High School Seniors Have Tried Illegal Drugs; Nearly Half Have Tried Marijuana (or Cannabis)*

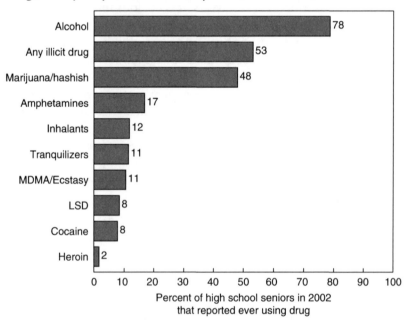

Source: Johnston, O'Malley, and Bachman (2003).

were designed to focus supervision and treatment resources on youth involved in, or headed toward, problematic substance abuse. Exactly what does this term mean? Should all teenage drug users be eligible for juvenile drug court? Should one incident of marijuana possession qualify a teenager for drug court? What about a single arrest for underage drinking? Should a youth's substance use have to be unusually serious to be eligible for drug court? What is considered usual, or "normative," substance use for adolescents? If most adolescents try psychoactive substances at some point, how should juvenile justice practitioners identify the level of substance use that goes beyond the expected or normative pattern? Should drug courts restrict their efforts to juveniles considered dependent on drugs (figure 5.2)?

These questions are important not only for juvenile justice professionals and policymakers, but also for youth. Drug courts involve young offenders and their families in an intense and expensive course of treatment and supervision. The process can last more than a year, and a youth's failure to comply with the program can result in increasingly punitive consequences, including secure detention. The strength and consistency of sanctions in juvenile drug courts may be one of their most appealing features, but it is also one of the main reasons to restrict their use. Drug courts could be powerful weapons in the struggle to contain substance abuse, but they could also harm juveniles and their families if drug courts deploy the power of the legal system in an overly intrusive and stigmatizing way. This axiom is especially true in the juvenile justice system where courts have broad powers to intervene, even in cases involving nonserious offenses.

Juvenile Drug Court Clients

The key question for anyone wishing to examine the use of juvenile drug courts is, "Who are the juveniles handled in juvenile drug courts and how serious are their drug problems?" Surprisingly, it can be very difficult to obtain this information. Most programs are relatively new, and statistics about their clients are not consistently reported. Most nationally available data come from self-report surveys of drug court program directors. Surveys sponsored by the federal Office of Justice Programs, for example, indicate only that juvenile drug court clients use a variety of illegal drugs, from cannabis and cocaine to amphetamines and prescription pain relievers (see, for example, Office of Justice Programs 1999). The surveys ask juvenile

Figure 5.2. *More Than 9 in 10 Drug Users Use Marijuana Only or Use Drugs Other Than Marijuana without Indications of Dependence*

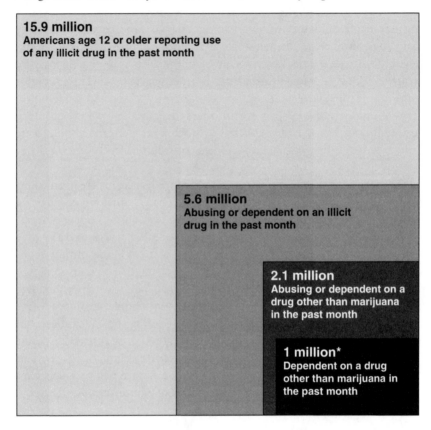

Source: Results from the 2001 National Household Survey on Drug Abuse (SAMHSA 2002).

Note: Number of youth dependent on a drug other than marijuana is estimated based on the proportion of dependent users among all respondents considered either substance abusing or substance dependent, regardless of drug type. Taking this estimate of 1 million, 14.9 million of the 15.9 million drug users, or 94 percent, use marijuana only or use drugs other than marijuana without exhibiting drug dependence.

drug courts to report the general pattern of drug use among their clients. This reporting is different from asking about the drug-use profiles of individual youth. For instance, how many juvenile drug court clients have used only alcohol? How many have used alcohol and cannabis, and nothing more? How many clients are considered "abusing" as opposed to "using" substances, and how many are thought "dependent?"

For answers to these questions, researchers must rely on information from individual drug court programs. Obtaining such information from published reports is rarely possible. Most studies of juvenile drug courts do not document the extent of substance abuse among program clients. Of the six juvenile drug court evaluations available from the web site of the OJP Drug Court Clearinghouse and Technical Assistance Project in April 2003, only one provided information about the drug use behavior of clients. This report, about a juvenile drug court in Tennessee, included just two sentences on the topic:

> The most prevalent drugs in the District are crack/cocaine and marijuana, with methamphetamine and LSD starting to be detected as well. Heroin is also present increasingly. (Taylor 1998)

No data were offered to support the report's suggestion that cocaine was used frequently by juvenile drug court clients, nor did the report clarify what was meant by the statement that other drugs were "starting to be detected" or were "present increasingly." Most reports and evaluations about juvenile drug courts use similar language to describe their client populations. The reports assess program operations and treatment models in detail, and often compare local practices with national guidelines, but they do not describe exactly how juvenile drug courts are used and who their clients are in terms of their drug use behaviors. Practitioners and policymakers have to make their own inquiries to identify the actual drug behaviors of juvenile drug court clients. The information generated by such inquiries is often at odds with the popular impression that juvenile drug courts deal with severe substance abuse.

During site visits for the National Evaluation of Juvenile Drug Courts Project, researchers from the Urban Institute routinely asked local judges, program directors, and other drug court staff about the characteristics of their juvenile clients. The researchers were told repeatedly that 80 to 90 percent of juvenile drug court clients have used only alcohol and marijuana when they are referred to juvenile drug court. The lowest such estimate offered by any program was 75 percent—i.e., just one in four youth in juvenile drug court have used a drug other than alcohol or marijuana. When clients use drugs other than marijuana, they tend to focus on inhalants and inappropriately obtained prescription drugs. The professionals in juvenile drug courts are far more concerned about the use of prescription drugs by juveniles than they are about the use of illegal narcotics such as cocaine and amphetamines. In most jurisdictions, only "a handful" of juvenile drug court clients are thought to be using these other drugs.

Juvenile drug court staff also report that very few youth qualify for a dependency diagnosis. Truly addicted youth, it turns out, are rare in juvenile drug courts. Nearly all youth referred to juvenile drug courts are either using or abusing drugs, but very few are considered dependent. Members of drug court teams are often gravely concerned about the lives and safety of their juvenile clients, but they are primarily worried about a youth being killed while driving drunk or taking an overdose of prescription drugs. Ecstasy, methamphetamine, and cocaine are pretty far down on their list of worries.

Whether these drug use patterns represent a problem for juvenile justice policy depends largely on how one defines the mission of juvenile drug courts. If juvenile drug courts are designed to provide treatment for adolescent drug addiction, the programs are apparently serving the wrong youth. If policymakers support juvenile drug courts out of concern for teenagers who abuse serious and harmful drugs, then the funds devoted to these programs may be misdirected. If, on the other hand, juvenile drug courts are designed to deliver prevention services for a broad cross-section of youth involved with alcohol and other drugs, then their current mode of operating may be appropriate, but such a broad mission would raise other questions about the risks of labeling, net-widening, and iatrogenic effects (i.e., the cure may be worse than the disease).

Unfortunately, it is difficult to know which interpretation is correct. Professional and governmental publications use inconsistent language to describe the purposes of juvenile drug courts. Some experts clearly believe that juvenile drug courts are intended for young offenders with serious substance abuse problems. Cooper (2001, 5), for example, suggests that the clients of juvenile drug courts should be similar to youth held in secure detention and include "youth who have serious problems and need the intensity of services and supervision provided by the [juvenile drug court] program."

Others take a broader view. In their recent report about juvenile drug court "strategies in practice," the National Drug Court Institute and National Council of Juvenile and Family Court Judges describe juvenile drug court clients as young offenders "identified as having problems with alcohol and/or other drugs" (NDCI/NCJFCJ 2003, 7). Not only does this description suggest that the use of alcohol alone could qualify a young person for juvenile drug court, but it also does not specify how severe substance abuse must be to warrant the use of juvenile drug court. In fact, the NDCI/NCJFCJ report implies that even the distinction between "use" and "abuse" is less than helpful:

> The term substance abuse may have many different meanings depending on the context and the person using it. . . . For the purposes of this publication, substance abuse is referred to broadly as youth involvement with alcohol and other drugs (AOD) at all problem levels. Although this definition differs from the strict diagnostic meaning of the term, it has two advantages. First, this broad definition avoids the designation of any particular level of use, acknowledging that youth who appear before the court differ in their levels of use. Second, it allows the consistent use of a single term rather than multiple terms that may confuse the reader and detract from the flow of the text. (NDCI/NCJFCJ 2003, 2)

The intent of the NDCI/NCJFCJ report is clear. Choosing the target population for juvenile drug courts can (or should) be left to local decisionmakers. Some jurisdictions may want to focus on young offenders with relatively severe substance abuse problems. Others may want to intervene with delinquent youth just as they are beginning to use alcohol or other drugs. In the view of the NDCI and the NCJFCJ, either strategy could fall within the mission of juvenile drug courts.

Given the potentially broad mission of juvenile drug courts, policymakers and practitioners must consciously design and implement their own programs. At a minimum, the implementation process should involve four steps: (1) developing a sound understanding of adolescent development and the prevalence of various risk behaviors among teenagers in general; (2) examining how the juvenile justice system may or may not accommodate the goals of the juvenile drug court process; (3) monitoring substance use among all young people as well as among youthful offenders and potential juvenile drug court clients; and (4) selecting an appropriate target population for juvenile drug courts and monitoring how well the program focuses on that population after implementation.

The use of alcohol and other drugs is a worrisome but common behavior among all adolescents. Drug use is probably even more widespread among delinquent youth. How many of these youth would benefit from the intensive intervention provided by juvenile drug court programs? How many would probably require such intervention to avoid serious drug problems? Juvenile justice agencies are responsible for making these important decisions. To do so, they must be able to differentiate between what is common or "normative" drug use by adolescents and what is problematic or potentially dangerous drug use. One of the first steps in meeting this challenge is to understand adolescent development.

Adolescent Development

Adolescence is the time of transition when individuals grow from children to adults. The term adolescence is derived from the Latin word for "growing up," and adolescent development is marked by numerous physiological, behavioral, intellectual, emotional, and social transformations. The idea of adolescence is relatively new. All cultures recognize differences between children and adults, but the concept of adolescence as a separate and definable stage of life did not exist in its present form until roughly the 1800s. In many developing countries, the concept is still relatively recent (McCauley and Salter 1995).

The exact timing of adolescence is not well defined in the United States. Some societies have initiation rites that signify the actual moment adulthood begins. In contemporary American society, there is no precise moment when adulthood begins, although a number of events during the teen years could be considered akin to a formal rite of passage, including church confirmations, bar/bas mitzvahs, obtaining a driver's license, getting a first job, and graduating from high school. Each marker represents movement toward adulthood, but none confers it completely. This ambiguity may lead American teenagers to work harder at defining the onset of adult status in their own way, perhaps by engaging in risky behaviors that are disapproved by parents and adult society in general.

The Ages of Adolescence

Researchers have identified three distinct periods within adolescence—early, middle, and late—each with its own developmental tasks, opportunities, and risks (Fenwick and Smith 1994; Committee on Community-Level Programs for Youth 2002; Rapp 1998). Individuals in one period are often quite different from those in another. The three periods of adolescence provide a broad timeline against which to track developmental progress. Youth-serving agencies, including those in the juvenile justice system, would be well advised to approach adolescents differently, depending on their position within each stage (box 5.1).

Early adolescence, between ages 10 and 14, is often the most stressful portion of adolescence (Committee 2002). The ego dominates the child's view of all issues and physical growth is rapid. Youth begin to show increased concern about their personal appearance, and self-consciousness

Box 5.1. Adolescent Development Occurs in Stages, Each with Its Own Challenges and Tasks

Early adolescence	Ages 10–14	• biological puberty • rapid physical growth, especially in females • increased concern about personal appearance • rebellious/defiant behavior • increased emphasis on friends and peer groups • growing independence from family
Middle adolescence	Ages 14–17	• greater awareness of others • increasingly independent decisionmaking • experimentation with self-image • increased emphasis on new experiences • emergence of morals and values • capacity for lasting friendships • sexual awareness • performance-oriented
Late adolescence	Ages 17–20	• more idealistic world view • growing interest in life beyond home and school • more stable personal relationships • increasing awareness of adults as equals • increased enjoyment of independence • growing career focus

Sources: Committee on Community-Level Programs for Youth (2002); Kipke (1999).

may increase. Youth at this age often exhibit rebellious or defiant behaviors and place great importance on acceptance by friends and peer groups. During this phase, adolescents begin to develop greater independence from their families and must deal with disruptive school transitions from elementary school to middle or junior high school (Committee 2002). When they leave elementary school, youth typically encounter larger schools, more controlling environments, less personal contact with adults, and more competitive grading systems. These transitions may be particularly challenging because they disrupt youth social networks at the very time early adolescents are beginning to place greater emphasis on peers, and they emphasize competition and social comparisons at a time when young adolescents are already highly self-critical.

Much of the turmoil experienced during early adolescence begins to subside during middle adolescence, or sometime between ages 14 and 17. Middle-stage adolescents are increasingly performance-oriented. They become less self-absorbed, begin to make their own decisions, and are more willing to experiment with a new self-image. Middle-stage adolescents are interested in new experiences and show more fully developed morals and values. They are also more capable of making lasting friendships, are more sexually aware, and can enjoy the development of new skills and interests. A growing interest in and awareness of their own experiences and perceptions could increase their curiosity about drugs and alcohol at this time.

Late-stage adolescents, between ages 17 and 20, often view the world more idealistically as they begin involvement in the world outside home and school. By this stage of adolescence, youth begin to have stable relationships, and they start to see adults as equals and enjoy their growing independence. Older teenagers are more focused on work and careers, but the rates of illegal behavior, including substance abuse, also peak during the late adolescent years. Late adolescence can sometimes extend into the early twenties for youth who delay their entry into adult roles through educational activities or other social factors (Kipke 1999). Alcohol and drug use, for example, are usually at their highest during a young adult's college years (Bachman et al. 2002).

Normative Development

Normally developing adolescents must cope with a unique set of tasks and challenges. Steinberg and Schwartz (2000) placed these challenges into four critical domains—physical, intellectual, emotional, and social.

PHYSICAL CHANGES

Adolescence is a time of accelerated growth and change. Youth experience puberty and acquire reproductive capabilities and secondary sexual characteristics. They grow to full adult height and experience changes in bodily proportions and physical changes in the brain. Physiological sexual maturity is a gradual process that appears to be occurring earlier and earlier, particularly in prosperous countries. Youth today achieve puberty two to three years earlier than young people did a century ago (Hetherington and Parke 1986). The most dramatic biological changes occur during early adolescence, beginning around age 12. The timing of these changes often differs by sex, race, and ethnic group (Money 1980; Susman 1997). An adolescent's social context may mediate the pace of maturation, and the timing of maturation can influence adolescent adjustment.

Physical development and the social consequences of maturation are a fundamental concern for teenagers, particularly those in early and middle adolescence. Adults who work in the juvenile justice system should be conscious of the powerful force of such concerns, and how their effects may differ for males and females. Research findings show early maturation among males is generally positive, as early maturing boys report more confidence, less dependence, and greater popularity with their peers (Perry 2000). The findings for early maturing females are mixed, but some studies indicate that early maturing girls experience more negative affect, lower self-esteem, and greater contact with deviant peers than girls who mature later (Perry 2000).

INTELLECTUAL CHANGES

A number of cognitive changes occur during adolescence, allowing youth to process more complex information and think about the world and themselves in more complicated ways (Committee 2002). The intellectual and cognitive changes experienced by adolescents are the result of continued brain growth and more efficient neural processing (Crockett and Petersen 1993). Young adolescents are still concrete thinkers. They learn from direct experience and have limited ability to generalize from abstractions. By middle to late adolescence, formal operational or abstract thinking becomes possible. As abstract thinkers, older youth can generate hypotheses, deduce consequences from a variety of alternative hypotheses, and assimilate and combine information from various sources. This flexible, efficient, and more effective thinking is part of what differentiates adolescents from children (Hetherington and Parke 1986; Perry 2000). Older adolescents begin to acquire a more complex and integrated notion of self, a greater ability for reflection, and an improved capacity for making social comparisons and contemplating the future (Burton, Allison, and Obeidallah 1995).

By age 16 or 17, an adolescent's raw intellectual abilities may compare to those of an adult. For this reason, court professionals often treat older teenagers differently when attempting to impart complicated information. They can speak about long-term consequences and ask youth to consider the risks of various behaviors. Adolescent development, however, is a continual and highly variable process. The intellectual abilities of many older adolescents may be comparable to those of adults, but not all adolescents have the necessary tools to engage in logical reasoning by age 16 or 17, and young people still have less life experience to draw upon for decisionmaking (Steinberg and Schwartz 2000). Adolescents tend to discount the future and weigh short-term consequences more heavily than long-term consequences (Fried and Reppucci 2001). Their short-term bias in calculating risks may relate to their lack of life experience and greater uncertainty about the future in general. Adolescents also may have a different risk-benefit calculus than adults, focusing more on possible gains than potential losses (Reppucci and Woolard 1999).

EMOTIONAL CHANGES

Adolescents have been characterized as audacious and insecure, lonely, psychologically vulnerable, moody, argumentative, and emotional (Konopka 1973). Adolescents experience more intense emotions than do adults, and this intensity may be one reason they process information differently (Kipke 1999). It is no surprise that adolescents experience emotional changes as they prepare to become autonomous individuals. In a few short years, they must achieve independence from adults, come to terms with the fact that their parents are not perfect, define themselves apart from their families, search for acceptance by peers, and navigate new adult-like roles in society (Elliott and Feldman 1990; Havighurst 1972; Stover and Tway 1992). Adolescents also experience the progressive maturing of sexual attitudes and behavior that allow them to form personal relationships and become fully functioning members of adult society (Gleitman 1991). Conventional wisdom suggests that adolescents have diminished self-esteem and are more insecure and self-critical than are children and adults. Research, however, indicates that self-esteem remains relatively stable after age 13, and an adolescent's self-concept is relatively complete by that time (Steinberg and Schwartz 2000).

SOCIAL CHANGES

Adolescents place greater emphasis on friends and peer groups as they try to increase their independence from parents and family. They begin to define their education and career aspirations, as well as their personal values and morals. Peer interaction is critical for these tasks. As teenagers work to achieve new and more mature relationships with age-mates, they acquire the interpersonal skills necessary for sexually intimate relationships (Stover and Tway 1992; Elliott and Feldman 1990; Havighurst 1972). Susceptibility to peer influence also peaks between ages 12 and 15 (Steinberg and Schwartz 2000). During this period, an adolescent's decisions are not always made independently or autonomously. Adolescents' growing attachment to peers combined with their desire for autonomy from parents can increase the risk of group-oriented problem behavior, including substance abuse and delinquency (Reppucci and Woolard 1999). Criminologists often blame peer-group dynamics for the high incidence of group offending during adolescence.

Obviously, parent-child relationships may also change dramatically during adolescence. Adolescents seek autonomy from their parents and begin to question family roles and responsibilities. These changes are often assumed to cause tremendous conflict between parents and their children, but recent research suggests that parents and their children agree with one another more often than not, particularly about core values (Committee 2002). Other studies suggest that emotional turbulence is far from universal among modern American adolescents (Steinberg and Schwartz 2000).

During the later teen years, youth begin to acquire experiences needed for adult work, and they spend more time thinking about the future and their specific career options. Youth begin the transition from social and economic dependence on family to increasing independence. A large part of adolescence includes defining oneself and developing a set of personal values and ethics. This process includes resolving issues of identity and sexuality; acquiring or determining an individual set of moral, ethical, religious, and political principles to guide behavior; desiring and achieving socially responsible behavior; and forging a niche in society (Stover and Tway 1992; Elliott and Feldman 1990; Havighurst 1972).

Developmental Variations and Social Context

Juvenile justice practitioners must be acutely aware of the variations in adolescent development and how they may affect a youth's responses to the lure of substance abuse, the threat of legal sanctions, and the provision of treatment or services designed to change behavior. Steinberg (1995) described adolescence as a continuum where each phase is inherently linked to what precedes and follows it. Adolescent development consists of multiple pathways shaped simultaneously by characteristics of the individual, influences of the immediate environment, and the opportunities and constraints present in the broader social context. Individuals negotiate these pathways at varying speeds and with different degrees of success. In particular, progress toward the completion of cognitive and moral development during adolescence can be delayed or detoured by social disadvantage (Grisso 1996). Skills and knowledge may accrue unevenly for different developmental tasks, and the ages at which competencies emerge can be influenced by differences in language ability, knowledge, experience, and culture. The importance of these differences will only increase as the adolescent population in the United States becomes more racially and ethnically diverse (table 5.1).

Burton, Allison, and Obeidallah (1995) suggested that within the social contexts of economically disadvantaged communities, distinct ideologies, role expectations, and behavioral practices shape individual and familial responses to adolescence. In middle- and upper-income communities, teen activities often prepare youth for adulthood, but adolescents are not expected or allowed to assume adult responsibilities (e.g., work and parenthood). In disadvantaged communities, on the other hand, expectations about adolescent behavior may be quite different and the demarcation between adolescent and adult responsibilities less distinct. As disadvantaged teens adapt the skills and responsibilities necessary to survive in their social environment, including earning an income and becoming the primary caregiver for younger siblings, they may move from childhood to adulthood without an extended intermediate stage of adolescence.

Table 5.1. *Increasing Diversity Means More Adolescents Will Belong to Racial and Ethnic Minority Groups*

Year	Population under 18	Percent minority[a]
1980	63.7 million	26
1990	64.2 million	31
2000	70.4 million	36
2010	72.1 million[b]	41[b]
2020	77.2 million[b]	45[b]

Source: Federal Interagency Forum on Child and Family Statistics (2002).
a. Non-Caucasian or Hispanic.
b. Projections by the U.S. Census Bureau.

In their review of historical and ethnographic accounts of African American families, Burton et al. (1995) identified five dimensions of ambiguity in social roles that could affect the lives of disadvantaged teenagers: (1) inconsistencies across different social institutions regarding normal adolescent behavior, (2) lack of clarity in developmental boundaries, particularly in age-condensed families, (3) overlapping social worlds of teens and parents, (4) perceptions of an accelerated life course, and (5) alternative contextual definitions of successful developmental outcomes. These five dimensions may be most salient in community and family contexts where insufficient resources preclude the luxury of adolescence.

All forms of behavior during adolescence, including substance abuse, should be viewed in context. Empirical knowledge about adolescence and social context suggests that juvenile justice policymakers and practitioners should consider not only the chronological and developmental status of the juveniles they encounter in juvenile drug courts, but also their cultural and social contexts. Although drug use varies only slightly by race and ethnicity, family and community context is an important component in assessing the severity of adolescent substance use (figure 5.3). In one com-

Figure 5.3. *Rates of Illegal Drug Use Are Slightly Higher among White, Non-Hispanic Youth than Black, Non-Hispanic Youth*

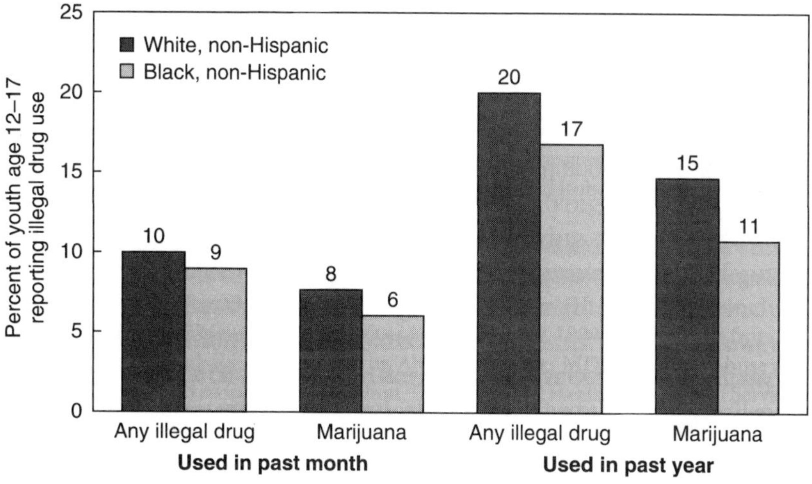

Sources: SAMHSA (1999, 2000).

munity, smoking cannabis or drinking alcohol at age 14 may be highly deviant and a red flag for intensive intervention. In another setting, such behavior could be more normative, suggesting a less intrusive and less punitive response. A 14-year-old binge drinker would require close attention regardless of context, but the pathological quality of such behavior should be assessed within each youth's social and developmental context.

Drug Use by Adolescents

The developmental characteristics of adolescents could make them more likely than adults to become involved in harmful abuse once they begin to use drugs, but how many adolescent drug users require intensive treatment to stop or control their behavior? National surveys suggest that nearly all teenagers try at least one psychoactive substance before age 18, mostly alcohol. Cannabis use is widespread among adolescents, with 29 percent of youth age 16 and 17 reporting use of cannabis in the previous year (figure 5.4). Are all these juveniles at risk of severe

Figure 5.4. *More than One in Three 16- and 17-Year-Olds Used an Illegal Drug in the Past Year; Most Were Marijuana Users*

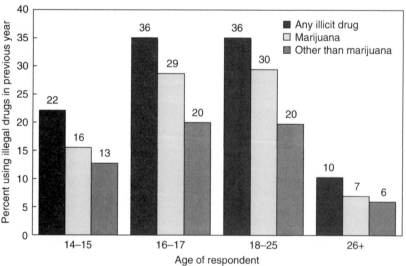

Source: National Survey on Drug Use and Health (SAMHSA 2003).

drug problems? How should practitioners identify those youth headed toward harmful and uncontrolled drug behavior? Which young offenders should practitioners refer to juvenile drug court?

One logical and obvious method of targeting the resources available in juvenile drug courts is to classify youth according to the severity of their current substance use behavior. Substance-related behavior is traditionally divided into three levels—use, abuse, and dependence. Successful control over the frequency and timing of consumption is a fundamental characteristic of drug use. A drug user, as opposed to abuser, can control his or her pattern of consumption and avoid negative consequences associated with drug use, including legal penalties, loss of employment, and family disruption. Many individuals use drugs without ever displaying symptoms of abuse or dependence. Most adults, for example, are able to use alcohol without abusing it.

Lack of control over the timing and frequency of consumption is a fundamental marker of drug use that has become drug abuse (Winters, Latimer, and Stinchfield 2001). Drug abusers may also consume larger quantities of psychoactive substances, but the critical distinction between use and abuse is consumption that is prolonged and uncontrolled, placing the drug abuser and others in jeopardy, including physical, emotional, mental, legal, social, and occupational hazards.

Both drug use and drug abuse can be precursors to drug dependence. Dependence may emerge because the use of psychoactive substances is reinforced over time by the physiological, emotional, and behavioral effects that accompany consumption (Crowley et al. 1998; Kenkel, Mathios, and Pacula 2001). Beyond the risk of sudden death from ingesting large amounts of certain drugs (alcohol, cocaine, and the like), the greatest risk associated with substance use is dependence. Dependence on psychoactive substances can result in profound developmental lags for adolescents, including mental distortion, cognitive confusion, impaired judgment, uncontrollable mood swings, and an inability to grow, develop, and mature into a healthy adult. Dependence can interrupt and even stop the developmental process (Pursley 1991).

Dependence is traditionally indicated by the difficulties drug users have in discontinuing their use of drugs. Whether a particular user is diagnosed as dependent, however, is also a function of the person's age, the type of drug he or she consumes, the family history and biochemistry, and exposure to negative consequences (e.g., legal penalties, loss of income, family conflict).

Ultimately, distinguishing drug use from drug abuse and dependence involves multiple factors viewed in combination. Some factors are physical or chemical, but others are based on social judgments. In fact, the role of social judgment in assessing drug abuse and dependence has increased in recent decades. The identification of abuse and dependence is partly governed by social context, which could have particularly profound consequences for adolescents, especially those from disadvantaged communities.

Drug Use, Abuse, and Dependence in the General Youth Population

According to the National Survey on Drug Use and Health (NSDUH), 46 percent of Americans age 12 and older have used at least one illicit drug in their lifetime and 15 percent are recent users, meaning they used an illegal drug at least once in the previous year (SAMHSA 2003).[1] Recent drug use varies considerably by age. Adolescents and young adults have substantially higher rates of recent drug use than older adults (figure 5.5).

Figure 5.5. *Drug Use Increases Sharply during Adolescence, Then Declines*

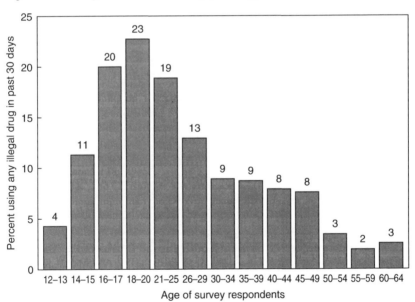

Source: National Survey on Drug Use and Health (SAMHSA 2003).

Rates of past-month drug use, for example, vary from 20 percent among youth age 16 and 17 to 23 percent among young adults between 18 and 20. Past-month drug use is reported by fewer than 10 percent of adults over age 30.

The NSDUH is a comprehensive examination of the use of alcohol, cigarettes, and illicit drugs among a representative sample of Americans age 12 and older. The study relies on interviews to estimate the extent of substance abuse and dependence among respondents. Interviews are conducted in person using procedures to ensure respondent confidentiality and truthfulness. To determine rates of substance abuse and dependence, the NSDUH uses criteria established by the fourth edition of the Diagnostic and Statistical Manual of Mental Disorders, known as the DSM-IV (American Psychiatric Association 1994). Interview questions focus on the individual's health status, emotional problems, reported attempts to cut down on substance use, tolerance, withdrawal, and other symptoms associated with the DSM definition of dependence.

According to the NSDUH, rates of drug dependence vary by age, increasing throughout the teen years, peaking at around age 20, and declining after the late twenties. The highest rate of dependence (i.e., within the past year) occurs at age 18 to 25 (table 5.2). Juveniles are less likely than adults to meet dependence criteria, either for marijuana or any illicit drug. In 2002, just over 3 percent of juveniles in the general population

Table 5.2. *More than One in Five 12- to 17-Year-Olds Used an Illegal Drug in the Past Year, but Three-Quarters Cannot Be Described as Drug Abusing or Drug Dependent*

	Used Any Illicit Drug in Previous Year (percent)			Used Marijuana Only in Previous Year (percent)		
Extent of drug use	Age 12–17	Age 18–25	Age 26+	Age 12–17	Age 18–25	Age 26+
Use	22.2	35.5	10.4	15.8	29.8	7.0
Use without abuse or dependence	16.6	27.3	8.6	11.5	23.8	6.2
Abuse or dependence	5.6	8.2	1.8	4.3	6.0	0.8
Dependence	3.2	5.5	1.2	2.5	3.9	0.4

Source: SAMHSA (2003), detailed tables, sections 1 and 5.

reported behavior consistent with substance dependence during the previous year, while nearly 6 percent could be described as having "abused" drugs during that period. Yet, more than 22 percent of youth between 12 and 17 reported using some type of illicit drug in the past year. These numbers suggest that three in four users of illegal substances are neither abusing nor dependent on drugs.

Drug Use, Abuse, and Dependence in the Juvenile Justice Population

Most information available about adolescent substance abuse is based on statistics from the general population (e.g., NSDUH) or from high school seniors (e.g., "Monitoring the Future"). Youth referred to juvenile drug courts, however, may not share the same characteristics as youth in the general population. They may be more deeply involved with substance use and their rates of abuse and dependence could be higher. The magnitude of this difference, however, is difficult to estimate. Surprisingly, researchers have never compared drug use among offenders and non-offenders using consistent methods.

Some research suggests that drug use among youth in the juvenile justice system could be as much as five times higher than among youth in general. In a study of 415 juvenile offenders from an unnamed western state, 37 percent of interviewed juveniles admitted using some form of hallucinogen within the past year (Jenson and Howard 1999). When high school seniors are asked a similar question, just 7 percent report use of hallucinogens within the past year (Johnston, O'Malley, and Bachman 2002, table 5). In fact, past-year hallucinogen use among high school seniors has never exceeded 12 percent since the "Monitoring the Future" surveys began in 1975. The interview techniques used in these studies may not be comparable, however, and it is difficult to compare one study's results with another's. Still, research suggests that illegal drug use may be more common among juvenile offenders than among youth in general. Of course, whether all these drug users have drug "problems" is a different question.

Other sources suggest that drug use among juvenile offenders may be two to three times higher than among youth in general. Approximately one in five adolescents age 16 and 17 admit using illegal drugs in the past 30 days, according to national surveys. On the other hand, data from the National Institute of Justice's Arrestee Drug Abuse Monitoring (ADAM) program suggest that in many U.S. cities, half of all juveniles taken into police custody have used illegal drugs recently enough to be detected in urinalyses or other physical tests (National Institute of Justice 2000). In 1999, for example, more than two-thirds (69 percent) of all juveniles arrested and detained in Phoenix tested positive for at least one illegal substance at the time of arrest. In other cities, including Cleveland and Denver, more than 60 percent of all detained juveniles tested positive for illicit drugs. These data, however, do not include youth that are released upon arrest rather than taken into custody. They likely exclude many youth charged with less serious offenses.

In addition, it may be inappropriate to compare drug test results with self-report surveys. By definition, test results for "any illicit drug" include figures for marijuana, which is detectable in the body far longer than most illegal drugs, up to several weeks after the most recent use (Iversen 2000). Thus, the rate of positive tests for "any illegal drug" at the time of arrest would be equivalent to a fully truthful self-reported 30-day prevalence rate for marijuana. A 30-day prevalence rate of approximately 50 percent among arrested juveniles would be more than twice the rate reported by youth in the general population, but is this comparison fair? Is it meaningful to compare drug testing data from one population (arrestees) and self-reported data from another population (youth in general)? The true difference between the drug use patterns of the two groups may be different, either greater (because self-reporters in the general population falsely exaggerate their drug use) or less (because they minimize it).

Further, a positive drug test at time of arrest does not necessarily indicate the presence of drug problems, either abuse or dependence. To gauge the prevalence of drug problems among young offenders, it is important to review the findings of research that uses clinical interviewing. For example, Teplin and her associates (2002) examined a sample of 1,800 youth held in the Cook County juvenile detention center in Chicago. The results indicated substance use disorders (abuse or dependence during the previous six months) in more than half of detained male juveniles (51 percent) and just under half of detained females (47 percent). The majority of these youth were users of alcohol and cannabis alone. Among males, for example, "marijuana use disorders" were seen in 45 percent of juvenile offenders and "alcohol use disorders" were seen in 26 percent. "Other substance use" disorders (i.e., drugs beyond alcohol and marijuana) were detected in just one of every 40 offenders (2.4 percent of detained males).

The data from Teplin et al., however, should *not* be used to generalize about the degree of abuse and dependence among all juvenile offenders. First, only one-fifth of all juvenile court cases on average involve secure detention (Harms 2003). Second, offenders chosen for secure detention are typically the most serious cases heard in juvenile court, either in terms of the youth's illegal behavior or the extent of his or her social and family problems (which would increase the odds of youth failing to appear for court hearings, thus prompting detention). Third, the probability that any particular youth would be selected for an interview during a study of detained youth would be related to the length of his or her stay in detention, and juveniles with long detention stays tend to be more seriously involved in delinquent behavior. Thus, a study that measures the prevalence of substance abuse disorders among a population of detained juvenile offenders is likely to find higher rates of substance abuse relative to the rates of juvenile offenders in general.

The degree of overestimation is compounded further in studies that rely on data from large, urban areas. Juvenile subjects in the Teplin study, for example, were interviewed while detained in a chronically overcrowded facility in one of the nation's largest cities.[2] In urban areas, high demand for confinement space combined with limited resources make local officials reserve their secure detention space for juveniles who prompt the greatest concern among judges and other court staff, usually those who have committed serious offenses and those with severe behavioral problems. A study measuring the extent of mental health and substance abuse disorders in an urban detention facility would very likely find prevalence rates exceeding those of an average, non-detained juvenile justice population.

This supposition is confirmed by the results of another recent study that relied on clinical interviews to assess the degree of substance abuse and dependence among a broad population of juvenile offenders. Aarons et al. (2001) used structured diagnostic interviews to assess the extent of mental health and substance use disorders among more than 1,000 troubled youth in an unnamed western county. Study subjects were selected at random from the population of all youth actively involved in at least one of five major service systems in the county (12,662 youth). The service systems were alcohol and drug services, adolescent mental health, school-based service for youth with serious emotional disturbances, child welfare, and juvenile justice. Youth involved with the juvenile justice system (419) represented an average group of adjudicated offenders from that county. Most had been placed out of their homes at some point in their lives, but one-third had not been detained or confined at any time during the previous year.[3]

As expected, the prevalence of substance abuse and dependence among this population was considerably lower than reported by Teplin and her colleagues. In the Chicago detention center, Teplin et al. asked about substance use behaviors over the previous six months and detected abuse and dependence in 51 percent of male juveniles and 47 percent of females. The Aarons et al. study calculated past-year prevalence rates, which should be much higher than six-month rates. Yet, Aarons and his colleagues found just 37 percent of youths had any form of substance use disorder, and most of these were alcohol disorders. Past-year alcohol use disorders were found in 28 percent of study subjects, while cannabis use disorders were seen in just 15 percent. Other disorders reported among the study sample were even less prevalent, including those involving the use of amphetamines (10 percent), hallucinogens (3 percent), and cocaine (0.5 percent).

In a more recent study, Wasserman and her colleagues used clinically sophisticated interviewing techniques to estimate the prevalence of various substance use and mental health disorders among a sample of 991 randomly selected youth from a juvenile justice intake population in Texas (i.e., youth not yet adjudicated or sentenced in court). Substance use disorders were detected in just 25 percent of the study sample. Most youth were abusing drugs but not dependent and most used alcohol and marijuana as opposed to "other substances" (Wasserman et al. forthcoming). Abuse of drugs other than marijuana was found in 3 percent of the sample, while "other substance dependence" was noted in 3.6 percent of sampled youths.

Implications for Juvenile Drug Court Operations

Whether the youth typically referred to juvenile drug courts are more similar to the youth in the Teplin study, those in the Aarons or Wasserman studies, or to youth in the general population is impossible to say without additional research. It is probably safe to assume that drug problems among juvenile drug court clients are higher than among the general youth population and lower than among youth held in secure confinement facilities, but this still leaves a lot to guesswork. The true difference between the drug problems of youth in general and those of juvenile drug court clients likely depends on the screening and assessment policies used by juvenile drug courts. If virtually any contact with an illicit drug is enough to qualify a youth for juvenile drug court (i.e., one possession charge), the proportion of substance abuse and dependence among juvenile drug court clients could be quite close to the prevalence rate among youth in general. If, on the other hand, juvenile drug court is reserved for youth with repeated or serious incidents of drug-related behavior, the incidence of abuse and dependence among juvenile drug court clients is likely higher than among youth in general. Without more information from juvenile drug court programs, these questions are impossible to answer with any degree of accuracy.

Drug Use and Other Risk Factors

For some juvenile offenders, the use of illegal drugs may be just one indicator of more complex problems. These youth may be disproportionately likely to have personality disorders, histories of physical or sexual abuse, and a range of mental health problems (Cote and Hodgins 1990; Abram 1989; Dembo et al. 1987). Problems sometimes correlated with the onset of adolescent substance abuse, such as teen pregnancy and school failure or dropout, may lead to escalating behavioral problems. It is important for practitioners to differentiate, however, between what could be considered normative health risk behaviors and behaviors associated with more serious problems.

Zweig and her colleagues (Zweig, Lindberg, and McGinley 2001; Zweig, Phillips, and Lindberg 2002) examined how frequently adolescent substance use co-occurs with other health risk behaviors. Drawing on data from the National Longitudinal Study of Adolescent Health, a nationally representative sample of students (12,955 total), the researchers used cluster analysis to examine how youth in grades 9 through 12 combined various health risk behaviors, including unsafe sexual activity, suicidal thoughts and behaviors, physical violence, and substance use (distinguishing among tobacco, alcohol, marijuana, and other illicit drugs). The results revealed four distinct combinations of risky behaviors among adolescent youth (table 5.3).

How "troubled" young people who used drugs were considered varied, as indicated by a range of social and developmental variables, including family and school "connectedness." One behavioral characteristic that generally identified troubled youth, or those with lower adjustment and connectedness scores, was the use of an illicit drug other than marijuana. While adolescent users of alcohol or marijuana may have had developmental and behavioral problems, as a group their troubles were

Table 5.3. *The Greatest Total Risks Associated with Adolescent Substance Use Appear When Youth Use Illegal Drugs Other than Marijuana or Cannabis*

Key risk behaviors reported by sample youth	Percent of sample	Total risk assessed across all factors
Males		
No risk or low risk across all forms of health risk behavior	66	No risk to low risk
Sexually active, substance using but primarily tobacco and alcohol with some marijuana use	17	Moderate risk
Higher levels of marijuana use, use of other illicit drugs, and suicidal thoughts or behaviors	4	High risk
High-risk on all behaviors except suicide	12	High risk
	100	
Females		
Sexually active, using effective birth control, no other risks	60	No risk to low risk
Sexually active, substance using but primarily tobacco and alcohol with some marijuana use	19	Moderate risk
Some physical fighting, suicidal thoughts and behavior	13	Moderate risk
All forms of risky behaviors, including use of illicit drugs other than marijuana	8	High risk
	100	

Sources: Zweig, Lindberg, and McGinley (2001); Zweig, Phillips, and Lindberg (2002).

similar to those experienced by low-risk adolescents who did not use alcohol or marijuana. Youth who used an illegal drug other than marijuana faced more severe risks, including participation in physical violence and suicidal thoughts and behaviors. They were more likely to engage in additional health risk behaviors and cause harm to themselves and others.

The fact that some youth have tried drugs other than marijuana is not a guarantee that they will have more serious problems, but it does increase their odds of having more serious problems. Perhaps juvenile drug courts should focus their efforts on youth who have gone beyond cannabis, while diverting marijuana users to less intrusive and voluntary services? Would this strategy be risky? Isn't marijuana a "gateway" to other forms of substance abuse? Based on the research evidence, the answer is no.

Gateway Myths

According to the enduring gateway hypothesis, drug users inevitably move through a sequence of progressively more severe substance use, with each stage drawing them to the next stage and the next drug. Some researchers find support for the gateway hypothesis in surveys of drug users. Using data from the former NHSDA (now the NSDUH), Kandel and Yamaguchi (2002) saw a sequence of worsening drug use across individuals users. Virtually all cocaine users, for example, first use marijuana and alcohol. Other researchers see confirmation of the gateway hypothesis in studies of twins with different drug use behavior. Lynskey and his associates examined several hundred pairs of same-sex twins and reported that the use of marijuana before age 17 in one sibling was associated with higher lifetime rates of drug use, drug dependence, and alcohol dependence in that sibling relative to the twin not using marijuana before age 17 (Lynskey et al. 2003).

Neither of these studies, however, actually supports the gateway hypothesis as it is commonly understood. The findings merely indicate that individuals more likely to use drugs at some point tend to begin using them at an early age, and tend to begin with alcohol and marijuana. This phenomenon is not the same one suggested by the gateway hypothesis. There may be a developmental pattern to drug initiation, with marijuana as the bridge between legal and illegal drugs for those who go on to other drugs, and it may be true that individuals that use drugs at very young ages are more likely to develop problems with abuse and dependence later in life. However, the use of any particular drug does not appear to cause or lead to the use of other drugs. Marijuana use does not signal the beginning of a progression toward the use of other drugs (Morral, McCaffrey, and Paddock 2002).

An apt analogy might be that most marathon runners once started out jogging, but jogging does not lead to or cause marathons. The vast majority of joggers, in fact, do *not* progress to marathon running. Similarly, very few drug users follow the entire drug progression sequence. Drug use during adolescence does not always lead to continued use over time, nor does it necessarily lead to serious drug problems in adulthood.

Most individuals stop voluntarily during the drug progression sequence (Iversen 2000; Labouvie and White 2002). Escalation from one substance to another is not even statistically likely. Indeed, once substance use has begun, users are far more likely to regress to earlier stages in the sequence than to advance to subsequent stages (Elliot 1993).

So why do so many people believe in the gateway hypothesis? The best explanation for the enduring appeal of the gateway hypothesis is relatively simple—opportunity. Based on data from the NHSDA, Wagner and Anthony (2001) found that marijuana users were more likely to find themselves in social situations where there could be an opportunity to use cocaine. In other words, cannabis smokers *are* more likely than non-smokers to use cocaine eventually, but this has nothing to do with the addictive properties of marijuana. It results from the friendship networks that develop among drug users. Cocaine users feel more socially compatible with marijuana users than with non-marijuana users. Thus, the typical marijuana smoker is more likely to be around when cocaine users make cocaine available. In fact, teenagers who use tobacco and alcohol are also more likely to be in social situations where cannabis is offered (Wagner and Anthony 2001). This relationship does not mean that tobacco and alcohol lead to or cause marijuana use.

Implications for Juvenile Drug Court Operations

Where should juvenile drug courts focus their treatment and supervision resources (figure 5.6)? By definition, all juvenile offenders have been arrested and charged with some delinquent offense, and many of them deserve some form of intervention, but what if their drug and alcohol behavior is relatively normal for their age? What if they are no more likely to develop serious drug problems than thousands of other youth in their community with similar behavior? Should juvenile offenders be forced to participate in an intensive (and expensive) drug treatment process simply because they happened to be arrested for shoplifting or vandalism? How bad should their substance use problems be to justify a referral to juvenile drug court? Given that resources are always limited, would it be cost-effective for juvenile drug court programs to restrict their services to clients that have used drugs other than alcohol and marijuana or those that exhibit indications of serious abuse and dependence? Ultimately, the decision rests on the accuracy of assessment and diagnosis.

Figure 5.6. *Where Should Juvenile Drug Courts Target Their Efforts?*

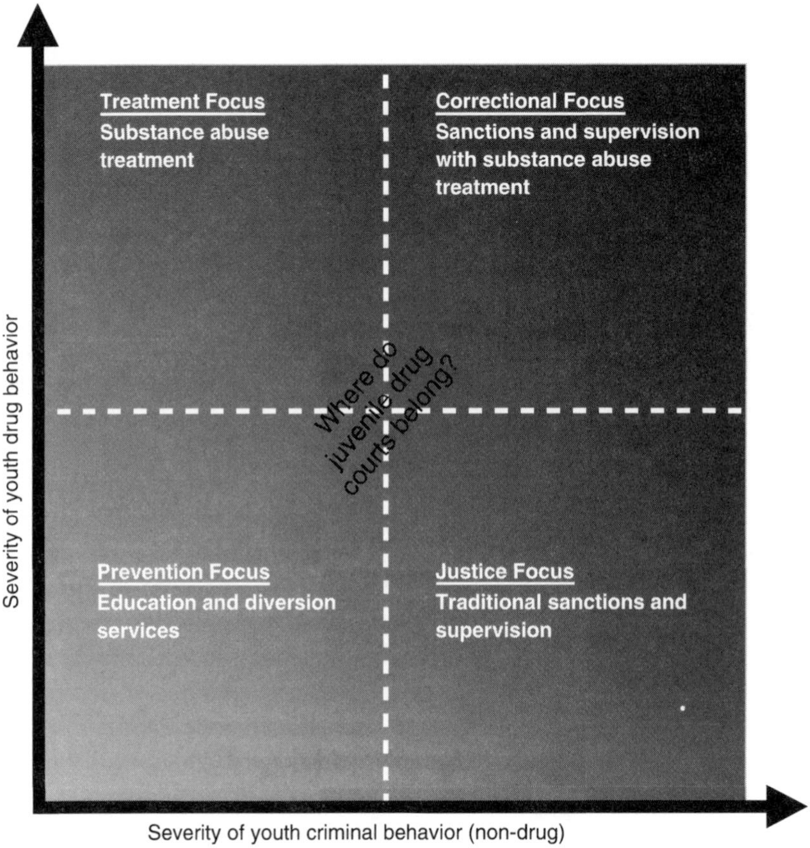

Source: Urban Institute National Evaluation of Juvenile Drug Courts.

Identifying Adolescent Drug Problems

The use of any drug is potentially dangerous, especially for young people who lack the knowledge and experience to make sound decisions about risky behavior. Some participation in health risk behaviors, however, is a common part of adolescent development. Within limits, engaging in risk behavior may even be adaptive for building self-confidence and social competence. Taking nonlethal risks during adolescence may help adolescents meet certain developmental needs such as the quest for autonomy. But participation in risky behavior ceases to be adaptive when it becomes persistent or pathological.

Where does adolescent substance use fall on the continuum from adaptive to maladaptive? It depends on the frequency and severity of the behavior, combined with the motivation for engaging in the behavior. Adolescents try drugs for many reasons, including the search for social or peer acceptance, the need to establish a group identity, the expectation of desirable outcomes, favorable attitudes toward deviant behavior, and a predisposition toward sensation seeking (box 5.2). Given adequate opportunities to obtain drugs, a number of these factors working in concert could propel many adolescents toward substance use. Not all drug users, however, will go on to engage in dangerous or maladaptive substance abuse, and not all will become dependent on drugs. Research shows, in fact, that most adolescent substance users do not become dependent, with or without treatment. Most stop their drug use the old fashioned way—they grow up and discover that life offers greater pleasures than inebriation.

In fact, an individual's interest in all health risk behaviors tends to decrease with age and maturity (Blum 1987; Elliot 1993; Hawkins et al. 2002). This pattern has also been observed in the progression of criminal behavior from adolescence into adulthood. Researchers from the state of Washington found that criminal behavior was widespread among young people. One of every four Washingtonians born in 1970 was charged with at least one delinquent offense before reaching the age of 18. Yet, only 6 percent of these delinquent youth were charged with serious crimes as adults, fewer than one in fifty residents overall (Barnoski, Aos, and Lieb 1997). In other words, for the vast majority of individuals, criminality ceases with maturation.

Similarly, most adolescents who use drugs stop on their own before they become dependent. Even most cocaine and heroin users stop using without ever reaching the point of dependence or addiction (ASREC 2003). Some drug users, however, may have difficulty stopping their use of drugs without structured interventions. A small proportion of adolescent drug users will develop lifelong substance abuse problems (Bachman et al. 2002). In fact, some researchers have estimated that 5 to 6 percent of cocaine users become dependent on cocaine within the first year of use (ASREC 2003). It is critical that juvenile justice agencies make every attempt to identify those youth headed toward severe drug problems, and as early as possible. Unfortunately, there is no foolproof way for courts or treatment agencies to intervene, and errors in the diagnostic process have serious consequences.

Box 5.2. Many Factors May Contribute to Drug Use by Adolescents

Attitudes about deviance	Personal attitudes regarding unlawful behavior are highly salient during adolescence and may shape a youth's propensity to experiment with drugs.
Social influences	Exposure to drug use by friends often contributes to an adolescent's decision to begin using drugs. Parental influence also plays a role in establishing basic norms regarding drug use and other forms of deviant behavior.
Perceived benefits	Vicarious learning from peers or past drug experiences may lead to an expectation of positive effects from drug use. Outcome expectancies may even develop in early childhood and lead to substance use during adolescence and early adulthood.
Predisposition for sensation seeking	Sensation seeking is characterized by a need for new and complex experiences as well as the acceptance of any physical and social risks associated with those experiences. Individuals measuring high in sensation seeking may even have a biologically based need for greater stimulation.
Drug use myths	False or inflated expectancies about the positive effects of drug use may encourage experimentation and early use. Beliefs in such myths could offset information about negative outcomes associated with drug use.
Perceived lack of control	Adolescents that believe they have a low degree of control over their lives may be more likely to experiment with drug use.
Co-morbidities	Drug use may represent a form of self-medication for other problems and disorders, including stress, anxiety, and depression.

Sources: Adalbjarnardottir and Rafnsson (2001); Ames, Sussman, and Dent (1999); Blum (1987); Jessor and Jessor (1975).

Diagnosis as a Social Construct

Juvenile justice and drug treatment agencies detect adolescent substance abuse using various screening and assessment instruments (see the discussion by Mears, in this volume). Some of the more popular instruments used in the juvenile justice system are the Substance Abuse Subtle Screening Inventory (or SASSI), the Global Assessment of Individual Needs (GAIN), the Massachusetts Youth Screening Instrument (MAYSI), and the Comprehensive Addiction Severity Index for Adolescents (CASI-A). Screening instruments, such as the SASSI and the MAYSI, help practitioners identify potential drug problems and select youth for further assessment. Assessment instruments, such as the GAIN and the CASI-A, are used to develop in-depth information about each youth's behavior and guide subsequent treatment efforts.

Most screening and assessment tools used in the juvenile justice system rely on the underlying logic of the DSM to categorize substance use into levels of varying severity (APA 1994).[4] The DSM is widely endorsed by clinicians, but few policymakers and other nonclinicians appreciate how much it has evolved over the past two decades. The DSM procedures for identifying drug abuse and dependence are not based strictly on medicine or pharmacology. They are derived from a consensus of practitioners and treatment researchers about the behavioral problems associated with substance use. As such, these procedures are subject to social judgments about the use of psychoactive substances. Especially after 1980, changing social mores and shifting policy values have affected how the DSM defines the severity of substance use (box 5.3).

In 1980, the DSM-III categorized drug behavior as either "nonpathological substance use," "abuse," or "dependence." To diagnose drug dependence required "the presence of physiological dependence, evidenced by either tolerance or withdrawal." An abuse diagnosis required a clinician to find "impairment in social or occupational functioning" that had lasted for at least a month. To declare a person's use of marijuana as "abuse," the 1980 version of the DSM required a clinician to report tolerance *and* either impairment (loss of job, family, friends, or repeated legal troubles) or "pathological use," which was defined as "intoxication throughout the day, use of cannabis nearly every day for at least a month, or episodes of Cannabis Delusional Disorder."

By 1994, the concept of nonpathological use no longer appeared in the DSM (DSM-IV). Substance dependence no longer required physiological dependence, but could be indicated by the presence of any three factors from a list of physiological, behavioral, and social symptoms, with or without the presence of tolerance and withdrawal. The definition of substance abuse evolved as well between 1980 and 1994.

(text continues on page 171)

Box 5.3. DSM Criteria for Substance Dependency in 1980, 1987, and 1994

1980—DSM-III

Substance dependence generally is a more severe form of Substance Use Disorder . . . and requires the presence of physiological dependence, evidenced by either tolerance or withdrawal.

Criteria for dependence vary slightly across five classes of substances: alcohol, barbiturates, opioids, amphetamines, and cannabis.

Dependence . . . requires only evidence of tolerance or withdrawal, except for alcohol and cannabis dependence, which in addition require evidence of social or occupational impairment or a pattern of pathological use.

1987—DSM-III-R

Some symptoms of the disturbance have persisted for at least one month, or occurred repeatedly over a longer period of time, *and* at least three of the following are present:

- persistent desire or one or more unsuccessful efforts to cut down or control substance use

- substance often taken in larger amounts or over a longer period than the person intended

- a great deal of time spent in activities necessary to obtain the substance (e.g., theft), taking the substance (e.g., chain smoking), or recovering from its effects

1994—DSM-IV

A maladaptive pattern of substance abuse, leading to clinically significant impairment or distress, as manifested by three (or more) of the following at any time in the same 12-month period:

- a persistent desire or unsuccessful efforts to cut down or control substance use

- substance often taken in larger amounts or over a longer period than was intended

- a great deal of time spent in activities necessary to obtain the substance (e.g., visiting multiple doctors or driving long distances), taking the substance (e.g., chain smoking), or recovering from its effects

Criteria for Cannabis Dependence
Tolerance and either of the following:

Impairment—marked loss of interest in activities previously engaged in, loss of friends, absence from work, loss of job, or legal difficulties (other than a single arrest due to possession, purchase, or sale of an illegal substance).

Pathological use—intoxication throughout the day; use of cannabis nearly every day for at least a month; episodes of Cannabis Delusional Disorder.

- Tolerance: markedly increased amounts of the substance are required to achieve the desired effect or there is a markedly diminished effect with regular use of the same dose

- important social, occupational, or recreational activities given up or reduced because of substance use

- continued substance use despite knowledge of having a persistent or recurrent social, psychological, or physical problem caused or exacerbated by the use of the substance (e.g., keeps using heroin despite family arguments about it, cocaine-induced depression, or having an ulcer made worse by drinking)

- Marked tolerance: need for markedly increased amounts of the substance (i.e., at least a 50 percent increase) to achieve intoxication or desired effect, or markedly diminished effect with continued use of the same amount

- important social, occupational, or recreational activities are given up or reduced because of substance use

- continued substance use despite knowledge of having a persistent or recurrent physical or psychological problem that is likely to have been caused or exacerbated by the substance (e.g., current cocaine use despite recognition of cocaine-induced depression, or continued drinking despite recognition that an ulcer was made worse by alcohol consumption)

- Tolerance, as defined by either of the following:
  (a) a need for markedly increased amounts of the substance to achieve intoxication or desired effect;
  (b) markedly diminished effect with continued use of the same amount of the substance

(continued)

Box 5.3. *Continued*

1980—DSM-III	1987—DSM-III-R	1994—DSM-IV
• Withdrawal: a substance-specific syndrome follows cessation of or reduction in intake of a substance that was previously regularly used by the individual to induce a psychological state of intoxication	• Frequent intoxication or withdrawal symptoms when expected to fulfill major role obligations at work, school, or home (e.g., does not go to work because hung over, goes to school or work "high," intoxicated while taking care of his or her children), or when substance use is physically hazardous (e.g., drives when intoxicated) *Note:* The following items may not apply to cannabis, hallucinogens, or phencyclidine: • characteristic withdrawal symptoms • substance often taken to relieve or avoid withdrawal symptoms	• Withdrawal, as manifested by either of the following: (a) the characteristic withdrawal syndrome for the substance (refer to criteria A and B of the criteria sets for withdrawal for the specific substances); (b) the same (or closely related) substance is taken to relieve or avoid withdrawal symptoms Specify if *with Physiological Dependence* (evidence of either tolerance or withdrawal) *without Physiological Dependence* (no evidence of tolerance or withdrawal)

Sources: American Psychiatric Association (1980, 1987, 1994).

170

In the DSM-IV, abuse could be indicated by any one of four indicators, as long as the indicator was present at some point during the previous 12 months. The indicators were

- recurrent substance-related legal problems (e.g., arrests for substance-related disorderly conduct);
- recurrent substance use in situations in which it is physically hazardous (e.g., driving an automobile or operating a machine when impaired by substance use);
- continued substance use despite having persistent or recurrent social or interpersonal problems caused or exacerbated by the effects of the substance (e.g., arguments with spouse about consequences of intoxication, physical fights);
- recurrent substance use resulting in a failure to fulfill major role obligations at work, school, or home (e.g., repeated absences or poor work performance related to substance use; substance-related absences, suspensions, or expulsions from school; neglect of children or household). (APA 1994)

These revisions to the DSM reduced the level of evidence needed for diagnoses of substance use disorders and introduced criteria that were increasingly social. The extent of the changes becomes clear when one considers the language used in 1980 to introduce the topic of substance abuse. In the DSM-III, the American Psychiatric Association stated that

> In our society, use of certain substances to modify mood or behavior under certain circumstances is generally regarded as normal and appropriate. Such use includes recreational drinking of alcohol, in which a majority of adult Americans participate, and the use of caffeine as a stimulant in the form of coffee. On the other hand, there are wide subcultural variations. In some groups even the recreational use of alcohol is frowned upon, while in other groups the use of various illegal substances for recreational purposes is widely accepted. In addition, certain substances are used medically for the alleviation of pain, relief of tension, or to suppress appetite.
>
> This diagnostic class deals with behavioral changes associated with more or less regular use of substances that affect the central nervous system. These behavioral changes in almost all subcultures would be viewed as extremely undesirable. Examples of such behavioral changes include impairment in social or occupational functioning as a consequence of substance use, inability to control use of or to stop taking the substance, and the development of serious withdrawal symptoms after cessation of or reduction in substance use. These conditions are here conceptualized as mental disorders and are therefore to be distinguished from nonpathological substance use for recreational or medical purposes. (APA 1980, 163)

This language was removed in later editions of the DSM. It would be difficult to find any official body today that would endorse a concept like "nonpathological substance use for recreational or medical purposes" (even though this is essentially why state and federal policies continue to permit the socially sanctioned, regulated use of tobacco and alcohol). The APA of 1980 clearly acknowledged the social and cultural foundations of drug use and the laws controlling it.

By the time of the DSM-IV in 1994, legal problems alone were enough to qualify an individual for a "substance abuse disorder," even in the absence of tolerance and withdrawal, and without any indications of school problems, occupational troubles, or family strife. Clinicians needed only to define how "recurrent" a person's legal problems had to be to diagnose abuse. Obviously, drug users living in communities where prohibitions against substance use are strictly enforced are more likely to encounter recurrent legal problems. According to the DSM-IV, therefore, a person's chances of being defined as a drug "abuser" rather than a drug user are partly determined by the strength and consistency of law enforcement in his or her city or neighborhood (box 5.4).

Diagnosing Adolescents

The utility of the DSM for diagnosing adolescent drug problems has long been debated. Researchers have suggested for 20 years that mental health professionals tend to overdiagnose substance abuse pathology in juveniles (Jessor and Jessor 1975; Offer, Ostrov, and Howard 1981; Blum 1987, 527). At the very least, the DSM may not produce consistent identification of drug problems across age cohorts (Fulkerson, Harrison, and Beebe 1999; Frances et al. 1995). Practitioners may err in diagnosing adolescent drug problems because diagnostic measures designed for adults fail to account for adolescent tendencies to engage in health risk behaviors of all varieties. Some critics have argued that the populations used to develop DSM diagnostic categories are unrepresentative clinical samples, and they may be very different from adolescents in general or even youth involved in the juvenile justice system (Fulkerson et al. 1999). Clinical samples include individuals who have already sought (or have been forced to accept) help for substance abuse. They are likely to have characteristics (such as strong motivation to change) that make them different from the broader population. Researchers continue to debate what impact these differences have on the understanding of adolescent substance abuse and its treatment.

Box 5.4. DSM Criteria for Substance Abuse in 1980, 1987, and 1994

1980—DSM-III	1987—DSM-III-R	1994—DSM-IV
Three criteria distinguish nonpathological substance use from substance abuse: 1. Pattern of pathological use 2. Impairment in social or occupational functioning caused by the pattern of pathological use 3. Minimal duration of disturbance of at least one month Criteria for substance abuse vary slightly across five classes of substances: alcohol, barbiturates, opiates, amphetamines, and cannabis. *Example: Criteria for Cannabis Abuse* Impairment—marked loss of interest in activities previously engaged in, loss of friends, absence from work, loss of job, or legal difficulties (other than a single arrest due to possession, purchase, or sale of an illegal substance).	The symptoms have never met the criteria for substance dependence for this class of substance. and Some symptoms of the disturbance have persisted for at least one month, or occurred repeatedly over a longer period of time. and A maladaptive pattern of psychoactive substance use indicated by at least one of the following: • recurrent use in situations in which it is physically hazardous (e.g., driving while intoxicated)	The symptoms have never met the criteria for substance dependence for this class of substance. and A maladaptive pattern of substance use leading to clinically significant impairment or distress, as manifested by one (or more) of the following, occurring within a 12-month period: • recurrent substance-related legal problems (e.g., arrests for substance-related disorderly conduct) • recurrent substance use in situations in which it is physically hazardous (e.g., driving an automobile or operating a machine when impaired by substance use)

(continued)

173

Box 5.4. *Continued*

1980—DSM-III

and

Pathological use—intoxication throughout the day; use of cannabis nearly every day for at least a month; episodes of Cannabis Delusional Disorder.

and

Duration of disturbance of at least one month.

1987—DSM-III-R

- continued substance use despite knowledge of having a persistent or recurrent social, occupational, psychological, or physical problem that is caused or exacerbated by use of the psychoactive substance

1994—DSM-IV

- continued substance use despite knowledge of having persistent or recurrent social or interpersonal problems caused or exacerbated by the effects of the substance (e.g., arguments with spouse about consequences of intoxication, physical fights)

- recurrent substance use resulting in a failure to fulfill major role obligations at work, school, or home (e.g., repeated absences or poor work performance related to substance use; substance-related absences, suspensions, or expulsions from school; neglect of children or household)

Sources: American Psychiatric Association (1980, 1987, 1994).

174

Some investigators have questioned whether adolescents can be assessed at all using DSM criteria. By definition, adolescents have shorter drug use histories. As much of the DSM depends on the duration of drug use behavior, it is unclear whether the DSM should be used to detect drug problems in adolescents (McBride et al. 1999). Fulkerson, Harrison, and Beebe (1999) argued that most adolescents will have likely matured into adulthood by the time a dependence designation is appropriate. Blum (1987) noted that withdrawal symptoms are rarely present in cases of adolescent drug users. Martin and Winters (1998) pointed out that key symptoms—withdrawal and drug-related medical problems—tend to emerge only after years of heavy use.

Another commonly noted limitation of the DSM for adolescents is that some indicators of abuse or dependence are inappropriate for teenagers, particularly younger teens. The dependence criteria in the DSM do not acknowledge differences in life responsibilities between adolescents and adults. One key indicator of abuse and dependence is a failure to fulfill important social, educational, and occupational responsibilities. Fulkerson et al. (1999) argued that it can be difficult to gauge whether adolescents are involved in appropriate amounts of work and family obligations. Moreover, judgments about a youth's school performance can be culturally relative and class specific. A particular grade point average or school attendance record that would cause great alarm in one family might be celebrated in another. Juvenile justice officials should look carefully at the substance abuse assessments used to classify young offenders referred to drug court. The differences between drug use, abuse, and dependence are becoming less and less precise, yet they can profoundly affect juvenile justice decisionmaking and the expenditure of program resources.

Implications for Policy and Practice

It will never be feasible or wise to provide court-sponsored substance abuse treatment for every juvenile that tries illegal drugs. Such a broad intervention strategy would spread resources too thin, stigmatize large numbers of youth unnecessarily, lock some nonserious offenders into a deviant life course, and expose others to punishments that could cause more harm than the substance use that precipitated their referral to juvenile drug court. Given their limited resources, juvenile drug courts have no choice but to focus their efforts where they can do the most good for the community. Drug courts must target the youth most likely to respond positively to intervention, and those most likely to escalate their substance abuse to dangerous levels without intervention. Juvenile drug courts are most effective when they focus on youth who are likely to continue using drugs until they suffer grave harm or cause serious harm to others.

Fulfilling the mission of juvenile drug courts presents a number of challenges for policy and practice. Some key challenges include the following:

- Adolescents are more likely than adults are to engage in health risk behaviors of all sorts, including drug use.
- Juvenile drug courts are designed to reduce a problem among young offenders that is highly prevalent among teenagers in general (substance use).
- The diagnostic methods used to distinguish drug use from abuse and dependence may be inexact and subject to social and cultural influence.
- The youth at greatest risk of severe problems from drug use appear to be those that go beyond alcohol and marijuana to use other illegal drugs.
- The majority (80 to 90 percent) of youth involved in juvenile drug court programs have used alcohol and marijuana only.
- Unless the target clients for juvenile drug courts are identified clearly, juvenile justice systems may end up using considerable shares of scarce resources to serve a broad population of young offenders, including many who are unlikely to have serious problems with substance abuse.

At the very least, these challenges suggest that policymakers and practitioners should clarify the intended purposes of juvenile drug court programs. Because the mission of juvenile drug court programs varies from community to community, it is not possible to assume that any youth referred to a juvenile drug court anywhere *must* have had a serious substance abuse problem. It is also not possible to assume that any youth who uses alcohol or other drugs at any time is inevitably headed toward more severe problems. Many individual and environmental factors influence whether a drug user will progress to more severe stages of drug use.

Compared with adults, adolescents have higher rates of accidents, suicides, and homicides, and are more likely to engage in unprotected sex, drive recklessly, and engage in criminal behavior (Gardner 1993). Practitioners must be aware of the wide range of adolescent risk behaviors and must attend to the differences between experimentation or limit testing and the dangerous behaviors sometimes associated with substance use. For some adolescents, antisocial risk taking may be a statement of independence from parents and authorities, while for others it may reflect a shortened frame of reference in assessing personal risks or an inadequate understanding of risks.

Interventions to reduce or stop risky behavior by adolescents should account for the developmental status and behavioral orientation of individual youth. First, interventions with juveniles must be informed by a general understanding of adolescent development. Second, intervention protocols must recognize the diversity of health risk behavior during adolescence and distinguish those behaviors associated with long-term harm from time-limited behaviors that may fall within the normative range of adolescent development. Third, intervention approaches should be consistent with empirical knowledge about the actual impact of substance abuse treatment on adolescent populations in the justice system. Treatment programs must be prepared to offer a range of interventions that address varying drug-related behaviors of young people, whether they are experimental, chronic, or life-threatening.

In designing effective interventions for drug and alcohol problems among adolescent offenders, practitioners must be able to identify the parameters of normative development and behavior within specific social contexts, and they should know how to ensure that their understanding is reflected in the timing, delivery, and purpose of the justice process, substance abuse treatment, and other services. For example, what cognitive and developmental capacities are necessary for young people to understand and participate in the juvenile justice system? How should juvenile drug courts adapt their processes to the needs and capacities of adolescent clients?

A juvenile's ability to comprehend complex information directly affects his or her experience in court. To maximize the effectiveness of services and sanctions, the courtroom process should be easy to interpret and relatively short. At a minimum, courtroom communications should be clear and jargon free, and the process should begin soon after the precipitating offense. Timeliness is especially important given adolescents' differing perceptions of time. Adolescents and adults experience similar lengths of time differently, and teenagers are likely to discount the negative effects of delayed consequences (Butts 1997; Fried and Reppucci 2001). Courtroom dynamics may be especially critical for younger adolescents.

Developmental variations may also directly affect how adolescents will likely react to group settings. The juvenile drug court process in particular depends on adolescent group dynamics for part of its effectiveness. The importance of peer groups at various stages of adolescence may affect an individual's response to the court process. Concern about peer approval may be highest during early adolescence (age 10 to 14) and substantially diminished by middle adolescence (age 14 to 17) when independence and autonomy become paramount concerns. Attempts to influence behavior through peer group dynamics, however, may be ineffective even for youth in the early stages of adolescence. Some research suggests that peer-oriented interventions for young adolescent substance users could actually be harmful, leading to increased rather than reduced risk behavior (Poulin, Dishion, and Burraston 2001).

Finally, regardless of the severity of substance use problems detected among clients of juvenile drug court programs, policymakers and practitioners should not lose sight of the illegal behaviors that brought youth into contact with the juvenile justice system. When young offenders fail to comply with the requirements of juvenile drug court, the court may place them in secure detention for a day or two as a sanction. Particularly defiant juveniles may be placed in detention repeatedly for longer and longer periods as the juvenile drug court attempts to secure cooperation. Detention decisions made in juvenile drug courts should be viewed in light of the youth's illegal behavior. Many youth referred to juvenile drug court programs have committed relatively minor acts of delinquency. In fact, those who have committed serious or violent crimes are often excluded from drug court eligibility. Some juvenile drug court clients may be charged with drug and alcohol possession alone or with other minor offenses typically seen in juvenile courts, including running away, curfew violations, vandalism, and shoplifting. Holding such offenders in a secure detention facility could cause them undue harm. For many youth, confinement in a secure facility with serious juvenile offenders would be far more harmful than the alcohol or marijuana use that brought them to drug court in the first place.

Conclusion

Adolescents that use drugs are engaging in potentially dangerous behavior that could create havoc in their lives and their families' lives. Ignoring the risks associated with this behavior is irresponsible, but overreacting is equally problematic. All juveniles using illicit drugs have broken the law, but this fact does not mean that they should all be drawn into the juvenile justice system for extended treatment and intervention. Juvenile drug courts may be a powerful tool in the fight against adolescent substance abuse, but they must be designed carefully and targeted precisely.

NOTES

1. Before 2002, the National Survey on Drug Use and Health was known as the National Household Survey on Drug Abuse.

2. Juvenile interview data for the study were collected during 1995–98 (Teplin et al. 2002, 1134), a period of conflict over population levels in the Cook County Juvenile Temporary Detention Center. In 1999, a class action lawsuit was filed on behalf of detainees placed in a facility that was designed to contain no more than 495 youth but often housed 600 to 800 juveniles at a time (*Jimmy Doe et al. v. Superintendent of the Cook County Juvenile Detention Center,* U.S. District Court for the Northern District of Illinois, Eastern Division, No. 99 C 3945).

3. Gregory Aarons, e-mail correspondence with Jeffrey Butts, May 2, 2003.

4. Some assessment instruments do not use the DSM and rely instead on the Addiction Severity Index (ASI). The ASI assesses problem behaviors across seven domains: employment, interpersonal relations, physical health, mental health, criminal behavior, alcohol abuse, and drug abuse. Another alternative to the DSM, the International Classification of Diseases (ICD), was developed by the World Health Organization to compile international statistics on the causes of death and illness, including those related to alcohol and drug abuse. The most recent version, ICD-10, includes indicators of drug dependence as well as a category called "harmful use" (Babor 1992; Rounsaville et al. 1993).

REFERENCES

Aarons, Gregory A., Sandra A. Brown, Richard L. Hough, Ann F. Garland, and Patricia A. Wood. 2001. "Prevalence of Adolescent Substance Use Disorders across Five Sectors of Care." *Journal of the American Academy of Child and Adolescent Psychiatry* 40(4): 419–26.

Abram, Karen M. 1989. "The Effect of Co-Occurring Disorders on Criminal Careers: Interaction of Antisocial Personality, Alcoholism, and Drug Disorders." *International Journal of Law and Psychiatry* 12(2–3): 133–48.

Adalbjarnardottir, Sigrun, and Fjolvar Darri Rafnsson. 2001. "Perceived Control in Adolescent Substance Use: Concurrent and Longitudinal Analyses." *Psychology of Addictive Behaviors* 15(1): 25–32.

Addiction Science Research and Education Center. 2003. "Drug Facts." Austin: University of Texas, College of Pharmacy. http://www.utexas.edu/research/asrec/index.html.

American Psychiatric Association. 1980. *Diagnostic and Statistical Manual of Mental Disorders,* 3rd ed. Washington, DC: American Psychiatric Association.

———. 1987. *Diagnostic and Statistical Manual of Mental Disorders,* 3rd ed. rev. Washington, DC: American Psychiatric Association.

———. 1994. *Diagnostic and Statistical Manual of Mental Disorders,* 4th ed. Washington, DC: American Psychiatric Association.

Ames, Susan L., Steve Sussman, and Clyde W. Dent. 1999. "Pro-Drug-Use Myths and Competing Constructs in the Prediction of Substance Use among Youth at Continuation High Schools." *Personality and Individual Differences* 26:987–1003.

APA. *See* American Psychiatric Association.

ASREC. *See* Addiction Science Research and Education Center.

Babor, Thomas F. 1992. "Substance-Related Problems in the Context of International Classificatory Systems." In *The Nature of Alcohol and Drug Related Problems,* edited by Malcolm H. Lader, Griffith Edwards, and D. Colin Drummond (83–99). New York: Oxford University Press.

Bachman, Jerald G., Patrick M. O'Malley, John E. Schulenberg, Lloyd D. Johnston, Alison L. Bryant, and Alicia C. Merline. 2002. *The Decline of Substance Use in Young Adulthood: Changes in Social Activities, Roles, and Beliefs.* Mahwah, NJ: Lawrence Erlbaum Associates, Inc.

Barnoski, Robert, Steve Aos, and Roxanne Lieb. 1997. *The Class of 1988, Seven Years Later: How a Juvenile Offender's Crime, Criminal History, and Age Affect the Chances of Becoming an Adult Felon in Washington State.* Olympia: Washington State Institute for Public Policy.

Blum, Robert W. 1987. "Adolescent Substance Abuse: Diagnostic and Treatment Issues." *Pediatric Clinics of North America* 34(2): 523–31.

Burton, Linda M., Kevin W. Allison, and Dawn Obeidallah. 1995. "Social Context and Adolescence: Perspectives on Development among Inner-City African-American Teens." In *Pathways through Adolescence: Individual Development in Relation to Social Contexts,* edited by Lisa J. Crockett and Ann C. Crouter (119–38). Mahwah, NJ: Lawrence Erlbaum Associates, Inc.

Butts, Jeffrey A. 1997. "Necessarily Relative: Is Juvenile Justice Speedy Enough?" *Crime and Delinquency* 43(1): 3–23.

Committee on Community-Level Programs for Youth. 2002. *Community Programs to Promote Youth Development,* edited by Jacquelynne Eccles and Jennifer A. Gootman. Washington, DC: National Academy Press.

Cooper, Caroline S. 2001. "Juvenile Drug Court Programs." *JAIBG Bulletin.* NCJ 184744. Washington, DC: U.S. Department of Justice, Office of Juvenile Justice and Delinquency Prevention.

Cote, Gilles, and Sheilagh Hodgins. 1990. "Co-Occurring Mental Disorders among Criminal Offenders." *Bulletin of the American Academy of Psychiatry and the Law* 18(3): 271–81.

Crockett, Lisa J., and Anne C. Petersen. 1993. "Adolescent Development: Health Risks and Opportunities for Health Promotion." In *Promoting the Health of Adolescents: New Directions for the Twenty-First Century,* edited by Susan G. Millstein, Anne C. Petersen, and Elena O. Nightingale (13–37). New York: Oxford University Press.

Crowley, Thomas J., Marilyn J. Macdonald, Elizabeth A. Whitmore, and Susan K. Mikulich. 1998. "Cannabis Dependence, Withdrawal, and Reinforcing Effects among Adolescents with Conduct Symptoms and Substance Use Disorders." *Drug and Alcohol Dependence* 50(1): 27–37.

Dembo, Richard, Lawrence la Voie, James Schmeidler, and Mark Washburn. 1987. "The Nature and Correlates of Psychological/Emotional Functioning among a Sample of Detained Youths." *Criminal Justice and Behavior* 14(3): 311–34.

Elliot, Delbert S. 1993. "Health-Enhancing and Health-Compromising Lifestyles." In *Promoting the Health of Adolescents: New Directions for the Twenty-First Century*, edited by Susan G. Millstein, Anne C. Petersen, and Elena O. Nightingale (119–45). New York: Oxford University Press.

Elliott, Glen R., and S. Shirley Feldman. 1990. "Capturing the Adolescent Experience." In *At the Threshold: The Developing Adolescent*, edited by S. Shirley Feldman and Glen R. Elliott (1–12). Cambridge: Harvard University Press.

Federal Interagency Forum on Child and Family Statistics. 2002. *America's Children: Key National Indicators of Well-Being 2002*. Appendix A: Detailed Tables. http:// childstats.gov/ac2002/pdf/appendixa.pdf.

Fenwick, Elizabeth, and Tony Smith. 1994. *Adolescence*. New York: Dorling Kindersley Publishing.

Frances, Allen, Avrum Mack, Michael B. First, and Cindy Jones. 1995. "DSM-IV Issues in Development." *Psychiatric Annals* 25(1):15–19.

Fried, Carrie S., and N. Dickon Reppucci. 2001. "Criminal Decision Making: The Development of Adolescent Judgement, Criminal Responsibility, and Culpability." *Law and Human Behavior* 25(1): 45–61.

Fulkerson, Jayne A., Patricia A. Harrison, and Timothy J. Beebe. 1999. "DSM-IV Substance Abuse and Dependence: Are There Really Two Dimensions of Substance Use Disorders in Adolescents?" *Addiction* 94(4): 495–506.

Gardner, William. 1993. "A Lifespan Rational-Choice Theory of Risk Taking." In *Adolescent Risk Taking*, edited by Nancy J. Bell and Robert W. Bell (66–83). Thousand Oaks, CA: Sage Publications.

Gleitman, Henry. 1991. *Psychology*, 3rd ed. New York: W. W. Norton and Company.

Grisso, Thomas. 1996. "Society's Retributive Response to Juvenile Violence: A Developmental Perspective. *Law and Human Behavior* 20(3): 229–47.

Harms, Paul. 2003. "Detention in Delinquency Cases, 1990–1999." OJJDP Fact Sheet 200307. Washington, DC: U.S. Department of Justice, Office of Juvenile Justice and Delinquency Prevention.

Havighurst, Robert J. 1972. *Developmental Tasks and Education*, 3rd ed. New York: David McKay Co.

Hawkins, J. David, Karl G. Hill, Jie Guo, and Sara R. Battin-Pearson. 2002. "Substance Use Norms and Transitions in Substance Use: Implications for the Gateway Hypothesis." In *Stages and Pathways of Drug Involvement: Examining the Gateway Hypothesis*, edited by Denise B. Kandel (42–64). Cambridge, U.K.: Cambridge University Press.

Hetherington, E. Mavis, and Ross D. Parke. 1986. *Child Psychology: A Contemporary Viewpoint*, 3rd ed. New York: McGraw Hill Boon Co.

Iversen, Leslie. 2000. *The Science of Marijuana*. New York: Oxford University Press.

Jenson, Jeffrey M., and Matthew O. Howard. 1999. "Hallucinogen Use among Juvenile Probationers: Prevalence and Characteristics." *Criminal Justice and Behavior* 26(3): 357–72.

Jessor, Richard, and Shirley Jessor. 1975. "Adolescent Development and the Onset of Drinking." *Journal of Studies on Alcohol* 36(1): 27–51.

Johnston, Lloyd D., Patrick M. O'Malley, and Jerald G. Bachman. 2002. "2002 Data From In-School Surveys of 8th, 10th, and 12th Grade Students." http://www.monitoringthefuture.org/data/02data.html#2002data-drugs.

———. 2003. *Secondary School Students.* Vol. 1 of *Monitoring the Future: National Survey Results on Drug Use, 1975–2002.* Bethesda, MD: National Institute on Drug Abuse.

Kandel, Denise B., and Kazuo Yamaguchi. 2002. "Stages of Drug Involvement in the U.S. Population." In *Stages and Pathways of Drug Involvement: Examining the Gateway Hypothesis,* edited by Denise B. Kandel (65–89). Cambridge, U.K.: Cambridge University Press.

Kenkel, Donald, Alan D. Mathios, and Rosalie L. Pacula. 2001. "Economics of Youth Drug Use, Addiction, and Gateway Effects." *Addiction* 96:151–64.

Kipke, Michele D., ed. 1999. *Risks and Opportunities: Synthesis of Studies on Adolescence.* Washington, DC: National Academy Press.

Konopka, Gisela. 1973. "Requirements for Healthy Development of Adolescent Youth." *Adolescence* 8(31): 291–316.

Labouvie, Erich, and Helene R. White. 2002. "Drug Sequences, Age of Onset, and Use Trajectories as Predictors of Drug Abuse/Dependence in Young Adulthood." In *Stages and Pathways of Drug Involvement: Examining the Gateway Hypothesis,* edited by Denise B. Kandel (19–41). Cambridge, U.K.: Cambridge University Press.

Lynskey, Michael T., Andrew C. Heath, Kathleen K. Bucholz, Wendy S. Slutske, Pamela A. F. Madden, Elliot C. Nelson, Dixie J. Statham, and Nicholas G. Martin. 2003. "Escalation of Drug Use in Early-Onset Cannabis Users vs. Co-Twin Controls." *Journal of the American Medical Association* 289(4): 427–33.

Martin, Christopher S., and Ken C. Winters. 1998. "Diagnosis and Assessment of Alcohol Use Disorders among Adolescents." *Alcohol Health and Research World* 22:95–105.

McBride, Duane C., Curtis VanderWaal, Yvonne M. Terry, and Holly VanBuren. 1999. *Breaking the Cycle of Drug Use among Juvenile Offenders.* Washington, DC: National Institute of Justice.

McCauley, Ann P., and Cynthia Salter. 1995. *Meeting the Needs of Young Adults.* Population Report J 41. Baltimore, MD: Johns Hopkins School of Public Health, Population Information Program.

Money, J. 1980. *Love and Love Sickness: The Science of Sex, Gender Difference, and Pair-Bonding.* Baltimore, MD: Johns Hopkins University Press.

Morral, Andrew R., Daniel F. McCaffrey, and Susan M. Paddock. 2002. "Reassessing the Marijuana Gateway Effect." *Addiction* 97:1493–1504.

National Drug Court Institute and National Council of Juvenile and Family Court Judges. 2003. *Juvenile Drug Courts: Strategies in Practice.* NCJ187866. Washington, DC: U.S. Department of Justice, Bureau of Justice Assistance.

National Institute of Justice. 2000. *1999 Annual Report on Drug Use among Adult and Juvenile Arrestees. Juvenile Program Findings.* Washington, DC: U.S. Department of Justice, Office of Justice Programs, National Institute of Justice. http://www.ncjrs. org/pdffiles1/nij/181426.pdf.

NDCI/NCJFCJ. *See* National Drug Court Institute and National Council of Juvenile and Family Court Judges.

Offer, Daniel, Eric Ostrov, and Kenneth I. Howard. 1981. "The Mental Health Professional's Concept of the Normal Adolescent." *Archives of General Psychiatry* 38(2): 149–52.

Office of Justice Programs. 1999. *Juvenile Drug Court Activity Update: Summary Information, June 1999.* OJP Drug Court Clearinghouse and Technical Assistance Project. Washington, DC: American University. http://www.american.edu/spa/justice/publications/Juvoverviewinsert.htm.

Perry, Cheryl L. 2000. "Preadolescent and Adolescent Influences on Health." In *Promoting Health: Intervention Strategies from Social and Behavioral Research,* edited by Brian D. Smedley and S. Leonard Syme (217–53). Washington, DC: National Academy Press.

Poulin, François, Thomas J. Dishion, and Bert Burraston. 2001. "3-Year Iatrogenic Effects Associated with Aggregating High-Risk Adolescents in Cognitive-Behavioral Preventive Interventions." *Applied Developmental Science* 5:214–24.

Pursley, William L. 1991. "Adolescence, Chemical Dependency, and Pathological Gambling." *Journal of Adolescent Chemical Dependency* 1(4): 25–47.

Rapp, Melanie. 1998. "Adolescent Development: An Emotional Roller Coaster." In *Young Adults and Public Libraries,* edited by Mary Anne Nichols and C. Allen Nichols (1–10). Westport, CT: Greenwood Press.

Reppucci, N. Dickon, and Jennifer L. Woolard. 1999. *Competence and Judgment in Serious Juvenile Offenders, Part I: Developmental Implications for Adolescent Offenders.* Washington, DC: U.S. Department of Justice, Office of Juvenile Justice and Delinquency Prevention.

Rounsaville, Bruce J., Kendall Bryant, Thomas Babor, Henry Kranzler, and R. Kadden. 1993. "Cross System Agreement for Substance Use Disorders: DSM-III-R, DSM-IV, and ICD-10." *Addiction* 88(3): 337–48.

SAMHSA. *See* Substance Abuse and Mental Health Services Administration.

Steinberg, Laurence. 1995. "Commentary: On Developmental Pathways and Social Contexts in Adolescence." In *Pathways through Adolescence: Individual Development in Relation to Social Contexts,* edited by Lisa J. Crockett and Ann C. Crouter (245–55). Mahwah, NJ: Lawrence Erlbaum Associates, Inc.

Steinberg, Laurence, and Robert G. Schwartz. 2000. "Developmental Psychology Goes to Court." In *Youth on Trial,* edited by Thomas Grisso and Robert G. Schwartz (9–31). Chicago: The University of Chicago Press.

Stover, L. T., and E. Tway. 1992. "Cultural Diversity and the Young Adult Novel." In *Reading Their World: The Young Adult Novel in the Classroom,* edited by Virginia R. Monseau and Gary M. Salvner (132–54). Portsmouth, NH: Boynton/Cook.

Substance Abuse and Mental Health Services Administration. 1999; 2000. Results from the National Household Survey on Drug Abuse. Rockville, MD: Substance Abuse and Mental Health Services Administration, Department of Health and Human Services.

———. 2002. *Summary of National Findings.* Vol. 1 of *Results from the 2001 National Survey on Drug Use and Health.* NHSDA Series H-17, DHHS Publication No. SMA 02-3758. Rockville, MD: Substance Abuse and Mental Health Services Administration.

————. 2003. *Summary of National Findings*. Vol. 1 of *Results from the 2002 National Survey on Drug Use and Health*. NHSDA Series H-22, DHHS Publication No. SMA 03-3836. Rockville, MD: Substance Abuse and Mental Health Services Administration.

Susman, E. J. 1997. "Modeling Developmental Complexity in Adolescence: Hormones and Behavior in Context." *Journal of Research on Adolescence* 7(3): 283–306.

Taylor, Ronald J. 1998. *Recommendations Regarding the Planning of a Drug Court for Juvenile and Youthful Adult Drug Offenders in the Twenty-Sixth Judicial District: Madison, Henderson, and Chester Counties, Tennessee*. OJP Drug Court Clearinghouse and Technical Assistance Project. Washington, DC: American University. http://www.american.edu/spa/justice/publications/96report_tenn.htm.

Teplin, Linda A., Karen M. Abram, Gary M. McClelland, Mina K. Dulcan, and Amy A. Mericle. 2002. "Psychiatric Disorders in Youth in Juvenile Detention." *Archives of General Psychiatry* 59(Dec): 1133–43.

Wagner, Fernando, and James C. Anthony. 2001. "Into the World of Illegal Drug Use: Exposure Opportunity and Other Mechanisms Linking the Use of Alcohol, Tobacco, Marijuana, and Cocaine." *American Journal of Epidemiology* 155(10): 918–25.

Wasserman, Gail A., Larkin S. McReynolds, Susan J. Ko, Laura M. Katz, and Jennifer R. Carpenter. Forthcoming. "Gender Differences in Psychiatric Disorders at Juvenile Probation Intake." *American Journal of Public Health*.

Winters, Ken C., William W. Latimer, and Randy Stinchfield. 2001. "Assessing Adolescent Substance Abuse." In *Innovations in Adolescent Substance Abuse Interventions*, edited by Eric Wagner and Holly B. Waldron (1–29). New York: Elsevier.

Zweig, Janine M., Laura Duberstein Lindberg, and Karen Alexander McGinley. 2001. "Adolescent Health Risk Profiles: The Co-Occurrence of Health Risks among Females and Males." *Journal of Youth and Adolescence* 30(6): 707–28.

Zweig, Janine M., Stacey D. Phillips, and Laura Duberstein Lindberg. 2002. "Predicting Adolescent Profiles of Risk: Looking Beyond Demographics." *Journal of Adolescent Health* 31(4): 343–53.

6

Identifying Adolescent Substance Abuse

Daniel P. Mears

Practitioners and policymakers are increasingly interested in effective drug treatment for young offenders, including strategies for providing treatment at earlier stages of the juvenile justice system. Researchers have responded by trying to identify drug treatment interventions that work, but evaluating the effectiveness of drug treatment first requires a method of establishing that a drug problem exists. The question arises: How do we know when a juvenile has a drug problem that requires treatment? To answer this question, this chapter addresses five more specific questions about the screening and assessment of drug problems among juvenile offenders: (1) What purposes do drug screening and assessment serve? (2) What are the elements of effective drug screening instruments and assessment instruments? (3) Which juvenile drug screening and assessment instruments are recommended? (4) What drug screening and assessment instruments are most often employed in juvenile justice settings? and (5) What are some primary challenges in implementing drug screening and assessment instruments? These questions are answered by reviewing research on drug treatment screening and assessment.

In 1998, roughly 138,000 youth age 12 to 17 entered publicly funded drug treatment facilities. This number was 45 percent higher than the number of admissions in 1993. Juvenile and criminal justice system referrals for drug treatment increased markedly during this period, growing from 39 to 49 percent of all admissions (Substance Abuse and Mental

Health Services Administration [SAMHSA] 2001). Increases in juvenile drug treatment have generated concern among policymakers that drug problems should be identified and treated before they lead drug users to become further involved in the criminal justice system (Horgan, Skwara, and Strickler 2001). In response, researchers have begun to focus on identifying and assessing prevention and early intervention programs that treat drug problems among at-risk juveniles and juvenile offenders (Winters 1999b). By focusing on what works, policymakers, researchers, and the public hope to significantly reduce delinquency and improve the physical, mental, and social health of young people (Tonry and Wilson 1990; Sherman et al. 1997; Crowe 1998; General Accounting Office [GAO] 1998). These efforts assume that there are physical, social, or development problems that can be objectively identified as "drug problems." They also assume that the severity of these problems, or more simply the difference between the existence and absence of these problems, can be reliably measured. But what are "drug problems" exactly, and how do practitioners identify and measure them?

This chapter examines the screening and assessment of drug problems and the corresponding need for drug treatment. It does not address methods of assessing all risks and needs among juvenile offenders, nor does it investigate the best techniques of choosing drug treatment modalities and strategies for specific types of offenders. Although these tasks entail a similar process of identifying and assessing key dimensions that may affect treatment effectiveness (Cullen and Gendreau 2000; Loeber and Farrington 2001), they are distinct from what might be viewed as the necessary precondition of effective drug treatment—the accurate identification of drug problems.

Screening and Assessment

Drug screening and assessment instruments facilitate a more general process aimed at identifying the drug treatment needs of juvenile offenders (Leccese and Waldron 1994; Peters and Peyton 1998; Shearer and Carter 1999; Grisso and Barnum 2000; Winters 1999a; Winters, Latimer, and Stinchfield 2001; Grisso and Underwood 2003; Poteet-Johnson and Dias 2003). The use of instruments, as opposed to purely subjective approaches, can ensure more consistent and accurate identification of drug problems.

Within the juvenile justice system, screening instruments aim to identify potential drug problems among youth—they essentially raise a flag,
through a brief evaluation process conducted by an intake officer, that a
problem may need to be addressed (Peters and Bartoi 1997). It should be
emphasized that drug screens differ from clinical screens—the former test
for the presence of a drug, while the latter test for the presence of a drug
problem. The initial screening is typically conducted by a practitioner with
relatively little training and usually does not involve a drug screen. Youth
with possible drug problems are then referred to clinically trained professionals for more in-depth assessment to determine if a problem exists.
If there is a problem, further assessment is undertaken to develop an
intervention plan.

Screening instruments often identify other potential problem areas
besides drug use, such as family conflicts and mental illness. They also can
identify a youth's major strengths and deficits, factors that may affect treatment (such as cognitive limitations and motivation), and the minimum
level of security needed to effectively supervise the youth (Peters and Peyton 1998). Assessment instruments provide more in-depth and accurate
information that can be used to guide the diagnosis and treatment of drug
problems and other areas of need, including education, mental health,
peer relationships, and family and school functioning. Assessments, which
are typically conducted by trained clinicians, may reveal that identified
drug problems appear linked to these different areas, either as a result or a
cause of problems in each. This information can in turn guide treatment
planning for drug problems and co-occurring disorders.

Screening and assessing juvenile offenders for drug problems is thus
part of a more general process that can be implemented to identify potential risks and needs, as well as appropriate sanctions and intervention
plans. Figure 6.1 outlines this process.

Although screening and assessment can occur at intake (i.e., when
youth are referred by the police or schools to a probation department),
they can also be conducted at other stages of the juvenile justice system,
such as entry into secure confinement facilities or residential treatment
programs. Screening and assessment involve distinct steps. At intake, for
example, youth are screened to identify their full range of potential risks
and needs. If a crisis is identified, such as a youth at risk of suicide or with
a medical situation requiring immediate action, it is dealt with before
proceeding. In the absence of a crisis, or after a crisis has been resolved, an
assessment plan is initiated. This plan reviews past assessments, current

Figure 6.1. *Effective Screening and Assessment Can Identify Drug Problems and Develop Interventions More Effectively*

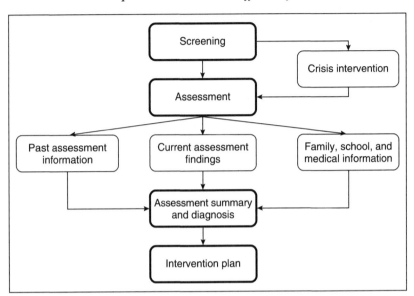

Source: Adapted from Winters (1999a, 20).

assessments that further investigate issues identified during screening, and information from families, schools, doctors, the child welfare system, and other sources. Based on this plan, an assessment summary and diagnosis is generated that provides the foundation for creating an intervention plan.

Developing an intervention plan may entail further assessment to evaluate a youth's full set of risk and protective factors as well as his or her amenability to treatment (Peters and Bartoi 1997), and to determine the most appropriate treatment approach (Winters et al. 2001, 6). Assessments can be undertaken periodically during treatment to gauge an individual's progress; they can also be undertaken after treatment to measure how well the intervention has improved outcomes. Inciardi (1993) makes a stronger recommendation, arguing that continuous and repeated assessments are important throughout all stages of the justice system.

Winters (1999a, 13) summarizes several guidelines for conducting and using screening and assessment instruments:

- Ensure that instruments are properly administered (e.g., in the recommended manner, with the appropriate populations);
- Train staff regarding the validity and reliability of the instruments and any limitations or cautions of the instruments;
- Use appropriate norm-based considerations (e.g., the test setting and conditions) and cut-off points for specific age, sex, race/ethnicity, or other populations;
- Ensure that instruments are accurately scored; and
- Train staff to interpret instrument results and effectively convey this information to individuals who have been tested.

Adherence to the guidelines is critical for several reasons. It means drug problems are identified more efficiently and effectively. It also ensures that youth with drug problems are accurately identified and that those without drug problems are not misidentified as needing drug treatment. As a result, scarce resources can be put to use more effectively, and potential unintended effects of treating offenders without drug problems can be avoided. Relying on trained professionals—who can ensure the correct administration, scoring, and interpretation of results—is essential for avoiding unintended misuse, especially in assessments. Trained professionals can also be important when using screening instruments, but not always. Indeed, screening instruments are typically constructed to minimize reliance on trained professionals. Even so, they must be administered by practitioners who have been trained to administer, score, and interpret the results correctly.

Screening and assessment processes are especially relevant for drug courts. As Peters and Peyton (1998, 6) emphasized,

> Candidates for drug court programs typically have a wide range of substance abuse, mental health, and other health-related disorders, in addition to many psychosocial problems. . . . Many of these deficits are not clearly apparent through examination of . . . records, but can be revealed through an individualized interview, drug testing, and use of specialized instruments.

Screening and assessment processes can link to all aspects of drug court operations. If implemented well, they can ensure the accurate identification of youth with drug problems and co-occurring disorders, and the sharing and dissemination of information critical to making decisions about treatment. If implemented poorly, problems can arise; indeed, even good implementation can result in potential misuse of the resulting information.

Elements of Effective Screening and Assessment Instruments

Screening and assessment instruments constitute a critical part of any process for identifying youth with drug problems. So, the question arises, what are the elements of effective screening and assessment instruments? The sections below describe the elements specific to each type of instrument.

Effective Screening Instruments

Screening "serves as a 'first look' at the possibility of a youth's special mental health needs, but typically it does not seek to diagnose a mental disorder or to provide information on which important and long-term interventions should be decided" (Grisso and Barnum 2000, 11). Screening instruments are flag-raisers, and effective ones thus cover a wide range of areas and issues. That is, they identify specific potential problems, such as drug abuse or mental illness, that may merit closer investigation. Validating screening instruments involves estimating how well they produce results associated with those from more in-depth, area-specific instruments that focus on drug addiction, mental disorders, or other problems.

By their very nature, screening instruments do not provide in-depth assessments. They do not, for example, confirm the presence of drug addiction. But, if they are effective flag-raisers, then they should correlate with area-specific assessment instruments.

It is generally best for screening instruments to err on the side of over-inclusiveness to ensure they include all youth who might have a serious problem—however a problem is defined—for more intensive assessment (Leccese and Waldron 1994; Grisso and Barnum 2000). That is, screening instruments should accurately identify all youth who may have a serious drug problem, even if that means incorrectly identifying some who in fact do not have problems, what statistically are called "false positives." But it is also necessary to minimize the number of false positives to avoid conducting unnecessary and more costly assessments. In addition, screening instruments should minimize "false negatives"—that is, cases in which youth are identified as not having drug problems when in fact they do. Failure to capture drug problems in an initial screening can mean youth will not receive treatment.

The basic psychometric properties or criteria used to validate and compare the relative utility of screening instruments are similar to those used for assessment instruments. In addition to standard measures of reliability and validity, these criteria include overall accuracy, sensitivity, positive predictive accuracy, specificity, and negative predictive accuracy. These criteria are discussed in the "Reliability and Validity of Assessment Instruments" section.

Effective Assessment Instruments

The goal of any assessment process is to consistently and accurately determine if an individual has a drug problem. So, a logical first step is to define a drug problem and then develop instruments that can reliably and validly measure the existence of the problem. Given a set of instruments, researchers then need criteria by which to compare them and determine which ones may work best in a particular population or setting.

CHALLENGES IN DEFINING A "DRUG PROBLEM"

Practitioners and researchers typically believe that drug treatment is appropriate when somebody has a drug problem. The challenge lies in identifying what exactly a "drug problem" is, and for that juvenile drug courts typically rely on assessment instruments and clinical judgment. Ultimately, however, any definition is arbitrary in the sense that reasonable people may disagree about what criteria must be met for a problem to exist. For some, drug use in the past week, month, or year may constitute an appropriate definition. From this perspective, a considerable portion of the youth population has a drug problem. For example, among high school seniors surveyed in 2001 about their drug experiences in the previous year, 73 percent reported that at least on one occasion they used alcohol, 37 percent reported smoking marijuana or hashish, 20 percent reported using any illicit drug except marijuana, and 11 percent said they used amphetamines (Johnston, O'Malley, and Bachman 2002, table 6.2).

Other people may find a definition focused solely on use too limiting. For them, the definition may center on the severity of drug use, as captured by such dimensions as frequency or volume. For still others, the definition may include several components, such as severity of use and its effects on personal, interpersonal, or social functioning. There is no single agreed-upon definition or measure of a drug problem, although some, such as the ones provided in the Diagnostic Statistical Manual, fourth edition (DSM-IV), are commonly used or have a relatively strong empirical foundation.

The Diagnostic Statistical Manual approach to defining a drug problem. The DSM-IV is perhaps the most widely used source for determining the need for drug treatment. The DSM-IV distinguishes between two types of drug problems: substance abuse disorder and substance dependency disorder, the latter more conventionally termed addiction (box 6.1).

For clinicians to classify individuals as having a substance abuse disorder, one or more of the specified conditions must be met during a 12-month period; to classify individuals as having a substance dependency disorder, three or more conditions must be met during a 12-month period. The conditions for substance abuse disorder focus on the frequency of drug use, the use of drugs in particular situations, negative outcomes that can be linked to the drug use, and pronounced drug use in the face of evidence that drugs are contributing to personal and interpersonal problems. In contrast, the conditions for *substance dependency disorder* are broader, including physical symptomatology, such as tolerance and withdrawal, and patterns of behavior aimed at either unsuccessfully reducing the influence of drugs or allowing for greater amounts of drugs to be taken.

It is important to emphasize that the "DSM-IV is not based on a gold standard" (Fulkerson, Harrison, and Beebe 1999, 495; Frances et al. 1995). That is, there is no single definition or measure of a drug problem, or types of drug problems, that can be used to validate the DSM-IV drug disorders. The lack of agreement about the most useful and appropriate definition stems from differing opinions among researchers about the classification scheme that best captures the full range and severity of possible drug problems (Winters et al. 2001).

The difficulty of identifying useful and widely agreed-upon definitions of drug problems is reflected in part by the considerable challenges the creators of the DSM faced in modifying the substance use disorder classifications. Fulkerson et al. (1999, 496) described some of the more prominent ones:

> In DSM-III, substance dependence was defined by the presence of either pathological use or substance-related impairments in social or occupational functioning in conjunction with manifestations of tolerance or withdrawal; abuse was defined as pathological use or impairment without tolerance or withdrawal (American Psychiatric Association 1980). In the revision of these criteria, the intent of the Sub-

stance Use Disorders Work Group was to drop the substance abuse diagnosis category (Rounsaville et al. 1986; Schuckit et al. 1991); however, the category was
retained because of insufficient data to support the change (Schuckit et al. 1991).
As a result, in DSM-III-R, the definition of substance dependence was broadened
substantially while substance abuse became a residual category (American Psychiatric Association 1987). In 1988, the Substance Use Disorders Work Group again
was faced with revision of the diagnostic schema and it "spent more of its time considering alternative concepts and definitions of substance abuse and dependence
and their impact on possible modifications in the criteria for abuse and dependence
than on any other single issue" (Nathan 1991:356).

The importance of classifications should not be underestimated. As
with any social program or policy, a drug intervention is significantly
more likely to be effective if the problem to be treated is clearly identified (Rossi, Freeman, and Lipsey 1999; Winters et al. 2001). It thus is
striking that researchers disagree about the relative utility of the definitions and classifications used in different versions of the DSM compared with those found in other sources. The disagreement reflects
different conceptual and theoretical orientations (Nathan and Langenbucher 1999). It also reflects the findings of studies that apply the
DSM-IV (and previous versions of the DSM) to adult populations and
clinical samples. This research suggests, for example, that more than
one type of dependence may exist. And studies have identified, through
factor analysis and other related statistical procedures, different arrangements of the clusters of behaviors listed in the DSM-IV, arrangements
that do not always conform to the abuse and dependence classifications
(Harrison, Fulkerson, and Beebe 1998; Fulkerson et al. 1999; Nelson
et al. 1999).

Definitional issues are even more pronounced in assessing drug problems among adolescent populations. The DSM-IV, for example, has been
critiqued for not taking into account the fact that some drug-related medical conditions, such as tolerance and withdrawal, emerge only after several years. Thus, these conditions cannot typically be applied to youth
(Martin and Winters 1998), although some youth, including those who
enter the juvenile justice system, may have long-standing histories of
drug use. The DSM-IV criteria also create "diagnostic orphans"—that is,
situations in which a youth may exhibit up to two dependence symptoms
and no abuse symptoms and yet not fall into either the abuse or dependence diagnostic category (Pollock and Martin 1999). By definition, then,
such youth do not have drug problems, although they clearly exhibit
symptoms that suggest they do. According to research, "diagnostic

Box 6.1. The Criteria for Defining Substance Abuse and
Substance Dependency Disorders Differ

Substance Abuse Disorder

A. A maladaptive pattern of substance use, leading to clinically significant impairment or distress, as manifested by one (or more) of the following, occurring within a 12-month period:

• recurrent substance use resulting in a failure to fulfill major role obligations at work, school, or home (e.g., repeated absences or poor work performance related to substance use; substance-related absences, suspensions, or expulsions from school; neglect of children or household)

• recurrent substance use in situations in which it is physically hazardous (e.g., driving an automobile or operating a machine when impaired by substance use)

• recurrent substance-related legal problems (e.g., arrests for substance-related disorderly conduct)

• continued substance use despite persistent or recurrent social or interpersonal problems caused or exacerbated by the effects of the substance (e.g., arguments with spouse about consequences of intoxication, physical fights)

-and-

Substance Dependency Disorder

A. A maladaptive pattern of substance use, leading to clinically significant impairment or distress, as manifested by three (or more) of the following, occurring at any time in the same 12-month period:

• tolerance, as defined by either of the following:
  – a need for markedly increased amounts of the substance to achieve intoxication or desired effect
  – markedly diminished effect with continued use of the same amount of the substance

• withdrawal, as manifested by either of the following:
  – the characteristic withdrawal syndrome for the substance
  – the same (or a closely related) substance is taken to relieve or avoid withdrawal symptoms

• the substance is often taken in larger amounts over a longer period than was intended

• a persistent desire or unsuccessful efforts to cut down or control substance use

• a great deal of time spent in activities necessary to obtain the substance (e.g., visiting multiple doctors or driving long distances), use the substance (e.g., chain-smoking), or recover from its effects

(continued)

Box 6.1. *Continued*

Substance Abuse Disorder	Substance Dependency Disorder
B. The symptoms have never met the criteria for substance dependence for this class of substance.	• important social, occupational, or recreational activities given up or reduced because of substance use
	• continued substance use despite knowledge of a persistent or recurrent physical or psychological problem that is likely caused or exacerbated by the substance (e.g., current cocaine use despite recognition of cocaine-induced depression, or continued drinking despite recognition that an ulcer was made worse by alcohol consumption)

Source: American Psychiatric Association (1994, 181–83).

orphans" are particularly prevalent among adolescent populations (Harrison et al. 1998).

The lack of research on the applicability of the DSM-IV definitions to juveniles contributes further to uncertainty about their usefulness (Pollock and Martin 1999). Although some research has examined the categories for certain drugs, such as alcohol and marijuana, few studies have examined a broader range of drugs across diverse adolescent populations (Fulkerson et al. 1999; Nelson et al. 1999; Cottler et al. 2001; Winters et al. 2001). Thus, despite the popularity of the DSM-IV, serious conceptual and empirical problems underlie the definition and classification of drug problems among young people. On the other hand, few if any comparable attempts have been subject to as much scientific research as the DSM-IV (Nathan and Langenbucher 1999).

Alternatives to the Diagnostic Statistical Manual approach. Other sources besides the DSM-IV can be used to define a drug problem. Another frequently used approach to defining a drug problem comes from the Addiction Severity Index, or ASI (McLellan et al. 1980), the "de facto standard instrument for assessment of alcohol and other drug addiction in the United States and beyond" (Leonhard et al. 2000, 129). By some estimates, ASI is the most commonly used instrument—and thus definition of a drug problem—in substance abuse clinics in the United States (Government Printing Office 1989).

The ASI's popularity can be attributed in part to an extensive body of research establishing its validity, reliability, and utility for diverse populations (Leonhard et al. 2000). A multidimensional assessment instrument, the ASI examines seven distinctive domains that each assess a problem associated with addiction (Bovasso et al. 2001). The domains are problems with employment, interpersonal relations, physical health, mental health, criminal behavior, alcohol abuse, and drug abuse. Several drug assessment instruments for juveniles have been modeled on the ASI, including the ADAD, APSI, CASI-A, T-ASI. Table 6.1 lists these instruments and others.

These instruments and most others have particular, designed uses that do not always accord with practice. For example, the ASI was developed primarily to assess treatment outcomes, not to provide a clinical diagnosis of a drug problem. But in practice, the ASI and other instruments are often used to assess the presence of a drug problem, even though most experts recommend that any assessment rely on clinical judgments, not just the results of particular instruments. In cases where clinical judgments are not systematically relied upon, the instruments provide a de facto definition of a drug problem through their particular measures and scoring systems.

Key elements in defining a "drug problem." Regardless of whether the DSM-IV or a particular instrument serves as the primary definition of a drug problem, most definitions attempt to capture the severity of a drug problem along the following continuum: abstinence, experimental use, early abuse, abuse, and dependence (Winters 1999b). Researchers increasingly argue that existing or new instruments should consider the developmental aspects of juvenile drug use and drug problems (Winters et al. 2001). Researchers note that youth typically use different drugs (e.g., alcohol and marijuana) than adults; use similar drugs differently (e.g., binge drinking is more common among youth); are less likely to recognize they have a problem; exhibit more co-occurring problems such as depression; undergo considerable biological and cognitive changes (e.g., changes in hormonal activity, transition from concrete to abstract thinking); and are subject to institutions, such as schools and the juvenile justice system, that are unique to adolescence (Dennis 2002, 2). Such differences indicate the need to conceptualize drug problems differently for youth, and in turn to create definitions and classifications that reflect adolescent-specific patterns of drug use and its consequences.

Winters et al. (2001, 2) argued that the "heterogeneity of adolescent drug involvement" indicates the need for a "broad definition of drug abuse." However, most youth who experiment with drugs do not develop more frequent or serious levels of drug use, and most "mature out" of drug use by age 21 (Leccese and Waldron 1994, 554). Such facts suggest caution in adhering to a broad definition. As Winters et al. (2001, 3) themselves observed:

> Because the majority of adolescents experiment with alcohol and many experiment with other substances, to define abuse as use implies that virtually every adolescent requires some sort of drug abuse intervention. This creates a definition of abuse that is too broad to be meaningful.

Despite the need for caution, some studies focus exclusively on drug use patterns and equate these patterns with drug problems, leading in turn to considerably larger, and likely overinflated, estimates of the extent of drug problems among youth. For example, a recent report summarizing trends in drug use among adolescents is titled, *Substance Abuse: The Nation's Number One Health Problem* (Horgan et al. 2001), suggesting the seemingly paramount importance of youth drug problems. Although this assessment may be true, it is based in part on an examination of drug use patterns, which simply indicate changes in, say, the number of youth who have "ever tried" a specific drug or used the drug in the past month. Of course, any use may be cause for concern, but almost all definitions of drug problems require a certain amount of drug use coupled with consequences that arise from that use, as the *Substance Abuse* report itself emphasizes.

Other reports focus on trends in processing drug offenses and assume that these trends measure drug problems. Researchers know, for example, the arrest rate for drug abuse violations among juvenile males more than doubled between 1990 and 1999, from 527 to 1,081 arrests per 100,000 males age 10–17 (Stahl 2001). However, the number of arrests for drug violations does not necessarily measure drug problems, nor does the number of juvenile court cases involving drug charges. Both figures can be driven by not only youth behavior but also the attention law enforcement gives to this behavior and the resources available to address drug use. Clearly, the priorities and funding of law enforcement agencies can vary. Consequently, changes in drug violations or court processing of drug-involved youth may reflect these dynamics rather than any underlying trends in drug problems among youth.

Whether broad or narrow, a definition or classification of drug problems with face validity ultimately must capture specific underlying patterns (e.g., drug use of various kinds and levels) that can be linked directly and causally to specific problems (e.g., medical conditions or psychological, personal, interpersonal, or social problems). Both are necessary for a "drug problem" to exist. Drinking frequency and levels, for example, are largely irrelevant if they do not contribute to or cause specific identifiable consequences. Similarly, the presence of various problems that co-occur with drug use is not evidence of a drug problem per se unless there is a causal relationship of some sort between the drug use and the problems.

Researchers have generated numerous classification schemes that frequently have intuitive appeal. Often these schemes involve statistical analyses and evaluations suggesting that the classifications and problems are linked. Yet, there remains relatively little firm evidence indicating causal relationships between drug use or various drug problem classifications on one hand and such problems as delinquency and crime on the other (White and Gorman 2000).

Of course, other criteria can be used to define a drug problem, most notably moral or religious perspectives. For example, if society views any drug use as intrinsically wrong or sinful, there is no need to specify underlying patterns or causal links to specific consequences. Rather, the drug use itself is the problem. From a scientific or health perspective, however, the relevant criteria for determining when a problem exists include whether the problem can be clearly defined and measured and whether it can be causally linked to negative or unhealthy outcomes.

VALIDATING AN ASSESSMENT INSTRUMENT AGAINST A SPECIFIC DEFINITION

Once a definition of "drug problem" has been identified, validation of an assessment instrument consists of creating measures that capture the elements of the definition (Winters et al. 2001). Conventionally, this type of validity is called "face validity," which involves examining how well questions or items in an instrument appear, "on the face of it," to measure a particular phenomenon, such as a drug problem.

Determining whether face validity is present depends entirely on the definition of the phenomenon under consideration, and thus can be viewed as a type of *definitional validation*. For example, instruments may be created that ask questions to measure the different DSM-IV conditions necessary for a diagnosis of drug abuse or dependence (see box 6.1). These questions must pass the face validity test as applied to the DSM-IV definition—that is, do they at face value seem to measure the specific conditions listed in the DSM-IV? The face validity of instruments and questions may vary considerably depending on the definition of a drug problem.

A further kind of definitional validation, *criterion* or *discriminative validation,* involves assessing whether specific types of drug problems can be identified under a particular classification scheme. The DSM-IV, for example, distinguishes between drug abuse and drug dependence. After identifying measures that capture the unique conditions associated with each type of drug problem, researchers can conduct statistical analyses of data from assessment instruments to determine whether the conditions cluster in an expected manner (Fulkerson et al. 1999). That is, do the conditions unique to one type of drug problem (e.g., abuse) cluster together, separate from the clustering of conditions unique to another type of drug problem (e.g., dependence)?

Since different classification schemes conceptualize drug problems in different ways, no single study can definitively demonstrate the superiority of one scheme over another, only that statistical approaches provide evidence for the existence of certain types of drug problems. For example, research on adult populations suggests that the DSM-IV category of drug dependence actually subsumes four distinct types of dependence (Caetano 1985; Nelson et al. 1999). And studies of youth populations have found relatively little support for the existence among youth of the two distinct types identified in the DSM-IV (Fulkerson et al. 1999; Winters 1999a; Mikulich et al. 2000).

RELIABILITY AND VALIDITY OF ASSESSMENT INSTRUMENTS
A range of statistical criteria are used to evaluate assessment instruments. These criteria, sometimes called psychometric properties, focus on two domains: reliability and validity. Reliability typically refers to the "capacity of an instrument to measure a relatively enduring trait with some level of consistency over time, across settings, and between raters" (Winters et al. 2001, 12). Some standard types of reliability include

- stability, or test-retest reliability (i.e., how well individuals' responses to an instrument remain largely consistent when given an instrument repeatedly over short periods);

- internal consistency (i.e., how well different questions or items that measure a particular scale in an instrument generate consistent responses); and
- inter-rater agreement (i.e., how well different administrators of an instrument obtain similar scores from the same individuals).

Instruments should have high stability, internal consistency, and inter-rater agreement to ensure that drug problems are assessed reliably.

As discussed above, validity refers to the notion that an instrument measures what it is supposed to measure. For example, if an instrument is supposed to measure a drug problem, or conditions that make up the definition of a drug problem, then it should in fact measure a drug problem or these conditions, not some other phenomenon. The earlier discussion mentioned face, or definitional, validity (i.e., how well an instrument "on the face of it" measures what it is supposed to measure) and criterion, or discriminative, validity (i.e., how well an instrument distinguishes or discriminates among groups that make up a particular classification scheme, such as individuals with no drug problems, abuse, and dependence). Other types of validity include *convergent validity,* which measures how well the results from an instrument correlate with other instruments or "gold standards," and *construct validity,* which measures how well theories of an identified phenomenon (such as drug use) explain that phenomenon, given that other forms of validation have been established (Rossi et al. 1999; Crowley et al. 2001; Winters 1999a).

Each type of validation can apply to any or all of a range of drugs. It is possible, for example, that some definitions, classifications, and instruments may be more valid with some drugs (e.g., alcohol) than with others (e.g., hallucinogens) (Winters 1999a; Cottler et al. 2001). Assessment of instruments should consider such possibilities and test instruments for different populations, with norms, such as mean scores and cut-off points, established for each (Leccese and Waldron 1994).

CRITERIA FOR EVALUATING AND COMPARING ASSESSMENT INSTRUMENTS
Additional criteria or psychometric properties of assessment instruments can be used to assess them and compare their validity and relative usefulness (Griner et al. 1981; Glaros and Kline 1988; Peters et al. 2000; Winters et al. 2001; Grisso and Underwood 2003). These criteria, described in box 6.2, capture different dimensions that juvenile justice practitioners and researchers may give greater or lesser weight, depending on their

Box 6.2. Different Criteria Can Be Used to Evaluate and Compare Whether One Screening or Assessment Instrument Is Better than Another

Criterion	Description	Formula
Overall accuracy	Proportion of participants identified correctly as having or not having a drug problem.	$= \dfrac{\left(\begin{array}{c}\text{\# correctly identified} \\ \text{drug problem + no problem}\end{array}\right)}{\left(\begin{array}{c}\text{\# actual drug problem} \\ \text{+ no problem}\end{array}\right)}$
Drug problem Sensitivity	Proportion of participants with a drug problem who are correctly identified as having one. (The higher the proportion, the higher the true positive rate.)	$= \dfrac{\left(\begin{array}{c}\text{\# correctly identified} \\ \text{drug problem}\end{array}\right)}{\left(\text{\# actual drug problem}\right)}$
Positive predictive accuracy	Proportion of participants identified as having a drug problem who actually have one. (The higher the proportion, the lower the false positive rate.)	$= \dfrac{\left(\begin{array}{c}\text{\# identified with actual} \\ \text{drug problem}\end{array}\right)}{\left(\begin{array}{c}\text{\# identified with} \\ \text{a drug problem}\end{array}\right)}$
No drug problem Specificity	Proportion of participants with no drug problem identified correctly as not having a drug problem. (The higher the proportion, the higher the true negative rate.)	$= \dfrac{\left(\begin{array}{c}\text{\# correctly identified with} \\ \text{no drug problem}\end{array}\right)}{\left(\begin{array}{c}\text{\# who actually have} \\ \text{no drug problem}\end{array}\right)}$
Negative predictive accuracy	Proportion of participants identified as having no drug problem who do not have one. (The higher the proportion, the lower the false negative rate.)	$= \dfrac{\left(\begin{array}{c}\text{\# identified who actually} \\ \text{have no drug problem}\end{array}\right)}{\left(\begin{array}{c}\text{\# identified without} \\ \text{a drug problem}\end{array}\right)}$

focus and needs. Each criterion is discussed below, and figure 6.2 provides an empirical example.

The first criteria, *overall accuracy*, captures the idea that practitioners want instruments that accurately classify youth with and without drug problems. From the standpoint of effectively targeting drug treatment, it is clearly important to identify not only youth who have drug problems, but also those who do not. To illustrate: if, among 100 youth entering intake, 20 have a drug problem and 80 do not, an instrument with good overall accuracy will identify accurately, or better than chance, a greater percentage of the youth with and without drug problems. For example, as figure 6.2 shows, an instrument might correctly identify 12 youth as having a drug problem and 74 as not having a problem. The overall accuracy thus would be 86 divided by 100, or 86 percent. In reality, even the best instruments will misclassify some youth because of the artificial imposition of cut-off scores with phenomena that may have a continuous distribution of values (Dwyer 1996).

Figure 6.2. *An Instrument with High Specificity and Negative Predictive Accuracy, but Low Sensitivity and Positive Predictive Accuracy*

		Actual		
		Problem	No problem	
Identified	Problem	12	6	18
	No problem	8	74	82
	Total	20	80	100

Overall accuracy	= (12 + 74)/100	= 86%
Sensitivity	= 12/20	= 60% (a higher value indicates more true positives)
Positive predictive accuracy	= 12/18	= 67% (a higher value indicates fewer false positives)
Specificity	= 74/80	= 93% (a higher value indicates more true negatives)
Negative predictive accuracy	= 74/82	= 90% (a higher value indicates fewer false negatives)

Setting aside for the moment the focus on identifying youth without drug problems, assessment instruments should correctly identify those youth who have drug problems. This dimension is termed *sensitivity* (the true positive rate). For example, if 20 of 100 youth who enter intake have a drug problem, the ideal instrument would identify all 20. In practice, however, a given instrument might identify 18 as having a drug problem, and only 12 of them might have actual drug problems. Thus, only 12 of 20 youth with drug problems were accurately identified, and the sensitivity, or true positive rate, is 60 percent.

Positive predictive accuracy is a related criterion for evaluating an assessment instrument. This criterion measures an instrument's false positive rate (i.e., how many youth are identified as having drug problems when in fact they do not). In the above example, 18 youth were identified as having a drug problem, but only 12 had a problem. The positive predictive accuracy is 12 divided by 18, or 67 percent. An example illustrates the relevance of this dimension: Two instruments have equal sensitivity (e.g., 60 percent), but the first one has much lower positive predictive accuracy and thus a higher false positive rate. All else equal, the second instrument is better because it has a similar level of sensitivity and fewer false positives. Practitioners save resources by not allocating them to youth with no drug problems.

Corresponding to these criteria are two additional ones—*specificity* and *negative predictive accuracy*—that focus on how well instruments identify youth *without* drug problems. Specificity (the true negative rate) refers to the ability of an instrument to identify correctly those youth with no drug problems. To continue the example from above, the assessment instrument identified 82 youth as having no drug problem, but only 74 in fact had no problem. This instrument's specificity (true negative rate) thus is 74 divided by 80, or 93 percent.

Negative predictive accuracy measures an instrument's false negative rate. In the example, 82 youth were identified as not having a problem, but 8 actually had a problem. The negative predictive accuracy thus is 74 divided by 82, or 90 percent, indicating that a relatively low percentage (10 percent) of classified cases represented false negatives.

The different criteria should be considered as a whole. For example, it was noted earlier that between two instruments with similar sensitivity, the better one has the higher positive predictive accuracy (i.e., a lower number of false positives). However, it is possible that a practitioner or researcher may be more interested in maximizing negative predictive accuracy (i.e., minimizing the number of false negatives). As a result, less weight may be given to positive predictive accuracy or the other criteria.

Figure 6.3 illustrates an instrument with lower overall accuracy, positive predictive accuracy, and specificity than the instrument in figure 6.2, but higher sensitivity and negative predictive accuracy. In the context of screening, the figure 6.3 instrument might be preferred because it better identifies all youth with a problem. With the figure 6.2 instrument, 8 youth with drug problems are misclassified, whereas with the figure 6.3 instrument, only 1 youth is misclassified. However, this high level of sensitivity comes at the expense of a high false positive rate, reflected in the lower positive predictive accuracy for the figure 6.3 instrument compared with the figure 6.2 instrument (39 percent versus 67 percent).

There are no hard and fast rules for which criteria are most important in all settings (Peters and Bartoi 1997; Winters 1999a). Ultimately, practitioners and researchers must consider the range of reliability and vali-

Figure 6.3. *An Instrument with High Sensitivity and Negative Predictive Accuracy, but Low Positive Predictive Accuracy and Specificity*

		Actual		
		Problem	**No problem**	
Identified	Problem	19	30	**49**
	No problem	1	50	**51**
	Total	**20**	**80**	**100**

Overall accuracy	= (19 + 50)/100	= 69%
Sensitivity	= 19/20	= 98%
Positive predictive accuracy	= 19/49	= 39%
Specificity	= 50/80	= 63%
Negative predictive accuracy	= 50/51	= 98%

dation measures, and the different criteria for comparison. They then must emphasize the most relevant measures for addressing their particular concerns. For example, practitioners in some jurisdictions may consider it important to err on the side of overinclusion, even if it means providing treatment to youth who in reality have no drug problem. In other jurisdictions, limited resources may dictate using an instrument that minimizes false positives.

The need for a case-by-case determination is reinforced by the fact that relatively few studies systematically compare screening or assessment instruments along these different domains (Peters et al. 2000). Fewer still compare instruments focusing on drug problems among youth (Winters et al. 2001). Such gaps in research do not mean that the different statistical considerations can be ignored. Indeed, statistical validation constitutes the cornerstone on which effective screening and assessment is built. But these gaps do mean that the statistical considerations generally must be undertaken case by case rather than through comparing the same set of statistical properties across several instruments.

Other, nonstatistical considerations may also apply. Time and resources, for example, are major concerns for practitioners (Grisso and Underwood 2003). When all else is equal, a better instrument will be one that requires fewer resources and staff. It is on the basis of these considerations, both statistical and nonstatistical, that significant progress has been made in recent years. Recent reviews have identified instruments that appear promising and have been tested and validated in real world settings.

Recommended Drug Screening and Assessment Instruments

Many screening and assessment instruments identify drug problems among youth in the juvenile justice system. Of these, many have been well-studied, are relatively easy to use, and have high reliability and validity. However, most have not been adapted for use with juvenile populations. Because of the unique ways drug problems may arise and manifest themselves in youth, developing youth-specific instruments is critical (Winters et al. 2001; Grisso and Underwood 2003).

Practitioners frequently want to know what the "best" instrument is, but no instrument is most effective in all situations, and any instrument typically should be used as part of a more general decisionmaking process involving clinicians. In addition, what is "best" will depend on the specific populations, staffing, resources, and needs of juvenile justice practitioners in particular contexts (Winters 1999b). Failure to address such issues can result in unnecessary expenditures and possibly harm to individuals through, for example, misuse of the resulting information. In selecting an instrument, practitioners should consider a range of factors—including the psychometric properties of a particular instrument, whether it has been developed for application to a particular population (e.g., girls or boys, different racial or ethnic groups), and pragmatic considerations such as the time and resources available to conduct assessments—and use the results appropriately.

Recommended Screening Instruments

Table 6.1 lists instruments recommended by the Center for Substance Abuse Treatment (CSAT) (Winters [1999a] and Winters et al. [2001]) as well as some identified by Dennis, White, and Titus (2001). Many other instruments exist or are in development (see, for example, Winters, Estroff, and Anderson 2003). Here, however, the discussion primarily covers CSAT's identified instruments because of how the agency created its recommendations. CSAT convened a panel of nationally recognized experts to review screening and assessment instruments for adolescents with drug problems. Although the panel did not endorse any one instrument (Winters 1999a, xvii), it recommended the listed instruments based on several criteria. For example, the panel focused on whether a given instrument was well-studied and if repeated studies demonstrated that the instrument had "favorable psychometric properties" with high reliability and validity (Winters et al. 2001, 13).

Screening instruments were selected based on additional criteria. For example, the panel focused on instruments that can be administered in a short period of time (e.g., 15 minutes), are easily understood, and can be administered, scored, and interpreted by nonclinicians. The panel did not, however, systematically compare instruments along each dimension discussed earlier (e.g., overall accuracy, sensitivity, positive predictive accuracy, specificity, negative predictive accuracy) and so could not determine which were better for each dimension.

Because CSAT's recommendations rely on a consensus panel of experts who consistently applied a set of scientific criteria, researchers can trust the identified instruments may be useful to practitioners in diverse settings. New and better instruments may have emerged recently, but they have not been systematically reviewed in a manner similar to that used by CSAT. This analysis, however, includes additional instruments identified by Winters et al. (2001), who extended the work of the CSAT panel and examined well-known and well-studied instruments widely used in different settings. (Ken C. Winters was the CSAT Consensus Panel Chair for the screening and assessment Treatment Improvement Protocol [Winters 1999a].) The discussion also included the MAYSI (Grisso and Barnum 2000) and the GAIN (Dennis 1998), both of which have garnered considerable interest in recent years. Dennis et al.'s (2001) review, which was sponsored by CSAT, provides a listing of additional instruments, as does a recent report by Drug Strategies (2003).

One example from table 6.1 is the Personal Experience Screening Questionnaire, or PESQ (Winters 1992). The PESQ was created to determine whether youth need additional assessment for the presence of drug problems. This instrument uses a "red flag" and "green flag" problem severity score and includes a brief overview of drug use frequency, psychosocial problems, and faking tendencies (Winters 1999a). The questionnaire is written at a fourth grade reading level and takes approximately 10 minutes to complete and 3 minutes to score.

The Drug and Alcohol Problem (DAP) Quick Screen paper-and-pencil test is a 30-item test with four items used to determine a need for further assessment of adolescent substance abuse problems (Schwartz and Wirth 1990). The questionnaire is designed for adolescents at a sixth grade reading level. Completing and scoring the instrument takes approximately 15 minutes.

The other instruments in table 6.1 have characteristics similar to the PESQ and DAP. They vary primarily in their precise focus, dimensions covered, length of time required to complete and score them, and cost (Winters 1999a; Winters et al. 2001). Readers interested in specific instruments or newer versions of them should consult the sources cited above.

Table 6.2 identifies several particular features of each recommended screening instrument in table 6.1—whether the instrument is used in the juvenile justice system, whether it uses DSM-IV as the "gold standard" for defining and thus identifying a drug problem, and whether it was designed for youth. As with table 6.1, sources for table 6.2 include Winters (1999a), Winters et al. (2001), and Dennis et al. (2001).[1]

According to these sources, existing screening instruments are not widely used in juvenile justice settings, few instruments use the DSM-IV as a "gold standard," and roughly half have been created for adolescent

Table 6.1. *Some Recommended Screening and Assessment Instruments*

	Authors[a]	Acronyms
Screening Instruments		
Adolescent Drug Involvement Scale	Moberg and Hahn (1991)	ADIS
Client Substance Index	Moore (1983)	CSI
Client Substance Index–Short	Thomas (1990)	CSI-S
Drug and Alcohol Problem Quick Screen	Schwartz (1990)	DAP
Drug Use Screening Inventory–Revised	Tartar (1990)	DUSI-R
Global Assessment of Individual Needs Quick Screener	Titus and Dennis (2001)	GAIN[b]
Massachusetts Youth Screening Instrument–2nd Version	Grisso and Barnum (2000)	MAYSI[c]
Personal Experience Screening Questionnaire	Winters (1992)	PESQ
Problem Oriented Screening Instrument for Teenagers	Rahdert (1991)	POSIT
Substance Abuse Subtle Screening Inventory	Miller (1985)	SASSI
Assessment Instruments		
Psychiatric Interviews		
Diagnostic Interview for Children and Adolescents	Herjanic and Campbell (1977)	DICA
Diagnostic Interview Schedule for Children	Costello et al. (1985)	DISC-C
Kiddie Schedule for Affective Disorders and Schizophrenia	Endicott and Spitzer (1978)	KSADS
Structured Clinical Interview for the DSM	Spitzer et al. (1987)	SCID
Substance-Use Disorder Interviews		
Adolescent Diagnostic Interview	Winters and Henly (1993)	ADI
Customary Drinking and Drug Use Record	Brown et al. (1998)	CDDR
Prototype Screening/Triage Form for Juv. Det. Centers	Dembo et al. (1993)	PSTFJDC
Substance Use Disorders Diagnostic Schedule	Hoffman and Harrison (1989)	SUDDS
Texas Christian U. Prevention Management and Eval. Sys.	Simpson and McBride (1992)	TCU/PMES

Table 6.1. *Continued*

	Authors[a]	Acronyms
Interviews Modeled after the Adult Severity Index (ASI)		
Adolescent Drug Abuse Diagnosis	Friedman and Utada (1989)	ADAD
Adolescent Problem Severity Index	Metzger et al. (1991)	APSI
Comprehensive Addiction Severity Index for Adolescents	Meyers (1991)	CASI-A
Teen-Addiction Severity Index	Kaminer et al. (1991)	T-ASI
Paper-and-Pencil Questionnaires		
Adolescent Self-Assessment Profile	Wanberg (1994)	ASAP
Hilson Adolescent Profile	Inwald et al. (1987)	HAP
Juvenile Automated Substance Abuse Evaluation	Ellis (1996)	JASAE
Personal Experience Inventory	Miller (1985)	PEI
American Drug and Alcohol Survey	Oetting et al. (1986)	ADAS

Sources: Winters (1999a) and Winters et al. (2001).

a. Complete references for each author are provided in Winters (1999a) and Winters et al. (2001).

b. Experts with whom Mears consulted identified the GAIN as a promising screening instrument for adolescents with drug problems. Tests of its reliability and validity currently are under way (Dennis et al. 2001).

c. The MAYSI includes a drug abuse scale and is one of the few general screening instruments designed for youth that has consistently shown significant reliability and validity (Grisso and Barnum 2000).

populations. However, no census of screening instruments in juvenile justice settings currently exists. Thus, these sources merely provide suggestive evidence about which instruments are used by juvenile justice practitioners. In some cases, an instrument may in fact use a DSM-IV "gold standard" or may be amenable to DSM-IV classification schemes, but was not designated as such by the different sources. For example, screening instruments typically attempt to capture many common domains associated with various definitions of drug problems (e.g., drug use frequency and amounts, type of drug use, impacts of drug use on self and others).

Recommended Assessment Instruments

Table 6.1 also lists assessment instruments recommended by the CSAT panel (Winters 1999a), Winters et al. (2001), and Dennis et al. (2001).

Table 6.2. *Despite an Abundance of Screening and Assessment Instruments, Few Rely on DSM Diagnostic Standards and Few Were Explicitly Designed and Tested for Adolescents*

	Used in juvenile justice system[a]	Relies on DSM[b]	Designed for adolescents[c]
Screening			
ADIS			✓
CSI			
CSI-S			
DAP			✓
DUSI-R		✓	
GAIN	•		
MAYSI	✓		✓
PESQ	✓		
POSIT	✓		✓
SASSI	✓		
Assessment			
ADAD			✓
ADAS			✓
ADI		✓	✓
APSI			
ASAP			
CASI-A	•		
CDDR		✓	
DICA		✓	
DISC-C	•	✓	
HAP	✓		✓
JASAE		✓	✓
KSADS		✓	
PEI	✓		
PSTFJDC	✓		✓
SCID		✓	
SUDDS		✓	
T-ASI			
TCU/PMES			✓

Sources: Winters (1999a), Winters et al. (2001), and Dennis et al. (2001).

a. A check (✓) indicates one source listed above identified the instrument as being used at some point in the juvenile justice system. A dot (•) indicates Mears has personal knowledge of an instrument being used in some jurisdictions, but no systematic empirical study has assessed its application in the juvenile justice system.

b. A check (✓) indicates that the DSM provides the primary basis for defining a drug problem. Some instruments without checks may allow for approximation of DSM definitions or diagnoses of a drug problem.

c. A check (✓) indicates that the instrument was created for youth, not adapted from an existing instrument for adults. These youth instruments are not necessarily better than adaptations of adult instruments.

As when they selected screening instruments, the CSAT panel focused on well-studied assessment instruments that exhibited favorable characteristics, such as high reliability and validity. The instruments are classified according to the methodology of assessment: psychiatric interviews, substance-use disorder interviews, interviews modeled after the ASI, and paper-and-pencil questionnaires (Winters et al. 2001).

The Adolescent Diagnostic Interview, for example, is a structured interview process that uses DSM-III-R and DSM-IV criteria to diagnose drug problems in adolescents. It measures several dimensions, including interpersonal, psychological, emotional, and behavioral functioning. Winters and Henly (1993) designed the instrument for use by professionals qualified by the American Psychological Association. The completion time of the instrument ranges from 30 to 90 minutes, with scoring requiring an additional 10 to 15 minutes.

The Adolescent Self-Assessment Profile (ASAP), by contrast, is a 225-item self-report instrument made up of 20 basic scales that collectively assess drug use and involvement across nine drug use categories (Wanberg 1991). The ASAP is a self-administered questionnaire but can also be completed in an interview. The reading level for this instrument is sixth to seventh grade. Certified addiction counselors, psychologists, social workers, physicians, and licensed professional counselors are recommended to administer the instrument.

As with the screening instruments, table 6.2 presents additional information about the assessment instruments listed in table 6.1. It shows, for example, that most assessment instruments use the DSM-IV as a "gold standard," but only about half have been created expressly for use with adolescents.

Screening and Assessment Practices in Juvenile Justice

Nationally, there is no current comprehensive or systematic census describing the full range of screening and assessment instruments used throughout the juvenile justice system. Towberman (1992) documented that screening and assessment practices vary considerably. A recent study by Drug Strategies (2003), a Washington, D.C., nonprofit research institute, reinforces this finding. The Drug Strategies study involved describing the characteristics and features of drug treatment programs that a panel of experts, national organizations, and state drug programming agencies had identified as effective. The resulting sample consisted of 144 programs using close to 40 different assessment instruments. The most popular instruments were the Substance Abuse Subtle Screening Inventory–Adolescent, "in-house" instruments (i.e., instruments that had been created by program staff or by others on behalf of the program), and the American Society of Addiction Medicine's placement criteria, as described in box 6.3 (ASAM 2002).[2]

Although not representative of all juvenile drug programs, the study nonetheless is notable for having focused on well-established programs that are thought or have been proved effective. These programs all used instruments of one kind or another, but in many instances the reliability and validity of the instruments has not been established. Many treatment programs likely do not use any instruments, but rather rely on subjective, intuitive assessments of need (Andrews and Bonta 1998).

Even if a comprehensive census of screening and assessment instruments used in the juvenile justice system existed, critical questions would still need to be addressed. For example, researchers would want to know precisely when during processing the instruments are used,

---

Box 6.3. American Society of Addiction Medicine
Placement Criteria

The American Society of Addition Medicine (ASAM) recently published a revised second edition of its patient placement criteria (ASAM PPC-2R). The ASAM criteria serve as a guideline for decisions concerning placement, continued care, and discharge of individuals with drug and other psychosocial problems. The ASAM PPC-2R has two sets of guidelines: one for adults and one for adolescents. There are five levels of care for each group. Each level prescribes a more intense treatment regimen. For example, level III requires the individual to participate in inpatient treatment. Level IV requires the individual to participate in medically managed intensive inpatient treatment. The language in the ASAM PPC-2R conforms to DSM-IV criteria for diagnosing adolescents with drug problems and placing them in a particular level of treatment. Available tools, such as the Level of Care Index (LOCI-2R), assist in implementing the ASAM PPC-2R criteria (Hoffman et al. 2002). The ASAM criteria and the LOCI-2R are not psychometric tools. Rather, they focus on assisting with placement decisions. They incorporate information from assessments, such as those identified in this chapter, but do not themselves provide an assessment.

why they are used, who administers them, and how the resulting information is used. In some cases, screening and assessment instruments and processes are sophisticated and well integrated into juvenile justice system operations. Juvenile assessment centers illustrate this approach (Rivers, Dembo, and Anwyl 1998). At the other end of the spectrum lie systems and programs that rely on untested and unvalidated instruments or that fail to use the information from validated instruments appropriately (Mears and Kelly 1999). These programs run the risk not only of inefficiency but also of making harmful decisions about whether and how to treat youth with drug problems (Winters et al. 2001). For these reasons, evaluating the current state of practice is a critical next step in improving knowledge and practice in juvenile drug screening and assessment.

Screening and Assessment Implementation Challenges

As the previous section shows, researchers currently lack information about the extent and nature of screening and assessment practices in the juvenile justice system. It appears evident, though, that screening and assessment instruments have not been universally adopted, and that when present they frequently may not be effectively or appropriately used (Towberman 1992; Grisso and Underwood 2003). Research on this issue provides several potential explanations.

A study of screening and assessment practices in Texas juvenile probation departments identified that many practitioners and administrators held different views about the purpose of a state-mandated screening instrument, when it was supposed to be used, and how and with whom the information was to be shared (Mears and Kelly 1999). In some jurisdictions, there were too few resources and staff to conduct and use the screening instrument appropriately. Other jurisdictions reported operating under numerous paperwork burdens, explaining their reluctance to adopt any practice that would impose even heavier loads. Still others reported that prosecutors often misused information from the screening instrument and more in-depth assessments to focus not on treatment but on punishment, and that information sharing between stages of the justice system was minimal.

Other studies examining juvenile and adult justice systems have documented similar issues (e.g., Peters and Bartoi 1997; Gendreau and

Goggin 1997). They document, for example, many barriers to effective screening and assessment, including limited time and resources; redundant assessment processes; lack of staff training; limited awareness of the importance and role of screening and assessment in facilitating improved decisionmaking; and reliance on unvalidated instruments or instruments not designed for youth.

Practitioners generally operate with limited resources and thus require instruments that are relatively inexpensive and easy to use, but that also have the characteristics of effective instruments (e.g., reliable, validated, normed for different populations). But few such instruments exist, and fewer still provide clear protocols for their use and interpretation. Experts have recommended many different instruments, such as those identified by CSAT (Winters 1999a). But practitioners must choose for themselves which ones they believe best suit their needs. In small departments with few resources, few people may be trained to evaluate the advantages and limitations of the different instruments or how to use them appropriately. Consequently, many juvenile justice probation departments, courts, and programs must develop their own instruments or rely on consultants or the intuition of in-house staff.

Finally, considerable challenges confront those who wish to streamline information sharing within the juvenile justice system and between the juvenile justice system and other agencies. Effective screening and assessment can be conducted using self-reported information from youth, but a more accurate and complete approach requires collecting information from multiple sources (Winters 1999a). Many times, however, links between agencies are not well-established. Some agencies may even be unwilling to share information, especially in contexts where court actors believe that information will be misused (Mears and Kelly 1999). The result can be incomplete and inaccurate assessments, as well as the unnecessary additional costs of collecting information that other agencies have already obtained.

Conclusion

This chapter examined how juvenile drug problems are and can be identified, focusing primarily on the role of screening and assessment instruments. The discussion presented five related topics: the purposes of drug screening and assessment; elements of effective drug screening and assessment instruments; recommended juvenile drug screening and assessment instruments; drug screening and assessment instruments commonly used in juvenile justice settings; and some challenges in implementing drug screening and assessment instruments.

Effective screening and assessment of young offenders with potential drug problems require using effective instruments. The ideal screening instrument provides, with relatively little cost and time, an initial "flag" of a potential drug problem. The ideal assessment instrument accurately identifies whether a drug problem exists. As part of a more general screening and assessment process, these and similar instruments can be used to develop treatment plans and monitor a youth's progress.

Researchers currently lack information on the full range of instruments in use among juvenile justice systems and stages within these systems. The available evidence indicates that many instruments are in use and that few have been rigorously validated. Meanwhile, practitioners have been given relatively little clear guidance about which instruments to use among the many available.

Regardless of the type of instrument used, many challenges and issues confront those who wish to create effective screening and assessment processes. There may be limited resources and few staff available qualified to determine what instruments best meet the jurisdiction's or program's needs or to ensure that the instruments are used appropriately. And the willingness or ability of different agencies and programs to share information may impede screening and assessment, and undermine the accuracy of assessments. These issues and others must be addressed to ensure an effective process that goes beyond the decision to use a well-studied and validated instrument.

Youth throughout the juvenile justice system suffer from various problems and have many needs (Loeber and Farrington 2001). An efficient and effective response to these needs involves identifying which youth have specific problems, while at the same time ensuring that youth without problems are not misdiagnosed. Research to date provides a solid foundation for creating effective screening and assessment processes, including the identification of a range of recommended instruments. However, much more research is needed to develop effective screening and assessment instruments, and to systematically address the numerous challenges associated with collecting and appropriately sharing and using information within the juvenile justice system.

NOTES

1. See also Grisso and Underwood (2003). Summary descriptions of most instruments in tables 6.1 and 6.2, including the time needed to use each and the credentials and training required to administer each correctly and interpret results appropriately, can be found in appendix B of Winters (1999a).

2. Rosalind Brannigan, vice president, Drug Strategies, personal correspondence with Daniel P. Mears, January 31, 2003.

REFERENCES

American Psychiatric Association. 1980. *Diagnostic and Statistical Manual of Mental Disorders,* 3rd ed. Washington, DC: American Psychiatric Association.

———. 1987. *Diagnostic and Statistical Manual of Mental Disorders,* 3rd ed. rev. Washington, DC: American Psychiatric Association.

———. 1994. *Diagnostic and Statistical Manual of Mental Disorders,* 4th ed. Washington, DC: American Psychiatric Association.

American Society of Addiction Medicine. 2002. *Patient Placement Criteria.* ASAM PPC-2R. Washington, DC: American Society of Addiction Medicine.

Andrews, Don A., and James Bonta. 1998. *The Psychology of Criminal Conduct,* 2nd ed. Cincinnati, OH: Anderson Publishing Company.

ASAM. *See* American Society of Addiction Medicine.

Bovasso, Gregory B., Arthur I. Alterman, John S. Cacciola, and Terry G. Cook. 2001. "Predictive Validity of the Addiction Severity Index's Composite Scores in the Assessment of 2-Year Outcomes in a Methadone Maintenance Population." *Psychology of Addictive Behavior* 15:171–76.

Caetano, Raul. 1985. "Two Versions of Dependence: DSM-III and the Alcohol Dependence Syndrome." *Drug and Alcohol Dependence* 15:81–103.

Cottler, Linda B., Sharon B. Womack, Wilson M. Compton, and Arbi Ben-Abdallah. 2001. "Ecstasy Abuse and Dependence among Adolescents and Young Adults: Applicability and Reliability of DSM-IV Criteria." *Human Psychopharmacology: Clinical and Experimental* 16:599–606.

Crowe, Ann H. 1998. *Drug Identification and Testing in the Juvenile Justice System.* Washington, DC: Office of Juvenile Justice and Delinquency Prevention.

Crowley, Thomas J., Susan K. Mikulich, Kristen M. Ehlers, Elizabeth A. Whitmore, and Marilyn J. Macdonald. 2001. "Validity of Structured Clinical Evaluations in Adolescents with Conduct and Substance Problems." *Journal of the American Academy of Child and Adolescent Psychiatry* 40:265–73.

Cullen, Francis T., and Paul Gendreau. 2000. "Assessing Correctional Rehabilitation: Policy, Practice, and Prospects." In *Policies, Processes, and Decisions of the Criminal Justice System,* Vol. 3 of *Criminal Justice 2000,* edited by J. Horney (109–75). Washington, DC: U.S. Department of Justice, National Institute of Justice.

Dennis, Michael L. 1998. *Global Appraisal of Individual Needs (GAIN).* Bloomington, IN: Chestnut Health Systems.

———. 2002. "Treatment Research on Adolescent Drug and Alcohol Abuse: Despite Progress, Many Challenges Remain." *Connection* May:1–2, 7. Washington, DC: Academy for Health Services Research and Health Policy.

Dennis, Michael L., Michelle K. White, and Janet C. Titus. 2001. "Common Measures That Have Been Used for Both Clinical and Research Purposes with Adolescent Substance Abusers." Unpublished manuscript (draft, 11/6/2001). Bloomington, IL: Chestnut Health Systems.

Drug Strategies. 2003. *A Guide to Adolescent Treatment Programs.* Washington, DC: Drug Strategies.

Dwyer, Carol A. 1996. "Cut Scores and Testing: Statistics, Judgment, Truth, and Error." *Psychological Assessment* 8:360–62.

Frances, Allen, Avrum Mack, Michael B. First, and Cindy Jones. 1995. "DSM-IV Issues in Development." *Psychiatric Annals* 25:15–19.

Fulkerson, Jayne A., Patricia A. Harrison, and Timothy J. Beebe. 1999. "DSM-IV Substance Abuse and Dependence: Are There Really Two Dimensions of Substance Use Disorders in Adolescents?" *Addiction* 94(4): 495–506.

GAO. *See* U.S. General Accounting Office.

Gendreau, Paul, and Claire Goggin. 1997. "Correctional Treatment: Accomplishments and Realities." In *Correctional Counseling and Rehabilitation,* 3rd ed., edited by Patricia van Voorhis, Michael Braswell, and David Lester (271–80). Cincinnati, OH: Anderson Publishing Company.

Glaros, Alan G., and Rex B. Kline. 1988. "Understanding the Accuracy of Tests with Cutting Scores: The Sensitivity, Specificity, and Predictive Value Model." *Journal of Clinical Psychology* 44:1013–23.

Government Printing Office. 1989. "Proposed Rules. Appendix: Pilot Study Proposal." *Federal Register* 54:8978.

Griner, Paul F., Raymond J. Mayewski, Alvin I. Mushlin, and Philip Greenland. 1981. "Selection and Interpretation of Diagnostic Tests and Procedures: Principles and Applications." *Annals of Internal Medicine* 94:553–600.

Grisso, Thomas, and Richard Barnum. 2000. *Massachusetts Youth Screening Instrument— 2: User's Manual and Technical Report.* Worcester: University of Massachusetts Medical School.

Grisso, Thomas, and Lee Underwood. 2003. *Screening and Assessing Mental Health and Substance Use Disorders among Youth in the Juvenile Justice System.* Delmar, NY: National Center for Mental Health and Juvenile Justice.

Harrison, Patricia A., Jayne A. Fulkerson, and Thomas J. Beebe. 1998. "DSM-IV Substance Use Disorder Criteria for Adolescents: A Critical Examination Based on a Statewide School Survey." *American Journal of Psychiatry* 155:486–92.

Horgan, Constance, Kathleen C. Skwara, and Gail Strickler. 2001. *Substance Abuse: The Nation's Number One Health Problem.* Princeton, NJ: The Robert Wood Johnson Foundation.

Inciardi, James A. 1993. "Classification, Assessment, and Treatment Planning for Alcohol- and Drug-Involved Offenders." Treatment Improvement Exchange communiqué. Rockville, MD: Center for Substance Abuse Treatment.

Johnston, Lloyd D., Patrick M. O'Malley, and Jerald G. Bachman. 2002. *Monitoring the Future: National Results on Adolescent Drug Use, 2001.* Bethesda, MD: National Institute on Drug Abuse.

Leccese, Monica, and Holly B. Waldron. 1994. "Assessing Adolescent Substance Use: A Critique of Current Measurement Instruments." *Journal of Substance Abuse Treatment* 11:553–63.

Leonhard, Christoph, Kevin Mulvey, David R. Gastfriend, and Michael Shwartz. 2000. "The Addiction Severity Index: A Field Study of Internal Consistency and Validity." *Journal of Substance Abuse Treatment* 18:129–35.

Loeber, Rolf, and David P. Farrington. 2001. *Child Delinquents: Development, Intervention, and Service Needs.* Thousand Oaks, CA: Sage Publications.

Martin, Christopher S., and Ken C. Winters. 1998. "Diagnosis and Assessment of Alcohol Use Disorders among Adolescents." *Alcohol Health and Research World* 22:95–105.

McLellan, A. Thomas, Lester Luborsky, George E. Woody, and Charles P. O'Brien. 1980. "An Improved Diagnostic Evaluation Instrument for Substance Abuse Patients: The Addiction Severity Index." *Journal of Nervous and Mental Disease* 186:26–33.

Mears, Daniel P., and William R. Kelly. 1999. "Assessments and Intake Processes in Juvenile Justice Processing: Emerging Policy Considerations." *Crime and Delinquency* 45:508–29.

Mikulich, Susan K., S. K. Hall, E. A. Whitmore, and T. J. Crowley. 2000. "Concordance between DSM-III-R and DSM-IV Diagnoses of Substance Use Disorders in Adolescents." *Drug and Alcohol Dependence* 61:237–48.

Nathan, Peter E. 1991. "Substance Use Disorders in the DSM-IV." *Journal of Abnormal Psychology* 100:356–61.

Nathan, Peter E., and James W. Langenbucher. 1999. "Psychopathology: Description and Classification." *Annual Review of Psychology* 50:79–107.

Nelson, Christopher B., Jurgen Rehm, T. B. Üstün, Bridget Grant, and Somnath Chatterji. 1999. "Factor Structures for DSM-IV Substance Disorder Criteria Endorsed by Alcohol, Cannabis, Cocaine, and Opiate Users: Results from the WHO Reliability and Validity Study." *Addiction* 94(6): 843–55.

Peters, Roger H., and Marla Green Bartoi. 1997. *Screening and Assessment of Co-occurring Disorders in the Justice System.* Delmar, NY: The National GAINS Center.

Peters, Roger H., and Elizabeth Peyton. 1998. *Guidelines for Drug Courts on Screening and Assessment.* Washington, DC: Drug Court Programs Office and American University's Justice Programs Office.

Peters, Roger H., Paul E. Greenbaum, Marc L. Steinberg, Chris R. Carter, Madeline M. Ortiz, Bruce C. Fry, and Steven K. Valle. 2000. "Effectiveness of Screening Instruments in Detecting Substance Use Disorders among Prisoners." *Journal of Substance Abuse Treatment* 18:349–58.

Pollock, Nancy K., and Christopher S. Martin. 1999. "Diagnostic Orphans: Adolescents with Alcohol Symptoms Who Do Not Qualify for DSM-IV Abuse or Dependence Diagnoses." *American Journal of Psychiatry* 156:897–901.

Poteet-Johnson, Deborah J., and Philomena J. Dias. 2003. "Office Assessment of the Substance-Using Adolescent." In *Principles of Addiction Medicine,* 3rd ed., edited by Allan W. Graham, Terry K Schultz, Michael F. Mayo-Smith, Richard K. Ries, and Bonnie B. Wilford (1523–34). Chevy Chase, MD: American Society of Addiction Medicine.

Rivers, James E., Richard Dembo, and Robert S. Anwyl. 1998. "The Hillsborough County, Florida, Juvenile Assessment Center: A Prototype." *Prison Journal* 78:439–50.

Rossi, Peter H., Howard E. Freeman, and Mark W. Lipsey. 1999. *Evaluation: A Systematic Approach,* 6th ed. Newbury Park, CA: Sage Publications.

Rounsaville, Bruce J., Robert L. Spitzer, and Janet B Williams. 1986. "Proposed Changes in DSM-III Substance Use Disorders: Description and Rationale." *American Journal of Psychiatry* 143:463–68.

SAMHSA. *See* Substance Abuse and Mental Health Services Administration.

Schuckit, Marc A., Peter E. Nathan, John E. Helzer, George E. Woody, and Thomas J. Crowley. 1991. "Evolution of the DSM Diagnostic Criteria for Alcoholism." *Alcohol, Health, and Research World* 15:278–83.

Schwartz, Richard H., and Philip W. Wirth. 1990. "Potential Substance Abuse Detection among Adolescent Patients: Using the Drug and Alcohol Problem (DAP) Quick Screen, a 30-Item Questionnaire." *Clinical Pediatrics* 29:38–43.

Shearer, Robert A., and Chris R. Carter. 1999. "Screening and Assessing Substance-Abusing Offenders: Quantity and Quality." *Federal Probation* 63:30–35.

Sherman, Lawrence W., Denise Gottfredson, Doris MacKenzie, John Eck, Peter Reuter, and Shawn Bushway. 1997. *Preventing Crime: What Works, What Doesn't, What's Promising.* NCJ 165366. Washington, DC: U.S. Department of Justice, Office of Justice Programs.

Stahl, Anne L. 2001. *Drug Offense Cases in Juvenile Courts, 1989–1998.* OJJDP Fact Sheet 200136. Washington, DC: Office of Juvenile Justice and Delinquency Prevention.

Substance Abuse and Mental Health Services Administration. 2001. "Coerced Treatment among Youths: 1993 to 1998." *The DASIS Report,* September 21. Rockville, MD: Substance Abuse and Mental Health Services Administration.

Tonry, Michael H., and James Q. Wilson, eds. 1990. *Drugs and Crime.* Chicago: University of Chicago Press.

Towberman, Donna B. 1992. "National Survey of Juvenile Needs Assessment." *Crime and Delinquency* 38:230–38.

U.S. General Accounting Office. 1998. *Drug Abuse: Research Shows Treatment Is Effective, but Benefits May Be Overstated.* Washington, DC: U.S. General Accounting Office.

Wanberg, Kenneth W. 1991. *Adolescent Self-Assessment Profile.* Arvada, CO: Center for Alcohol/Drug Abuse Research and Evaluation.

White, Helene R., and D. M. Gorman. 2000. "Dynamics of the Drug-Crime Relationship." In *The Nature of Crime: Continuity and Change,* Vol. 1 of *Criminal Justice 2000,* edited by Gary LaFree (151–218). Washington, DC: U.S. Department of Justice, National Institute of Justice.

Winters, Ken C. 1992. "Development of an Adolescent Alcohol and Other Drug Abuse Screening Scale: Personal Experience Screening Questionnaire." *Addictive Behaviors* 17:479–90.

———. 1999a. *Screening and Assessing Adolescents for Substance Use Disorders.* Treatment Improvement Protocol (TIP) 31. Rockville, MD: Substance Abuse and Mental Health Services Administration, Center for Substance Abuse Treatment.

———. 1999b. *Treatment of Adolescents with Substance Use Disorders.* Treatment Improvement Protocol (TIP) 32. Rockville, MD: Substance Abuse and Mental Health Services Administration, Center for Substance Abuse Treatment.

Winters, Ken C., and George A. Henly. 1993. *Adolescent Diagnostic Interview Schedule and Manual.* Los Angeles: Western Psychological Services.

Winters, Ken C., Todd W. Estroff, and Nicole Anderson. 2003. "Adolescent Assessment Strategies and Instruments." In *Principles of Addiction Medicine*, 3rd ed., edited by Allan W. Graham, Terry K Schultz, Michael F. Mayo-Smith, Richard K. Ries, and Bonnie B. Wilford (1535–46). Chevy Chase, MD: American Society of Addiction Medicine.

Winters, Ken C., William W. Latimer, and Randy D. Stinchfield. 1999. "The DSM-IV Criteria for Adolescent Alcohol and Cannabis Use Disorders." *Journal of Studies on Alcohol* 60:337–44.

———. 2001. "Assessing Adolescent Substance Use." In *Innovations in Adolescent Substance Abuse Interventions,* edited by Eric Wagner and Holly B. Waldron (1–29). New York: Elsevier.

7

Shaping the Next Generation of Juvenile Drug Court Evaluations

Jeffrey A. Butts, John Roman,
Shelli Balter Rossman, and Adele V. Harrell

To build an adequate knowledge base for the future development of juvenile drug courts (JDCs), policymakers and practitioners need research that tests explicit hypotheses about how drug courts influence offender behavior. In other words, exactly how do drug courts reduce substance abuse among young offenders? This question has not been answered by research because previous evaluations have been limited to descriptions of program operations and comparisons of aggregate, postprogram differences between treatment and comparison samples. These studies have allowed researchers to answer some questions about *if* juvenile drug courts work, but they provide little guidance about *how* they work.

Future evaluations should use conceptual frameworks to specify what juvenile drug courts do and how each program component or activity is believed to help change offender behavior. Conceptual frameworks for JDC programs will have to be relatively complex. Juvenile drug courts involve the combined efforts of the justice system and the treatment or service-delivery system. Some activities pursued by drug courts are designed to affect youth directly, while others modify service delivery structures and agency cooperation. To be useful for research and practice, conceptual frameworks for JDC programs have to represent all the components that might contribute to behavioral changes among youthful offenders.

This chapter introduces a conceptual framework developed by the National Evaluation of Juvenile Drug Courts project at the Urban Institute (UI). The framework specifies the conceptual underpinnings of drug court activities and identifies causal mechanisms that might enable these activities to achieve program outcomes. It does this by specifying the chain of events leading from program activities to program outcomes. It identifies hypothesized links between JDC practices, systems of treatment, and key outcomes such as treatment participation, client retention, and program graduation. The framework is essentially a description of how JDCs *might* change offender behavior. Researchers should use the framework to narrow the scope of future juvenile drug court evaluations and identify case processing and service delivery variables that may be most closely linked to program effectiveness. The conceptual framework can be used to refine empirical assumptions about JDC operations, guide the measurement of key influences on offender behavior, and develop data collection methods for evaluation studies.

Hypotheses of Program Impact

Evaluations of juvenile drug courts should be developed in accord with clearly articulated hypotheses of program impact. In other words, an evaluation's efforts to measure the association between program activities and client outcomes should be consistent with established hypotheses that represent a reasonable explanation of cause and effect. Ideally, program planners would have identified such hypotheses before any program elements were implemented, and all JDC program activities would have been built around the empirical findings in support of each hypothesis. In practice, however, social programs are almost never designed this way. Program development takes a more intuitive course, and evaluators are compelled to devise their own hypotheses after the fact. Policymakers and practitioners usually hear about a successful program used in another jurisdiction and program planners adapt the model to local constraints (political, operational, legal, etc.). Empirical connections between program activities and client outcomes are usually assumed, and theories about how the program actually achieves these outcomes are rarely articulated. After repeated cycles of replication and adaptation, the original rationale for program activities may even be forgotten. Gaps between stated objectives and practice may appear, making evaluation difficult and forcing evaluators to reconstruct the reasons why only certain activities survive.

The failure to ground program development on clearly articulated hypotheses of cause and effect has at least three negative consequences. First, it may never be entirely clear to practitioners and managers why one program activity should be undertaken and another should not. Without a clear, causal orientation to guide the selection of program modifications, program strategies are likely to evolve through the unplanned accumulation of innovations, some of which may even conflict. Second, without clear hypotheses of cause and effect to guide their research designs, evaluators may not measure the right combination of program and client variables, and this may prevent them from ascertaining how program outcomes are or are not achieved. Third, without a causal explanation of how client outcomes are achieved, it is impossible to know whether the behavioral changes offenders exhibit during drug court will persist after they leave the program. To avoid these problems, juvenile drug courts should be developed around explicit hypotheses of cause and effect.

To build viable and testable hypotheses of program impact, evaluation researchers have to look beyond the concept of "therapeutic jurisprudence." If drug court researchers address theory in any way, it is usually to describe how drug courts developed in concert with the goals of therapeutic jurisprudence (Hora, Schma, and Rosenthal 1999; Senjo and Leip 2001). Therapeutic jurisprudence, however, is not a theory of program impact. It is a legal philosophy and an approach to justice. At best, therapeutic jurisprudence provides a justification for evaluators to look beyond a court's stated goal of imposing appropriate penalties for infractions of the law, and for extending the concerns of court professionals to the secondary effects of the process—i.e., the mental, emotional, and social well-being of court participants. It may be advisable to make court processes consistent with the principles of therapeutic jurisprudence in order to guard against negative secondary effects, but therapeutic jurisprudence does not provide any clear guidance for practitioners developing drug court programs or for researchers seeking to evaluate them.

In fact, very few studies are available to guide the efforts of future evaluators of juvenile drug court programs. Researchers have not agreed on an adequate conceptualization of how JDCs work and what makes them effective, nor have they agreed how to measure program operations across the various models of drug courts to detect meaningful differences in client outcomes. There are, however, two good sources of information for building hypotheses of program impact: the common sense and experience of practitioners and drug court researchers, and theoretical insights from the social and behavioral sciences (box 7.1).

Guidance from Practitioner and Researcher Experience

Juvenile drug courts spread rapidly across the country in the late 1990s. One reason for their immediate popularity may be that the drug court concept just makes sense to practitioners and policymakers. Using the authority of the court to engage offenders in an aggressive program of substance abuse treatment is appealing from the perspectives of the justice system and the treatment system.

Practitioners generally endorse juvenile drug court models that share the following five elements:

1. Individualized and informal *courtroom procedures* allow judges and other drug court staff to motivate young offenders to confront and change their harmful drug-related behavior and then to sustain those changes.
2. Juvenile drug users change their behavior more successfully when they are engaged in high-quality substance abuse *treatment* and when that treatment is consistent with the goals established for each youth during court hearings.
3. A visible and consistent system of *sanctions and rewards* (both in and out of the courtroom) encourages pro-social behavior while deterring deviant behavior among juvenile clients.
4. An effective system of *case management* services can match offenders and services and ensure consistent application of rewards and sanctions.
5. Courts, and especially judges, are uniquely suited to using their community standing and leadership skills to ensure that high-quality treatment and supervision services are available and accessible to drug-involved youth and that the services system as a whole is *accountable* to youth, their families, and the community.

COURTROOM PROCEDURES

Many distinguishing features of drug courts are found in the courtroom. Drug court procedures are quite different from traditional courts. The bureaucratic, sometimes impersonal process of a traditional courtroom is replaced in drug courts by a very personal, team-oriented courtroom

Box 7.1. Why Do Researchers Need Conceptual Frameworks?

Conceptual frameworks help researchers decide which components of social programs are the most important to measure. Without such frameworks, evaluators would have too many possible factors to measure and something important would likely be missed. If evaluators fail to measure a program's most important components, research findings will never be able to detect the principal influences on program outcomes. Even if a program appears effective, its methods would likely remain a mystery and it would be difficult to replicate.

An Analogy—The Drive-Through Car Wash
Imagine we had no idea how drive-through car washes worked. All we knew was that cars went in dirty at one end and came out clean at the other. Suppose it was your job to find the most effective car wash in your area and to build another one just like it in a nearby town.

One way to perform this task would be to stand by the exits of various automatic car washes and measure how clean the cars are as they come out. After choosing the brand with the best results, you could simply ask a contractor to build one just like it—a single-story building about 50 feet long with garage doors on both ends—and then you could drive cars through it to see whether they came out clean.

Obviously, this would not be your strategy. You would look inside the various drive-through car washes and watch them operate. You would do more than measure the cleanliness of cars at the end of the process, you would observe the components of each washing process and estimate how important they were in cleaning the cars.

You also would likely control for the relative dirtiness of cars as they entered various car washes. You would not want to be tricked into thinking that one car wash was effective just because it happened to be in a part of town where people wash their cars more frequently and thus the average car presents less of a challenge.

So, how would you identify the key components of the car wash process? What if all the manufacturers of various car washes argued that their products were the best, and each had a different explanation for how car washes worked?

When you walked into a car wash, you would be faced with a vast array of equipment and activities, but you would not know how important each part was to the overall process. You might notice, for example, that some car washes had vacillating brushes and others did not. Some had water jets beside and above the cars, while others had jets only above.

Should you estimate the effect of these differences? Are they the most important variations? What other variations should you measure and attempt to correlate with car wash outcomes? Should you keep track of the brand of soap? Should you measure the pressure of the water? Which factors are most critical to outcomes?

(continued)

Box 7.1. *Continued*

What if the final outcome depends on more than the washing process? Perhaps you should measure how long the attendant waits before wiping each car with a dry towel. If you begin your efforts with an incomplete understanding of the process, you might spend a lot of time and money collecting information but still miss the most important factors.

A conceptual framework identifies these important factors. It helps an evaluator understand a program so data collection efforts target the right activities and components. Even if mistakes are made in particular studies, over time the accumulation of evaluation findings will shed light on the principal ingredients of program effectiveness.

---

where procedures are highly interactive, even theatrical. Many drug court procedures seem to be inspired by the concepts of therapeutic jurisprudence, in which the court process itself supports the social and psychological well-being of court participants (Hora et al. 1999; Wexler 1990). Practitioners often place great value on the dynamic interaction between offenders and judges in drug court proceedings.

Juvenile drug court judges try to motivate clients by maintaining close and frequent communication with youth and keeping track of each offender's personal situation. Judges convey important information to offenders and their families during court hearings. A judge may confront a young offender with the results of a failed drug test and discuss an incident report from school, or praise the youth for a clean drug test and the completion of other program milestones. During court hearings, the judge plays the role of a concerned authority figure, compassionate when possible but always ready to impose punitive sanctions (including detention) so offenders understand their actions have consequences.

One critical factor in the effectiveness of the courtroom is its conformance to the concepts of "procedural justice." According to Hirst and Harrell (2000), a court that maximizes procedural justice can result in positive client outcomes independently of other factors, including the severity of sanctions. Courts provide effective procedural justice when they ensure that

- mutual "trust" exists among all court participants;
- all participants have sufficient opportunities to be heard ("voice");

- the fact-finding process operates with demonstrable "accuracy";
- the hearing and sanctioning process is transparent, impartial, and fair ("neutrality"); and
- participants are granted "standing" by being treated with respect.

TREATMENT

Practitioners believe the drug court process encourages offenders to begin and remain in treatment. This belief has been supported by a wide range of evaluation research (Belenko 2001; GAO 2002; Roman and DeStefano, in this volume). According to the growing treatment literature, effective drug treatment programs can significantly reduce drug use and criminal activity among offenders who remain in treatment for the recommended length of time. For example, the Drug Abuse Treatment Outcome Study found that regular cocaine use is cut in half following long-term residential treatment, and the percentage of clients reporting predatory illegal activity also falls after treatment (Anglin, Hser, and Grella 1997). The National Treatment Improvement Evaluation Study, a five-year study of more than 4,000 drug treatment clients, found that up to half of regular cocaine and heroin users spending at least three months in treatment were mostly drug-free in the year after treatment, regardless of the treatment received (CSAT/SAMHSA 1997).

The quality and consistency of treatment is obviously important for client outcomes. Of course, drug treatment is not effective in all circumstances. Client outcomes depend on the extent and nature of client problems, the appropriateness of available treatments for those problems, how successfully clients are engaged in the treatment process, and the use of supportive services during and following treatment.

Research suggests, however, that even coerced treatment may increase the likelihood of client success. Researchers once believed that voluntary clients would be more motivated than coerced participants, and consequently would be more likely to stay and succeed in treatment. Evidence is mounting, however, that coerced treatment can be just as effective (Anglin, Brecht, and Maddahian 1989; Belenko 1999; Collins and Allison 1983; Hubbard et al. 1989; Lawental et al. 1996; Miller and Flaherty 2000; Siddall and Conway 1988; Swartz, Lurigio, and Slomka 1996; Trone and Young 1996). For example, treatment combined with urinalysis and court monitoring may be more successful than treatment alone (Falkin 1993). Some research has shown that even multiple layers of coercion (incarceration, removal of children from family, etc.) can be effective in facilitating client success (Rempel and DeStefano 2000). Research generally supports the notion that the interaction of treatment and criminal justice supervision (i.e., coercion) can be positive in drug court programs.

SANCTIONS AND REWARDS

One of the founding principles of the justice system is that people adjust their behavior according to how effectively the law rewards desirable conduct and punishes unwanted conduct (Nagin 1998). The three classic ingredients of punishment are certainty, severity, and celerity (or swiftness). Of these, the most important may be certainty. When individuals perceive that punishments will likely follow illegal or unwanted behavior, they are less likely to engage in such behavior. In fact, once certainty is taken into account, the severity and speed of punishment seems to have less effect on behavior.

The drug court movement takes much inspiration from these concepts. Practitioners believe, and an extensive body of research confirms, that drug courts are most effective when they employ a system of sanctions and rewards that offenders believe will be implemented reliably and as intended (Taxman 1999). Youthful offenders will adjust their behavior—i.e., follow program rules and reduce their substance abuse—when they see the consequences for prohibited behaviors are highly certain and become more certain and more serious with each infraction.

The research literature also confirms that individuals in drug court settings will change their behavior in response to rewards, or even the promise of rewards (Marlowe and Kirby 1999). In fact, rewards may be even more effective than punishments. Rewards are used frequently in juvenile drug court, and most are of little monetary value. The most common rewards offered to successful clients are small token gifts, applause, and public recognition in front of the courtroom with family and other offenders in attendance. The behavioral changes associated with the receipt of rewards are thought to occur as offenders internalize the goals of drug court and adopt the pro-social values stressed in recovery programs. Rewards are used with varying frequency in juvenile drug courts, but their positive effects on motivating program compliance are widely endorsed by practitioners and researchers.

CASE MANAGEMENT

Practitioners often see case management as the mortar that binds together the bricks of the drug court process. Case management plays at least two roles in drug court—gatekeeper for the criminal justice system and facilitator of client services (Roman, Harrell, and Sack 1998). A case manager's role includes assessing clients for program eligibility and treatment needs, identifying other social service needs, linking clients to appropriate treatment, monitoring client progress in treatment, and reporting client status in courtroom hearings. Case managers often recommend sanctions and rewards to the drug court judge, and they play a key role in determining a client's progression through treatment, including graduation and dismissal decisions. In addition, some drug courts maintain a secondary sanctioning schedule for program rule violations deemed not serious enough to warrant an appearance in front of a judge, and case managers may be responsible for imposing these sanctions.

Given the central role of case management in drug courts, it is somewhat surprising that evaluation research only occasionally explores its value (Taxman 1999). A study on the value of case management in publicly funded substance abuse treatment in Boston, however, concluded that case management was an effective, low-cost means of retaining clients in treatment and reducing the incidence of short-term relapse (Shwartz et al. 1997). Other studies have reported similar results (Kofoed et al. 1986; Siegal et al. 1996).

SYSTEM ACCOUNTABILITY

Practitioners also express great confidence in the ability of drug court programs to coordinate the efforts of the broader drug treatment and juvenile justice systems. The leadership and influence of the judge, in particular, is considered an indispensable ingredient in the effectiveness of juvenile drug courts (NDCI/NCJFCJ 2003). In most communities, the services offered through the juvenile drug court program existed before the program began, but they were usually not well coordinated and agencies involved in purchasing or providing the services did not collaborate effectively. When juvenile drug court programs are introduced, the agencies that form the juvenile justice system and those in the adolescent drug treatment system become accountable to a common authority—the court and, more directly, the judge.

Guidance from Social and Behavioral Sciences

Evaluators of JDCs will find considerable guidance in the social and behavioral sciences. Many theoretical questions that could be asked about the impact of JDCs are similar to questions asked of all programs designed to reduce illegal behavior among young people. Namely, what mechanisms lead young people to engage in illegal and deviant acts and how can intervention programs stop or reverse those mechanisms? Some theoretical perspectives question the operations of the justice system itself and what factors might increase the impact of the court process on the perceptions and behavior of participants. These theories, and the quality of the evidence in support of them, can facilitate the development of conceptual frameworks for juvenile drug courts (Akers 2000; Gibbons 1994; Vold, Bernard, and Snipes 1998).

A theory of drug court impact should lead to testable hypotheses about the factors that produce behavioral change in drug court clients. Ideally, it should reasonably explain how program activities produce client outcomes, and each explanation should be grounded in a developed field of research and a body of empirical literature. The Urban Institute identified two theoretical perspectives that seem to have informed the JDCs' methods of achieving client behavioral change: rational actor (or deterrence) theory, and learning theory. Neither perspective completely explains juvenile drug court practices, but together they suggest how the effects of juvenile drug court might change client behavior.

RATIONAL ACTOR (DETERRENCE) THEORY

Criminological adaptations of economic theory suggest a straightforward explanation of how juvenile drug courts might alter the drug-related behaviors of young offenders (Becker 1968; Clarke and Cornish 1985; Cornish and Clarke 1986). From an economic perspective, "agents" or individuals (i.e., drug court clients) learn about the costs and benefits of various behaviors from the drug court process. With this information, agents embark upon whatever course yields the highest ratio of benefits to costs. In other words, clients are encouraged to weigh the benefits of drug use against the risks of detection and punishment. When the drug court process can provide agents with complete information, they should be more likely to seek the benefits of complying with program requirements while avoiding the costs of noncompliance.

Elements of rational actor theory are clearly at work in the operations of JDCs. The established legal concept of deterrence assumes the existence of rational actors responding to known risks of punishment. The basic proposition of deterrence theory is that individuals are independent, rational actors, and their behavior arises from the exercise of choice and free will. Moreover, people choose to violate rules based on their perceptions of the costs and benefits associated with such behavior. Tittle (1980) suggested that an actor's perceptions of cost can be more important than actual costs, as people act upon what they believe is true. The immediate and consistent application of sanctions alters how offenders estimate the value of drug use, making costs (sanctions) high enough to offset benefits (inebriation and group affiliation).

The clarity and transparency of program rules improves each offender's assessment of costs and benefits. The transparency of the drug court process could be viewed as a mechanism for resolving the "principal-agent problem" (Pindyck and Rubinfeld 1994). In the economics literature, the principal-agent problem describes the negative effects of asymmetric information in situations with different incentives for one party (the principal) who directs the actions of another (the agent). As a result, not all the information available to one party may be available to the other. The principal-agent problem in criminal justice generally takes the form of hidden actions and the measures that reveal them. In the case of drug courts, hidden actions would be the illegal activities of the agent, and drug court activities would be directed in large measure toward discovering these actions. Program participants are aware of their actions surrounding drug use or criminal activity but the court is not. Routine drug tests, for example, can be viewed as a way to increase the amount of information available. Increasing information reduces uncertainty for both the principal and the agent.

The drug court process creates a situation in which clients are expected to behave strategically. In fact, strategic behavior is an integral part of the drug court process. Any situation where an actor makes decisions based on expected payoffs is considered strategic. In the case of juvenile drug courts, a youth's decision to comply with program rules can be seen as a strategic choice based on the expected response of actors in the court (the judge, case manager, etc.). An explicitly theoretical approach to understanding JDCs would view client responses to court rules by modeling how clients view payoffs in particular situations. Most drug courts approach such questions intuitively.

LEARNING THEORY

A second class of theories that may aid in the understanding of JDCs can be described collectively as "learning theory." Learning theory describes how individuals respond to environmental conditions and how their response may lead to behavioral change. Unlike economic models of behavior, the principles of learning theory do not presume rationality. They focus on how various environmental cues—either physical or psychological—shape individual responses. In a theoretical framework for JDCs, learning theory could help shape court operational structures, the content of services, and the methods used to link treatment and social services.

Two important ideas form the basis of learning theory—operant conditioning (Skinner 1954) and social learning (Bandura 1977). Operant conditioning involves stimulus-response learning, which is guided by rewards (positive or negative reinforcements) or punishments (punitive consequence for particular behaviors). "Shaping" is the provision of frequent small rewards to achieve a larger desired result. "Stimulus generalization" describes how individuals learn that similar behaviors lead to similar outcomes, although conditions need not be replicated exactly to generate similar outcomes.

Social learning theory suggests that individuals will model the behavior of others in the hope of achieving a desired result or outcome. A role model such as a peer or an authority figure demonstrates the way to achieve outcomes through desired behaviors, which the individual agent then learns to adapt. Observers are more likely to model the behaviors of role models they admire, or to adapt behaviors that have functional value.

Two distinct paths can facilitate "learning" within a therapeutic or intervention context—a cognitive path and a cognitive-behavioral path. Cognitive interventions are typically short-term and symptom-focused (Beck 1963; McGinn and Sanderson 2001). The goal of cognitive intervention is to facilitate greater understanding of the nature of events or the dysfunctional behavior at issue. Interventions focus on how individuals interpret events in their lives and what assumptions they make about themselves and others. The cognitive therapeutic path consists of a series of interactions designed to lead individuals to better understand the causes and consequences of their actions. Through increased awareness of cause and effect, individuals learn to engage in rewarding behavior while avoiding detrimental behavior.

Cognitive-behavioral interventions rely on a two-tiered approach to spark learning. They combine the cognitive approach (strategies to reduce negative symptoms directly) with a behavioral approach in which individuals are introduced to strategies and techniques to replace negative cognition with positive skills and experiences (McGinn and Sanderson 2001). Specific and measurable goals are defined at the beginning of intervention, and success is defined in terms of achieving those goals. Once standing goals are met, the next task of cognitive-behavioral intervention is to prevent recurrence of negative symptoms or behaviors. Cognitive-behavioral interventions typically follow a highly structured format using a staged model in which progression from one stage to the next is contingent on completing particular milestones. Individuals learn techniques to prevent relapse of negative cognition and behaviors. They are encouraged to anticipate situations that might be difficult and use role-playing activities to prevent negative thoughts or behaviors. Cognitive-behavioral interventions make individual clients responsible for improving their situations, but interventions also include efforts to teach clients how to apply therapeutic techniques in their everyday lives.

The links between cognitive-behavioral techniques and JDC activities are clear. Most interventions include a system of phases to monitor and evaluate participant progression through the program, and many include participant instruction as a fundamental goal (Gottfredson, Jones, and Gore 2002). Juvenile drug courts may be particularly suited to the application of cognitive-behavioral approaches given the educational focus of most adolescents' daily lives.

Recognizing that individuals shape their environment and their behavioral response to the environment through action, Bandura (1999) noted the importance of "efficacy" in achieving learning and behavioral change. Self-efficacy is an individual's capacity to believe that a particular action will achieve a desired outcome. Perceived self-efficacy is the foundation of human agency. Belief that an action will produce a desired outcome leads a person to pursue that outcome. Improved self-efficacy affects motivation, aspirations, outcome expectancies, and perceptions of opportunity in the social environment (Bandura 2000). Adequate self-efficacy would encourage juvenile drug court clients to believe that they could succeed in becoming drug free, facilitating their actions to achieve that goal.

OTHER THEORETICAL CONCEPTS

Authority and legitimacy. Milgram (1974) defined a legitimate authority as a person who is recognized as having the *right* to give commands to others, and whom others feel obliged to obey. A legitimate authority is granted leverage over subordinates (individual agents or participants), and that leverage can be applied to varying degrees depending on the extent to which the authority's power is seen as legitimate. The relationship between authority and subordinate is a fundamental component of human organization, whether the relationship is between parent and child, teacher and student, manager and employee, or many other combinations of actors within hierarchical structures.

Both rational actor theory and learning theory suggest that interventions should involve an individual (or principal) at the center of the process with a legitimate claim to authority. In drug courts, the authority and visibility of the judge is pivotal, as is the perceived legitimacy of the therapist or treatment provider. In learning theory, the role of authority is critical. People who do not have control over their lives or their immediate situation may seek to improve their well-being or security through a proxy agency. In this socially mediated form of agency, people try to get others with authority, expertise, or influence to act on their behalf to achieve the outcomes they desire. Thus, successful learning can be facilitated by the effective use of legitimate authority.

Motivation and coercion. Drug courts use two mechanisms to apply cognitive-behavioral principles: motivation and coercion. Motivation is required for any change in behavior. It is at the root of any substance abuse treatment protocol. For courts, coercion is often the mechanism used to retain clients in a therapeutic environment. By keeping clients in a therapeutic environment, courts ensure that clients have opportunities to develop the internal motivation necessary to prevent relapse.

Motivation to begin or receive treatment was once thought to come entirely from within the individual. Failure in treatment was the responsibility of the client. Practitioners applied rewards and punishments to promote internal motivation. Current theories recognize two types of motivation: intrinsic and extrinsic (Donahoe and Palmer 1993). Intrinsic motivation originates internally, where an individual has (or develops) an independent desire to change his or her behavior. Extrinsic motivation originates from persuasion or coercion by an outside party, and it can be positive (e.g., offenders are paid to attend a treatment program) or negative (e.g., offenders are jailed if they fail to attend). Either source of motivation may be effective and lead to positive outcomes.

Drug court clients may respond to a mix of intrinsic and extrinsic sources. The authority of the court can be an extrinsic source of motivation, and this authority can be derived in turn from two sources of legitimacy: referent power and expert power (Raven 1965). Referent power is wielded when a subordinate obeys an authority because of respect and admiration. This type of authority does not rely on coercion or reward. Rather, the subordinate (or drug court client) develops respect and admiration from continued interaction over time with the authority (or judge). Expert power, in contrast, develops from the client's recognition that the authority has superior knowledge or ability. Obedience to this type of authority, however, takes time to develop.

Drug courts develop and support all forms of intrinsic motivation. An offender's desire to become drug free plays a critical role in both the successful completion of drug court and the persistence of the drug court's effects. The most successful programs may use the legitimate authority of the court to leverage multiple forms of power and motivation. While development of internal motivation is the ultimate goal of the drug court process, coerced treatment may also be a vehicle for that development. How do clients develop internal motivation, however, when they are forced to seek treatment? This tension, along with the tension experienced by a judge mandated to both motivate clients and maintain public safety, are at the heart of most criticisms of drug courts (e.g., Hoffman 2000). While the concept of extrinsic motivation may help explain this paradox, coerced treatment should be considered within the framework of an explicit theory, rather than simply applied ad hoc. If the application of coercion is inconsistent with the development of intrinsic motivation, the court process may not lead to positive and persistent outcomes.

Changing human behavior. Experts in substance abuse and chemical dependency once believed that the best way to promote behavior change was to aggressively break through "denial" and confront individuals with the consequences of their behavior. In practice, however, this technique could accelerate the process of failure and withdrawal for many clients, and those clients remaining may have been prone to succeed even without intervention. Current thinking about promoting behavior change in substance abusing clients accepts the cyclical nature of change, and recommends that intervention programs help clients move through the stages of change, often several times, before expecting them to achieve lasting improvement. A recurrence of unwanted behavior (i.e., a relapse into drug or alcohol use) is not seen as "failure," but as the end of one cycle and the beginning of the next.

In the popular "Transtheoretical Model of Change" developed by Prochaska and his colleagues (1982, 1992, 1994), people go through several stages on their way to lasting change:

- *Pre-contemplation.* No intention to take action to achieve long-term change.

- *Contemplation.* Intending to take action in the near future.
- *Preparation.* Intending to take action immediately and already taking some steps in that direction.
- *Action.* Completed changes in overt behavior during recent past.
- *Maintenance.* Completed long-term changes in overt behavior.
- *Termination.* Overt behavior will never return, and individual has complete confidence of ability to function without fear of relapse.

Other researchers have developed similar models of behavioral change. Fishbein (1997) focused on the relationship between intentions and behavior, since intentions are the underlying fabric of behavior. An individual's intentions, in turn, are determined by three factors: attitudes toward the behavior; norms (i.e., societal constraints) concerning the behavior; and perceived behavioral control (i.e., self-efficacy beliefs, or one's confidence in his or her ability to perform the behavior). Fishbein suggested that intentions could accurately predict behavior if an actor perceives the behavior as reasonable and achievable, but intentions may be a less-than-accurate predictor if an actor believes the behavior is not reasonable (e.g., lack of ability or negative environmental factors). An effort to change behavior needs to start by changing intentions, but it must also recognize whether those intentions are consistent with attitudinal and self-efficacy considerations. For example, intentions that spring from personal attitudes may be easier to modify than those rooted in societal norms or cultural expectations.

Still other models of behavior change could serve as a lens for viewing the behavioral change goals of juvenile drug courts. Rosenstock, Strecher, and Becker's (1988) three-stage health belief model, for example, saw perception as a key factor in behavior change. The first stage in the model starts with a person who may or may not have concern about a health issue or health-related behavior. A specific and salient motivator (either internal or external) is necessary to make a potential health issue relevant. The second stage begins with the onset of risk perception, when the individual (or someone close to the individual) becomes aware that a specific issue makes the individual vulnerable to illness or harm. For example, a perceived threat of illness often galvanizes people to assist their loved ones to lose weight, stop smoking, or quit drinking alcohol. Finally, the third stage in the model emerges with the belief that a given plan of action will sufficiently reduce the perceived threat at a subjectively acceptable cost (i.e., perceived barriers that must be overcome to reach the health goal).

As in most models, Rosenstock and his colleagues saw self-efficacy as critical in successful behavior change.

Finally, practitioners in juvenile drug courts should remember several pertinent facts that may alter their assessment of client motivation. First, JDC clients are adolescents. Their daily lives are spent accommodating and resisting adult authority in ways older clients may remember only vaguely. Traditional methods of assessing motivation may fail to detect an adolescent's true intentions. Second, very few juveniles have been abusing drugs long enough or severely enough to suffer the type of devastating personal consequences often seen in adults (divorce, loss of a home, unemployment, etc.). Convincing an adolescent of the risks accompanying drug use may be challenging. Third, even if they have started to experience negative consequences, it may be difficult for this reality to penetrate the veil of adolescent invincibility. Youth appearing in juvenile drug court are usually coerced to participate under the threat of legal sanctions, but their appreciation of such a threat may be less predictable than that of adult clients. Together, these observations underscore the importance of designing juvenile drug court evaluations with a conceptual framework that accounts for the unique influences on youth behavior.

Existing Frameworks for Evaluating Drug Courts

The next task in developing a conceptual framework for juvenile drug court evaluations is to consider all existing frameworks. While no frameworks exist for evaluating JDCs, practitioner organizations have published recommended program components for juvenile drug courts, and some work on conceptual frameworks for adult drug courts has emerged recently. These key component lists and beginning frameworks were developed for two purposes—to guide drug court practitioners and identify variation in drug court models that may be related to outcomes. Insights from these frameworks were helpful in developing the UI conceptual framework presented later in this chapter.

Frameworks Developed by Professional Consensus

In the past decade, several frameworks have been proposed for identifying the important features of drug court operations. Some frameworks are nontheoretical, normative lists of "best practices" derived from professional consensus. Two such frameworks were published by the former Drug Courts Program Office in 1997 and the National Drug Court Institute in collaboration with the National Council of Juvenile and Family Court Judges in 2003.

DRUG COURTS PROGRAM OFFICE

In a widely disseminated report, the former Drug Courts Program Office within the U.S. Department of Justice suggested there were 10 key components of drug courts (box 7.2). The DCPO key components, based on the work of an interdisciplinary committee, were intended as a set of professional guidelines for practitioners seeking to develop new drug court programs. The components in the list were not theoretically derived, nor were they linked empirically to program outcomes. The DCPO list simply

---

Box 7.2. Key Drug Court Components Identified by the Drug Courts Program Office

1. The drug court integrates alcohol and other drug treatment services with justice system case processing.
2. Using a nonadversarial approach, prosecution and defense counsel promote public safety while protecting participants' due process rights.
3. Eligible participants are identified early and promptly placed in the drug court program.
4. The drug court provides access to a continuum of alcohol, drug, and other related treatment and rehabilitative services.
5. Abstinence is monitored by frequent alcohol and other drug testing.
6. A coordinated strategy governs drug court responses to participants' compliance.
7. Ongoing judicial interaction with each drug court participant is essential.
8. Monitoring and evaluation measure the achievement of program goals and gauge effectiveness.
9. Continuing interdisciplinary education promotes effective drug court planning, implementation, and operations.
10. Forging partnerships among drug courts, public agencies, and community-based organizations generates local support and enhances drug court program effectiveness.

Source: Drug Courts Program Office (1997).

described a number of program components and structural features that committee members *believed* were important for program effectiveness (DCPO 1997). As such, the list summarized practitioner hypotheses about factors that *might* affect participant outcomes.

NATIONAL DRUG COURT INSTITUTE AND THE NATIONAL COUNCIL OF JUVENILE AND FAMILY COURT JUDGES

In 2003, the National Drug Court Institute collaborated with the National Council of Juvenile and Family Court Judges to draft a set of key components explicitly for juvenile drug courts. Their efforts resulted in a list of 16 elements, or "strategies in practice," that JDCs were encouraged to consider for their program operations (box 7.3). As with the DCPO key components, the NDCI/NCJFCJ framework was not designed to assist in evaluation design or hypothesis testing, but it did provide a checklist for developers of juvenile drug court programs.

Most of the elements proposed by NDCI/NCJFCJ described program characteristics that could affect the ability of JDCs to meet their primary goal of behavioral change. Some elements in the NDCI/NCJFCJ framework, however, were only indirectly related to a JDC program's potential effect on offender behavior. Elements 5 and 16, for example, may be important for program administration, but it would be hard to argue that their presence or absence would have an immediate and direct impact on a program's capacity to change offender behavior.

Frameworks Developed by Researchers

Two other conceptual frameworks for evaluating drug courts were developed by researchers, drawing on their studies of drug court outcomes. Developed by researchers associated with the RAND Corporation in California and Temple University in Pennsylvania, the two frameworks were directly applicable for evaluation design and represented important developments in the growing conceptual understanding of drug courts and their impact on offender behavior.

RAND FRAMEWORK

A team of researchers coordinated by the RAND Corporation developed an explicitly theoretical framework for drug courts based on the concept of therapeutic jurisprudence, which underlies the methods and practices of many drug courts (Longshore et al. 2001). The RAND framework iden-

Box 7.3. Juvenile Drug Court Strategies Identified by the National Drug Court Institute and the National Council of Juvenile and Family Court Judges

1. Collaborative planning	Engage all stakeholders in creating an interdisciplinary, coordinated, and systemic approach to working with youth and their families.
2. Teamwork	Develop and maintain an interdisciplinary, nonadversarial work team.
3. Clearly defined target population and eligibility criteria	Define a target population and eligibility criteria aligned with the program's goals and objectives.
4. Judicial involvement and supervision	Schedule frequent judicial reviews and be sensitive to the effect that court proceedings can have on youth and their families.
5. Monitoring and evaluation	Establish a system for program monitoring and evaluation to maintain quality of service, assess program impact, and contribute to knowledge in the field.
6. Community partnerships	Build partnerships with community organizations to expand the range of opportunities available to youth and their families.
7. Comprehensive treatment planning	Tailor interventions to the complex and varied needs of youth and their families.
8. Developmentally appropriate services	Tailor treatment to the developmental needs of adolescents.
9. Gender-appropriate services	Design treatment to address the unique needs of each gender.
10. Cultural competence	Create policies and procedures that are responsive to cultural differences and train personnel to be culturally competent.
11. Focus on strengths	Maintain a focus on the strengths of youth and their families during program planning and in every interaction between the court and those it serves.

(continued)

Box 7.3. *Continued*

12. Family engagement	Recognize and engage the family as a valued partner in all components of the program.
13. Educational linkages	Coordinate with the school system to ensure that each participant enrolls in and attends an educational program appropriate to his or her needs.
14. Drug testing	Design drug testing to be frequent, random, and observed. Document testing policies and procedures in writing.
15. Goal-oriented incentives and sanctions	Respond to compliance and noncompliance with incentives and sanctions designed to reinforce or modify the behavior of youth and their families.
16. Confidentiality	Establish a confidentiality policy and procedures that guard the privacy of the youth while allowing the drug court team to access key information.

Source: NDCI/NCJFCJ (2003).

tified key structure and process factors that researchers believed would facilitate offender rehabilitation. The authors designed their approach to satisfy five criteria. First, they proposed that a conceptual framework for drug court evaluations should be systematic and comprehensive, addressing all relevant program characteristics. Second, they believed that a useful framework should be parsimonious, or simple enough for researchers to test its utility. Third, they argued that a good framework should allow investigators to study factors that can be compared across drug courts. Fourth, they felt that a conceptual framework should lead researchers to measure program characteristics as implemented, not as designed or intended. The fifth and final criterion proposed by the RAND researchers was that a conceptual framework should suggest testable hypotheses relevant for policy and practice.

With these criteria in mind, the RAND team devised a relatively simple, yet robust conceptual framework consisting of five separate dimensions: leverage, population severity, program intensity, predictability, and rehabilitation emphasis (table 7.1). Each dimension focused evaluation *(text continues on page 244)*

Table 7.1. *Elements of the RAND Conceptual Framework*

Dimension	Description	Measures/Indicators	Hypothesis
Leverage	Severity of punishment for non-compliance, including program discharge. Depends on how adverse discharge is perceived, and how participants enter drug court—whether pre-plea or post-plea.	• Percent of pre-plea versus post-plea participants. • Perceived harm of discharge.	Drug courts that have greater leverage (whether actual or perceived) will have better outcomes.
Population severity	Characteristics of drug court participants, including criminal history and drug use behavior.	• Severity of drug use. • Severity of criminal history (current charge and prior charges).	Courts that handle offenders with less severe histories will have better outcomes.
Program intensity	Extent of requirements for participation and completion of drug court. (Does not refer to consequences for noncompliance, but what participants perceive as minimum requirements for completion.)	• Required frequency of urine testing. • Required frequency of court appearances. • Required hours of treatment. • Required employment activities.	Drug courts with more intensive requirements will have better outcomes than courts that are perceived as more lenient.

	Description	Indicators	Hypothesis
Predictability	Degree to which drug court participants know about and believe in the likelihood of responses to compliant and noncompliant behavior.	• Consistency of rewards and sanctions. • Conformance of actual rewards and sanctions with program protocol. • Time between noncompliance and response. • Perceived predictability.	Drug courts with more predictable rewards and sanctions will have better outcomes.
Rehabilitation emphasis	As the avowed agenda of drug courts is therapeutic jurisprudence, the primary agenda should be helping participants with substance abuse problems rather than other concerns.	• Strength of collaborative decisionmaking. • Attention to multiple needs. • Flexibility in procedure. • Concern for reentry. • Drug court dynamics (observed).	Courts with greater emphasis on rehabilitation will have better outcomes.

Source: Longshore et al. (2001).

studies on measurable, relevant, and consistently defined questions about the structure and process of drug court programs. Each dimension was accompanied by sample research hypotheses about the main effects expected for that dimension.

Several elements of the RAND framework (leverage, program intensity, and predictability) reflected standard theories of behavior change and were consistent with practitioner principles found in the DCPO and NDCI/NCJFCJ frameworks. Of course, to be implemented, the RAND elements would need to be more specific. The framework suggested several methods, for example, that *could* be used to measure program intensity (frequency of urine testing, frequency of court appearances, hours of treatment, etc.). It did not suggest how many program elements *should* be measured for their intensity.

Which elements of service delivery need to be emphasized, and which do not? Which aspects of the courtroom process or case management need to be maximized? Is the relationship between the judge and other drug court staff part of program intensity? By maximizing the framework's first two criteria simultaneously—i.e., comprehensiveness and parsimony—and by limiting the contents of the framework to five conceptual dimensions that were by definition broad and nonspecific, RAND made the framework almost too simple to provide practical guidance for future drug court evaluators.

The RAND framework implied that drug court outcomes were linearly related to rehabilitation emphasis and population severity, but evaluators would have to explore nonlinear associations as well. Perhaps the most positive client outcomes are likely among offenders with the *most* severe as well as the *least* severe drug abuse problems and offense histories. It is also possible that drug court programs can be too rehabilitative, and that the strongest effects on client behavior may be discovered in programs that use an effective balance of rehabilitation and deterrence, or even incapacitation. These and other unresolved issues in the RAND framework underscore the challenges faced by researchers as they attempt to develop frameworks that are parsimonious while still complex enough to offer practical assistance to evaluators.

TEMPLE UNIVERSITY FRAMEWORK

Drawing on their own experiences in conducting drug court evaluations, a team of researchers associated with Temple University developed an innovative framework for understanding and measuring drug court effectiveness (table 7.2). The researchers proposed that the most effective drug courts would be those programs in which certain features were present, and that comparing programs using these elements would help evaluators focus on the key characteristics of drug court operations. By tracking whether each element was present in a sample of drug court programs, and measuring client outcomes in those programs, investigators could learn how internal and external program factors influence client outcomes.

Table 7.2. *Elements of the Temple University Conceptual Framework*

Dimensions of program structure and process	Sample indicators
Target problem	• Specific drug-crime problem program addresses—e.g, AOD-related crime, homelessness and heroin addiction, property crime. • Problem that led to creation of drug court.
Target population	• Type of client focused on by drug court—e.g., felony defendants, probation or parole revocation cases, etc.
Court processing focus and adaptations	• Stage of court processing at which drug court intervention is offered to defendants—diversion, post-conviction, probation/parole and revocation.
Identification, screening, and evaluation of candidates—reaching the target	• Criteria or procedures used to locate and enroll clients. • Use of clinical assessments to evaluate substance abuse involvement of potential program clients.
Structure and content of treatment	• Treatment programs associated with drug court. • Range of options for treatment, substantive services provided, and types of supporting services. • Program phases, graduation requirements, and ways to fund treatment services. • Courtroom dynamics, as observed.
Responses to performance—participant accountability	• How program rewards positive achievements in treatment versus poor performance or noncompliance.
Extent of systemwide support for program	• Political, financial, and bureaucratic support and/or participation by criminal justice actors and non–justice system agencies (health, treatment, social services).

Source: Goldkamp (1999).

According to Goldkamp (1999), internal factors are those characteristics of drug courts and drug court offenders that directly affect outcomes. There are two types of internal factors: offender attributes (age, race/ethnicity, gender, etc.) and drug court program elements (contact with the judge, frequency of drug tests, etc.). External factors, on the other hand, are forces outside the control of a drug court that could also affect outcomes, including political, fiscal, organizational, and cultural influences. For example, a jurisdiction might change the legal penalties for particular forms of drug use, thereby altering the range of people willing to risk drug use and their willingness to participate in drug court and treatment if apprehended. Researchers should monitor both internal and external factors during drug court evaluations to avoid misinterpreting patterns in client outcomes.

The Temple University researchers also proposed that researchers should develop an understanding of how the drug court process affects client behavior. In a series of analyses conducted with client-level data from two drug court programs, the authors designed and tested various models of the drug court process, or the chain of events leading from program activities to program outcomes. The model that seemed most supported by the data portrayed the drug court process as a series of relationships among several clusters of factors, including offender attributes, drug court elements, drug court outcomes, and offender behavior (figure 7.1).

According to the analysis, offender behavior is at least partly a result of the attributes offenders bring into the drug court process, such as their demographic characteristics, their economic and social contexts, and their specific experiences with substance abuse and criminal offending (path A). According to the model, the association between pre-court offender attributes and post-court offender behaviors should be mediated or interrupted by the impact of the drug court process. Drug courts are designed to have an independent effect on offender behavior (path B) as long as they implement particular program elements, which result in certain outcomes (path C). Finally, of course, drug court outcomes may be partly shaped by the prior attributes of offenders (path D).

The approach taken by the Temple University project was an important contribution to the research literature and to developing an understanding of how drug courts function. If a researcher were responsible for disseminating the ideal drug court model to state and local officials,

Figure 7.1. *Temple University Framework for Analyzing the Impact of Drug Courts*

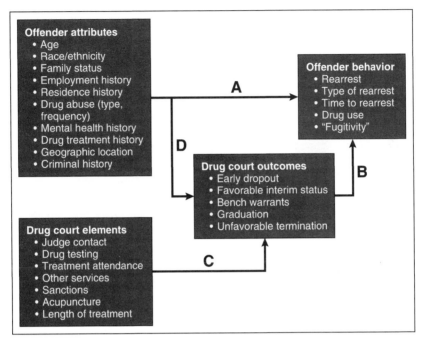

Source: Goldkamp, White, and Robinson (2001, 50).

the Temple framework would provide some conceptual guidance and at least a beginning explanation of how drug court programs may achieve their primary goal of client behavior change. The Urban Institute framework extends this form of analysis by adding variables on court practices and interim outcomes that may help explain the links between various program elements.

The Urban Institute Framework

To devise a theoretically oriented conceptual framework that will facilitate hypothesis testing, the Urban Institute reviewed the previously published frameworks from the RAND Corporation, Temple University, and NDCI/NCJFCJ. In addition, researchers gathered information during site visits to six juvenile drug court programs as part of the National Evaluation of Juvenile Drug Courts project (see Rossman et al. in this volume). The site visits involved reviews of program records and operations; interviews with judges, program staff, and treatment agencies; and direct observations of client staffings and drug court hearings. These combined efforts resulted in a new conceptual framework for evaluating juvenile drug courts (figure 7.2).

The Urban Institute's conceptual framework is designed to

- direct researchers' attention to the most important ingredients of program operations;
- encourage the formulation and testing of viable hypotheses about the relationships between program activities and outcomes; and
- suggest measurement approaches and data collection techniques that may be used to establish causal links between program outcomes and changes in client behavior.

Whether guided by this framework or another, future evaluation research on juvenile drug courts must be guided by some coherent framework. The Urban Institute conceptual framework may not be definitive, but it is one approach that could allow researchers to advance knowledge about juvenile drug court effectiveness through the systematic accumulation of empirical findings. The UI framework encourages researchers to consider the theoretical underpinnings of program activities and program outcomes. It specifies a potential causal chain of events leading from program activities to program outcomes and suggests a research agenda that could allow evaluators to reject some of the many hypotheses currently competing to explain drug court impacts.

The UI framework is divided into four basic elements: inputs, outputs, intermediate outcomes, and end outcomes. Inputs (staff, salaries, expertise, etc.) lead directly to program outputs, which would be measured by tracking the results of program activities (participants served, treatments delivered, hearings held, etc.). Outputs lead to intermediate outcomes, which would generally be measured as participant experiences and perceptions of the juvenile drug court process. These experiences and perceptions lead participants to internalize the lessons of drug court and motivate them to change their behavior. As a result, program participants begin to alter their behavior (end outcomes) in ways hypothesized by drug court theories.

Figure 7.2. *Urban Institute Conceptual Framework for Evaluating Juvenile Drug Courts*

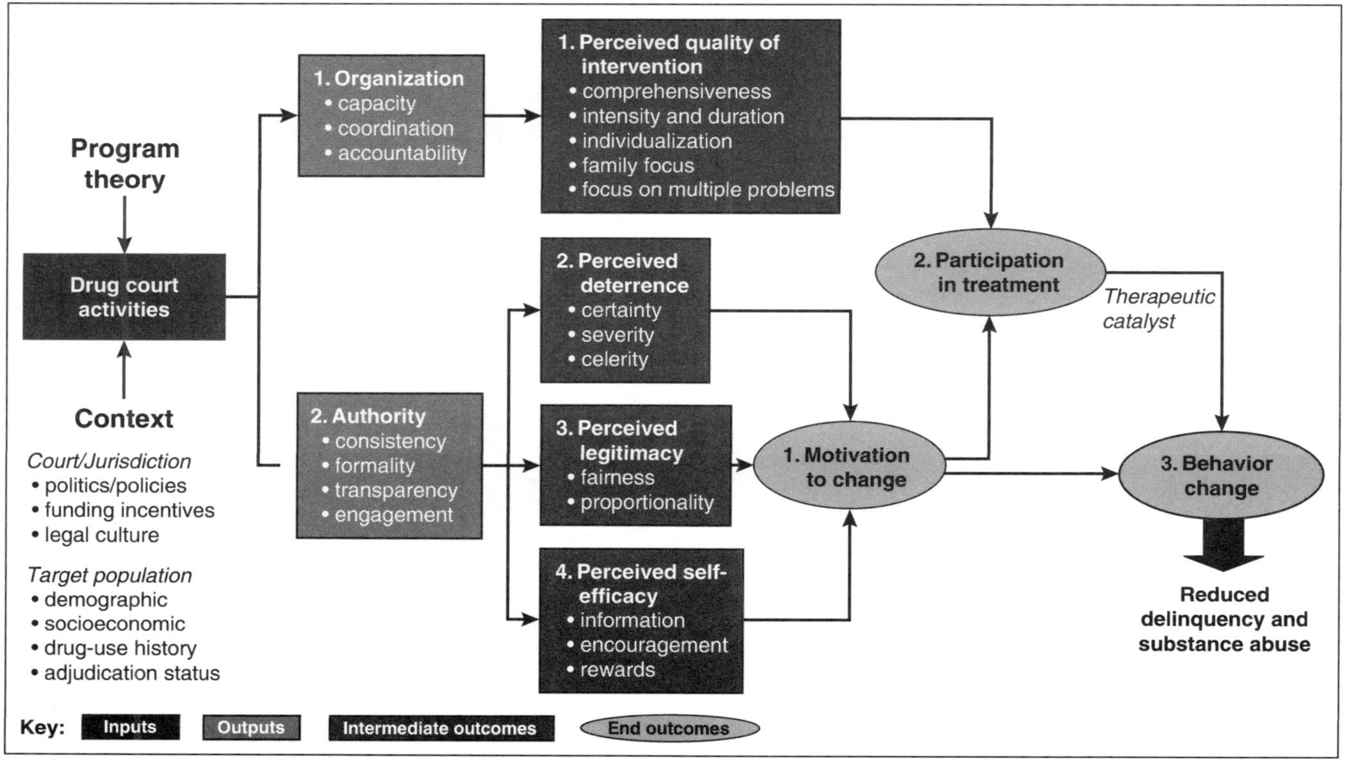

Source: Urban Institute National Evaluation of Juvenile Drug Courts.

Background Elements—Program Theory and Context

Before evaluators measure program inputs and client outcomes, they may want to specify the contextual and theoretical factors that underlie program designs and operations. These factors often shape local choices about juvenile drug court activities. Juvenile drug courts can significantly change the philosophy and orientation of the juvenile justice system. Drugs courts require complex interactions among agencies, individuals, and community members, and the policies and practices adopted by individual drug courts will reflect these environmental factors. Each interaction, in turn, is likely shaped by budgetary politics, local political values, and demographic or economic trends. External forces, whether theoretical (rehabilitation versus punishment), structural (judicial control versus staff control), or communal (urban versus rural, affluent versus impoverished), contribute to the approach a drug court adopts. Whenever relevant, these factors should be included in evaluation studies as potential influences on program inputs and, therefore, outputs and outcomes.

Input—Drug Court Activities

Identifying the individual activities that make up a juvenile drug court is critical in evaluation research. Evaluators need to track how various resources are used in a juvenile drug court program and how the program handles its cases. The Urban Institute framework does not provide any further detail about inputs because they are the most thoroughly analyzed part of juvenile drug courts and drug court programs in general. Inputs are also probably one part of evaluation that practitioners and program managers are capable of managing completely independently, without assistance from outside evaluators or research specialists.

The fact that program inputs are represented by a single box in the conceptual framework should not be interpreted to mean they are less important than other elements. Evaluations must measure what happens to program clients during their drug court participation. How many hearings do they attend? How many community supervision contacts are made? How many times are they drug tested, and when? How many days do they spend in detention, and why? It is only by measuring inputs carefully that evaluation studies can explain a program's effects on client behavior.

Collecting consistent data on program activities and examining their relationship to client behavior allow an evaluator to test hypotheses about cause and effect. Which of the many program components involved in a juvenile drug court influences the court's ability to achieve client outcomes? Would JDCs be just as effective, for example, if cases were heard one at a time with no audience, or is the fact that juveniles witness the handling of each other's cases in open court a crucial ingredient in the drug court process? Would JDCs be just as successful if they abandoned positive reinforcements and tangible rewards? Must the court's authority be backed up with the threat and actual use of secure detention, or would offenders be just as likely to respond to other sanctions? Which parts of the juvenile drug court process encourage offenders to continue their behavioral changes after they leave the program?

MEASURABLE PROGRAM ACTIVITIES

No two juvenile drug courts are identical, but all juvenile drug courts share some basic operational features that should be tracked by evaluation studies and measured at the individual level. All courts have procedures for identifying and recruiting eligible offenders. All require client involvement in a treatment program. All use a collaborative team to monitor treatment progress and program compliance, and have judicial involvement, a graduated sanctioning scheme, and a form of program graduation. In addition to these common elements—which should be measured in detail—drug courts vary on a number of other dimensions that evaluation studies should consider. These dimensions include the following:

- *Oversight.* Some drug courts establish formal oversight boards to develop and direct their operations. These boards may include various stakeholders. Advisory boards may be established for specific functional areas, such as clinical or educational boards.
- *Leadership.* In many drug courts, the judge is the charismatic leader, directing all aspects of court operations. Other courts rotate hearing authorities, and program leadership may be staff-driven.
- *Legal eligibility.* Some drug courts are limited to misdemeanor cases or first-time offenders. Others accept felony cases and offenders with long criminal histories. Guidelines vary from place to place, reflecting local politics, public safety concerns, and the availability of treatment and social services.
- *Legal incentives at recruitment.* Legal penalties may be reduced in exchange for drug court completion, including case dismissal, a

shorter period of probation, probation instead of incarceration, or a shorter period of incarceration.

- *Clinical eligibility.* Some drug courts require a diagnosis of abuse or dependence. Others admit offenders if they report drug use, test positive for drugs, or request treatment. These courts may accept occasional drug users. A few drug courts admit participants based on legal charges alone, without evidence of personal drug use, or as a diversion program for offenders with a history of drug sales.

- *Treatment availability, appropriateness, and quality.* Juvenile drug courts may develop their own treatment, or they may purchase treatment from other providers. Some drug courts establish formal Memoranda of Understanding with treatment providers, while others maintain informal relationships.

- *Program duration and intensity.* Generally, juvenile drug court programs last at least six months. Some require more than a year of participation. Many include a "phase" structure, where the intensity of program requirements is gradually reduced as participants achieve predetermined indicators of compliance. The phase structures may be formally incorporated into drug court protocols, or vary across participants.

- *Drug testing.* Drug testing policies vary from court to court. Frequency of testing may depend on treatment mode and phase. The drugs included in tests may be limited to as few as three substances or as many as 10.

- *Judicial monitoring.* The timing and frequency of court reviews depends on drug court policies. Docketing of cases, length of hearings, order of appearances, and other aspects of the judicial review process may vary.

- *Compliance.* Most drug courts track participant compliance, treatment progress, drug test results, and program attendance. Drug courts may also track educational participation and attainment, compliance with parents or guardians, community service participation, payment of program fees, and other requirements.

- *Sanctioning protocols.* Failure to comply with program requirements usually prompts a set of graduated sanctions, where penalties increase in severity with each new infraction. Sanctioning schedules may be formal and predetermined, or may vary across participants and across time. The actual penalties faced by participants may vary considerably across courts.

- *Termination policies.* Participants may be terminated from drug court for a new arrest, positive drug tests, or failing to appear at court hearings or treatment appointments. The rules vary from one drug court to another. Some courts permit offenders to reenter after an unsuccessful termination, but many do not.
- *Graduation requirements.* Abstinence is only one of several requirements for graduation. Some juvenile drug courts require that participants receive a high school diploma or a GED, maintain employment or enrollment in an educational or vocational program, be current in all financial obligations (which often includes drug court fees and child support payments), and have a sponsor in the community. Many programs also require participants to perform community service.

In addition to client-specific variables, each relevant aspect of program structure or policy should be measured separately for each client in the study. In other words, client-level databases should be constructed so the presence or absence of important program characteristics can be attributed to each client. Was the client in a program with a single judge or rotating judges? Was the client in a program that excluded felony charges or one that accepted them, independently of the charge involved in his or her case? By tracking how program-related factors as well as case-related factors vary over time and across jurisdictions, and how they correlate with client outcomes, researchers will be able to accumulate evidence that establishes how juvenile drug court components combine to generate the outputs and outcomes desired by program planners.

Output 1—Organization

Juvenile drug court programs operate at more than one level of intervention. They use their legal authority to directly affect the behavior of individual offenders but they also work to improve service-delivery systems in their communities. The Urban Institute's conceptual framework portrays the first principal output of juvenile drug court activities as the effective organization of resources to serve program clients.

Juvenile drug courts, and especially the judges in juvenile drug courts, are often deeply involved in the design and management of service-delivery systems in their communities. Instead of merely selecting from available treatment programs and ordering youth to participate in those programs, juvenile drug courts work to develop needed programs and hold treatment providers accountable by reviewing treatment plans and determining whether each drug court case is properly managed. By actively supervising the adequacy of case management and service delivery, JDCs ensure that clients receive the services they need to change their behavior.

Key elements in organizational oversight include interagency client staffings, communication with outside providers, interactions of judges and other staff during courtroom hearings, judicial responses to failed service plans, and court management of the contracting process for service providers. Researchers could measure these elements in many ways, but they should at least assess the resource *capacity* of the service delivery system and how it responds to court intervention, the *coordination* of services (from the perspective of the judge, the youth, and the family), and the *accountability* of the entire system. Measurement of these indicators should be coded at the individual case level so the data can be correlated with intermediate outcomes (i.e., whether the various elements of effective organization are associated with participant experiences and perceptions as hypothesized).

- *Capacity.* The capacity of the service-delivery system refers to the size and diversity of treatment resources and other services available for drug court clients, as well as the intensity and adequacy of those resources and services. Measures of capacity could include the percentage of juvenile drug court cases in which services ordered by the court are available and credible. These indicators would likely vary at the court or program level, but the values of each indicator should be included in client-level data files.
- *Coordination.* The coordination of the treatment and services system refers to the strength and frequency of interagency relationships among service providers in the community, and how well providers respond to court supervision. Again, these system characteristics should be attached to client-level records.
- *Accountability.* Do drug court clients receive services as ordered by the court, and does the court possess and actually exercise the authority to enforce its orders? Researchers should assess not only what a program does and why, but also how these actions affect the behavior of other organizations within the service-delivery system,

and how the system responds in individual cases. To measure these factors, evaluators will likely need to survey judges, drug court staff, and treatment providers.

Output 2—Authority

The second program output is authority. The defining characteristic of JDCs is how they combine the authority of the court process with constructive social interventions and effective drug treatment. Legal authority encourages young offenders to participate and remain in treatment, but it is also thought to exert an independent effect on offender behavior. In particular, JDCs are designed to motivate behavior change in offenders with dramatic, yet supportive courtroom routines and close, repeated attention from the judge and other courtroom participants.

Juvenile drug courts maintain many of the data elements required to measure authority in their management information systems. *Consistency* can be measured by examining sanctions administered in response to a youth's first, second, and third infractions of program rules. Other indicators, such as *transparency, engagement,* and *formality,* can be measured at regular intervals through participant surveys or questionnaires. Surveys administered at regularly scheduled case manager meetings or graduations, for example, could assess whether participants believe the drug court process is fair, if they know the program rules, and if court hearings hold their interest.

Most intermediate outcomes hypothesized to result from the effective use of authority will have to be measured through surveys or interviews with participants. While some authority measures should determine whether the drug court did what it intended (e.g., was the drug court process transparent as intended), participant surveys should measure whether participants believe the court's authority influences their behavior. For example, clients could be asked whether the court's response to their behavior is fair and proportional. Surveys and interviews should determine whether court operations are consistent with theories of behavioral change.

- *Consistency.* Program staff, youth, and their families should report that the imposition of sanctions, the granting of rewards, and other procedures are consistent and predictable, and that the court process appears fair and equitable. Consistent implementation of court procedures should indicate to offenders that the imposition of sanctions is a dependable consequence of failure to follow program requirements.

- *Formality.* Courtroom procedures and any other court activities witnessed by young offenders should be perceived as formal and youth should report that the court possesses legitimate legal and social authority to intervene and sanction their behavior.

- *Transparency.* Young offenders should see the process itself as clear and easy to follow, with minimal legal jargon and procedural complexity. Decisionmaking about individual cases should be conducted in open court whenever possible and offenders should report that they are free to ask questions in open court. Youth and their families should report that they witness not only their own hearings but those of other youth as well.

- *Engagement.* Juvenile drug courts are designed to be engaging, at times even entertaining, for young offenders and their families. This element of the drug court process is sometimes referred to as "the theater effect." The court process is designed to hold the attention of offenders in order to facilitate behavioral change, and some researchers suggest that the quality and intensity of interaction between judges and offenders has an independent effect on offender behavior (Senjo and Leip 2001). Youth descriptions of the juvenile drug court process should reflect this attribute. Youth should also understand that tangible rewards are used to reinforce positive behavior, and the entire process should be memorable and provoke visceral reactions.

Intermediate Outcome 1—Perceived Quality of Intervention

By leveraging or establishing adequate services and supervision for drug-involved offenders, JDCs presumably encourage young offenders to participate and remain in treatment. Youth handled in an effective system of intervention, and professionals who work in that system, should be able to confirm the presence of effective system characteristics, such as whether the juvenile drug court delivers on its promises regarding services and treatment. Program evaluators should measure several indicators of intervention quality, including *comprehensiveness, intensity and duration, individualization, family focus,* and a *focus on multiple problems.*

- *Comprehensiveness.* Youth in an effectively organized service-delivery system should report that their treatment plan deals with a wide range of individual, family, and community problems thought to be associated with substance abuse problems. Treatment professionals and court staff could also be asked to rate the comprehensiveness of each youth's treatment experience, and their ratings could be attached to client-level data records.
- *Intensity and duration.* The service-delivery system should be equipped to work with young offenders as long as, and as much as, each youth requires. In addition, juvenile drug court judges should report satisfaction with their ability to secure adequate services for youthful offenders.
- *Individualization.* Treatment providers should supply services and supervision programs that meet the needs of a wide variety of individual offenders in varying family and community contexts.
- *Family focus.* At least some service providers available to the juvenile drug court should employ methods that are family-focused, and youth and their families should be able to describe this feature of their program experience.
- *Focus on multiple problems.* Service providers should employ methods that focus on a range of potential problem areas for each youth. These areas could include educational issues, mental health problems, and family violence.

Intermediate Outcome 2—Perceived Deterrence

The intermediate outcomes associated with an effective use of authority are perceived deterrence, perceived legitimacy of authority, and the perceived self-efficacy of participants. As all these intermediate outcomes rely on internal, subjective perceptions of clients, measuring them will require evaluators to use questionnaires or interviews with juvenile clients.

Classical deterrence theory suggests that sanctions and punishments are more effective when delivered with the proper combination of certainty, severity, and celerity. To some extent, these elements can offset each other. Sanctions that are certain may not have to be as severe or swift, those that are very severe may not have to be as certain or swift, and so on. Deterrence theory presupposes that, by nature, people act to minimize pain and are sufficiently rational to develop expectations about the consequences of their actions. People weigh the expected benefits of criminal or deviant acts against expected benefits and perform only those acts for which the benefits seem to exceed costs. Thus, increasing the certainty, swiftness, or severity of punishment should affect the cost-benefit calculus of would-be offenders and deter them from acting illegally.

In empirically connecting deterrence and drug court program outcomes, researchers should measure each offender's perceptions of the *certainty, severity,* and *celerity* of sanctions. Each youth's beliefs and opinions should be measured more than once during his or her involvement with the drug court to detect changes that may occur as a result of experiences in the program.

- *Certainty.* Youth involved with the juvenile court should report in interviews or surveys that they understand the consequences for program rule violations. They should report high levels of confidence that sanctions will be imposed as announced.
- *Severity.* Each youth's impressions of sanction severity should be measured. The measures should include sanctions imposed by treatment and service delivery agencies in addition to those imposed by the court process.
- *Celerity.* Interviews and survey questionnaires should measure each youth's perceptions about the scheduling of program sanctions, and whether sanctions appear to be imposed as scheduled.

Intermediate Outcome 3—Perceived Legitimacy

To ensure their compliance with authority, individuals must perceive the authority as legitimate, which is partly a function of how transparently and fairly decisions are made. Offenders may comply with drug court requirements not only to avoid unwanted consequences (self-interest) but also because they believe the court (usually the judge) has behaved in accordance with shared norms regarding the administration of justice. Drug court consultant Michael Smith of New York's Lincoln Hospital has endorsed this view by saying, "The drug court model creates a very healthy and transparent system of authority. The actions of the judge depend directly on the patient's own performance; it's all observable: the urine screens, the attendance, how the patient relates to other patients" (as quoted by Satel 1998, 47).

The primary indicators of perceived legitimacy are *fairness and proportionality.*

- *Fairness and proportionality.* Whether a court process (and the court's authority) is perceived as legitimate must be assessed by measuring the attitudes and opinions of individuals subjected to the process and whether it is procedurally just. Tyler (1997) identified four key dimensions of procedural justice: trustworthiness of the decisionmaking authority, opportunity for personal participation in the proceedings, being treated with respect/dignity by authorities, and the neutrality of authority. These indicators should be collected via questionnaires or face-to-face interviews with participants.

Intermediate Outcome 4—Perceived Self-Efficacy

Social psychological theory asserts that individuals attempt to shape their environment through action, and their willingness to engage in action depends in part on self-efficacy, or their subjective belief in the likelihood of success. Perceived self-efficacy would naturally be associated with motivation, goals, aspirations, outcome expectancies, and perceptions of opportunity in the social environment.

Information, encouragement, and *rewards* are all indicators of perceived self-efficacy.

- *Information.* Youth should report that they have information relevant to change their substance use behaviors, and they should be able to demonstrate comprehension of such information in interviews or questionnaires.
- *Encouragement.* Youth should believe that they have the ability to change, and their personal opinions and beliefs should suggest that the juvenile drug court program has encouraged them to make behavioral changes.
- *Rewards.* Interviews and survey questionnaires should measure each youth's perceptions about the scheduling of program rewards, and whether he or she believes that program youth receive timely and tangible inducements or rewards for making behavior changes.

End Outcome 1—Motivation to Change

The four intermediate outcomes (intervention, deterrence, legitimacy, and self-efficacy) hypothetically affect three end outcomes. The first logically necessary end outcome is motivation to change. Successful behavioral change depends on an individual receiving considerable support and encouragement to change and directly experiencing successful change. A key concept in most behavioral change models suggests that individuals are more likely to succeed when they believe they will get some tangible benefit from changing their behavior. These "outcome expectations" can be defined as a person's estimate that a given behavior will lead to a particular outcome.

Each prominent behavioral change model discussed above, as well as others not described here, could offer something to practitioners seeking more systematic methods of conceptualizing change for program design and client impact assessment. Regardless of which model seems to fit best, it is important that conceptual frameworks for juvenile drug courts include some formal model of behavior change and the motivations for change.

End Outcome 2—Participation in Treatment

The second end outcome is participation in treatment. The principal goal of the juvenile drug court process is to ensure that clients become engaged, and remain, in treatment, or at least that they persist through the stages of behavior change. Juvenile clients often begin and remain in treatment through coercion. Coercion is rarely effective on its own, but it can entice or restrain a client to continue in a program of treatment, and the longer a client remains in treatment, the greater the chance that treatment can facilitate and sustain change.

Researchers should collect enough data about each youth's subjective experience of the juvenile drug court process to specify the form of motivation that appears most relevant in each case (i.e., whether behavior change was in response to the coercion of the court process alone or to the therapeutic catalyst of the treatment process as well). By establishing empirical connections between program activities, client motivation, and changes in actual behavior, juvenile drug court evaluations will identify the most effective pathways to behavior change.

End Outcome 3—Behavior Change

Juvenile drug courts must state their goals and intended outcomes carefully. Some programs may be tempted to present themselves as remedies for a long menu of problems facing adolescents. The interventions offered by most drug courts, however, can reasonably be expected to affect only a small range of behaviors directly related to drug use and delinquent offending. The problem faced by drug courts is similar to that facing most school systems. To have a real impact on the lives of the lowest achievers, schools would have to intervene in every facet of a child's life. Many schools find the challenge overwhelming and unrealistic, and they set goals of a lower order (attendance, test scores, etc.).

Similarly, juvenile drug courts cannot transform their clients into young pillars of the community. Drug courts are designed to prevent youth from using drugs and committing new crimes associated with their drug use. Behavior change goals are most appropriately conceptualized within these bounds. The inputs, outputs, intermediate outcomes, and end outcomes in the conceptual framework are designed to measure the efficacy of drug courts in achieving these more limited goals. Of course, the measurement of behavior change may include self-reported measures and clinical, diagnostic inventories about substance abuse, but it should also focus on justice-related behavior, such as reported arrests, court referrals, and adjudications.

Conclusion

Drug courts are based on the hypothesis that active court oversight and the effective use of legal authority, combined with high quality treatment, will encourage offenders to change their drug-related behavior more effectively than either the court or the treatment system can do alone. This hypothesis has broad, intuitive appeal, but more evidence is needed to establish its authenticity. A number of evaluation studies have suggested that drug courts may be effective, but few studies have come close to providing convincing evidence (see Roman and DeStefano, in this volume). To develop sound evaluation findings for policymakers and practitioners, evaluation researchers must document the effects of specific program elements on offender behavior. To do so, researchers need to identify how drug courts work and exactly how they achieve their primary goal of changing offender behavior.

Without conceptual frameworks, there would be an endless supply of potential factors to consider in evaluating juvenile drug courts. Research designs must be built theoretically and empirically, not from assertions about "best practices" or the biases of individual researchers or practitioners. Conceptual frameworks can help evaluators disaggregate the potential causal influences and interactions among various program components and expected outcomes. By collecting data within such a framework, evaluators can test empirical relationships, identify causal connections, and discard unproven hypotheses along with the unnecessary program components that support them. This chapter has described a conceptual framework that could help future evaluation studies focus on detecting and explaining differences in the success of varying juvenile drug court models and identify those aspects of the juvenile drug court process most related to outcomes.

Conceptual frameworks provide a roadmap for evaluation design, but every evaluation does not need to explore every nook and cranny of the mapped terrain. The measurement and analysis of every element described in a framework would require a sophisticated and expensive evaluation design involving large subject samples and extensive data collection, including client interviews, questionnaires, direct observations, and paper and electronic records from multiple agencies. Evaluators and court practitioners may find that certain elements of their chosen framework can be disregarded in some studies, or perhaps some elements can be measured using less-than-ideal methods to reduce the cost of a particular evaluation. This strategy could be acceptable as long as every evaluation is at least designed to test some explicit hypothesis of program impact. Knowledge of program impact will only be advanced by rejecting hypotheses, not by generating new hypotheses that are never tested.

REFERENCES

Akers, Ronald L. 2000. *Criminological Theories: Introduction, Evaluation, and Application,* 3rd ed. Los Angeles: Roxbury.

Anglin, M. Douglas, Mary-Lynn Brecht, and Ebrahim Maddahian. 1989. "Pre-treatment Characteristics and Treatment Performance of Legally Coerced versus Voluntary Methadone Maintenance Admissions." *Criminology* 27(3): 537–56.

Anglin, M. Douglas, Yih-Ing Hser, and Christine E. Grella. 1997. "Drug Addiction and Treatment Careers among Clients in the Drug Abuse Treatment Outcome Study (DATOS)." *Psychology of Addictive Behaviors* 11(4): 308–23.

Bandura, Albert. 1977. *Social Learning Theory.* Englewood Cliffs, NJ: Prentice Hall, Inc.

———. 1999. "A Sociocognitive Analysis of Substance Abuse: An Agentic Perspective." *Psychological Science* 10(3): 214–17.

———. 2000. "Exercise of Human Agency through Collective Efficacy." *Current Directions in Psychological Science* 9(3): 75–78.

Beck, Aaron T. 1963. "Thinking and Depression: I. Idiosyncratic Content and Cognitive Distortions." *Archives of General Psychiatry* 9(4): 324–33.

Becker, Gary S. 1968. "Crime and Punishment: An Economic Approach." *The Journal of Political Economy* 76(2): 169–217.

Belenko, Steven. 1999. "Research on Drug Courts: A Critical Review, 1999 Update." *National Drug Court Institute Review* 2(2): 1–58.

———. 2001. *Research on Drug Courts: A Critical Review, 2001 Update.* New York: Columbia University, National Center on Addiction and Substance Abuse.

Clarke, Ronald V., and Derek B. Cornish. 1985. "Modeling Offenders' Decisions: A Framework for Research and Policy." In *An Annual Review of Research,* Vol. 6 of *Crime and Justice,* edited by Michael Tonry and Norval Morris (147–85). Chicago: University of Chicago Press.

Collins, James J., and Margaret Allison. 1983. "Legal Coercion and Retention in Drug Abuse Treatment." *Hospital and Community Psychiatry* 34(12): 1145–49.

Cornish, Derek B., and Ronald V. Clarke, eds. 1986. *The Reasoning Criminal: Rational Choice Perspectives on Offending.* New York: Springer-Verlag.

CSAT/SAMHSA. *See* Substance Abuse and Mental Health Services Administration, Center for Substance Abuse Treatment.

DCPO. *See* Drug Courts Program Office.

Donahoe, John W., and David Palmer. 1993. *Learning and Complex Behavior.* Boston: Allyn and Bacon.

Drug Courts Program Office. 1997. *Defining Drug Courts: The Key Components.* Washington, DC: U.S. Department of Justice, Office of Justice Programs, Drug Courts Program Office.

Falkin, Gregory P. 1993. *Coordinating Drug Treatment for Offenders: A Case Study.* New York: National Development and Research Institutes, Inc.

Fishbein, Martin. 1997. "Predicting, Understanding, and Changing Socially Relevant Behaviors: Lessons Learned." In *The Message of Social Psychology Perspectives on Mind in Society,* edited by Craig McGarty (77–91). Malden, MA: Blackwell Publishers, Inc.

GAO. *See* U.S. General Accounting Office.

Gibbons, Don C. 1994. *Talking about Crime and Criminals: Problems and Issues in Theory Development in Criminology.* Englewood Cliffs, NJ: Prentice Hall, Inc.

Goldkamp, John S. 1999. "Challenges for Research and Innovation: When Is a Drug Court Not a Drug Court?" In *The Early Drug Courts, Case Studies in Judicial Innovation,* edited by W. Clinton Terry III (166–77). Thousand Oaks, CA: Sage Publications.

Goldkamp, John S., Michael D. White, and Jennifer B. Robinson. 2001. "Do Drug Courts Work? Getting Inside the Drug Court Black Box." *Journal of Drug Issues* 31(1): 27–72.

Gottfredson, Gary D., Elizabeth M. Jones, and Thomas W. Gore. 2002. "Implementation and Evaluation of a Cognitive-Behavioral Intervention to Prevent Problem Behavior in a Disorganized School." *Prevention Science* 3(1): 43–56.

Hirst, Alexa, and Adele V. Harrell. 2000. "Measuring Perceptions of Procedural Justice among Court-Monitored Offenders." Paper presented at the 52nd annual meeting of the American Society of Criminology, San Francisco, Nov. 14–18.

Hoffman, Morris B. 2000. "The Drug Court Scandal." *North Carolina Law Review* 78:1437–1534.

Hora, Peggy F., William G. Schma, and John T. A. Rosenthal. 1999. "Therapeutic Jurisprudence and the Drug Treatment Court Movement: Revolutionizing the Criminal Justice System's Response to Drug Abuse and Crime in America." *Notre Dame Law Review* 74(2): 439–537.

Hubbard, Robert L., Mary Ellen Marsden, J. Valley Rachal, Henrick J. Harwood, Elizabeth Cavanaugh, and Harold M. Ginzburg. 1989. *Drug Abuse Treatment: A National Study of Effectiveness.* Chapel Hill: The University of North Carolina Press.

Kofoed, Lial, Joyce Kania, Thomas Walsh, and Roland M. Atkinson. 1986. "Outpatient Treatment of Patients with Substance Abuse and Coexisting Psychiatric Disorders." *American Journal of Psychiatry* 143(7): 867–72.

Lawental, Eli, A. Thomas McClellan, Grant R. Grissom, Peter Brill, and Charles O'Brien. 1996. "Coerced Treatment for Substance Abuse Problems Detected through Workplace Urine Surveillance: Is It Effective?" *Journal of Substance Abuse* 8(1): 115–28.

Longshore, Douglas, Susan Turner, Suzanne Wenzel, Andrew Morral, Adele Harrell, Duane McBride, Elizabeth Deschenes, and Martin Iguchi. 2001. "Drug Courts: A Conceptual Framework." *Journal of Drug Issues* 31(1): 7–26.

Marlowe, Douglas B., and Kimberly C. Kirby. 1999. "Effective Use of Sanctions in Drug Courts: Lessons from Behavioral Research." *National Drug Court Institute Review* 2(1): 1–29.

McGinn, Leta K., and William C. Sanderson. 2001. "What Allows Cognitive Behavioral Therapy to be Brief: Overview, Efficacy, and Crucial Factors Facilitating Brief Treatment." *Clinical Psychology: Science and Practice* 8(1): 23–37.

Milgram, Stanley. 1974. *Obedience to Authority: An Experimental View.* New York: Harper and Row.

Miller, Norman S., and Joseph A. Flaherty. 2000. "Effectiveness of Coerced Addiction Treatment (Alternative Consequences): A Review of the Clinical Research." *Journal of Substance Abuse Treatment* 18:9–16.

Nagin, Daniel S. 1998. "Deterrence and Incapacitation." In *The Handbook of Crime and Punishment,* edited by Michael H. Tonry (345–68). New York: Oxford University Press.

National Drug Court Institute and National Council of Juvenile and Family Court Judges. 2003. *Juvenile Drug Courts: Strategies in Practice.* NCJ187866. Washington, DC: U.S. Department of Justice, Bureau of Justice Assistance.

NDCI/NCJFCJ. *See* National Drug Court Institute and National Council of Juvenile and Family Court Judges.

Pindyck, Robert S., and Daniel L. Rubinfeld. 1994. *Microeconomics,* 3rd ed. Englewood, NJ: Prentice Hall, Inc.

Prochaska, James O., and Carlo C. DiClemente. 1982. "Transtheoretical Therapy: Toward a More Integrative Model of Change." *Psychotherapy: Theory, Research, and Practice* 19(3): 276–87.

Prochaska, James O., Carlo C. DiClemente, and John C. Norcross. 1992. "In Search of How People Change: Applications to Addictive Behaviors." *American Psychologist* 47(9): 1102–14.

Prochaska James O., John C. Norcross, and Carlo C. DiClemente. 1994. *Changing for Good.* New York: William Morrow and Company, Inc.

Raven, Bertram H. 1965. "Social Influence and Power." In *Current Studies in Social Psychology,* edited by Ivan D. Steiner and Martin Fishbein (371–82). New York: Holt, Rinehart, and Winston.

Rempel, Michael, and Christine DeStefano. 2000. "Predictors of Engagement in Court-Mandated Treatment: Findings at the Brooklyn Treatment Court, 1996–2000." *Journal of Offender Rehabilitation* 33(4): 87–124.

Roman, John, Adele Harrell, and Emily Sack. 1998. *The Brooklyn Treatment Court and Network of Services Interim Process Evaluation Report.* New York: City of New York.

Rosenstock, Irwin M., Victor J. Strecher, and Marshall H. Becker. 1988. "Social Learning Theory and the Health Belief Model." *Health Education Quarterly* 15(2): 175–83.

Satel, Sally. 1998. "Observational Study of Courtroom Dynamics in Selected Drug Courts." *National Drug Court Institute Review* 1(1): 56–87.

Senjo, Scott R., and Leslie A. Leip. 2001. "Testing and Developing Theory in Drug Court: A Four-Part Logit Model to Predict Program Completion." *Criminal Justice Policy Review* 12(1): 66–87.

Shwartz, Michael, Gregg Baker, Kevin P. Mulvey, and Alonzo Plough. 1997. "Improving Publicly Funded Substance Abuse Treatment: The Value of Case Management." *American Journal of Public Health* 87(10): 1659–64.

Siddall, James W., and Gail L. Conway. 1988. "Interactional Variables Associated with Retention and Success in Residential Drug Treatment." *International Journal of the Addictions* 23(12): 1241–54.

Siegal, Harvey A., James H. Fisher, Richard C. Rapp, and Casey W. Kelliher. 1996. "Enhancing Substance Abuse Treatment with Case Management: Its Impact on Employment." *Journal of Substance Abuse Treatment* 13(2): 93–98.

Skinner, B. F. 1954. "The Science of Learning and the Art of Teaching." *Harvard Education Review* 24(2): 86–97.

Substance Abuse and Mental Health Services Administration, Center for Substance Abuse Treatment. 1997. *The National Treatment Improvement Evaluation Study.* SMA 97-3154. Rockville, MD: Substance Abuse and Mental Health Services Administration.

Swartz, James A., Arthur J. Lurigio, and Scott A. Slomka. 1996. "The Impact of IMPACT: An Assessment of the Effectiveness of a Jail-Based Treatment Program." *Crime and Delinquency* 42(4): 553–73.

Taxman, Faye. 1999. "Unraveling 'What Works' for Offenders in Substance Abuse Treatment Services." *National Drug Court Review* 2(2): 93–134.

Tittle, Charles R. 1980. "Labeling and Crime: An Empirical Evaluation." In *The Labeling of Deviance*, 2nd ed., edited by Walter R. Gove (241–69). Beverly Hills, CA: Sage Publications.

Trone, Jennifer, and Douglas W. Young. 1996. *Bridging Drug Treatment and Criminal Justice*. Vera Institute Program Brief. New York: Vera Institute of Justice.

Tyler, Thomas R. 1997. *Social Justice in a Diverse Society*. Boulder, CO: Westview.

U.S. General Accounting Office. 2002. *Drug Courts: Better DOJ Data Collection and Evaluation Efforts Needed to Measure Impact of Drug Court Programs*. Washington, DC: General Accounting Office.

Vold, George B., Thomas J. Bernard, and Jeffrey B. Snipes. 1998. *Theoretical Criminology*, 4th ed. New York: Oxford University.

Wexler, David B. 1990. *Therapeutic Jurisprudence: The Law as a Therapeutic Agent*. Durham, NC: Carolina Academic Press.

8

Building Better Evidence for Policy and Practice

John Roman and Jeffrey A. Butts

Juvenile drug courts face many challenges. They are criticized from all directions. From the left, juvenile drug courts may be scolded for widening the net of intervention and using secure detention too often with youth who are not a threat to public safety. A liberal critic might argue that a courtroom is not an appropriate place to implement therapeutic interventions and that judges are not properly equipped to serve as de facto social workers and substance abuse counselors. From the right, juvenile drug courts could be maligned as soft on crime. Conservative critics may view treatment as an inadequate response to crime and might share liberals' concerns about the role of judges in the drug court process, although for different reasons. Asking judges to "do social work" from the bench needlessly diminishes the court's authority, conservatives might argue.

All these criticisms *may* be true, but none is inherently true. Certainly, the juvenile drug court process is imperfect, but it could be improved. Evaluation research has yet to generate definitive proof that drug courts work—i.e., that they reduce drug use and prevent future offending—but more studies are finding that drug courts (for adults at least) seem to influence offender behavior, particularly while participants are actually under program supervision. Research about juvenile drug courts is even less compelling. There have been fewer juvenile drug court studies, generating much less evidence about the impact of juvenile programs. In addition, criticisms of drug court are often more persuasive in the case of juvenile programs, particularly the concern that they contribute to net widening.

Even if researchers could prove juvenile drug courts reduce offending and prevent future substance abuse by delinquent youth, drug court practitioners would still not be able to explain exactly how they do it. Does the charismatic leadership of the judge make offenders change their behavior? Are the case managers responsible for whatever positive outcomes are seen in juvenile drug courts? Is it the quality and quantity of treatment? Is it the consistent application of graduated sanctions? Maybe the simple threat of punishment keeps youth on the right path. On the other hand, perhaps juvenile drug courts are simply an exercise in skimming—their eligibility rules and client screening procedures may allow them to select those offenders who would have done well even without drug court. Until the evidence base is stronger, policymakers and practitioners will not know whether juvenile drug courts actually reduce adolescent drug use, if some programs are better than others, or if juvenile drug courts represent a cost-effective approach to adolescent substance abuse and juvenile crime.

Current Policy Environment

As stated elsewhere in this book, the popularity of the drug court model was unmistakable during the 1990s. Lawmakers and practitioners across the country voted with their time and their money as they worked to design and implement hundreds of drug court programs for adults and juveniles. Clearly, there is something appealing about using the court process to supervise drug-involved offenders and coerce them into treatment.

Despite drug courts' attractiveness in theory, however, in practice they have drawn serious criticism. Chriss, for example, argued that it was impossible to reconcile the conflicting goals of coercion and compassion as easily as drug court proponents claim (Chriss 2002, 199). The same point was made powerfully by Denver Judge Morris Hoffman. In a widely circulated article from the *North Carolina Law Review,* Hoffman suggested that bringing therapeutic motives into the courtroom was inappropriate as a matter of law:

> If addiction is really a disease, then the most diseased defendants are precisely the defendants most likely to fail many, and perhaps even all, treatment attempts. Drug courts thus may be performing a kind of reverse moral screening—those

defendants who do not respond to treatment, and therefore may be the most dis-
eased, go to prison, while those defendants who respond well to treatment and
whose use of drugs may have been voluntary, escape prison . . . [C]ourts simply
should not be in the business of forcing medical treatment on people convicted of
crimes as a condition of a favorable sentence. They most certainly should not be
in the business of forcing treatment on defendants who have not yet been convicted as a condition of being released on bond. Yet, this is exactly what drug
courts are all about . . . [W]e are judges, not social workers or psychiatrists. We
administer the criminal law because the criminal law is its own social ends. It is
not, or at least ought not to be, a means to other ends. (Hoffman 2000, 1476–78)

Of course, such compelling arguments may not apply to juvenile drugs
courts, which are housed in a juvenile justice system that already embraces
the duality of purpose that so disturbs critics of adult drug courts. It would
be curious if adult drug courts ultimately fail because of these mission
incompatibilities while their juvenile counterparts survive.

There have also been practical reservations about using federal funds
to support drug court programs and the evidence base underlying the
drug court movement. In 2003, the U.S. General Accounting Office
released a highly critical assessment of the federal Drug Courts Program
Office operated by the U.S. Department of Justice. As part of a broad
review of DOJ, the report criticized DCPO's oversight function and
implicitly questioned the efficacy of drug courts themselves. In a section
titled, "Better Data Collection and Evaluation Efforts Needed to Measure
Impact of Federally Funded Drug Court Programs," the GAO criticized
the lack of information about drug court programs. The GAO seemed
especially piqued that DOJ failed to attend to earlier GAO recommendations that may have improved the quality of drug court evaluations, including methods of selecting comparison groups, data collection and analysis
techniques, and rigorous designs with adequate statistical power:

Despite the increasing number of drug court programs required to collect and
maintain performance and outcome data, and despite our recommendations in
1997 to improve evaluation efforts, Justice's DCPO continues to lack vital information on the impact of its programs. . . . Also, because of various administrative and research factors that have hampered Justice's ability to complete the
two-phase National Institute of Justice–sponsored national impact evaluation
study, Justice cannot provide Congress and drug court program stakeholders
with reliable information on program performance and impact. . . .

[W]e believe that it is unclear whether Justice's plans will address all of the
insufficiencies we have cited or how well Justice will monitor grantee compliance
with data collection, reporting, and evaluation requirements. Until Justice fully
implements our recommendations, Congress, the public, and other stakeholders

will continue to lack sufficient information to measure long-term program benefits and to assess how these programs affect criminal behavior of substance abuse
offenders and whether these programs are an effective use of federal funds. (GAO
2003, 31–32)

Shortly before the GAO released its report, the Bush administration closed the Drug Courts Program Office and transferred its employees to other bureaus and offices throughout the Department of Justice, scattering the department's knowledge of drug court programs and policy. Responsibility for drug court funding was moved to the Bureau of Justice Assistance, which administers federal funding across all criminal justice areas. The rationale for closing DCPO was never clearly articulated, although it is logical to assume that the expected findings of the GAO report played a part. At a minimum, however, the decision to close DCPO indicated that federal crime policy would not emphasize drug court program development and leadership as it had in the past. Drug court grants continued to flow out of DOJ, but it was no longer obvious who would be responsible for guiding and developing future drug court models. Compared with the 1990s, the current drug court environment looks less friendly.

How will juvenile drug courts fare in this environment? It will probably be even more difficult for judges and program directors to show their programs are effective. Without federal leadership and a coordinated program of demonstration and evaluation, juvenile drug court practitioners will be on their own—clearly a concern given that the state of research evidence for juvenile drug courts is already wobbly.

In an effort to develop reliable funding sources during the 1990s, juvenile drug courts had no choice but to claim success without a firm base of empirical support. It is easy to see how this scenario developed. New drug courts typically receive a year of planning money, followed by two or three years of federal funding for implementation and program operation. At the end of three years, the programs need to be able to sell themselves to state and local funding agencies in order to continue operating. Unfortunately, juvenile drug court evaluations take much longer than three years to produce useful, defensible findings. New juvenile drug courts often require a year or more just to work out their procedural kinks and establish a routine. Then, it may take another year or two to recruit even a minimal sample of drug court cases and comparison cases for an evaluation. The average youth takes 12 to 18 months to graduate from juvenile drug court, and good evaluation designs usually follow every client for one year after program completion. Thus, the earliest evaluation data for a new program may take five or six years to develop. By the time an evaluator can analyze the data and report any findings, federal program grants have long since expired.

As a result, juvenile drug court programs have been forced to replace their federal grants by approaching state and local funding agencies with claims of effectiveness before they have any real evidence. Often, programs rely on evaluation shortcuts. An evaluation may compare the recidivism of graduating clients with clients who were removed from the program for rule violations or new offenses. Of course, this approach is not credible. It creates a strong bias in favor of positive findings. Graduates and nongraduates may be different when they come into drug court. Any differences they exhibit during or after the program are partly the result of these preexisting differences and not the effectiveness of the program. Sorting out whether lower recidivism rates among drug court graduates are the result of preexisting differences or of the drug court requires sophisticated statistical techniques that are rarely used. In addition, unless follow-up periods are standardized, program failures by definition have longer post-court exposure to the risks of recidivism, raising their risk of a new arrest. It is not surprising that evaluations employing this design find significant differences in rearrest rates that favor drug courts.

Another evaluation shortcut relies on comparing individual offending rates before and after drug court. An evaluator may report that the average number of arrests per year among a group of drug court graduates is lower than it was before they entered the program. Hearing that a program is associated with a 20 or 30 percent reduction in offending, policymakers may believe they have discovered an effective solution. Again, however, such a conclusion is unfounded. This pre-post research design takes advantage of a statistical artifact known as selection regression. Individual offending rates are known to fluctuate, going from periods of high activity to low activity and back again. By definition, drug courts are more likely to receive clients shortly after a period of high-rate offending, when the probabilities of detection and arrest are also high. Based only on "regression to the mean," therefore, offenders are likely to exhibit reduced rates of offending after program referral, but this reduction may not be attributable to the effects of the program itself. Unless a pre-post evaluation has a very good comparison group to control for selection regression, its findings are not very reliable.

Widespread use of such inappropriate research designs has had serious consequences for juvenile drug courts. First, the results of the earliest evaluations are probably unsustainable. Drug courts using flawed research designs may report large reductions in recidivism and they may gain short-term political benefits as a result, but they set themselves up for failure. If subsequent evaluations and new data analyses do not match the first results, policymakers may conclude the programs allowed their effectiveness to slip. Second, poorly designed, shortcut evaluations often fail to measure exactly how a drug court works. Lawmakers, funders, and the public will eventually question why, after a substantial investment of time and money, evaluators cannot say which program components are important and whether the same effects could be achieved with fewer costs.

The lack of compelling evidence frustrates drug court practitioners, funders, and researchers. Despite a growing body of evaluation studies, few solid conclusions can be drawn about the effectiveness of drug court programs, either for adults or for juveniles. Our own work (see Roman and DeStefano, in this volume) confirms the embryonic quality of the research evidence. Using relatively lenient standards to review drug court evaluation designs (we required only that some effort was made to control for baseline differences in treatment and comparison groups), we were able to identify just a handful of credible evaluations out of more than 100 reviewed. Few studies had made their way into the peer-reviewed literature and it is unclear what influence they may have had on drug court policy and practice.

Although the drug court evaluation field remains underdeveloped, most knowledgeable observers are still optimistic about the long-term prospects of drug court programs, particularly those working with seriously addicted adult offenders. The most recent evidence supports the idea that drug courts help control drug use and reduce recidivism, especially during and immediately after an offender's participation in the program. Wilson and his colleagues at the University of Maryland recently mapped the effect sizes identified by 42 drug court evaluations (Wilson, Mitchell, and MacKenzie 2002). They found 41 evaluations with positive effects, most of which were statistically significant. Studies with weaker research designs were more likely to show large program effects, but even the most rigorous designs showed some positive outcomes from drug court participation.

New Research Agenda

Drug courts are held to a higher standard of efficacy than other interventions in the justice system. Every drug court receiving federal assistance is now required to conduct an outcome evaluation to test whether it has a positive aggregate effect on its clients. How many other justice programs could live up to such scrutiny? How many are even asked to try? Established, traditional system components—including probation and incarceration—are not expected to justify themselves with evaluation studies. Their next budget appropriation does not depend on the strength of their evaluation findings. Perhaps it is time to reconsider the need to evaluate every drug court program. Perhaps the funds used in all those evaluations could be put to better use. Certainly, requiring more and more outcome evaluations that add little to the literature is not an efficient strategy for long-term program development. Given the limited efficacy of drug court evaluations to date, it may be time to pursue a new course.

As full-time researchers, the authors of this volume naturally would be expected to call for more research, and more evaluation is certainly needed. None of the currently available evidence about drug courts is clear and unassailable. The future of drug court practice and policy depends on continued investment in high-quality evaluation studies. There is a limit, however, to the number of quality studies that can be funded and completed. The number of competent researchers available to do the work is finite, and given shortages in time, expertise, and funding, even the best studies can answer only a few key questions at a time. It is not enough simply to generate larger numbers of studies. This strategy has resulted in a glut of poorly conceived and underfunded evaluations, none of them capable of resolving key disputes about program design and court procedures. Rather than continuing to divide the pool of evaluation resources across an uncoordinated array of small studies, policymakers may want to concentrate research funds on a few, well-designed, theoretically oriented investigations of program impact and cost-effectiveness.

The juvenile drug court field should look beyond individual evaluations and start to build a system of research-based program accreditation. An effective accreditation process could relieve juvenile drug courts of the burdens imposed by constant evaluation. Standards could be set at the national level, and individual programs could demonstrate whether they meet the standards. Courts meeting the standards would then receive a credential. If the standards were carefully developed, accredited juvenile drug courts could use their credentials to demonstrate their competence and effectiveness to local stakeholders. Such a system would free resources for client services and program management that are currently diverted to inadequate and redundant evaluation studies. Policy and practice could be informed by a smaller number of carefully designed studies as long as those studies were used to inform a process of accreditation.

An accreditation process for juvenile drug courts would have to be sophisticated. It could not be simply an extension of "best practices," in which program design principles are extrapolated from the opinions and beliefs of practitioners. A rigorous system of accreditation would have to be empirical, based on a foundation of solid evaluation findings. Given the early stage of drug court research, it could be years before the drug court field is capable of implementing an effective accreditation regime, but the design and development work could start immediately.

Once established, however, accreditation would profoundly affect juvenile drug courts and the policy environment in which they operate. The strength of the evaluation literature underlying accreditation would put pressure on programs to forgo anecdotal evidence and personal preference in designing their procedures. If evaluators found, for example, that consistency in sanctioning was positively associated with decreased drug use, the accreditation process would encourage drug courts to implement sanctions consistently, even if judges preferred broad discretion. Accreditation would also help insulate individual programs against political attack. Currently, a state or local official who wishes to redirect juvenile drug court funds to another purpose has only to challenge local programs to produce evidence of their effectiveness. Unless the local courts are fortunate enough to have a recent study, they appear vulnerable. A respected accreditation process would allow any court to demonstrate its value using outcome data from other jurisdictions.

A national entity should manage juvenile drug court accreditation, backed by a panel of experienced practitioners and researchers. The accreditation body would synthesize and update drug court research, create a theoretically driven and empirically proven juvenile drug court model, use that model to create a set of standards, and determine whether individual juvenile drug courts meet the standards. While standardization may diminish the individual creativity that helped spark the juvenile drug court movement, it would free drug court resources for more productive uses. Rather than devoting substantial resources to debating the best approach for each client and responding to one case at a time, programs could rely on standards to govern their daily operations while they focused their energies on developing and implementing more strategic goals, such as creating community-justice partnerships and responding to emerging substance abuse issues in the community.

An accreditation-focused evaluation agenda would free researchers to investigate critical questions about program effectiveness, to identify precisely *how* drug courts work. Currently, a significant amount of research on juvenile drug courts is undertaken not to illuminate the elements of program effectiveness, but to fulfill funding requirements and provide support for future funding requests. Studies conducted under these circumstances are rarely carried out with a true spirit of discovery. Investigators cannot afford the luxury of building an evidence base with precise measurements of a few key program components at a time. They must develop broad indicators of effectiveness, and they must do it as quickly as possible. An accreditation process would allow evaluation researchers to focus on measuring the fundamental components of program effectiveness.

Future evaluations should test hypotheses of program impact. In chapter 7, we suggested a possible approach to conducting such evaluations. The Urban Institute conceptual framework provides a feasible theory of how drug courts might change individual behavior and how researchers might measure associations between program efforts and client behavior. The evaluation literature about juvenile drug courts does not yet include studies using this kind of framework, but the findings of drug court research to date are strong enough to at least support continued funding of drug court programs.

In the next decade, evaluators need to test explicit hypotheses about the impact of various drug court components, not only program-level effects. Some research of this type has already begun on adult drug courts. The Treatment Research Institute (TRI) in Philadelphia has two ongoing studies testing the effects of individual drug court components on participant outcomes. With support from the National Institute on Drug Abuse, TRI is using randomized designs to model the effects of different sanctioning strategies and drug court hearing procedures. More of this research is critical for the future of the drug court movement. Once the findings of such evaluations are available, court practitioners can use them to shape program designs and operations.

To implement an accreditation process properly, judges and other practitioners must be willing to cede some control over court operations. Most drug courts retain significant discretion in their operational approach.

New cases and new situations are dealt with independently, often in a committee setting with the judge as the final decisionmaker. Each participant's case processing is unique. Although this process is highly flexible, it is an inefficient way to discover effective procedures and practices. Even when juvenile drug court practitioners are aware of research findings, they may implement new research-based procedures selectively and haphazardly.

An accreditation system could standardize the scheduling and delivery of treatment services and allow judges to focus on the quality of decisionmaking. Unchained from their responsibilities as lead counselors and social workers, judges could turn their attention to strategic objectives. They could work to develop expanded prevention and intervention programs for juvenile offenders. The accreditation agency itself could look beyond the drug court movement for help in answering questions about the effectiveness of drug court components. Behavioral psychologists, for instance, have studied the effects of reinforcements on behavior for decades. A great deal of knowledge from other disciplines can be brought to bear on questions of drug court efficacy. It is not necessary for drug court researchers to continually reinvent the wheel. Some group or organization, however, must be authorized to identify, synthesize, and disseminate related research, and a drug court accreditation entity could do just that.

Conclusion

Using juvenile drug courts to address adolescent substance abuse is a gamble. Asking the justice system to pursue treatment goals involves significant risks. As young people are drawn deeper into the justice system, they may come to think of themselves as outlaws, and their families, schools, and communities may eventually agree with them. In choosing to refer youth to a juvenile drug court program, a community is gambling that formal, legal intervention to stop juvenile drug use will be less harmful and less costly than nonlegal intervention or even no intervention at all.

At some point, virtually every adolescent does something that could result in arrest and prosecution, but most youth "age out" of these behaviors on their own. The first challenge for juvenile drug courts—indeed, for all juvenile justice agencies—is to restrict their efforts to youth who are unlikely to stop risky behavior on their own and may go on to inflict serious damage on themselves and their communities. Clinical assessments may help with this task, but there is no such thing as an error-proof or even highly accurate prediction tool. Identifying youth for substance abuse interventions is inherently subjective, often laden with social, cultural, and class bias.

The second challenge facing juvenile drug courts is to demonstrate their own success. Good intentions are not enough. Juvenile drug courts must develop and rely on empirically validated approaches to measure how effectively they change youth behavior and whether they minimize the harm they could cause in attempting to do so.

Despite more than a decade of research, drug courts, and particularly juvenile drug courts, have not sufficiently documented whether they are successful and how they achieve their successes. Rather than continue spending resources on a haphazard program of inadequate and potentially redundant evaluations, researchers need a new paradigm. Impact evaluations are costly and time intensive. Outcome evaluations are cheaper and quicker, but only help determine who is doing well within an existing drug court model. Performance measures help institutionalize research into practice, but are only as helpful as their underlying concepts are thoughtful. A better way to evaluate and improve juvenile drug courts would be to conduct a few high quality evaluations, use these evaluations to establish operational principles, and create strong incentives for programs to implement those principles.

REFERENCES

Chriss, James J. 2002. "The Drug Court Movement: An Analysis of Tacit Assumptions." In *Drug Courts in Theory and Practice,* edited by James L. Nolan Jr. (189–213). New York: Aldine de Gruyter.

Hoffman, Morris B. 2000. "The Drug Court Scandal." *North Carolina Law Review* 78:1437–1534.

U.S. General Accounting Office (GAO). 2003. *Major Management Challenges and Program Risks: Department of Justice.* GAO-03-105. Washington, DC: GAO.

Wilson, David, Ojmarrh Mitchell, and Doris MacKenzie. 2002. "A Systematic Review of Drug Court Effects on Recidivism." Paper presented at the annual meeting of the American Society of Criminology, Chicago, Nov. 15.

The Drug Court Evaluation Literature

1993–2004

Description	*Design*

JUVENILE DRUG COURT EVALUATIONS

Delaware juvenile drug court program
(Miller, Scocas, and O'Connell 1998)

This program targeted juveniles with misdemeanor drug arrests and brief criminal histories. Drug court offered individual and group counseling, family counseling, and random urinalysis.

Post-only design

Treatment group

Drug court participants (sample size varies based on follow-up period)

Comparison group

Matched comparison group of like offenders arrested for misdemeanor drug possession ($n = 90$)

Findings	Issues

Recidivism

New arrests

21% of the treatment group ($n = 81$) and 30% of the comparison group ($n = 90$) were rearrested during the treatment period.[a]

Rearrests

Reported at 3-, 6-, 9-, and 12-month follow-up intervals. Sample sizes for the comparison group were not reported.

At 3 months, 14.8% of the treatment group (81) and 21.1% of the comparison group were rearrested.

At 6 months, 24.2% of the treatment group (62) and 32.2% of the comparison group were rearrested.

At 9 months, 38.1% of the treatment group (42) and 43.3% of the comparison group were rearrested.

At 12 months, 33.3% of the treatment group (18) and 51.1% of the comparison group were rearrested (not significant).

Selection bias

It is unclear how similar the comparison group was to the drug court participants at baseline.

Small sample size

Only 18 participants completed or were terminated from drug court at the 12-month follow-up.

Outcome analysis

Rolling outcome period creates potential selection and attrition effects. For example, 10 cases made it into the 12-month group and none recidivated. However, 22.7% recidivated at 9 months, 19.4% at 6 months, and 8.5% at 3 months. It is unclear whether treatment and comparison groups are comparable for each period.

Description	Design
Delaware juvenile drug court diversion program (O'Connell, Nestlerode, and Miller 1999)	**Post-only design**
	Treatment group
The program targeted juvenile offenders with misdemeanor drug possession charges. During the program, participants are expected to maintain abstinence, and relapse triggers more intensive treatment protocol. The program had three levels of involvement: (1) Some juveniles receive case management and treatment at other facilities if they were receiving treatment before arriving in drug court; (2) Juveniles who are arrested for drug possession but are not addicts (as defined by the DSM-IV) are provided psycho-educational counseling on drug use, peer interactions, and avoiding peer pressure; (3) Addicted juveniles are in treatment that includes group sessions, individual counseling, and family counseling.	Drug court participants that complied with the program ($n = 200$)
	Drug court participants that did not comply with (complete) the program ($n = 111$)
	Comparison group
	Sample of offenders matched on similar demographic characteristics (criminal history, race, and gender) ($n = 154$)
Orange County (Florida) juvenile drug court (Saunders et al. 2001)	**One-group design**
	Treatment group
This program targeted first-, second-, third-, or fourth-time nonviolent juvenile offenders in need of substance abuse treatment services. A description of the treatment program was not provided in the report.	Drug court participants ($n = 126$)

Findings	*Issues*
Recidivism	**Selection bias**

Recidivism

36.4% of the comparison group was rearrested within the treatment period (the first 200 days following their drug possession arrest), compared with 25.9% of the treatment group. This difference was statistically significant ($p < .05$).

60.5% of the comparison group, 67.3% of the treatment group that did not comply with the drug court, and 47.7% of the treatment group that complied with the drug court were rearrested within 18 months of completing or being terminated from treatment.

The cumulative recidivism rates 18 months after the treatment period were 55% for the entire treatment group and 60.5% for the comparison group.

The cumulative recidivism rate during and after treatment was 60.7% for the entire treatment group and 67.9% for the comparison group.

Selection bias

No information was provided about why the matched sample was not included in the drug court.

No statistical tests confirmed that the matched sample was similar to the treatment group.

Recidivism

7.9% of participants were arrested while in the program.

One participant was arrested following graduation.

Outcome analysis

"Of the 126 participants, 105 were selected to represent recidivism rates for the drug court program" (Saunders et al. 2001, 5). It is unclear why the analysis did not include all 126 participants, and how the 105 participants used to represent recidivism were selected.

Follow-up period used to calculate recidivism post graduation is not specified.

Description	Design
Orange County (Florida) juvenile drug court (Applegate et al. 1999) This program targeted first-, second-, or third-time nonviolent offenders in need of substance abuse treatment services. Fourth-time offenders may be eligible depending on individual circumstances. Treatment varied from four to eight months, with an average stay of six months. Services included intensive outpatient and residential services including individual sessions, group sessions, family meetings, and educational services.	**One-group design** *Treatment group* Drug court participants ($n = 100$) Graduates ($n = 28$) Failures ($n = 38$)
Santa Clara County (California) juvenile drug treatment (Community Crime Prevention Associates 1998) Four-phase, 12-month program for juveniles arrested on drug- or alcohol-related charges. Probation officer handling the case recommends juveniles believed to need treatment to the drug court. Type of treatment services offered was not discussed.	**Nonexperimental design** *Treatment group* Graduates ($n = 9$) *Comparison groups* Failures ($n = 20$) Still active ($n = 32$)

Findings	*Issues*

Recidivism

10% of participants were arrested while in the program.

15.2% of participants, 10.7% of graduates, and 21.1% of failures were arrested post-discharge from drug court.

Follow-up time ranged from 20 to 434 days with an average discharge time of 180 days at follow-up.

Graduates spent an average of 134 days arrest-free from point of discharge, compared with 88 days for failures.

Retention

41.8% of participants graduated and 56.7% failed.

Inconsistent follow-up period

Follow-up time ranged from 20 to 434 days. Therefore, at the time of analysis, some participants had a much lower time at risk.

Small sample size

Recidivism data only available on 66 participants.

Retention

After the first 17 months of operation, 15% ($n = 9$) had graduated, 52% ($n = 32$) were still active, and 33% ($n = 20$) had failed.

Relapse

Clients who graduated remained clean an average of 9.5 months, those who failed remained clean an average of 4.2 months, and those still in the program remained clean an average of 3.5 months.

On average, urinalysis results indicated that clients who graduated tested clean 92% of the time. Clients that failed treatment tested clean 70% of the time. Clients in the program remained clean 83% of the time, if in the regular program, and 51% of the time, if in placement.

Selection bias

No comparisons were made to persons who did not participate in the drug court. Comparisons were only made between graduates, failures, and actives.

Short follow-up period

Study examined outcomes after first 17 months of program. Since the program was 12 months long, at most, graduates would have been discharged 5 months, thereby greatly reducing available time at risk. However, authors note that the results are preliminary.

Small sample size

$n = 61$

Description	Design
Hudson Vicinage Superior Court (New Jersey)–Juvenile Division (Andes undated) Three-phase, individualized treatment program developed for juveniles with strong encouragement from family members to participate in treatment. Phase one consists of two days to one week of assessment and stabilization, phase two consists of two to three months of intensive outpatient treatment, and phase three is three to six months of transition/aftercare.	**Post-only design** *Treatment group* Drug court participants ($n = 79$) Graduates ($n = 31$) Failures ($n = 48$) *Comparison groups* Refusers—those who were eligible but refused ($n = 20$) Probation—juveniles on probation for drug-related offenses ($n = 40$)
Utah juvenile drug court (Parsons and Byrnes 1998) A description of the treatment program was not provided in the report.	**Pre/post design** *Treatment group* Drug court participants discharged from the program for at least one year ($n = 74$) *Comparison group* Juveniles matched according to demographic variables (age, race, and gender) as well as criminal history ($n = 74$)

Findings	Issues
Recidivism	**Selection bias**
42% of graduates ($n = 31$), 60% of failures ($n = 48$), 70% of refusers ($n = 20$), and 90% of those on probation ($n = 40$) were rearrested during the follow-up period (statistical significance not reported).	The similarities between the 40 juveniles on probation and the 20 eligible for juvenile drug court were unclear.
	When comparing recidivism data, analysis separates out drug court graduates from failures rather than reporting the entire sample of participants, thus inflating the success of the drug court.
	Inconsistent follow-up period
	Follow-up time for recidivism varied for participants and in some cases may have overlapped with time that participants were in program.
Recidivism	**Selection bias**
Drug court participants had 1.1 fewer charges and the comparison group had 0.6 fewer charges between one year before drug court participation and one year after discharge ($p < .001$).	Although authors matched the comparison group to the treatment group, the treatment group had significantly more serious criminal histories than the comparison group. Treatment group had 4.6 times more felony arrests and 1.6 times more general arrests than the comparison group.

Description	Design

EXPERIMENTAL DESIGNS

Baltimore City (Maryland) drug treatment court
(Gottfredson and Exum 2000)

This program targeted nonviolent, substance abusing offenders. Treatment is made up of four modalities: intensive outpatient, methadone maintenance, inpatient, and transitional housing. Depending on the modality, treatment may consist of acupuncture, GED training, treatment, job readiness and placement, life skills training, and housing assistance.

Randomized experiment

Treatment group

Drug court participants ($n = 139$)

Comparison group

Traditional parole and probation services ($n = 96$)

Findings	*Issues*

Recidivism

Rearrests

44% of the treatment group and 56% of the comparison group were arrested for new offenses during the 12 months after deposition (marginally significant, $p = .06$).

The researchers maintain that "this difference, larger than the differences reported for similar follow-up periods in other drug treatment courts, is a conservative estimate of the effects of the program because drug treatment court cases spent fewer days incarcerated and therefore had more opportunity to re-offend than control group cases."

Re-convictions

Although drug treatment court cases had fewer rearrests, participants were more likely to be re-convicted. The treatment group had 1.0 re-convictions; the comparison group had .63 ($p < .05$).

Selection bias

Those in the treatment group had more serious criminal backgrounds than those in the comparison group.

Short follow-up period

The 12-month follow-up period included time in treatment and therefore greatly reduced time at risk for arrest. However, this report was preliminary, and many in the treatment group will be followed for 36 months.

Description	Design
Baltimore City (Maryland) drug treatment court: year 1 results (Gottfredson and Exum 2002) "The Baltimore Drug Treatment Court (BDTC) is a program for district and circuit court cases supervised by the Baltimore City Division of Parole and Probation" (Gottfredson and Exum 2002, 341). The BDTC uses an increased frequency of court status hearings, urinalysis, and treatment as sanctions for relapse, and 60% of BDTCs use short periods of incarceration.	**Randomized experiment** *Treatment group* Participants assigned to the BDTC ($n = 139$) *Comparison group* Participants assigned to "treatment as usual in the criminal justice system" ($n = 96$)

Findings	Issues
Recidivism	**Selection bias**

Recidivism

48% of BDTC study participants were rearrested, compared with 64% of the comparison group ($p < .05$).

The number of new arrests and new charges for the treatment group were 0.9 and 1.6, respectively. The number of new arrests and new charges for the comparison group were 1.3 and 2.4, respectively. The differences between the two groups were significant ($p < .05$).

Selection bias

Randomization was halted periodically as a result of staff turnover in one of the many court offices participating in the process. When randomization was stopped, participants were assigned to the BDTC according to procedures that were in place before the study. The authors suggested that this might have affected generalizability.

Ethical considerations

Ethics must be considered when randomly assigning participants to a condition that may lead to less desirable outcomes.

Time frame of the report

This report covers the first year of a three-year study. A more detailed analysis of the BDTC is not yet available.

Description	Design
Maricopa County (Arizona) First-Time Drug Offender Program (Deschenes et al. 1995) Program targeted first-time felony drug offenders. The three-phase, 6- to 12-month program consists of drug education, social skills training, relapse prevention, and attendance at 12-step programs. Phase advancement and graduation is based on a point system.	**Randomized experiment** *Treatment group* Drug court participants ($n = 180$) *Comparison groups* Standard probation, no drug testing ($n = 180$) Standard probation with random monthly drug testing ($n = 180$) Standard probation with scheduled biweekly testing ($n = 180$)

Findings	Issues
Recidivism	**Implementation problems**
31% of the treatment group and 33% of the comparison groups were rearrested during the 12-month follow-up (not significant).	"The results, especially those involving recidivism, fail to establish strong effects of testing and treatment. Part of the reason for this may be due to the fact that various programs were not always implemented as designed" (GAO 1997, 102).
Retention	
One-year follow-up study found that 61% of treatment group either had completed or was still active in the program.	
Relapse	
48% of the treatment group versus 47% of the comparison groups tested positive at least once during 12-month follow-up (not significant).	
Technical violations	
40% of the treatment group versus 46% of the comparison groups received technical violations at 12-month follow-up (not significant).	

Description	Design
New South Wales (Australia) drug court (Freeman, Karski, and Doak 2000) Three-phase, 12-month program tailored to address the specific needs of each participant. Services include community and/or residential methadone and naltrexone programs in addition to abstinence programs such as detoxification, residential services, and group and individual counseling.	**Randomized experiment** *Treatment group* Drug court participants ($n = 224$) *Comparison group* Persons who were found eligible for the drug court program but due to space limitations were not admitted. The comparison group received traditional criminal justice processing ($n = 121$)

Findings	Issues

Recidivism

13% of the treatment group was sentenced for a new offense while in drug court. Recidivism data for the comparison group were unavailable when this study was published.

Relapse

Of the 224 members in the treatment group, 193 had been tested for drug use and 45.1% tested positive at their last court appearance. Results are suspect because some service providers gave participants several days notice before a urine test was conducted.

Retention

42.4% of the treatment group was terminated unsuccessfully, 8.9% absconded, and the court terminated the remaining 33.5% for unspecified reasons.

Short follow-up period

This report is preliminary. Recidivism will be analyzed at 15 months, starting from referral to the drug court. Since the program is 12 months and many take longer to complete, many were still in the program during the analysis.

Outcome analysis

Analysis examined new sentences rather than new arrests. Since arrests typically outnumber convictions, arrests would have been a more sensitive measure of recidivism.

Description	Design

QUASI-EXPERIMENTAL DESIGNS—STRONG DESIGN

Chester County (Pennsylvania) drug court (Brewster 2001)

Three-phase, post-plea program targeted offenders charged with nonmandatory drug offenses. Persons under probation or parole supervision when charged with the drug offense were ineligible. Drug offenders with past violent offenses were ineligible.

Pre/post design

Treatment group

Drug court participants ($n = 184$)

Comparison group

Comparable offenders placed on probation before the inception of the drug court

Findings	Issues

Recidivism

5.4% of the treatment group, compared with 21.5% of the comparison group, was rearrested (statistical significance not reported).

When controlling for time at risk, the treatment group had an annualized arrest rate of .108, compared with .199 for the comparison group ($p < .01$).

Revocations for offenders at risk

16.9% of the treatment group and 14% of the comparison group were removed from their respective supervision statutes (statistical significance not reported).

Relapse

The mean number of positive drug tests was 2.8 for the treatment group and 1.7 for the comparison group. These results are based on a sample of 125 drug court participants and 30 comparison group participants (statistical significance not reported).

The rate of positive drug tests for the treatment group (.17) was lower than the rate for the comparison group (.40) ($p < .01$).

Retention

Survival analysis found that at the end of 12 months, the cumulative proportion of the treatment group surviving was 75%, compared with 81% of the comparison group (not significant, $p = .056$).

Selection bias

Unemployment rates for participants were significantly different from the comparison group. Unemployment rate at intake was higher for the comparison group than for the treatment group sample (45% versus 28%). Due to the pre/post design, variables such as income, education, and marital status were unavailable for the comparison group. Earlier studies have found a link between such variables and treatment success.

History

The comparison group is from an earlier cohort of defendants.

Description	Design
Dade County (Florida) drug court #1 (Smith, Davis, and Goretsky 1991) (as described in GAO 1997) Three-phase, 12-month program targeted offenders charged with third-degree felony drug possession with no prior convictions. Treatment consisted of detoxification, counseling, acupuncture, and educational/ vocational assessment.	**Pre/post design** *Treatment group* A subgroup of persons assigned to the drug court who participated in the court $(n = 148)$ *Comparison group* A sample of pre-drug court narcotics cases from early 1988 $(n = 99)$
Dade County (Florida) drug court #2 (Goldkamp and Weiland 1993) Three-phase, 12-month program targeted offenders charged with third-degree felony drug possession with no prior convictions. Treatment consisted of detoxification, counseling, acupuncture, and educa- tional/vocational assessment.	**Multiple designs** *Treatment group* Drug court participants $(n = 326)$ *Comparison groups* Felony drug defendants in the same period who were ineligible for the program because of more serious offenses $(n = 199)$ Non-drug felony defendants in the same period $(n = 185)$ Felony drug defendants from a period several years earlier $(n = 302)$ Felony non-drug defendants from a period several years earlier $(n = 536)$ Offenders who opted out (n unknown)

Findings	*Issues*

Recidivism

The treatment group had the lowest recidivism rate at 15%, persons assigned to the drug court had a recidivism rate of 32%, and pre-drug court narcotic cases had a recidivism rate of 33% (statistical significance not reported).

Selection bias

Participants differed significantly from comparison group on such variables as offense seriousness and criminal history; such variables have been found to affect treatment outcomes (Babst 1971, Young et al. 1996).

Eligibility requirements for drug court changed over time; thus, the consistency of the results comes into question, as the participant population potentially changed.

Recidivism

33% of the treatment group was rearrested during the 18-month follow-up period, compared with between 48% and 55% of the comparison groups (statistical significance not reported).

Time to recidivism

During the 18-month follow-up period, the treatment group had 235 days to first recidivism event. The comparison groups had between 45 and 114 days to first recidivism event (significance not reported).

Failure to appear (FTA) rates

More than 50% of the treatment group FTA, compared with 2% to 11% of the comparison groups (significance not reported). Authors suggest that this result might be due to the higher requirements to appear for the drug court participants.

Selection bias

Eligibility requirements for drug court were flexible; thus, the consistency of the results over time comes into question as the participant population potentially changed.

Authors estimate that between 17% and 31% of defendants identified as eligible were not admitted to the program; it was unclear why this was the case.

Persons who dropped out within the first three weeks were excluded from the analysis.

History

Two comparison groups are from an earlier cohort of defendants.

Description	*Design*
D.C. Superior Drug Court Intervention Program (Harrell, Cavanagh, and Roman 1998) Program targeted drug felony defendants, many of whom had extensive criminal histories. The intensive outpatient treatment included acupuncture, structured treatment activities, and additional support services lasting a minimum of 6 months.	**Random assignment/quasi-experimental** *Treatment group* Drug court participants (eligible $n = 346$; participated $n = 140$) *Comparison groups* Sanctions docket included judicial monitoring of drug use, and referrals to treatment (eligible $n = 365$; participated $n = 240$) Standard docket included drug testing and judicial monitoring
Denver (Colorado) drug court (Granfield and Eby 1997) Three-phase, tailored treatment program in which convicted offenders were assessed on their drug use pattern and level of criminal risk and then recommended to one of seven treatment levels. The levels ranged from no treatment but judicial supervision (level 1) to therapeutic community placement (level 6). Level 7 consisted of intensified surveillance but no treatment.	**Pre/post design** *Treatment group* A random sample of drug court participants ($n = 100$) *Comparison groups* A random sample of subjects from pre-drug court years 1992–93 ($n = 100$) A random sample of subjects from pre-drug court years 1993–94 ($n = 100$)

Findings	Issues
Recidivism	**Selection bias**
27% of standard docket participants were rearrested by the 12-month follow-up, compared with 26% of treatment program participants (not significant), and 19% of sanctions participants ($p < .01$).	Although dockets were randomly assigned, defendants volunteered for the program. This is potentially problematic because "comparisons of participants to the standard docket eligible participants represent quasi-experiment comparisons and . . . although statistical procedures are used to adjust for potential bias, these adjustments may not fully control for self-selection into treatment" (Harrell et al. 1998, 140).
Reported drug use among users	
11% of standard docket participants tested negative the month before sentencing, compared with 17% of the treatment group ($p < .01$) and 21% of the entire comparison group ($p < .01$).	
Recidivism	**Small sample size**
At 12-month follow-up, 58% of drug court participants, 53% of the 1993–94 cohort, and 53% of the 1992–93 cohort were rearrested at least once (not significant).	Because the small sample size "significantly restricts the statistical power of the analysis, the results from this evaluation should be considered preliminary" (Granfield and Eby 1997, 2).
Revocations for violations of probation	**Short follow-up period**
22% of the participants versus 15% and 14% of the two previous cohorts experienced revocations within 6 months (not significant).	A 12-month follow-up period was used for rearrests. Treatment was designed to last up to 24 months. Collecting arrest data at 12 months meant that persons assigned to treatment may still have been in the program.

Description	Design
Douglas County (Nebraska) drug court (Martin et al. 1999) A description of the treatment program was not provided in the report.	**Multiple designs** *Treatment group* Drug court participants ($n = 285$) *Comparison groups* Traditional adjudication participants ($n = 194$) Diversion program participants ($n = 232$)
Hamilton County (Ohio) drug court (Johnson and Latessa 2000) Three-phase, 15-month treatment program consisted of inpatient, outpatient, and aftercare. Services included group and individual counseling, sobriety meetings, educational services, and family involvement. The program targeted fourth or fifth degree felony defendants whose criminal behavior was drug-driven.	**Matched design** *Treatment group* Drug court participants ($n = 226$) *Comparison group* Matched comparison group ($n = 230$)

Findings	*Issues*
Recidivism	**Selection bias**

42.1% of the treatment group, 60.8% of the traditional adjudication group, and 28.9% of the diversion group were rearrested at 12-month follow-up ($p < .05$).

Treatment group had 1.09 mean arrests, compared with 1.88 for traditional adjudication and 0.52 for diversion ($p < .05$).

20.7% of the treatment group, 28.0% of the traditional adjudication group, and 10.3% of the diversion group were convicted ($p < .05$).

Selection bias

On average, diversion program participants were lower risk offenders than those in the treatment group.

The three groups differed in distribution by gender.

Originally, 391 drug court participants, 301 diversion participants, and 326 traditionally adjudicated offenders were selected. Criminal history data were missing on 107 of the drug court participants and 69 of the diversion cases, and these cases were eliminated from the analyses.

History

One comparison group (diversion program participants) is from an earlier cohort of defendants.

Recidivism

29% of the treatment group was rearrested, compared with 39% of the comparison group ($p < .05$).

Average number of days until recidivism was 205 for the treatment group and 218 for the comparison group (not significant).

Outcome analysis

Time at risk for treatment group was 92%, compared with 77% for the comparison group. The follow-up period for recidivism rates is unknown; the treatment group may have had less opportunity to reoffend.

Unknown follow-up period

The timing of the recidivism analysis was not indicated. It is unclear what percentage of the treatment group was still in treatment during the recidivism analysis because the treatment program was 15 months long.

Description	Design
Kentucky drug court (Logan, Hoyt, and Leukefeld 2001)	**Pre/post design** *Treatment group*

Kentucky drug court
(Logan, Hoyt, and Leukefeld 2001)

Three drug court programs were analyzed. The results from these three drug courts were aggregated to provide a composite outcome evaluation for the state of Kentucky. Treatment and comparison groups were analyzed at two separate times: 1995–96 and 1997–98.

Fayette drug court program: This court began in 1996 as a three-phase program that took an average of 12 to 24 months to complete. Treatment in this drug court involved Individualized Program Plans (IPP), which outlined specific responsibilities and goals for the offender. This plan may include group, family, and individual counseling and frequent and random drug testing. Participants had input in phases I and II. In phase III participants had the most input.

Jefferson County drug court program: This drug court started in 1993. A three-phase program that, on average, took 18 months to complete. Treatment in this drug court involved IPP. Every offender received an IPP for his or her substance abuse problem. Other parts of the Jefferson County drug court were individualized based on client need.

Warren drug court program: Established in 1997, this drug court only admitted clients through a probation track. Criteria for inclusion include nonviolent criminal history, drug-related current charges, and judge's consent. The IPP defines particular goals in the three phases of the program.

Pre/post design

Treatment group

1997–98 sample:
    Graduates ($n = 189$)
    Terminators ($n = 283$)

1995–96 sample:
    Graduates ($n = 33$)
    Terminators ($n = 88$)

Comparison group

The comparison group was made up of offenders that were assessed but did not enter the program. Participants that were terminated from the drug court in less than three weeks were also part of the assessed but not entered group.

1997–98 sample:
    Assessed ($n = 114$)

1995–96 sample:
    Assessed ($n = 38$)

Findings	*Issues*
Sample characteristics	**Selection bias**

Sample characteristics

1997–98—There were several significant demographic differences between the three groups: Graduates had significantly fewer felony convictions than did terminators or the assessed. Graduates also had significantly fewer misdemeanor convictions than the terminators or the assessed group before entering drug court.

1995–96—There were significant demographic differences for felony and misdemeanor convictions, with graduates having fewer felony and misdemeanor convictions than the terminators or the assessed.

Recidivism

According to logistic regression analyses, graduates in both time groups were less likely to be in prison, less likely to enter into a new probation period, and less likely to have felony, misdemeanor, and other convictions. Termination status was positively associated with prison (authors concede, however, that this might be due to the sentence imposed after exiting drug court). Graduates were in prison and jail fewer days than the other two groups; had fewer days of probation supervision; had fewer felony, misdemeanor, and other charges; and had fewer felony charges than the other two groups in the 12 months after exiting the drug court program.

Selection bias

With significant differences on demographic variables for the graduates, terminators, and assessed, it is unclear whether results from significant outcomes were based on these differences or on the program itself.

The assessed group was compared because offenders in this group had been evaluated by the drug court but were not selected. The explanation for their nonparticipation in the drug court was not provided. This is potentially problematic when considering the composition of the comparison group.

Short follow-up period

The authors suggest that the 12-month period is inadequate for accurately assessing the outcomes of the drug court. However, they maintain that at the time of the write-up, two of the three programs were still relatively new (Fayette and Warren drug courts). Thus, it was difficult to follow up beyond 12 months.

Cross-sectional analysis

Data were analyzed over two periods: 1995–96 and 1997–98. The analyses performed were cross-sectional, making it difficult to establish causation. Given that data were available, a longitudinal design would have been more desirable. With this design the effects on the treatment and comparison group could be examined over time.

Description	Design
Los Angeles County (California) drug court: initial results (Fielding et al. 2002)	**Three-group matched design**
	Treatment group
	Drug court participants ($n = 242$)
Pre-plea program designed for felony offenders charged with possession of narcotics or a controlled substance. Participants in the drug court program must complete four distinct phases to successfully complete the program. Treatment averages 12 months. Typically treatment includes a minimum of 125 drug tests, attendance at a pre-specified number of self-help meetings, individual and group counseling, paying the program fee in full, and enrolment in an educational or vocational program.	*Comparison groups*
	PC 1000 diversion comparison group ($n = 298$)
	Felony defendant comparison group ($n = 251$)
Outcomes were evaluated for the County's first four drug courts: the Los Angeles Municipal Court Central Division, the Rio Hondo Municipal Court, the Pasadena Municipal Court, and the Santa Monica/West District Superior Court. The two comparison groups were made up of defendants charged with felony possession that participated in Penal Code (PC) 1000 drug diversion education, and defendants that went to trial. Each comparison group was matched with the sample of drug court participants on risk scale scores.	

Findings	Issues
Program completion	**Composition of matched samples**
65% of those admitted to drug court successfully completed the program and graduated.	The composition of participants in the drug court program ranged fairly evenly from low-risk to high-risk offenders. Those in the diversion group were more likely to be low- to medium-risk offenders. The majority of the felony defendant group was rated as very high risk. It is unclear whether results from significant outcomes were based on these differences or on the program itself.
Recidivism	
Drug court participants were less likely to be rearrested than drug court diversion participants or felony defendants ($p < .001$).	

Description	Design
Multnomah County (Oregon) STOP Drug Diversion Program (Finigan 1998) Twelve-month, three-phase diversion program targeted defendants charged with felony possession with no evidence of drug dealing and no violent crime charges pending at arrest. Treatment consisted of group and individual counseling, acupuncture, and life skills training. Inpatient treatment was available to those in need.	**Three-group matched design** *Treatment group* Drug court participants (n not specified) Graduates ($n = 150$) *Comparison groups* Failures ($n = 150$) A matched sample of arrestees who were eligible for the program but did not receive it ($n = 150$)
Oakland (California) (FIRST) drug court (Bedrick and Skolnick 1999) The program targeted first-time possession-for-use cases eligible for diversion. Treatment consisted of AIDS and drug education classes, counseling, and group probation sessions.	**Pre/post design** *Treatment group* Drug court participants ($n = 110$) *Comparison group* Defendants sent to diversion before inception of the drug court ($n = 110$)

Findings	Issues

Recidivism

At 24-month follow-up, drug court partici-pants had .59 new arrests (.23 for serious felony arrests) per 100 participants, com-pared with 1.53 (1.17 serious felony arrests) per 100 matched sample members ($p < .001$). Recidivism data between gradu-ates and failures found that graduates had .36 arrests per 100, compared with .71 per 100 failures ($p < .001$). Recidivism data between graduates and comparison group found that graduates had .36 arrests per 100, compared with 1.53 per 100 for the comparison group ($p < .001$).

Selection bias

The matched sample comparison group consisted of persons declared ineligible for drug court, suggesting they differed on criteria variables that may adversely affect outcomes.

Recidivism

Felony rearrests were compared among the two groups at 12, 36, and 48 months after arraignment.

During 12-month follow-up, 18% of the treatment group was rearrested, compared with 35% of the comparison group (statis-tical significance not reported).

At 36 months, 41% of the treatment group, compared with 55% of the compari-son group, had a new felony arrest ($p < .05$).

48 month results showed 47% of the treatment group was rearrested, compared with 55% of the comparison group (statistical significance not reported).

Selection bias

Authors note that eligibility requirements were waived for some defendants, demon-strating an inconsistency in how some par-ticipants were eligible for the court.

Authors note that one-third or more of those eligible for drug court failed to show for placement. It is unclear how these par-ticipants were treated in the statistical analyses.

History

Comparison group is from an earlier cohort of defendants.

Description	Design
Orange County (California) drug court (Deschenes et al. 1999) The program targeted nonviolent, felony drug possession cases. Report did not provide specifics about the type of treatment offered but did mention it was a four-phase, 12-month program.	**Matched design** *Treatment group* Drug court participants ($n = 236$) *Comparison group* Matched group of defendants charged with felony drug possession and sent to a diversion program ($n = 234$)

Findings	Issues

Recidivism

Rearrest was analyzed from the time of program entry to 12 months post-release. 22% of the treatment group was rearrested, compared with 34% of the comparison group ($p < .05$).

The treatment group had an average of 346 days to recidivism, compared with 244 days for the comparison group ($p < .05$).

Retention

33% of the treatment group was retained at 12-month follow-up, compared with less than 10% of the comparison group (statistical significance not reported).

21% of the treatment group failed to complete the program, compared with 31% of the comparison group (statistical significance not reported).

37% of the treatment group was terminated unsuccessfully, compared with 71% of the comparison group (statistical significance not reported).

Selection bias

Significant differences were found between the treatment and comparison groups on such variables as race, family stability, and seriousness of criminal risk. Such variables have been found to affect treatment outcomes in previous studies.

Diversion participants must take a six-week drug education course.

Description	Design
Polk County (Iowa) drug court (Stageberg et al. 2001)	**Multiple design**
	Treatment group
Drug court targeted probationers recommended for revocation with a history of alcohol or drug abuse and substance abuse-related technical violations or a new arrest.	Drug court participants ($n = 124$; 63 men and 61 women)
	Comparison groups
Drug court consists of ISP, community services, and treatment services ranging from residential treatment, mental health treatment, residential programs specifically for women and women with children, and outpatient services.	Referrals—those referred but did not enter ($n = 188$; 125 men and 63 women)
	Pilots—those who met target population criteria but were identified before drug court development ($n = 124$; 102 men and 22 women)

Findings	Issues
Recidivism	**Selection bias**
New conviction data for both within-program and post-program follow-up periods found that 47.6% of the treatment group versus 54.6% of referrals and 74.8% of pilots received new convictions (statistical significance not reported).	Participation in drug court was voluntary and therefore motivation, rather than drug court, may be driving the results.
	Significant differences existed between the three groups across three variables: sex, previous felony convictions, and previous probation sentences or charged with new felonies while on probation. Such variables have been found to affect treatment outcomes in previous studies.
	History
	Pilot comparison group is from an earlier cohort of defendants.
	Outcome analysis
	Analysis examined new convictions rather than new arrests. Since arrests typically outnumber convictions, arrests would have been a more sensitive measure of recidivism.

Description	Design
Riverside County (California) drug court (Sechrest et al. 1998) Twelve-month, three-phase, pre-plea program targeted nonviolent felony drug offenders age 18 to 25. The first phase of the program consisted of a day reporting program where defendants spend eight hours a day for six months before transitioning to community supervision. Services included drug abuse counseling, acupuncture, job skill development, employment searches, and GED preparation.	**Pre/post design** *Treatment group* Drug court participants ($n = 102$) *Comparison group* Probationers—random selection of drug offenders arrested in 1995 who received probation and might have gone to drug court if it were available ($n = 243$)

Ventura County (California) drug court (Cosden, Crothers, and Peerson 1999)
 	
A description of the treatment program was not provided in the report.
	Pre/post design
	
	Treatment group
	Drug court participants ($n = 235$)
	   Graduates ($n = 111$)
	   Failures ($n = 124$)
	
	Comparison group
	Group considered appropriate for drug court, but there were no vacancies ($n = 66$)

Findings	*Issues*
Recidivism	**Selection bias**
5.3% of graduates and 34.2% of failures recidivated at 24-month follow-up. Overall, 14.7% of all 102 drug court participants reoffended (statistically significant, exact *p*-value not reported).	Participation in drug court was voluntary and therefore motivation, rather than drug court, may be driving the results.
	Outcome analysis
Retention	Follow-up period for the comparison group was at least six months longer, thereby increasing their time at risk.
After 12 months, 62.7% of admissions graduated or were still enrolled. Retention data for probationers were not provided.	Follow-up period for some of the treatment group was only 12 months. Since the program is 12 months long, some were still in the program at the time of the analysis, thereby greatly reducing their time at risk.
Relapse	
Of all admissions, 56.1% tested positive during the program. When comparing graduates to failures, 42.1% tested positive compared with 25% of failures (statistical significance not reported).	
Recidivism	**Selection bias**
Graduates of the drug court had fewer charges, arrests, convictions, and days incarcerated than did the comparison group at 12-month follow-up.	There were several demographic differences between the treatment and comparison groups. The two groups demonstrated significant differences in sex, ethnicity, drug of choice, and type of drug consumed.
Graduates of the drug court had fewer subsequent illegal activities than failures at the 12-month follow-up.	Graduation rates suggest that particular trends predicted graduation or failure: women were more likely to graduate than men, Latinos were less likely to graduate than individuals of other ethnicities, heroin users were less likely to graduate than participants that consumed other substances.
Failures had subsequent levels of illegal activity that were similar to the comparison group.	

Description	Design

QUASI-EXPERIMENTAL DESIGNS—WEAK DESIGN

Akron municipal drug court: outcome evaluation findings
(Listwan, Shaffer, and Latessa 2001)

Treatment in the Akron Municipal Drug Court is predicated on substance abuse screening. Participants that receive "no diagnosis" for abuse enter a 10-week outpatient program. Participants diagnosed as chemically dependent or as drug abusers are placed in either outpatient programming or intensive outpatient services. The outpatient group meets for 12 weeks. The intensive outpatient group meets for four weeks, but the frequency and length of the meetings are longer for this group. Once the participant is assigned to treatment, he or she advances to the aftercare phase, which lasts 12 weeks. The third phase is the maintenance or step-down phase which lasts 26–36 weeks. The final phase, the maintained sobriety phase, generally lasts three months.

Pre/post design

Treatment group

Participants in the drug court ($n = 334$)

Comparison group

People who were eligible for drug court, but for various reasons did not receive drug court services. These reasons include individuals with too many cases pending against them, and those denied for other reasons by the narcotics unit, prosecutor, police department, or probation department ($n = 137$)

Findings	Issues

Sample characteristics

Significant differences between treatment and comparison groups in gender (more males and fewer females in comparison group), education (treatment group was more likely to have graduated from high school), and employment status (treatment group more likely to be employed).

Significant differences in arrest records. Control group more likely to have multiple felony arrests.

Graduation results

43% of the treatment group graduated the drug court while 33% were terminated unsuccessfully, 0.3% had their sentences expire before completion, 21% absconded, and 3% were listed as failing for other reasons.

Recidivism

40% of the treatment group was rearrested during the follow-up period, compared with 52% of the control group ($p < .05$). Significantly more comparison group members than treatment group members were arrested on felony charges. Logistic regression analysis deduced the following: education, employment, group membership, and time to rearrest were significantly related to probability of rearrest.

Selection bias

The significant differences between the treatment and comparison groups provide statistical evidence that these two groups are different. These differences make any comparisons between the two groups problematic. It is difficult to make inferences or predictions regarding the effectiveness of the drug court when the two groups analyzed are very different.

Comparison group

Increasing the size of the comparison group, collecting drug use and abuse data for the comparison group, extending the follow-up period, and tracking the services received by the comparison group would provide more information on the effectiveness of the Akron drug court.

Description	Design
Broward County drug court (Terry 1999) The program targeted defendants arrested for the purchase or possession of cocaine. Persons with prior felony convictions were ineligible. Treatment was a 12-month, three-phase program consisting of group and individual counseling, fellowship meetings, case staffing, and acupuncture.	**Matched design** *Treatment group* Graduates ($n = 230$) *Comparison group* Opt-outs—persons arrested for the purchase and/or possession of cocaine that received and completed probation ($n = 73$)

Findings	*Issues*
Recidivism	**Selection bias**
12-month follow-up found that 19% of the treatment group was rearrested, compared with 28% of the comparison group (not statistically significant).	Compared successful participants to failures and refusers.

Eligibility requirements changed over time. |
| | **Outcome analysis** |
| | Analysis was limited to those who graduated from drug court and those who successfully completed probation. |

Description	Design
Erie County (Ohio) drug court (Listwan, Shaffer, and Latessa 2001)	**Pre/post design**
	Treatment group
Individuals eligible for the drug court were required to attend status review hearings in front of the judge and attend four phases of chemical dependency treatment. In the first phase of treatment, participants engaged in six to eight weeks of intensive outpatient services. Phase two, called continuing care, offered group and individual counseling. Phase three, also called continuing care, offered group and individual counseling. Phase four offered services once a week for the remainder of the program.	Participants in the drug court ($n = 39$)
	Comparison group
	Matched sample made up of individuals with a reported substance abuse problem and those eligible for the drug court program (however, they either refused drug treatment or were rejected by the treatment provider) ($n = 48$)

Findings	Issues

Court-reported violations

18% of the treatment group received a court violation while under the supervision of the court. Of those with a technical violation, 4% were rearrested, 2% failed to appear in court, 25% had a positive urine screen, 3% absconded, 37% were non-compliant with treatment, and 28% received a technical violation that was defined as 'other' by the drug court staff.

Program completion

The 5 clients that successfully completed the program had their original charges dismissed and one graduate had his or her record expunged.

Of those that did not successfully complete the program, 33% were terminated, 7% absconded, and 27% were listed as failing for other reasons.

Recidivism

40% of the treatment group was rearrested during the follow-up period versus 69% of the comparison group ($p < .01$). Of those rearrested, 67% of the treatment group and 56% of the comparison group were charged with a drug-related offense.

A logistic regression analysis revealed group membership (treatment or comparison) was the only variable that predicted the likelihood of rearrest.

Selection bias

"Despite efforts to match the two groups on important characteristics, the fact remains that the offenders selected for the comparison group were either not willing or not deemed appropriate by the treatment provider to participate in the drug court" (Listwan et al. 2001, 10).

The court did not collect supervision data or court-reported data on comparison cases. Thus, it is not known what treatment and supervision services the comparison group received.

The treatment group was more likely to be charged with theft, while the comparison group was more likely to be charged with drug trafficking.

Small sample size

"The small sample size prohibited the use of treatment completion and dropout rates as a measure of outcome among the drug court population . . . The Erie County drug court has been in existence since 1996, the data indicated that the court has only graduated five participants. The small number of graduates limits that analyses that could be conducted" (Listwan et al. 2001, 9–10).

Description	Design
Florida's First Judicial Circuit drug court (Peters and Murrin 1998)	**Multiple matched design**
	Treatment groups
Three-phased treatment program lasting approximately one year. Treatment consisted of counseling, group therapy, peer support, community support systems, aftercare groups, vocational training, and referral to professional ancillary services.	Graduates from the Okaloosa County program ($n = 31$)
	Graduates from the Escambia County program ($n = 81$)
	Comparison groups
	Failures from Okaloosa County ($n = 27$)
	Failures from Escambia County ($n = 87$)
	A sample of persons matched to program graduates [Okaloosa ($n = 31$) and Escambia ($n = 81$)] under probation for at least one year on drug-related charges. The two groups were matched according to their county of residence, gender, race, and type of offense.

Findings	*Issues*

Recidivism

Recidivism data for the 30-month follow-up period (including the 12 months of drug court) found that in Escambia, 48% of graduates were rearrested, compared with 63% of matched and 86% of failures ($p < .001$). In Okaloosa, 26% of graduates were rearrested, compared with 55% of matched and 63% of failures ($p < .01$).

In the 30-month follow-up period, Escambia graduates averaged 82 arrests per 100 participants, compared with 164 for matched probationers and 274 for failures ($p < .001$). In Okaloosa, graduates averaged 46 arrests per 100 participants, compared with 117 for matched probationers and 219 for failures ($p < .001$).

Retention

48% of Escambia and 53% of Okaloosa drug court participants graduated. Failures averaged 311 days in Escambia and 137 days in Okaloosa.

Relapse

Drug use information was available for Escambia drug court participants only. 3% of graduates tested positive and 8% of failures tested positive (statistical significance not reported).

Selection bias

Graduates differed significantly from failures on variables such as education, race, employment, and arrest history.

No comparisons were made between all drug court participants and the comparison group. Rather, comparisons were made between graduates, failures, and matched sample, thereby inflating the success of the drug court.

Small sample sizes

Sample sizes range from 27 to 81.

Description	*Design*
Jackson County drug court diversion program (Jameson and Peterson 1995) Three-phase, 12-month program consisted of drug testing; acupuncture; individual, group, and family counseling; and AA/NA meetings.	**Pre/post design** *Treatment group* Drug court participants ($n = 450$) *Comparison group* Program-eligible offenders admitted to the Jackson County Department of Corrections between 1991 and 1994 with comparable eligibility and recidivism risk ($n = 4,755$)
Jefferson County (Kentucky) drug court (Vito and Tewksbury 1998) Twelve-month, three-phase program consisted of detoxification, stabilization, and aftercare. The treatment program included acupuncture, medication, individual counseling, group therapy, AA/NA, and chemical dependency education.	**Nonexperimental design** *Treatment group* Graduates ($n = 56$) *Comparison groups* Failures ($n = 163$) Opt-outs—persons who were screened for but opted out of the program ($n = 76$)

Findings	Issues
Recidivism	**Selection bias**
4% of the treatment group was rearrested at the 12-month follow-up, compared with 13% of the comparison group (statistical significance not reported).	It was unclear how similar the comparison group was to the treatment group.
	Short follow-up period
Relapse	At the time of the report, only one client had successfully graduated from the program, thereby greatly reducing time at risk.
Data were only provided for the treatment group. Clients with a higher level of participation in the drug court program had fewer positive urinalysis rates than those with lower levels of participation.	
	History
	Comparison group is from an earlier cohort of defendants.
Recidivism	**Selection bias**
At 12-month follow-up, 13.2% of graduates had new convictions, compared with 55.4% of opt-outs and 59.5% of drug court failures (statistical significance not reported).	Compared successful participants to failures and refusers.
	Significant differences were found between drug court participants and the comparison groups on demographic variables (sex, prior mental health treatments, and mental health history). Such variables have been found to affect treatment outcomes in previous studies.
	Biased comparison
	When comparing recidivism, analysis separated drug court graduates from failures, thereby inflating the success of the drug court.
	Outcome analysis
	Analysis examined new convictions rather than new arrests. Since arrests typically outnumber convictions, arrests would have been a more sensitive measure of recidivism.

Description	*Design*
King County (Washington) drug court (M. M. Bell, Inc. 1998) Program targeted offenders arrested for possession of drugs, serious alcohol or drug addiction, or abuse. Clients placed in one of three phases of treatment based on their treatment needs. Treatment consisted of weekly group sessions, case management, acupuncture, and participation in support groups.	**Nonexperimental design** *Treatment group* Graduates ($n = 108$) *Comparison groups* Failures ($n = 193$) Opt-outs—persons who were screened for but opted out of the program ($n = 198$)
Mobile County (Alabama) drug court (Johnson et al. 1997) No information provided regarding target population or treatment services.	**Two-group comparison design** *Treatment group* Graduates ($n = 119$) *Comparison group* Non-eligibles and decliners ($n = 286$)

Findings	Issues
Recidivism	**Selection bias**
9% of graduates received new charges versus 22% of failures and 33% of opt-outs (statistical significance not reported).	Compared successful participants to failures and refusers.
	Outcome analysis
	Recidivism analysis did not compare all drug court participants and both comparison groups. Comparisons were made between graduates and failures, thereby inflating the success of the drug court.
Recidivism	**Selection bias**
25.2% of graduates were rearrested *since graduation*, compared with 87.8% of the comparison group *since their first contact with drug court*.	The comparison group consisted of persons declared ineligible for drug court, indicating they differed significantly on criteria variables that may adversely affect outcomes. Graduates differed from the comparison group on such variables as race, education, employment, and criminal history.
The average length of time to recidivism for participants was 10 months after initial contact with the drug court, compared with 6 months for nonparticipants.	
	Outcome analysis
	Recidivism analysis did not compare all drug court participants and the comparison group. Comparisons were made between graduates and the comparison group, thereby inflating the success of the drug court.
	In comparing recidivism rates between the treatment and comparison groups, follow-up period for the treatment group is from the *point of graduation* and for the comparison group is *since their first contact with drug court*. Thus, the comparison group is likely to be at risk considerably longer than the treatment group.

Description	Design
Mobile County (Alabama) drug court (Johnson, Formichella, and Bowers 1998) The treatment program is designed to last 12 months for the typical drug offender and is conducted on an outpatient basis. Treatment is divided into three phases: assessment and evaluation, intensive outpatient treatment, and transition and aftercare.	**Three-group comparison design** *Treatment group* Graduates ($n = 119$) *Comparison groups* Failures ($n = 105$) Non–drug court participants ($n = 181$)

Findings	*Issues*
Demographic differences	**Selection bias**

Demographic differences

There were several statistically significant differences between the treatment and comparison groups. For example, the treatment group was more likely to have a higher level of education and have employment. The authors posit that the treatment group was more likely to have "socially advantaged characteristics" than the comparison group. However, the two groups were similar in criminal histories and income.

Recidivism

Non–drug court participants were more likely to have multiple rearrests than those that participated in the drug court.

After six months, nonparticipants were more than three times as likely to have been rearrested; after 18 months they were more than twice as likely to have been rearrested.

At 12 months, 69% of nonparticipants had been rearrested, compared with 61% of those receiving some treatment ($p < .001$). Graduates were less likely to be rearrested than non–drug court participants at 6, 12, and 18 months.

Selection bias

Participation was voluntary, therefore motivation may be driving the results. This might have caused some of the significant difference between the treatment and comparison groups.

Reasons given for those not participating in the drug court: one of four non-participants declined treatment, one of six were rejected because they had too serious a criminal record (definition of too serious not provided), and almost 10% were rejected because of extensive records as drug traffickers.

These results suggest that there are some fundamental differences between those that participated in the drug court and those that did not. The statistical comparison suggests that some differences lead to statistically significant results. Thus, the non-participant group may not be an ideal comparison group.

Description	Design
New York State drug court (Fox and Rempel 2001) A description of the treatment program was not provided in the report.	**Pre/post design** *Treatment group* Graduates of five New York State drug courts: Brooklyn ($n = 685$) Queens ($n = 219$) Suffolk ($n = 259$) Syracuse ($n = 135$) Ithaca ($n = 56$) *Comparison group* Failures of five New York State drug courts: Brooklyn ($n = 666$) Queens ($n = 98$) Suffolk ($n = 167$) Syracuse ($n = 215$) Ithaca ($n = 66$)

Findings	Issues

Recidivism

The average arrest warrant rate for each drug court:

Brooklyn:
  Graduates: 0.80
  Failures: 7.65

Queens:
  Graduates: 0.10
  Failures: 2.02

Suffolk:
  Graduates: 0.00
  Failures: 4.55

Syracuse:
  Graduates: 0.38
  Failures: 2.84

Ithaca:
  Graduates: 0.00
  Failures: 2.52

Percent of positive drug tests for graduates before and after 100 days of participation:

Brooklyn:
  Pre: 26%
  Post: 4% ($p < .01$)

Queens:
  Pre: 8%
  Post: 1% ($p < .01$)

Suffolk:
  Pre: 9%
  Post: 3% ($p < .01$)

Syracuse:
  Pre: 16%
  Post: 4% ($p < .01$)

Ithaca:
  Pre: 9%
  Post: 1% ($p < .01$)

Unknown follow-up period

There is no information about a follow-up period for the average arrest warrant comparison between graduates and failures.

Selection bias

The selection criteria for each court are different; however, further differences between the courts are not explicated (e.g., do the average times in drug court differ across courts).

Description	Design
Salt Lake County (Utah) drug court (Utah Substance Abuse and Anti-Violence Coordinating Counsel 2001)	**Pre/post design** *Treatment group* Graduates ($n = 143$)
A description of the treatment program was not provided in the report.	*Comparison groups* Control group of similar offenders that did not participate in the drug court program ($n = 150$) Individuals who were involved with, but did not complete, the drug court program ($n = 56$)
Tarrant County (Texas) drug court (Bavon 2001) The mission of the Tarrant County DIRECT project was to break the cycle of substance abuse of minor drug offenders age 17 and over. Offenders that volunteered for the program agreed to participate in a 12-month treatment program. "The rationale behind the drug court is that participants will react to the incentives and disincentives in ways that will ultimately result in reduced relapse in drug use and criminal recidivism" (Bavon 2001, 14).	**Pre/post design** *Treatment group* Graduates ($n = 72$) Dropouts ($n = 85$) *Comparison group* Opt-outs ($n = 107$)

Findings	Issues
Recidivism	**Selection bias**
Within 18 months of graduation, 39.2% of graduates had a new arrest for any type of offense. 78.0% of the control group had a new arrest. 55.4% of those who did not complete the program had a new arrest.	The control group was made up of individuals that had similar criminal histories to those that participated in the drug court. The authors maintain that the control group is matched according to race, gender, age, and criminal history. It is not clear why these participants were not considered for the drug court.
Within 18 months of graduation, 15.4% of participants had a new arrest for a drug-related offense. 64.0% of the control group had a new arrest for a drug-related offense. 39.3% of those not completing drug court had a new drug-related offense.	There is no information suggesting the drug of choice for the treatment and the control groups.
Recidivism	**Selection bias**
14.4% of the treatment group was arrested and charged with a crime within a year of graduating or dropping out of the DIRECT project. 55% of the recidivists were rearrested for drug- or alcohol-related offenses. 26% of the rearrests were arrested for property offenses (not significant).	Opt-outs, while given the opportunity to participate in the drug court, represent a population distinct from those that chose to participate in the drug court. Comparing the two groups is potentially problematic as the groups might be very different.
The rearrest rate for graduates was 12.7%. The rearrest rate for the comparison group was 16.8% (not significant).	It does not appear that the treatment and comparison groups were compared along demographic criteria. Demographic similarities or differences cannot be inferred.
The time to arrest was 5.3 months for DIRECT participants and 8.2 months for the comparison group.	**Small sample size**
	The small sample size restricts the statistical power of the analyses.

Description	Design
Travis County (Texas) drug diversion court (Kelly 1996) (As described in GAO 1997) Three-phase, 12-month program targeted addicted offenders with limited criminal histories. Treatment consisted of counseling, acupuncture, AA/NA meetings, and drug education.	**Pre/post design** *Treatment group* Participants ($n = 455$) Graduates ($n = 22$) *Comparison group* Individuals who would have been eligible but were arrested before the program was established ($n = 27$)
Ventura County (California) drug court (Oberg 1996) (As described in GAO 1997) Program targeted nonviolent, misdemeanant offenders. Treatment program was 12 months long and consisted of inpatient and outpatient programs offering counseling coupled with random drug tests and attendance at 12-step programs.	**Two-group comparison design** *Treatment group* Drug court participants ($n = 75$) *Comparison group* Offenders who applied for entrance into the drug court program, but were not accepted (n not specified)

Findings	*Issues*
Recidivism	**Selection bias**

Recidivism

Evaluation only included rearrest data for 22 of the 223 program graduates and a comparison group of 27. Of those, 27% of the graduates had been rearrested at 12-month follow-up, compared with 59% of the comparison group (statistical significance not reported).

Retention

Graduation rate data showed that of the 455 participants, 33% (74) had graduated and 232 were still active.

Selection bias

A significant number of eligible defendants either refused or failed to participate from the outset.

Outcome analysis

Recidivism analysis did not include a comparison between all drug court participants and the comparison group. Comparisons were made between graduates and the comparison group, thereby inflating the success of the drug court.

Small sample size

Study used a sample of 22 of the 223 graduates.

History

Comparison group is from an earlier cohort of defendants.

Recidivism

12% of participants were rearrested within the eight-month follow-up period, compared with 32% of the comparison group (statistical significance not reported).

Relapse

9% of the treatment group tested positive during the first eight months of the program.

Retention

During the first eight months of the program, 35% of the treatment group was terminated.

Selection bias

The comparison group consisted of persons not accepted to the drug court, indicating they differed significantly on eligibility criteria variables. This may have adversely affected outcomes.

Short follow-up period

Follow-up period included eight months of a 12-month program. Consequently, none of the participants had graduated at the time of the report, thereby greatly reducing their time at risk.

Outcome analysis

Analysis on relapse reported the number of positive drug tests. It is unknown what percentage of participants tested positive.

Description	Design

NONEXPERIMENTAL DESIGNS

Clark County (Nevada) drug court
(Choices Unlimited 1996)
(As described in GAO 1997)

Twelve-month, four-phase program initially targeted offenders charged with possession or under the influence of a controlled substance. Admission criteria changed over time to include persons charged with possession with intent to sell, low-level trafficking, and non-drug-related property offenses. Treatment phases varied and consisted of detoxification; individual, group, and family counseling; wellness education sessions; and job training. Advancement to the next phase was dependent upon completing requirements of each phase.

One-group design

Treatment group
Graduates ($n = 382$)

Delaware drug court
(Whillhite and O'Connell 1998)

Program targeted offenders under probation for prior convictions arrested for new charges in addition to drug users. Treatment ranged from substance abuse education programs to individual and group therapy, residential treatment, detoxification, and incarcerated treatment, if necessary. Information such as length of treatment and number of phases was not included in the report.

One-group design

Recidivism rates of a random sample of offenders ($n = 200$) who entered the program were examined. These results compared program graduates to failures.

A random sample of violation of probation cases ($n = 100$) was compared to a random sample of offenders receiving diversion ($n = 100$)

Findings	Issues

Recidivism

Recidivism for graduates during the 42 months of the court's operation was 6%.

Retention

Of the 1,544 offenders referred to the program, 24.7% graduated, 18.7% were terminated, 51% were still active, and 5% never enrolled.

Selection bias

Eligibility requirements changed over time, thereby reducing the ability to generalize conclusions to all participants.

Nonexperimental design

No comparisons were made to persons who did not participate.

Outcome analysis

When analyzing recidivism data, analysis only included results for graduates, thereby inflating the success of the drug court.

Recidivism

Recidivism for urban offenders who recently violated Superior Court probation was 39% for graduates versus 52% for failures (statistical significance not reported).

Recidivism for urban offenders with current and misdemeanor histories was 19% for graduates versus 55% for failures (statistical significance not reported).

Nonexperimental design

No comparisons were made to persons who did not participate.

Data problems

Findings are reported on a sample missing between 12% and 19% of criminal offending data.

Authors note that the reliability and validity of the arrest data sets were questionable.

Description	*Design*
Hawaii drug court (Okamoto Consulting Group 1998) Nine- to 12-month individualized treatment program targeted nonviolent, drug-involved felony offenders. Treatment ranged from outpatient, intensive outpatient, or inpatient services. All clients received Life Skills Training and 3–4 months of aftercare services.	**Nonexperimental design** *Treatment group* Graduates ($n = 36$)
Josephine County (Oregon) drug court (Martin 2001) All participants attended drug court once a month. In addition, each participant participated in intensive outpatient chemical dependency treatment for a minimum of one year following entry into drug court. Treatment included individual and group counseling services, and regular attendance at a 12-step recovery program.	**Nonexperimental design** *Treatment group* Graduates ($n = 82$) The author states that "graduates [are used] as their own 'control' or comparison group to explore the extent to which drug court participation changed drug offenders behavior patterns for the better over time."
SODAT—Delaware, Inc., drug court diversion program (Reed 1995) (As described in GAO 1997) Five- to 6-month program that targeted first-time offenders with no prior drug convictions. The report did not provide a description of the treatment program.	**Nonexperimental design** *Treatment group* Participants ($n = 127$) Graduates (n not specified) *Comparison group* Failures (n not specified)

Findings	Issues
Recidivism Of the 40 graduates, 4 were rearrested within six months of graduation. **Relapse** Six-month follow-up data found that 8% of graduates tested positive. 48% of the sample was not tested.	**Selection bias** Participation in drug court was voluntary and therefore motivation, rather than drug court, may be driving the results. **Small sample size** Only 40 persons had graduated, of whom 36 were included in the evaluation. **Short follow-up period** Six months
Recidivism Of the 82 graduates, 21% were rearrested at least once within a one- to two-year follow-up period, nearly 75% of graduates out of drug court for two or more years were not arrested for another offense, and nearly 50% of all graduates did not re-offend for a minimum of three years.	**Selection bias** There was no comparison group, therefore no baseline group was provided from which comparisons can be made. There is no way to tell if the court is effective without examining a similar population that is not in the drug court.
Recidivism 4% of participants and 8% of failures had been discharged due to rearrests (statistical significance not reported). **Relapse** Approximately 50% of the 80% tested positive during the program. Graduates were less likely than failures to have one or more positive tests (35% versus 80%).	**Nonexperimental design** No comparisons were made to persons who did not participate.

Description	Design
Stanislaus County (California) adult drug court (Shaver and Helfer 2000)	**Nonexperimental design** *Treatment group* Graduates ($n = 170$)
An intensive outpatient drug rehabilitation program lasting a minimum of one year. Clients participated regularly in AA/NA. Participants were also given employment readiness counseling.	
Los Angeles County (California) drug court (Los Angeles County Municipal Courts Planning and Research Unit 1996) (As described in GAO 1997)	**Nonexperimental design** *Treatment group* Graduates ($n = 47$) *Comparison group* Failures ($n = 47$)
Program targeted nonviolent, felony drug offenders. Persons charged with trafficking or sales, or who had prior convictions for these offenses, were not eligible. The three-phased program was designed to last a minimum of 12 months and consisted of random drug testing, individual and group counseling, 12-step programs, and educational and vocational guidance.	

Findings	*Issues*
Recidivism	**No comparison group**
Eight graduates of the drug court have recidivated since its inception (1995). This represents 5% of all graduates. Also, seven (1%) of all graduates committed new offenses while in the program.	There is no comparison group.
	Selection bias
	There is no demographic information presented on those accepted or not accepted into the drug court.
	Time at risk
	There was no indication of time at risk to accompany the graduates recidivism rates. This is problematic as time at risk validates the recidivism results.
Recidivism	**Nonexperimental design**
Rearrest data was compared between the first 47 graduates of the program and 47 failures.	No comparisons were made to persons who did not participate.
11% of the graduates had been rearrested compared to 64% of those terminated (statistical significance not reported).	**Outcome analysis**
Report does not indicate the length of time for the follow-up period.	No comparisons were made between all drug court participants and the comparison group. Rather, comparisons were made between graduates and failures, thereby inflating the success of the drug court.
Retention	
Of the 413 offenders admitted to the program, 29% graduated, 28% were still in the program, and the remaining 51.1% were terminated.	**Small sample size**
	Study provided data on 47 of the 116 graduates.

Description	Design
Santa Barbara County (California) #1 (Cosden, Peerson, and Crothers 1997)	**One-group design** *Treatment group*
Three-phase, 12- to 18-month intensive outpatient program included case management, 12-step meetings, relapse prevention, and vocational training. Program targeted alcohol- or drug-related arrestees (other than drunk driving or certain burglary offenses). Persons with a history of drug sales, violent crime, sex crimes, or two or more felonies were ineligible.	Participants ($n = 221$) Active ($n = 108$) Inactive ($n = 29$) Failures ($n = 85$)
Santa Barbara County (California) #2 (Cosden, Peerson, and Orliss 2000)	**Nonexperimental design** *Treatment group*
Five phase, 18-month intensive outpatient program including case management, 12-step meetings, relapse prevention, and vocational training. Program targeted alcohol- or drug-related arrestees (other than drunk driving or certain burglary offenses). Persons with a history of drug sales, violent crime, sex crimes, or two or more felonies were ineligible.	Total participants ($n = 663$) Graduates ($n = 171$)

Findings	*Issues*
Recidivism	**Nonexperimental design**

Study analyzed differences in arrests between clients who remained active in the drug court program for at least 12 months and clients who were discharged before 12 months (failures). The mean number of arrests among active clients in Santa Barbara was .50, compared with 1.42 for the failures ($p < .01$). In Santa Maria, the mean number of arrests for active clients was .67 versus 1.55 for the failures ($p < .01$).

Change in recidivism rates was analyzed for individuals that remained in the program for at least 12 months (actives). The mean number of arrests in the 12 months before the program was 2.56, compared with .65 during the 12 months after the program ($p < .05$).

Nonexperimental design

No comparisons were made to persons who did not participate.

Short follow-up

Treatment program is 12–18 months long, and only one person was discharged at the time of follow-up. Thus, the majority of participants had no time at risk. It should be noted that this was a year 1 report.

Small sample sizes

For comparison of recidivism rates at 12-month follow-up, discharged sample size was 31 for Santa Barbara and 27 for Santa Maria. For active clients, sample was 16 for Santa Barbara and 16 for Santa Maria.

Recidivism

Within-group comparisons (100 graduates and 146 failures) with a follow-up period of at least 12 months.

   Graduates had 2.4 arrests 12 months before and 0.2 arrests 12 months after completion (significant, *p*-value not reported).

   Graduates had 0.5 convictions 12 months before and 0.1 convictions 12 months after completion (significant, *p*-value not reported).

Selection bias

Participation was voluntary, therefore motivation may be driving the results.

Description	*Design*

Findings	Issues

Failures had 2.4 arrests 12 months before and 0.8 arrests 12 months after discharge. Failures had 0.7 convictions before and 0.6 convictions after discharge. Finally, failures had 39 days in jail before and 68 days in jail 12 months after discharge. (Arrests and number of jail days significant, *p*-values not reported).

Between-groups comparisons

84% of graduates and 41% of failures had no new arrests ($p < .01$)

85% of graduates spent fewer days in jail the year after they graduated, compared with 21% of failures after discharge from the program ($p < .01$).

Participants averaged 2.26 arrests before and 1.60 arrests during the 12-month drug court. There were 0.57 convictions 12 months before and 0.38 during the 12 months of drug court. Days in jail were 33.3 12 months before and 20.2 during 12 months in drug court (significant, *p*-value not indicated).

Retention

Of the 663 participants entering drug court during the study period, 25.8% graduated, 41.2% failed, and 33% were still active.

Graduates averaged 580 days in treatment (362 to 997), whereas failures averaged 223 days in treatment (1 to 798).

Description	Design
Twenty-third judicial circuit of Virginia (Shoemaker 1999) Twelve-month, three-phase program targeted persons charged with nonviolent, felony drug offenses and persons accused of other crimes and determined to be addicted to drugs. Eligible participants must have no record of violent crime and no conditions that would preclude completion of the program.	**One-group design** *Treatment group* Graduates ($n = 125$) Failures ($n = 84$)
Second judicial district drug court of New Mexico (Denman and Guerin 1998) Three-phase, six-month treatment program consisted of acupuncture, group and individual therapy, intensive outpatient, and 12-step meetings. The mean length of time in the program was 9.5 months.	**One group post-test design** *Treatment group* Participants (n not specified) Graduates ($n = 66$) Failures ($n = 130$) Active ($n = 145$)

Findings	Issues
Recidivism	**Nonexperimental design**
12% of graduates were convicted of a new offense after graduating from the program, 55.9% of failures received a new criminal conviction after leaving the program (significance not provided).	No comparisons were made to persons who did not participate.
	Selection bias
Retention	Participation was voluntary, therefore motivation may be driving the results.
59.8% of participants graduated.	**Outcome analysis**
	Analysis examined new convictions rather than new arrests. Since arrests typically outnumber convictions, arrests would have been a more sensitive measure of recidivism.
Recidivism	**Nonexperimental design**
6% of participants were rearrested while in the program.	No comparisons were made to persons who did not participate.
Retention	**Selection bias**
19.6% had graduated, 37.8% had failed, and the remaining 42.5% was still active.	Participation in drug court was voluntary, and therefore motivation, rather than drug court, may be driving the results.
Relapse	
The mean proportion of positive drug tests was .03 for graduates, .30 for failures, and .12 for active clients ($p < .001$).	

Description	Design
Washington State drug courts (Cox et al. 2001)	**Nonexperimental design**

Washington State drug courts
(Cox et al. 2001)

This evaluation examined six counties in Washington State (King, Pierce, Spokane, Skagit, Thurston, and Kitsap counties). Of those six, only three were examined in the outcome analysis portion of the report (King, Pierce, and Spokane counties).

King County–Treatment lasted between one year and 18 months and was divided into three levels or phases. Level 1 focused on developing abstinence and engagement in the treatment process. Level 2 focused on stabilization and establishing a drug-free lifestyle. Level 3 focused on developing skills and abilities to develop a drug-free lifestyle.

Pierce County–A three-phase program where phases 1 and 2 lasted 18 weeks and phase 3 lasted 16 weeks. Each phase consisted of group counseling, urinalysis, and court appearances.

Spokane County–A five-phase program where phases 1 and 2 lasted about three months each, phases 3 and 4 lasted about five months each, and phase 5 lasted about four months. Participants attended AA/NA meetings; in phases 1, 2, and 5 two meetings a week were required. During phases 3 and 4 the frequency increased to three meetings a week.

Nonexperimental design

Treatment group

Graduates (*n* not specified)
   Actives (persons who were still active in the drug court at the time of the study) (*n* not specified)
   Opt-outs (persons who were offered entry, but declined) (*n* not specified)
   Did not finish (persons that were in the program but did not complete it) (*n* not specified)
   Ineligibles (persons that were not eligible for drug court) (*n* not specified)

Findings	*Issues*
Recidivism	**Sample numbers and statistical analysis**
In King and Spokane counties, graduates showed the largest mean number of arrests of any group (no *p*-value provided).	The number of participants in each treatment group is not provided. This is problematic considering comparisons are made between groups. There is no indication of the magnitude of these results.
Graduates had significantly lower rates of rearrest than opt-outs in all three counties (no *p*-value provided).	
Graduates had significantly lower rearrest rates than the did not finish group in King and Spokane counties, but not in Pierce (no *p*-value provided).	There is no information suggesting that the sample populations in each group are similar or different. No statistical comparison is offered.
Graduates had significantly lower rearrest rates than ineligibles in Pierce County, but not in King or Spokane (no *p*-value provided).	
Graduates had significantly lower rearrest rates than actives in King County, but not in Pierce or Spokane (no *p*-value provided).	

Description	Design

DRUG COURT COST-BENEFIT ANALYSIS

Multnomah County drug court
(Carey and Finigan 2004)

Instituted in 1991, the Multnomah County drug court is the second oldest drug court program in the United States. The program is offered to drug offenders. The program is pre-plea, requiring clients to waive their right to trial by jury. The drug court requires participants to make regular court appearances, regularly undergo drug testing, and participate in mandated drug and alcohol treatment. The treatment program consists of three phases. As participants progress, court appearances and scheduled treatment sessions become less frequent. Successful completion of the program takes at least one year.

Pre/post design

Treatment group

Drug court participants: (1) a small, intensive sample drawn from a random sample of ~120 individuals who were eligible for drug court; (2) a larger random sample of 1,200 drug court–eligible individuals for the purposes of power analysis

Comparison groups

(1) Offenders from the sample of ~120 who chose not to participate in drug court; (2) offenders from the random sample of 1,200.

Proxy for costs/savings

Researchers used three levels of proxies to estimate costs. The first sample (~120) was for a high-intensity proxy in which individuals were intensively tracked by researchers. The moderate-intensity proxy used individual-level administrative data. The low-intensity proxy used expert opinion, policy, and aggregate administrative data.

Findings	Issues

Cost-benefit

Investment costs during drug court/probation

The average investment cost of the drug court program was $1,441 less per participant than the cost of the 'business as usual' process ($5,927 for drug court, $7,369 for business as usual). Cost comparison by agency indicated that the largest savers were law enforcement (−$1,179) and probation (−$908).

Outcome costs including victimization costs

Drug court participation resulted in $3,630 less in costs per participant ($15,658 for drug court participants, $19,288 for non–drug court participants).

Selection bias

Participation was voluntary.

Comparison group was made up of those offenders who did not choose to enter the drug court.

Description	Design
St. Louis City adult felony drug court (Loman 2004)	**Pre/post design**

St. Louis City adult felony drug court (Loman 2004)

This program began in April 1997 and targets adults charged with felony drug arrests. The drug court requires participants to make regular court appearances, regularly submit to urinalysis for drugs and breath testing for alcohol, participate in prescribed drug and alcohol treatment, and maintain employment. Successful completion of the program takes an average of a year and a half and results in dismissal of original charges.

Pre/post design

Treatment group

First drug court graduates who completed by November 2000 ($n = 219$)

Comparison groups

Matched comparison group (used paired matching technique) of offenders selected from probation records. Comparisons selected pled guilty to drug crimes, entered probation during same period, and successfully completed probation ($n = 219$). Variables used in matching included gender, race, date of birth, prior convictions, same major charge, and same ZIP code.

Note

a. Authors used four months as the treatment period for the comparison group because it was the average time drug court participants were in treatment.

Findings	*Issues*

Cost-benefit

Overall costs during drug court/probation

The average cost to successfully complete the drug court program was $1,449 more per participant than the cost of successful completion of probation ($7,793 for drug court, $6,344 for probation).

Cost-benefit ratios

During the two-year period following drug court/probation, for each dollar of drug court costs, a benefit of $2.80 in outcome savings was reported.

During the four-year period following drug court/probation, for each dollar of drug court costs, a benefit of $6.32 was reported.

Recidivism–arrests

Reported at two years pre-drug court/probation, during program/probation, and two years following graduation/completion of probation. Sample sizes were not reported.

At two years pre-drug court/probation, probation completers had an average of 2.1 felony arrests, compared with 1.7 for drug court graduates (significant).

During drug court/probation, probation completers averaged .373 felony and .184 misdemeanor arrests, compared with .175 felony and .062 misdemeanor arrests per drug court graduate.

At two years post-drug court/probation, rearrests were only slightly lower for drug court graduates and differences were not significant.

Selection bias

Participation was voluntary.

Differences were found between the criminal history of drug court graduates and completers. Matching was based on having no prior convictions versus any prior convictions. However, variables from each individual's previous history were introduced as statistical controls.

Cost-benefit analysis

Costs were calculated only for successful completers of the drug court program or probation. While this analysis reveals the benefits of the drug court for successful participants, findings cannot be generalized to the larger population of all drug court participants.

About the Editors

Jeffrey A. Butts is director of the Urban Institute's Program on Youth Justice and a senior research associate in the Justice Policy Center. In addition to the National Evaluation of Juvenile Drug Courts, he has directed Urban Institute projects on teen courts and the methods used to forecast bed space in juvenile detention and corrections facilities. He is currently directing the national evaluation of the Robert Wood Johnson Foundation's "Reclaiming Futures" program, an effort to improve the coordination of services for drug-involved juvenile offenders. Before joining the Urban Institute in 1997, Dr. Butts was a senior research associate at the National Center for Juvenile Justice in Pittsburgh, Pennsylvania.

John Roman is a senior research associate in the Urban Institute's Justice Policy Center, where his work focuses on evaluating innovative criminal justice policies and programs. He was the principal investigator for a national study of drug court recidivism rates, and has worked on a number of evaluations of drug treatment courts throughout the United States. Mr. Roman recently prepared a systematic review of existing drug court research for the Campbell Collaboration's Crime and Justice Group, and he has participated in developing curricula for the National Drug Court Institute's research and evaluation workshops.

About the Contributors

Christine DeStefano is a research associate in the Urban Institute's Justice Policy Center and has been involved in research on substance abuse treatment for offenders since 1996. She has experience in large-scale studies, including experimental and quasi-experimental design. Her current research focuses on assessing how enhanced judicial oversight of felony domestic violence cases reduces recidivism, increases the defendant's and the criminal justice system's accountability, and enhances victim safety.

Adele V. Harrell is a principal research associate at the Urban Institute and was the founding director of the Justice Policy Center. She has been actively engaged in research on the criminal justice system and drug abuse treatment since 1975. Her recent studies have included an evaluation of the Brooklyn Treatment Court services for female offenders, an evaluation of the "Breaking the Cycle" program that links the court process with treatment services for drug-involved defendants, a five-year experimental evaluation of the Washington, D.C., drug court, and an experimental evaluation of Children at Risk, a comprehensive drug prevention program for youth.

Cynthia Mamalian is an independent consultant to the Urban Institute and other criminal justice and victim service agencies in the Washington, D.C., area. Her primary research interests include domestic violence and child abuse and neglect. Before consulting, Dr. Mamalian worked as a senior analyst and social science analyst for five years for the Office of Research and Evaluation at the National Institute of Justice within the U.S. Department of Justice. She also previously served as associate director for the Center for Crime Prevention Studies at Rutgers University.

Daniel P. Mears is a senior research associate in the Justice Policy Center at the Urban Institute. He has conducted research on a range of juvenile and criminal justice issues, including screening and assessment, sentencing, drug treatment, mental health treatment, immigration and crime, and prison programming. His current research focuses on juvenile justice, drug treatment, domestic violence, and prevention and early intervention programming targeting youths with mental health, substance abuse, and other needs. Before joining the Urban Institute in 2001, he was a post-doctoral research fellow with the Center for Criminology and Criminal Justice Research at the University of Texas at Austin.

Alison S. Rebeck is a research analyst at MDRC and is currently evaluating school-based interventions in low-income communities. Before joining MDRC, Alison was a research assistant at the Urban Institute, where she conducted research on juvenile justice and drug treatment issues. She previously worked at the Vera Institute of Justice in New York City.

Shelli Balter Rossman is a senior research associate in the Urban Institute's Justice Policy Center, focusing on community-based services related to public health and safety issues. Over the past decade, she has directed several research projects that emphasize integrated services for juvenile and adult offenders as well as other high-risk populations. She was the principal investigator for the Opportunity to Succeed project, funded in California, Florida, Missouri, and New York by the National Institute of Justice and the Robert Wood Johnson Foundation. Ms. Rossman is currently principal investigator for the National Evaluation of Drug Courts, which is funded by the National Institute of Justice.

Ruth White is a research associate at ETR Associates in San Francisco. Previously, she was a research associate in the Justice Policy Center at the Urban Institute. Her interests include community policing, survey research, and geographical analyses of crime data.

Janine M. Zweig is a senior research associate in the Justice Policy Center at the Urban Institute. Her research and evaluation experience includes quantitative and qualitative methodologies, longitudinal studies, and multisite evaluations. Her work often addresses issues relating to vulnerable populations, intimate partner violence, sexual victimization, substance use, sexuality development, and adolescent and young adult development. Before joining the Urban Institute, Dr. Zweig conducted reviews of programs targeting high-risk youth funded by the Center for Substance Abuse Prevention.

Index

accountability, system, 224, 229, 254–55
acupuncture, 101, 103
addictions receiving facility (ARF), 70
Addictions Severity Index (ASI),
    179n.4, 196
adjudication of delinquency versus guilt, 4
adolescent development, 144, 177–78
  and developmentally appropriate
      services, 240
  normative, 146
    developmental variations and social
        context, 149–52
    emotional changes, 148
    intellectual changes, 147–48
    physical changes, 146–47
    social changes, 148–49
  substages, 144–46
Adolescent Diagnostic Interview, 211
Adolescent Self-Assessment Profile
    (ASAP), 211
adult drug court evaluations, 115
  evaluation typology, 116–17
    nonexperimental designs, 120–21
    quasi-experimental designs, 118–20
    randomized/experimental designs,
        117–18
  methodology, 115–16

adult drug courts
  compared with JDCs, 7–8
  contrasted with JDCs, 5–6, 8
Adult Severity Index (ASI)
  interviews modeled after, 209
Akron municipal drug court, 316–17
Alcohol, Drug Abuse, and Mental Health
    Administration (ADAMHA), 42
Alcohol and Drug Abuse Education
    amendments, 43
alcohol prohibition, 38–39
American Bar Association (ABA), 41
American Medical Association (AMA), 41
American Society of Addiction Medicine
    (ASAM) placement criteria, 212
animal-assisted therapy, 104
Anslinger, Harry
  drug policies enacted during tenure of,
      39, 40
arrests, drug, 31–33
  juvenile, 11–12, 31, 33
  rates of drug use versus, 32–34
assessment instruments, 191. See also
    screening and assessment instru-
    ments
  challenges in defining "drug problem,"
      191–92, 196–98

alternatives to DSM approach,
195–96
DSM approach to defining a drug
problem, 192–95
criteria for evaluating and comparing,
200–205
recommended, 205–6, 208–11
reliability and validity, 199–200
validating them against a definition,
198–99
attorneys, 61–62
authority, 233–34

Baltimore City (Maryland) drug treatment court (BDTC), 122, 123,
288–89, 290–91
behavior change, 235–37, 261
stages in change process, 235–36
behavior management, 87–92
behavioral therapy for adolescents, 99
BKOM (Best Kid of the Month) lottery,
88
black youth, drug use among, 151
Boggs Act of 1951, 39
Broward County drug court, 318–19
Bureau of Justice Assistance (BJA), 47,
48
bureaucracies, 29

case management, 95–97, 224, 228–29
Center for Substance Abuse Treatment
(CSAT), 206–7
change. See also behavior change
transtheoretical model of, 235–36
Charleston Juvenile Drug Court, 59, 65,
66, 68, 74, 84, 95. See also juvenile
drug court (JDC) programs
Chester County (Pennsylvania) drug
court, 296–97
Clark County (Nevada) drug court,
336–37
cocaine arrests, 32, 34
coercion, 234–35
cognitive-behavioral interventions,
232–33

collaborative planning, 240
collateral services, 57, 97–104
communities, disadvantaged, 150–51
community-level benefits of JDCs, 10
community partnerships, 55–56, 240
community program coordinator (CPC),
60, 61
Community Reinforcement Approach
(CRA) plus vouchers, 99
community service, 91–92
comparative change designs (evaluation
methodology), 118–19
compliance, 252
Comprehensive Drug Abuse and Control
Act, 42, 43
confidentiality, 241
conflict resolution program for parents
and kids, 103
consistency, 255–56
construct validity, 200
convergent validity, 200
coordination of services, 254
cost-benefit analysis (CBA), 128–31,
350–53
court hearings, 8, 9. See also judicial
hearings
courtroom procedures, 224, 226–27
courts, different missions of various, 4–7
criminal justice system, factors leading to
alternatives and innovations in,
44–48
criminal records, expunging, 87–88
criterion population designs (evaluation
methodology), 118, 119
criterion validation, 199
cultural competence, 240

Dade County (Florida) drug court,
298–99
Dayton Juvenile Drug Court, 59, 61, 65,
68, 70, 96–97. See also juvenile
drug court (JDC) programs
definitional validation, 198–99
Delaware drug court, 336–37

Delaware juvenile drug court diversion program, 282–83

Delaware juvenile drug court program, 280–81

delinquency versus guilt, adjudication of, 4

Denver drug court study, 125, 300–301

deterrence, perceived, 257–58

deterrence theory. *See* rational actor (deterrence) theory

developmentally appropriate services, 240

diagnosing adolescents, 172–75

diagnosis as social construct, 166–72

Diagnostic and Statistical Manual of Mental Disorders (DSM), 175, 192–93
    approach to defining a drug problem, 192–93, 195
    diagnostic criteria for substance abuse, 18–19, 167, 171–75, 192–95
    diagnostic criteria for substance dependency, 167–70, 192, 194–95

"diagnostic orphans," 193, 195

disadvantaged teens and communities, 150–51

discriminative validation, 199

dismissal of charges, 87

disposition, 4

Douglas County (Nebraska) drug court evaluation, 125, 302–3

Drug Abuse Office and Treatment Act, 43

Drug Abuse Prevention, Treatment, and Rehabilitation amendments, 43

drug abuse problems. *See also* substance abuse disorders
    JDCs' capacity to deal with, 10

drug abuse versus non-pathological drug use, 18–19, 143, 153–55, 167

Drug and Alcohol Problem (DAP) Quick Screen, 207

drug court evaluation, 19–22, 107–8, 133. *See also* adult drug court evaluations; juvenile drug court (JDC) evaluations; Urban Institute
    "black box" model, 21, 133
    challenges in, 108–9
        design issues, 110–14
        resource constraints, 109–10
        stakeholder requirements, 109
    frameworks for, 261–62. *See also under* Urban Institute
        developed by professional consensus, 237–39
        developed by researchers, 239, 241–47
    literature on
        cost-benefit analysis (CBA), 350–53
        experimental designs, 288–95
        JDC evaluations, 280–87
        nonexperimental designs, 336–49
        quasi-experimental designs, 296–335
    problems with existing impact evaluations, 132–33
    results of, 121–22
        cost-benefit analysis (CBA), 128–31, 350–53
        difficulties interpreting variation in existing studies, 131–32
        experimental designs, 122–24
        measuring the effectiveness of drug court activities on outcomes, 126–27
        meta-analysis, 128
        quasi-experimental (strong) designs, 124–25
        quasi-experimental (weak) and experimental studies, 125–26

drug court expansion, 48–51

drug court mission, 29–30

drug court model applied to juvenile offenders, 105

drug court movement, 1–3

drug court teams, 58, 60–63

drug courts, ix, 22–23
    contrasted with other courts, 5–6
    finances, 3, 49, 50, 66, 269–72. *See also* cost-benefit analysis
    history, x, 27, 51–52
    nature of, 2

popularity, 3
reasons for expansion of, 2–3, 28, 34
reasons for having, 27–28
Drug Courts Program Office (DCPO),
    49, 269–70
    key drug court components identified
        by, 238–39
drug dependence, 140
    diagnostic criteria, 168–70
    drug use, drug abuse, and, 153–59,
        167, 192, 194–95
"drug-involved" offenders, 11–14
Drug Offenders Act, 43
drug offense cases, increasing number of,
    34, 35
drug policy, U.S.
    history, 34, 36–37
        from tolerance to punishment,
            37–40
        the next era in, 39–44
drug problem(s), 187. See also under
        assessment instruments
    identifying, 16–19, 164–65. See also
        screening and assessment
    process of, 187, 188
Drug Strategies study, 211–12
drug test results, 156–57
drug testing, 57, 92–95, 241, 252
drug treatment. See treatment
drug use
    age and, 33, 35, 154, 155
    among adolescents, 137–39, 152–54
        factors contributing to, 165, 166
        in general population, 154–56
        increased, 33–35
        and JDC operations, 159–60, 163
        in juvenile justice population,
            156–59
        and other risk factors, 160–63
    among high school seniors, 12, 13, 138
    among juveniles arrested, 12–14
    history, 34, 36
    non-pathological, 18, 140
    severity, 57
drug users in justice system, 30–34

educational linkages, 241. See also school
    representatives
eligibility, 240
    clinical, 252
    legal, 251
engagement, 255, 256
Erie County (Ohio) drug court, 320–21
ethnic minority adolescents, 150, 151
exclusions. See eligibility
Expedited Drug Case Management
    (EDCM), 47–48
experimental designs, 117–18,
    122–24, 288–95. See also quasi-
    experimental designs

fairness, 259
family drug courts, 50
family focus, 257
family-friendly strategies, 58
family involvement, 57–58, 84, 104, 241.
    See also parent education and
    support
family therapy, multidimensional, 98, 126
federal funding. See drug courts, finances
Florida's First Judicial Circuit drug court,
    322–23
formality, 255, 256
funding. See drug courts, finances

gateway hypothesis, 15, 161–63
gender-appropriate services, 240

Hamilton County (Ohio) drug court,
    302–3
Harrison Narcotics Tax Act (Harrison
    Act), 37–38, 41
Hawaii drug court, 338–39
health belief model, 236–37
health risk behaviors, 160
hearings. See court hearings; judicial
    hearings
Heroin Trafficking Act, 43
Hoffman, Morris, 268–69
Hudson Vicinage Superior Court (New
    Jersey)—Juvenile Division, 286

incentives, 57, 87–88, 241, 251–52
individualization of treatment, 240, 257
Individualized Drug Counseling (IDC), 98
intensive outpatient program (IOP), 101
Intensive Supervision Probation (ISP),
    45–46
inter-rater agreement, 200
internal consistency, 200
International Classification of Diseases
    (ICD), 179n.4
interventions. *See also* treatment
    with adolescents, 177
    perceived quality of, 256–57
interviews
    psychiatric, 208, 211
    substance-use disorder, 208, 209

Jackson County drug court diversion
    program, 324–25
Jefferson County (Kentucky) drug court
    program, 324–25
Jersey City Juvenile Drug Court, 59, 62,
    65, 67, 68, 86, 87, 95–96, 100. *See
    also* juvenile drug court (JDC)
    programs
    a day in, 81–83
Josephine County (Oregon) drug court,
    338–39
judges, 84
judicial hearings, 73–74, 80. *See also* court
    hearings
    important of process, 80, 83–85
judicial monitoring, 57, 252
juvenile assessment center (JAC), 69–70
Juvenile Automated Substance Abuse
    Evaluation (JASAE), 70
juvenile courts, traditional
    contrasted with JDCs, 5–6
juvenile drug court (JDC) clients, 139–43
juvenile drug court (JDC) evaluations,
    121–22, 221, 240, 261–62, 270–72.
    See also under drug courts
    literature on, 280–87
    new research agenda, 273–75
juvenile drug court (JDC) process, 8–9

juvenile drug court (JDC) program
    development, 222–23
juvenile drug court (JDC) program
    impact, hypotheses of, 222–26
    guidance from practitioner and
        researcher experience, 224,
        226–29
    guidance from social and behavioral
        sciences, 229–37
juvenile drug court (JDC) programs, 105
    admission, 70–71
    duration and intensity, 252
    eligibility requirements and exclusions
        for, 57, 64–67
    future of, 221. *See also* juvenile drug
        courts, challenges facing
    graduation requirements, 253
    purposes/mission, 176
    screening, assessment, and referral,
        63–73
    steps in implementing, 143
juvenile drug courts (JDCs), 1, 22–23,
    276. *See also* drug courts
    challenges facing, 176, 267–68, 276–77.
        See also juvenile drug court
        (JDC) programs, future of
    differences among, 57–58
    flexibility, 4
    harmful effects, 10–11
    history and evolution, 49–52
    implications for the operations of,
        159–60, 163, 175–78
    number of, 2, 3
    questions regarding, 10–11
    reasons for growth and popularity of,
        28–31
    reasons for having, x–xi, 7–10
    where they should target their efforts,
        163, 164
    who should be referred to, 138–39
juvenile justice goals, 5–6
Juvenile Moral Reconation Therapy
    (MRT), 66, 98, 101, 102
juvenile probation officer (JPO), 60–62
juvenile records, expunging, 87–88

Kennedy, John F., 41–42
Kentucky drug court, 304–5
King County (Washington) drug court, 326–27

Las Cruces Juvenile Drug Court, 59, 61, 65, 66, 68, 71, 74, 80, 84–92, 94, 96, 100, 104. *See also* juvenile drug court (JDC) programs
  rules, 72
  treatment in, 102–3
law enforcement representatives, 62
leadership, 251
learning theory, 231–34
legitimate authority, 233–34
leverage, 242
Los Angeles County (California) drug court, 306–7, 340–41

Maricopa County (Phoenix, Arizona) First Time Drug Offender Program, 122–23, 292–93
Marihuana Tax Act, 39
marijuana, as "gateway" drug, 15, 161–63
marijuana education group, 103
marijuana laws
  problems with, 15
  why they are enforced, 15–16
marijuana problem, 14–16
marijuana use, 140, 152, 161
  among high school seniors, 12, 13, 138
  among juveniles arrested, 13, 14
Martinson, Robert, 42–43
matched designs (evaluation methodology), 119
minority groups, adolescents from, 150, 151
Missoula Youth Drug Court, 59–62, 65, 67, 68, 71, 86, 87, 94, 100, 104. *See also* juvenile drug court (JDC) programs
  a day in, 75–76
  sanctions grid, 91
  self-administered strengths-based assessment and inventory of personal resources, 67, 69

Mobile County (Alabama) drug court, 326–29
monitoring
  judicial, 57, 252
  program, 240
Montgomery County Juvenile Drug Court, a day in, 77–80
Moral Reconation Therapy (MRT), 66, 98, 101, 102
motivation, 234–35, 260
  assessment of, 237
Motivational Enhancement Therapy (MET), 99
Multi-Systemic Therapy (MST), 98, 100, 126–27
Multidimensional Family Therapy (MFT), 98, 126
Multnomah County (Oregon) drug court, 350–51
Multnomah County (Oregon) STOP drug diversion program, 308–309

"N Parts" (Narcotics Parts), 46–47
Narcotics Control Act of 1956, 39
narcotics farms, 39
National Drug Court Institute and National Council of Juvenile and Family Court Judges (NDCI/NCJFCJ), 239
  JDC strategies identified by, 239–41
  report, 142–43
National Evaluation of Juvenile Drug Courts (NEJDC) project, xv, xviii–xx, xix–xx, 55, 58, 61, 62, 84–86, 90, 141, 164. *See also* juvenile drug court (JDC) programs
  advisory committee, xviii–xix
  data from, 5–6, 9, 21, 75–83, 91, 102–103
  programs participating in, 59
National Survey on Drug Use and Health (NSDUH), 154–55
neuro-feedback, 104
New South Wales, Australia, drug court, 122–23, 294

New York State drug court evaluation, 330–31
Nixon, Richard M., 42

Oakland (California) (FIRST) drug court, 308–309
Office of Justice Programs (OJP), 49
Omnibus Crime Control and Safe Streets Act, 50
operant conditioning, 232
Orange County (California) drug court, 310–11
Orange County (Florida) juvenile drug court, 284
Orlando Juvenile Drug Court, 59, 61, 65, 66, 68–71, 73, 87, 96, 100, 104. *See also* juvenile drug court (JDC) programs
overall accuracy (assessment), 201, 202
oversight, 251

parent education and support, 103. *See also* family involvement
parks and recreation adventure program, 103
perception and behavior change, 236–37
Personal Experience Screening Questionnaire (PESQ), 207
police officers, 62
policy environment, current, 268–72
policy implications, 175–78. *See also* juvenile drug courts (JDCs), implications for the operations of
Polk County (Iowa) drug court, 312–13
Portland, Oregon, drug court in, 130
post-adjudication programs, 56
pre-adjudication programs, 56
predictive accuracy (assessment), 201–4, 243
principal-agent problem, 231
problem-solving approach, 4
procedural justice, 226–27
Prohibition, 38–39
proportionality, 259
psychiatric interviews, 208, 211

quasi-experimental designs, 118–20
strong design, 124–25, 296–315
weak design, 125–26, 316–35
questionnaires, paper-and-pencil, 209

race and drug use, 151
racial minority adolescents, 150, 151
RAND conceptual framework for evaluating drug courts, 239, 241
elements, 241–43
rational actor (deterrence) theory, 230–31, 234
rehabilitation emphasis, 243
relapse prevention, 98
reliability, types of, 199–200
research agenda, new, 273–76
research designs, inappropriate, 271–72
research evidence (of JDC effectiveness). *See also* drug court evaluation
need for, 19–22
researchers, need for conceptual framework, 223–26
rewards, 88–89, 224, 228, 259. *See also* incentives
Riverside County (California) drug court, 314–15
Robinson v. California, 42

Salt Lake County (Utah) drug court, 332–33
sanctions grid, 91
sanctions/sanctioning, 57, 89–92, 224, 228, 241, 252, 257–58
Santa Barbara County (California), 342–45
Santa Clara County (California) juvenile drug treatment, 284–85
school representatives, 62–63
screening and assessment, 63, 67–68, 185–89, 214–15
screening and assessment implementation challenges, 213–14
screening and assessment instruments designed for adolescents, 207, 210, 211

effective, 190–91. *See also* assessment instruments
guidelines for conducting and using, 188–89
recommended, 205–11
screening and assessment practices, in juvenile justice, 211–13
second judicial district drug court of New Mexico, 346–47
self-efficacy, 233, 259
sensitivity (assessment), 201–4
social learning theory, 232
SODAT—Delaware, Inc., drug court diversion program, 338–39
specificity (assessment), 201–4
St. Louis adult felony drug court, 130, 352–53
stability (reliability), 199
Stanislaus County (California) adult drug court, 340–41
state attorney's office (SAO), 70
strengths, focus on, 240
substance abuse
    DSM criteria, 172–74
    impact of JDCs on, 10
substance abuse disorders, 13–14. *See also* drug abuse problems
Substance Abuse (Horgan et al.), 197
Substance Abuse Subtle Screening Inventory (SASSI), 70
substance dependency. *See* drug dependence
substance dependency disorder. *See under* Diagnostic and Statistical Manual of Mental Disorders
substance-use disorder interviews, 208
substance use disorders, classification of, 192–93. *See also Diagnostic and Statistical Manual of Mental Disorders*
Summit County JDC evaluation, 121
Superior Drug Court Intervention Program (SDCIP), 130
Supportive-Expressive Psychotherapy (SEP), 98–99

Tarrant County (Texas) drug court, 332–33
team meetings and case reviews, 85–87
teamwork, 240
Temple University framework for evaluating drug courts, 244–47
    elements, 245
termination from drug court, 57, 253
Terry, Clinton, 48
test-retest reliability, 199
"theater effect," 256
therapeutic jurisprudence, 40–41, 223, 268–69
transparency, 255, 256
Travis County (Texas) drug diversion court, 334–35
treatment, 227–28. *See also* interventions
    availability, appropriateness, and quality, 252
    and legal system, 41–44
    and treatment modalities, 97–104
Treatment Accountability for Safe Communities (TASC), 44–45, 70, 96
Treatment Alternatives to Street Crime, 44–45
treatment-oriented interventions in criminal justice system, emergence of, 44–48
treatment planning, individualized, 240, 257
Treatment Research Institute (TRI), 275
twenty-third judicial circuit of Virginia, 346–47

Urban Institute (UI), xix, 32, 33, 72, 130. *See also* National Evaluation of Juvenile Drug Courts (NEJDC) project
    researchers, 15
Urban Institute (UI) framework for evaluating JDCs, 247–49
    background elements (program theory and context), 250
    end outcomes
        behavior change, 261

motivation to change, 260
    participation in treatment, 260
goals of, 248
input (drug court activities), 250–51
    measurable program activities,
        251–53
intermediate outcomes
    perceived deterrence, 257–58
    perceived legitimacy, 258–59
    perceived quality of intervention,
        256–57
    perceived self-efficacy, 259
output
    authority, 255–56
    organization, 253–55
Utah juvenile drug court evaluation, 121,
    286–87

validity, 198–200
    types of, 198–201
Ventura County (California) drug court,
    314–15, 334–35
violent crime arrests, 11, 12
Volstead Act, 38

Washington, D.C., Superior Drug Court
    Intervention Program (SDCIP),
    130, 300–01
Washington State drug courts, 348–49
Washington's criminal justice system,
    129
writing workshop, 103

Youth Level of Service/Case Management
    Inventory (YLoSI), 70